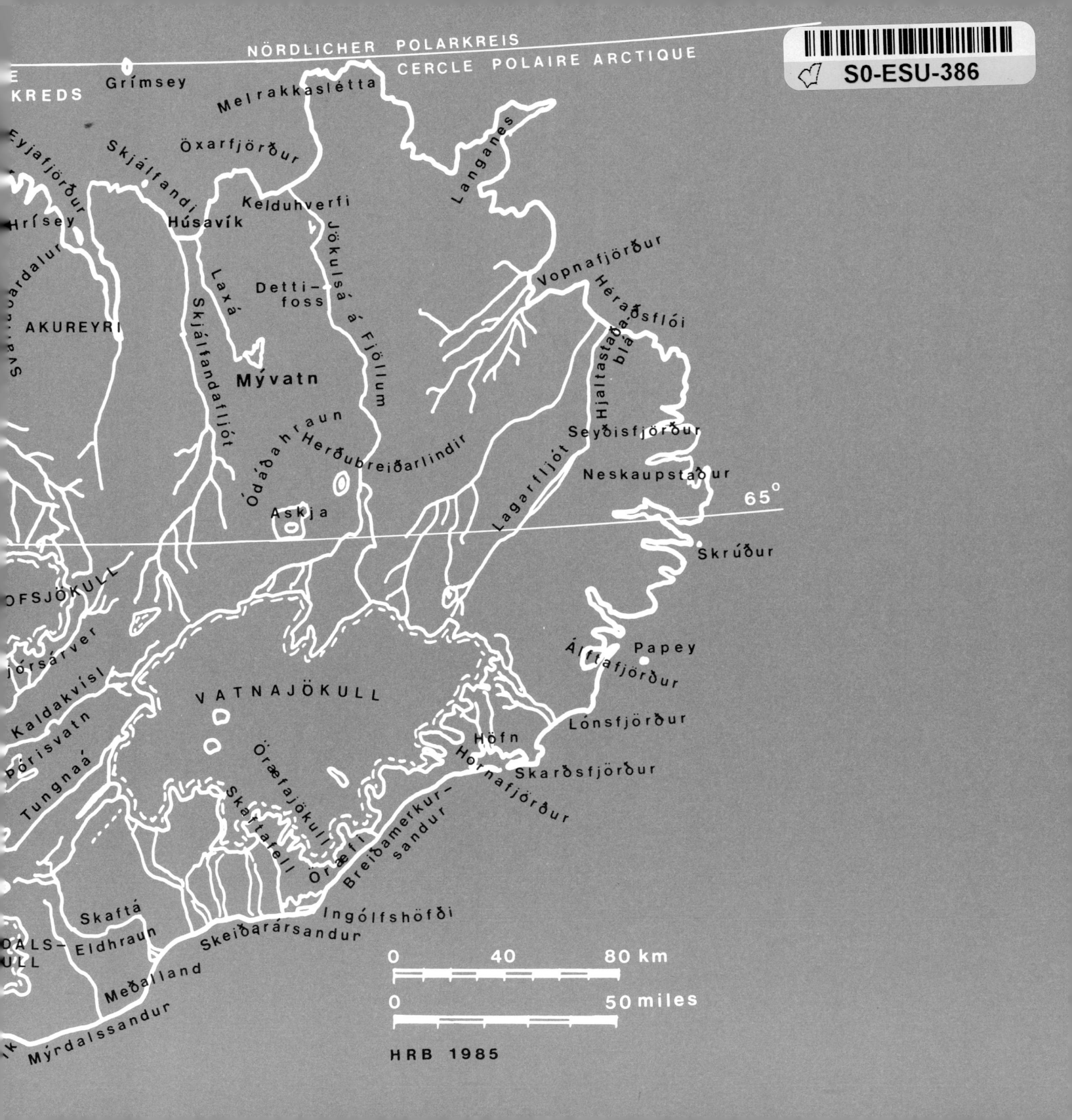

birds
of ICELAND

This book is dedicated to the memory of
my relative, the ornithologist
Dr. Finnur Guðmundsson.
It was he who encouraged me to specialise
in photographing birds and who,
on our many expeditions, taught me
so much about their distinctive features
and behaviour.

birds
of ICELAND

text and pictures by
Hjálmar R. Bárðarson

PUBLISHED BY: HJÁLMAR R. BÁRÐARSON, REYKJAVÍK

ENGLISH TRANSLATION: JULIAN MELDON D'ARCY, M.A.

FIRST ENGLISH EDITION 1986. SECOND EDITION 1987.

PUBLISHER: HJÁLMAR R. BÁRÐARSON
P.O. BOX 998, IS-121 REYKJAVÍK -1, ICELAND

PUBLISHED IN ICELAND AND COPYRIGHT ©1986
BY HJÁLMAR R. BÁRÐARSON
P.O. BOX 998, IS-121 REYKJAVÍK-1

ALL RIGHTS RESERVED

No part of this book may be reproduced by any mechanical, photographic, or electronic process, or in the form of a phonographic recording, nor may it be stored in a retrieval system, transmitted or otherwise copied for public or private use, without written permission from the publisher.

COLOUR SEPARATION:
PRENTMYNDASTOFAN H. F., REYKJAVÍK

PRINTED IN THE NETHERLANDS BY
JOH. ENSCHEDÉ EN ZONEN
GRAFISCHE INRICHTING B.V., HAARLEM

Contents

1. The world of birds and man ... 7
2. The last great auk ... 18
3. Icelandic birds ... 27
4. Islands and skerries ... 38
5. Cliff-birds ... 83
6. Shore-birds ... 108
7. Marshland-birds ... 133
8. Ducks ... 174
9. Moorland-birds ... 214
10. Town and farm birds ... 232
11. The highlands ... 250
12. Lava-fields and woodlands ... 262
13. Birds of prey ... 279
14. Visitors and irregular breeding birds ... 299
15. Postscript ... 321
16. Dr. Finnur Guðmundsson ... 323
17. Bird photography ... 325
18. Bibliography ... 327
19. Index ... 330
20. Glossary of bird names ... 334

Bird photography on Skrúður Island, the mainland in the distance.

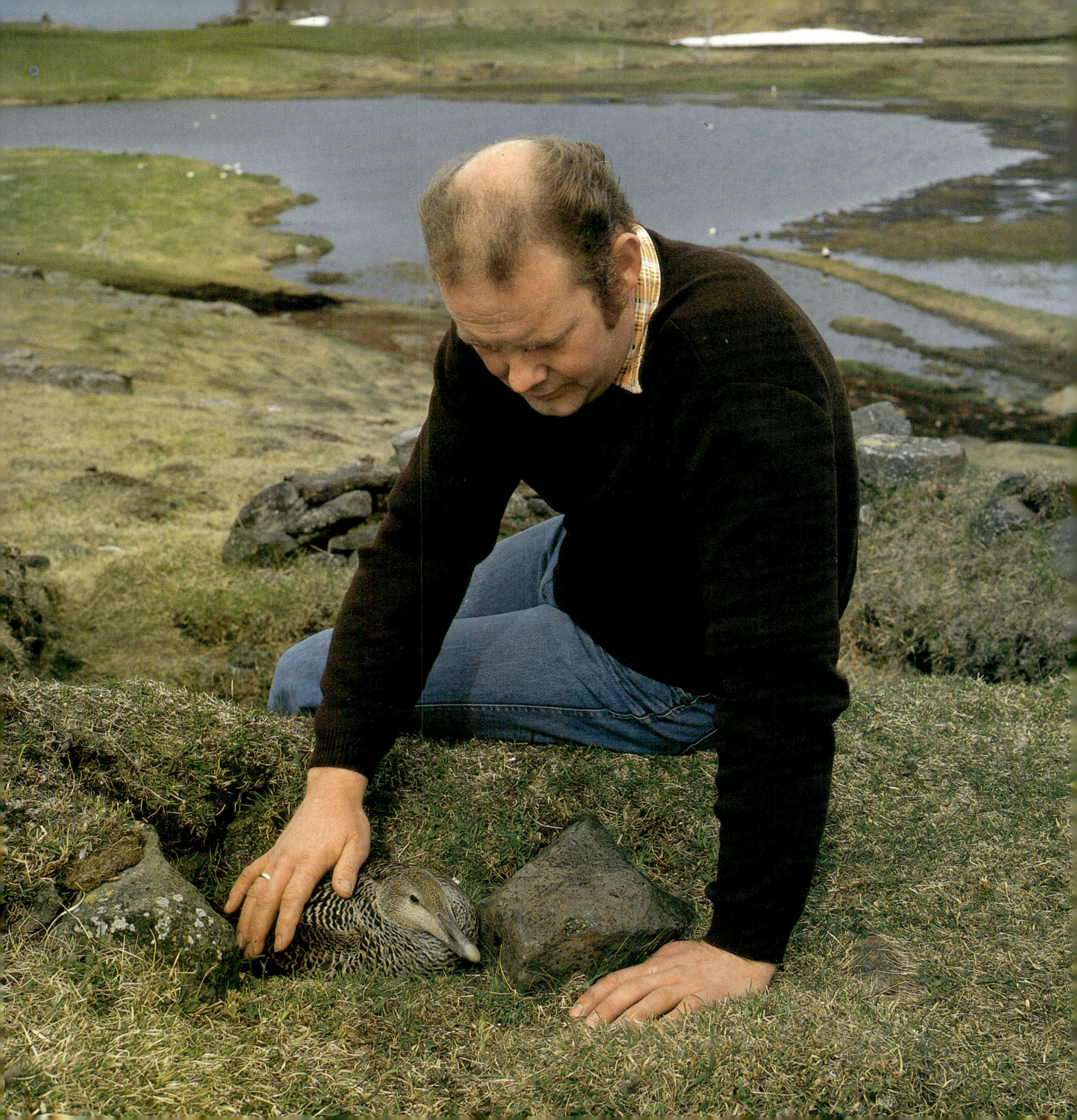

1 The world of birds and man

From time immemorial the flight of birds has enchanted the spirit of man. For thousands of years he has dreamed of taking the shape of a bird and flying freely through the skies. He has longed to escape from this earthbound existence and to soar swiftly on extended wings over the surface of the earth. Indeed in his imagination gods and mythological beings were often endowed with the ability to fly; in Ancient Egypt they were depicted as flying birds with human heads.

It is not known for certain when or where man first attempted to make his dreams of flying a reality. It is often difficult in ancient stories to distinguish between simple fairy-tales and what may be sound evidence of man's first attempts to fly.

Icelandic farmers collect the valuable eider down shed by eider ducks in their nests in specially tended nesting sites. Only small amounts are removed during the early part of the breeding season; the remainder is harvested after the duck and her young have left the nest and gone to sea. The farmers who collect the down take great care of the nesting grounds and protect them from predatory birds. The eider ducks fully appreciate the farmer's kindness and care and will allow him to stroke them in their nests without flinching.

The tale of Daedalus and Icarus is one of the best known of such stories. Daedalus made his son Icarus wings out of birds' feathers glued together with wax. Icarus's youthful impetuosity and carelessness led him to fly too near the sun, however, and the wax melted and he fell to his death in the sea. His father kept to a more prudent height and reached his destination.

Most of men's first attempts at flight involved the use of bird skins or flying outfits and trying to copy the birds' method of flying by flapping movable wings. In the Middle Ages a number of people were killed or seriously injured when they donned various kinds of artificial wings and leaped off rooftops or towers.

The first man known to have realistically studied the possibilities of man's being able to fly was Leonardo da Vinci. He soon realised that it was impossible to understand the flight of birds without a complete knowledge of the nature and force of air currents, and he painstakingly tried to ascertain not only exactly how birds used their wings, but also what effect air currents had on them. The science of aerodynamics, however, was completely unknown in his time.

From time immemorial man has been captivated by the flight of birds. The picture on the title-page is of a gannet gliding through the air as it observes the sea near its home; gannets will often range much further from their breeding grounds in search of food. Birds which are especially good flyers generally have proportionately larger wing-surfaces. Sea-birds such as gulls are noticeably rather slow flyers, but they have great aerobatic skills and the larger species are expert gliders. Above is a **herring gull** on a relaxed reconnaisance flight near the cliff-tops, intently scrutinising its surroundings should any food be in sight.

Leonardo also realised that man's arm muscles were not strong enough for him to fly and that he would need to use his leg muscles as well. He therefore constructed a flying machine in which the wings were to be operated by both the arms and legs, but it was never actually tried out, probably because he knew that it would not work. Leonardo da Vinci died in 1519, and for almost a century after his death men continued to put on various artificial wings and leap from the tops of towers.

It was not until the latter half of the 17th century that man finally accepted that it was completely impossible for him to fly with movable wings powered by his own bodily strength. It is the ratio between man's weight and muscular power which makes him totally incapable of flight, for in comparison with a bird his skeleton is heavy and his muscular power slight. It has been estimated that for man to be able to fly he would need such large chest muscles that his shoulders would have to be almost 2 m wide, and to provide enough attachment for these great muscles he would need a T-shaped breastbone, as birds have, and its keel would probably have to be about a metre in depth.

The ability to fly demands more than just strong muscles and highly developed wings, however. The bird's respiratory system has evolved in such a way that it is especially effective in the transference of oxygen into the blood stream. Its lungs are also an important cooling device as flying generates great body heat. A bird remains cool and maintains the oxygen levels in its blood in flight by breathing much faster than when on the ground, or at 300 times a minute as opposed to 130 times a minute when earthbound. Birds' flying skills have evolved according to their needs and environments. Thus larger birds, such as gulls, use rising air currents to a much greater degree than smaller birds, especially as they have relatively less muscular power in proportion to their weight.

Flying speeds vary according to the shape and structure of the wings. Fast flying birds are reminiscent of modern aircraft; they have thin, sharp-pointed wings with little surface area in relation to their weight. The aerobatic skills of smaller birds are very impressive, especially their ability to turn sharply in mid-air and to come to a sudden stop. Some birds can fly straight into their nests at up to 60 km per hour. Such precision at high speed depends on very quick reactions, and for these a bird needs a superbly developed brain, fast nerve impulses to the wing muscles, and a very sensitive eye-retina and sharp sight capable of swiftly recording and interpreting visible data. Among the fastest Icelandic birds is the starling, which, over long distances, can reach a speed of 75 km per hour. The gyrfalcon can reach much higher speeds whilst hunting, right up to 200–300 km per hour. The gannet can also reach great speeds when plunging into the sea after prey. Generally speaking, however, the bigger birds do not fly any faster than the smaller ones.

Most birds usually take off into the wind just like aircraft, but if there is no wind they can often just spring up and spread their wings to take to the air. Birds with large wing-surfaces need only to extend them when it is very windy in order to take off. Black guillemots, red-throated divers, diving ducks and whooper swans all take off by running on the surface of the water into the wind.

If in the beginning man had not concentrated so much on birds' wing movements, but had noted instead their ability to soar on outstretched wings, the art of gliding may well have been developed sooner. It was not until experiments were made with fixed, immovable wings that gliding became a reality for man; it only then needed the development of a motor light enough to power a propeller for the age of mechanical flying to begin.

Even though man failed to fly with movable wings it is still a fact that, to all our knowledge, the flight of both birds and aircraft is based on similar principles. The main difference is that, with an aircraft, the wings bear the weight whilst propellers or air-pressure (in jets) thrust the plane forwards; with a bird the wings are used both to bear the weight and as a means of propulsion. The basal part of the wing keeps the bird aloft whilst the feathers of the wing-tip propel the bird forwards.

It took over 150 million years of evolution for birds to attain the ability to fly. A bird's skeleton is light compared with its strength because the bones are hollow and filled with air. They have a hard outer shell and the inner walls are strengthened with spongy tissues. Aircraft wings are designed on exactly the same principles. Moreover birds are used as models for many other aspects of aerotechnology, for example air-stability and steering techniques. It is not only poets and artists, therefore, who have sought inspiration in the majestic flight of birds. The best aerotechnicians still look to the birds for knowledge and solutions to technical problems.

Although man has succeeded in producing the technology to enable him to fly and reach even greater heights than any bird (beyond earth's atmosphere and to the moon), he still remains basically an earthbound creature and it is only in his imagination, in myths, fairy-tales and folklore that he can fly by his own strength. He will always continue to admire the flight of birds, therefore, for he will never attain their aerobatic skills himself.

Man's admiration of birds' ability to fly forms only one aspect of his relationship with them. From time immemorial he has availed himself of birds and their eggs for food, especially birds which nest on cliffs or in crowded colonies, as they provide greater opportunities for hunting and collecting. In former times, for example, auks and puffins have been an important means of sustenance for Icelanders; indeed in many places in Iceland they have often saved people from starvation. Birds and eggs were collected on the great cliffs of the Vestfirðir (Westfjords) to provide both fresh food and an important store for the winter. Although they are no longer a dire necessity, auks' eggs and puffins are still regarded by many as tasty food and a useful addition to the larder.

Fowling in Iceland is no longer so extensive as to seriously reduce or exterminate any species. In earlier times unrestricted persecution could deplete the numbers of edible birds and the great auk, for example, was actually exterminated. Other species, such as the shag, have begun to increase once more after excessive persecution. Man has usually seen the advantage of sensibly utilising birds, however, and of avoiding making a species extinct. In recent years he has nonetheless considerably disturbed the ecology of bird life by interfering with natural food supplies. This has caused a dramatic increase in the population of some species, making them a problem. A good example of this in Iceland is the great black-backed gull which has learnt to find food in open-air rubbish tips and in the fish waste from harbours and fish-factories. When such bird populations increase out of all proportion men start to regard them as pests and killing them is considered legitimate.

Most people want to safeguard small birds as they feel they give an added beauty to their sur-

1. THE WORLD OF BIRDS AND MAN

Nordic vikings valued the raven highly and endowed it with the gift of prophecy. Ravens are mentioned at the very beginning of the history of Iceland. **The Book of Settlements** (**Landnámabók**) relates how Flóki Vilgerðarson leaves Rogaland in Norway in search of the land which later became known as Iceland. Before leaving Norway he sacrificed to 3 ravens which were to show him the way, for at that time no one in Scandinavia had a loadstone (a kind of compass) for navigating the seas. Flóki set sail with the ravens, first calling at the Shetlands and then later the Faroes. From there he sailed north and released one of the ravens. It flew past the stern and back towards the Faroes. When the second one was released it flew into the air, but returned to the ship. The third one flew forwards past the bow in the direction of land – Iceland. From then on Flóki Vilgerðarson was known as Raven-Flóki.

roundings. The ptarmigan is highly prized by hunters for its tasty meat, but others wish to have it protected as they see it as part of the beauty of Icelandic nature. Some people see sea-birds as dispensable because they compete with man for an important source of food: fish. Man's appreciation of birds thus depends on whether he sees them as a means of sustenance, a competitor for food, or as a beautiful addition to his surroundings.

In former times, when birds' eggs were an important part of the household diet, traditions were established to ensure that no species would be endangered. Around Lake Mývatn, for example, there was an unwritten rule that at least 4 eggs were to be left in ducks' nests, a rule which was later incorporated into legislation on bird protection. The same legislation also stipulates that only the first clutch of eggs could be taken from the nests of black-headed gulls and arctic terns. There are no laws limiting egg-collecting on bird-cliffs as these nesting sites are protected by other circumstances, such as the difficult terrain, the dangers of rock falls, and even local superstitions and taboos.

Man's relations with the eider duck in Iceland is also a good example of the sensible utilisation of birds. It is first and foremost the eider down which is collected from their nests, and only sparingly at first whilst the eider duck is still incubating her eggs. The remainder is taken once she and her young have left the nest. Farmers who collect eider down look after the breeding grounds by preparing nesting sites for the ducks, tending them in their nests, and protecting them from such predators as great black-backed gulls and ravens.

Falconry is a centuries old sport which only the nobility or men of rank could pursue. In earlier times, when Iceland still belonged to the Danish Crown, it was a national duty to provide the King with hunting falcons. Icelandic gyrfalcons were considered a great treasure throughout the world and the monarch often used them as gifts. There was a special aviary for falcons at Bessastaðir in which the birds were kept whilst awaiting exportation. This was later moved to Reykjavík in 1763 and there is a falcon carved in wood on the building which now stands where the aviary was situated (Hafnarstræti 1–3). The export of Icelandic gyrfalcons ceased after 1800.

The taming of hunting falcons entailed a great deal of care and patience. The birds were kept in semi-darkness and a black leather hood was placed over their heads when they were taken outside for training; this was only removed when the bird was to hunt. The falcon would then immediately soar into the sky and seize in its claws anything which flew into its range of vision.

Falconry is still practised in some countries, and the Icelandic falcon remains much in demand as a hunting bird. Unfortunately this has meant the appearance of thieves in Iceland in search of falcon eggs or young. Falcon eggs can be hatched abroad and fetch very high prices indeed. Gyrfalcons are completely protected by law in Iceland, however, and there are many vigilant bird-watchers determined to protect them.

A great number of people in many countries have bird-watching as a hobby or interest. It is no real surprise that birds are so fascinating to men, for they are an integral part of his environment everywhere. The beauty of their form and colours delights his eyes, and the music of their singing enchants his ears. In spring they are busy making their nests, hatching eggs, and feeding their young, all tasks which have to be finished by the beginning of autumn. The arrival of migratory birds heralds the spring for many people, a fact often reflected in the works of poets.

Anyone can enjoy bird-watching who has an open mind and alert eyes and ears. There is one essential rule which must always be observed, however. One's enthusiasm must never allow one to actually disturb the birds. One must always move slowly and carefully and watch in silence. This is the only way to become acquainted with the natural life of birds. By using a hide it is possible to get very close to a nest or colony and study birds' behaviour whilst remaining concealed. Good but light binoculars are also necessary, together with a

1. THE WORLD OF BIRDS AND MAN

note-book for jotting down observations. One can thus, with patience, succeed in entering the world of birds – a world which has proved a charming one for many bird-watchers.

Bird-watching can be more than just a hobby, however. When one has the opportunity to study birds' behaviour for days, weeks, or even months at a time, one is really taking part in research. In such instances one also quickly perceives that the behaviour of individual birds of the same species is much more variable than most people would believe. A close scrutiny of birds reveals, for example, that they can communicate with each other through body movements and changes of tone in their calls.

Sight and hearing are the vital senses for every bird as they are dependent on them for their entire existence. A blind bird is a doomed one. Their sense of sight and hearing is thus acute; their sense of smell and taste, on the other hand, is imperfect.

The eyes of most birds are positioned in such a way that only a very restricted area of their range of vision is actually shared by both eyes (i.e. binocular). This restricted area is usually immediately ahead of them so as to enable them to judge distances. The remainder of their range of vision is

The arctic tern is extremely deft and graceful in flight.

1. THE WORLD OF BIRDS AND MAN

This little pinkfoot gosling is exploring its surroundings in the pink-footed geese breeding grounds by the River Þjórsá, south of Hofsjökull glacier. If the gosling is separated from its mother its natural instinct will make it follow anything which moves – including man!

monocular. Predatory birds have considerable binocular vision as it is imperative for them to judge distances accurately when attacking prey. Owls have total binocular vision, but their eyes are relatively immovable and they have to move their heads to change their range of vision. They can easily turn their heads through 180 degrees to be able to see directly behind them; moreover their sight is very keen, especially in poor light.

There is no doubt that birds can easily distinguish colours, otherwise there would be little point in nature endowing many of them with such beautiful plumage. Colours are important, in fact, in birds' relations with each other.

Hearing, as well as sight, plays an important role in the life of all birds. Research seems to have established that birds are capable of hearing much higher tones than man, and some smaller birds' alarm-calls are probably – and very conveniently – above the range of human hearing. They appear to use these sounds when an enemy approaches which they conceal themselves from rather than flee. Birds can distinguish the direction of sounds just as man can, an important factor when in search of prey.

Like many other animals, birds have personalities which are sometimes extraordinarily like those of man. Their courtship rituals often remind one of human feelings and impulses. Birds also have a great ability to learn. Once a bird has discovered an easy way to obtain food it is certain to use the same method again.

Birds' behaviour is otherwise controlled to a great extent by natural instinct. Each bird is born with these instincts, they are not learned from older birds. It is a natural instinct, for example, for a hungry bird to seek food. Sex hormones direct their instincts to look for a mate, secure territory, build a nest, breed, lay eggs, hatch them, and feed and defend their young until they are capable of looking after themselves.

When an egg has tumbled out of the nest it is natural instinct which makes the bird push it back into the nest with its bill. It will only do this, however, if the egg is not too far from the nest, and the decisive distance may vary; some birds will roll back an egg which is up to a metre away from the nest whilst other species will ignore an egg which is only 10 to 15 cm away.

Small birds remove the excreta of their young from the nest. When parent birds arrive at the nest with food the young chicks automatically open their beaks. When they are young and blind it is believed to be the sound and vibration of their parents' arrival which stimulates them to do so, but once they can see it is the specific colour patterns of their parents which attract their attention.

Goslings, and some ducklings, will follow the first living creature they see after they emerge from the egg, and it can be difficult to make them accept their own mother if she is not that first object. Anyone walking in the marshy regions of the River Þjórsá in the central highlands of Iceland is often resolutely followed by newly hatched pinkfoot goslings, and it can be problem to shake them off! In their natural environment and under normal circumstances, of course, the mother is the first creature they see and so they follow her.

The singing of birds is also a natural instinct, although the actual tunes they sing are learned from older birds of their species. Many birds even try to imitate the songs of other species. A bird will make a special danger-call when it sees an enemy, even if there is no other bird in the vicinity. If a bird of its species does hear the call, however, it will immediately prepare to defend itself, the methods varying depending on the species involved and the vehemence of the call. Birds will sometimes respond with a ferocious counter-attack, but at other times they will just flee precipitately. Many kinds of birds also respond to the danger-call of other species, even though the call is totally different from their own. This means that either birds are born with a natural understanding of the danger-calls of other species, or that they learn to recognise them through experience. In a colony of gulls, arctic terns and waders, almost all the birds will become agitated if any one of them gives the danger-signal.

Many birds with protective colouring merge easily with their background and just crouch down and remain motionless if there is any danger in the vicinity. Their young will do the same if the parents give the danger-signal.

It is interesting to speculate as to why different species of birds will breed together in colonies. Some birds will only nest in groups of their own species, but others will nest within colonies of even wholly unrelated species. Gulls, arctic terns, shags, cormorants and black guillemots, for example, all nest in crowded colonies in which all the birds have a much larger feeding territory than any single one of them could either lay claim to or defend. Moorland-birds are completely the opposite, however, readily laying claim to an area which they tenaciously defend from birds of their own species. Perhaps it is the sociability of the birds forming mixed breeding colonies which determines how crowded their nesting sites are, though it could well be that social harmony has evolved through necessity because of a shortage of convenient breeding grounds near plentiful food supplies. A packed colony also provides a better defence against enemies as there are more birds to defend it, though on the other hand the larger the colony the more attention it will attract as it gives greater opportunities for predatory birds to find eggs or young.

Another curious phenomenon is that various species of waders choose their nesting sites within colonies of black-headed gulls and arctic terns, perhaps because they seek the defence of these aggressive and lively birds which vigilantly defend their territories. The black-headed gulls and arctic terns are far from being friendly towards these intrusive waders, however, the gulls often pecking the waders as they return to their nests. Nonetheless it seems that waders' nests are less likely to be raided when amidst colonies of gulls and terns than if they breed by themselves elsewhere. It could also be, of course, that waders nest among black-headed gulls and arctic terns simply because they like the same kind of breeding habitat as they do.

With a closer acquaintance with birds the question soon arises as to whether they have an intelligence like man does, or if all their actions and behaviour are due to natural instincts.

It is difficult to avoid comparing birds with men, because in studying the way their minds appear to work one can only relate them to humans. One soon realises, for example, that birds can be frightened, even terrified, and will react like humans do in similar circumstances. Parents are always on guard against threats to their young, and they will often take greater risks than usual when gathering food for them. Birds can sometimes show amazing courage when their young are in danger, though the extent of their courage varies according to the individual bird, some birds of the same species being braver than others, a very human characteristic.

Birds can clearly show their dislike for other individuals of the same species, but they can also establish great friendships and appear to be able to recognise each other at a distance, even if they have not seen each other for a while. Birds can also recognise their own young, even if they are dispersed amongst others.

Birds can also evidently grieve, especially for a dead mate, as many birds are faithful to their partners for life. The drawing power of the same breeding ground, however, may play some part in their relationship.

Some birds are tame and trust man immediately; others can take a long time to allay their fears and suspicions. The more intimately one gets to know individual birds, the more obvious it becomes that they have, in varying degrees, their own idiosyncracies, and that although much of their basic behaviour is inborn and instinctive, some of their actions are clearly governed by intelligent thought and individual character. All of which seems to indicate that the variability of the natural distribution of such characteristics as sensitivity, courage, intelligence and memory, so commonly found in mankind, has its parallel in the world of birds.

Both summer and winter there is always colourful bird life on the small Lake Tjörnin in central Reykjavík. When frozen in the winter, there is usually a large hole in the ice where the natural hot water from the town's heating system is discharged into the lake. Many birds gather there, especially ducks, geese and swans. Both the young and old of Reykjavík enjoy their company and children often feed them with bread. Older children come alone, but the very youngest come with their parents and grandparents.

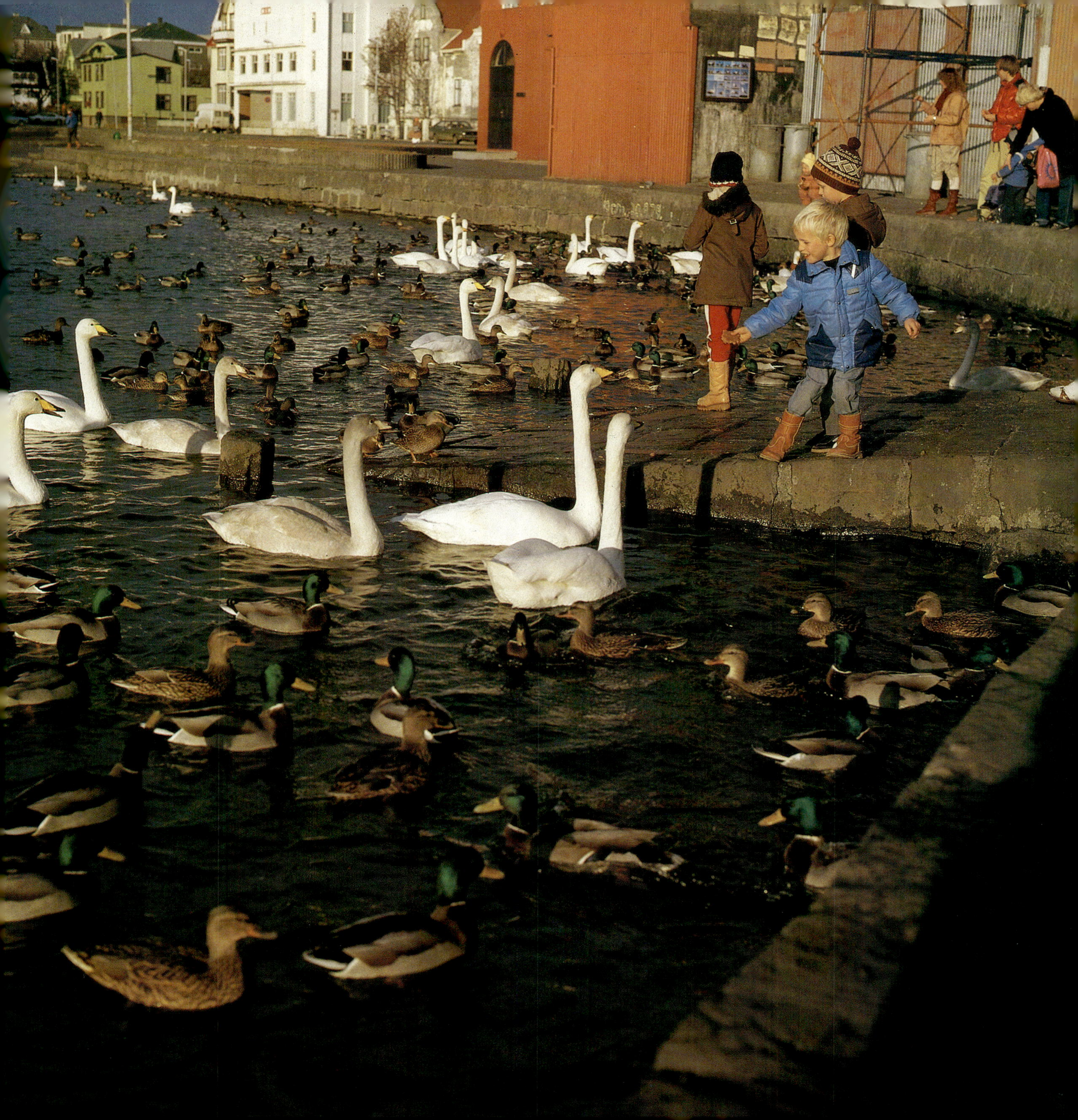

2 The last great auk

The last great auk in Iceland was killed on Eldey (Fire Island) in 1844, and there has been no known sighting of the bird anywhere in the world ever since.

There are now in museums and collections about 80 stuffed great auks, 75 eggs, 10 complete skeletons, and quite a number of various bones found in old kitchen middens, as well as 2 carcasses complete with internal organs. The great auk was a rather large bird, about 70 cm long and with a similar build to a razorbill, only much bigger and with a longer neck and bill. The wings were very small, about 16 cm long. A fully-grown bird in its summer plumage had a black back, neck and head, but a white breast and belly and a distinctive white patch in front of the eyes. The bill was black, but with 8–10 white transverse furrows on an adult bird. Both male and female birds had the same appearance. The young were said to be very similar in appearance to the adults except for fewer transverse furrows on the bill.

The **breeding grounds** of the great auk were on the east and west coasts of the North Atlantic, as the distribution map shows. Its nesting sites in

2. THE LAST GREAT AUK

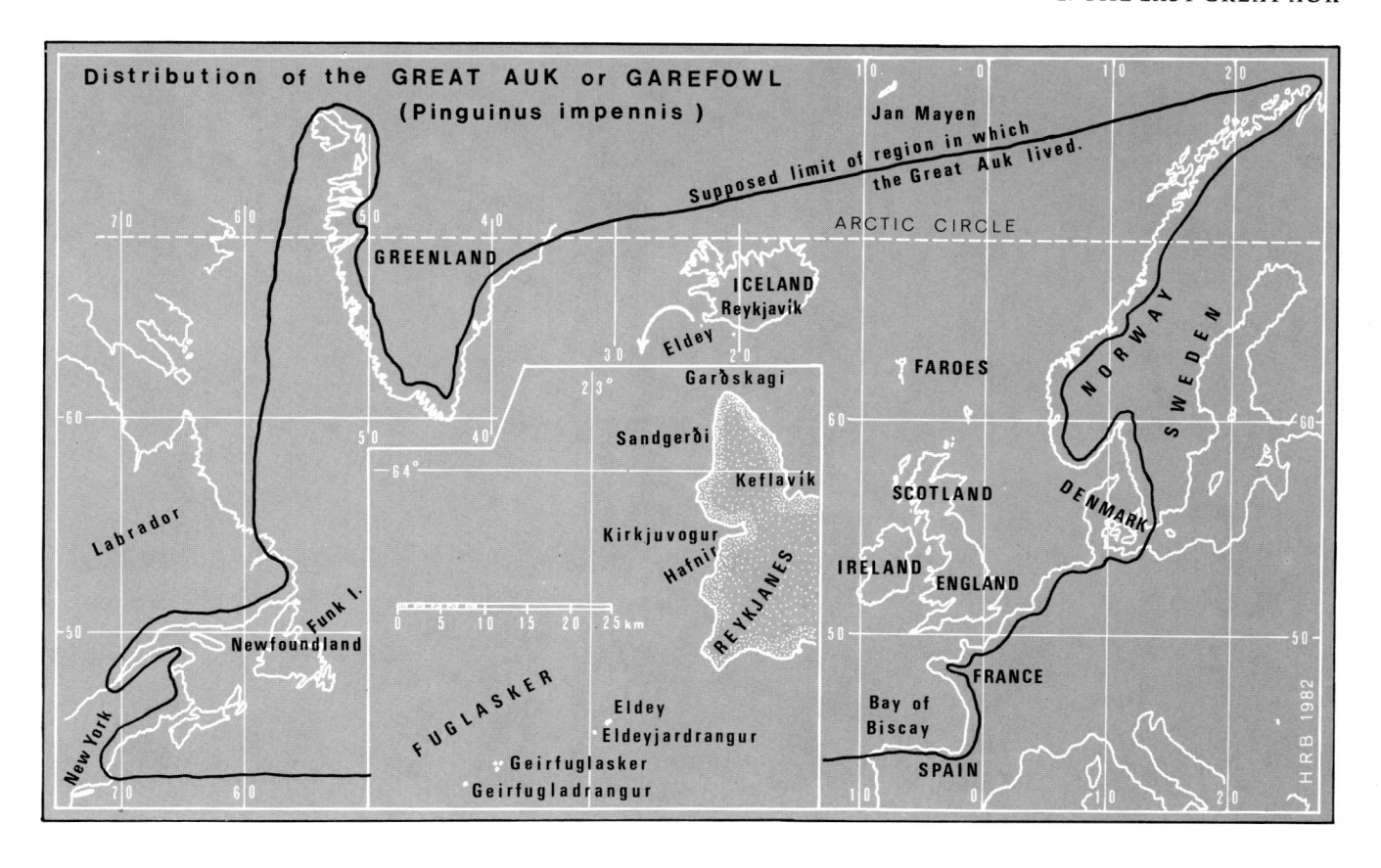

Distribution of the GREAT AUK or GAREFOWL (Pinguinus impennis)

Supposed limit of region in which the Great Auk lived.

Jan Mayen, ARCTIC CIRCLE, GREENLAND, ICELAND, Reykjavik, Eldey, Garðskagi, Sandgerði, Keflavík, Kirkjuvogur, Hafnir, REYKJANES, FUGLASKER, Eldey, Eldeyjardrangur, Geirfuglasker, Geirfugladrangur, FAROES, NORWAY, SWEDEN, SCOTLAND, DENMARK, IRELAND, ENGLAND, FRANCE, Bay of Biscay, SPAIN, Labrador, Funk I., Newfoundland, New York

HRB 1982

these areas were on islands and skerries. In the Stone Age it is believed that the great auk was distributed along all the shores of this area, in Europe as far south as the northern coast of Spain, and on the western seaboard as far south as where New York now stands. In later times the great auk's main breeding grounds were along the shores of Newfoundland and Labrador. Primitive peoples on both sides of the Atlantic undoubtedly hunted the bird for food whilst it actually nested on the mainland, and later pursued it to offshore islands in reach of their small boats. Once the great auk had thus been exterminated along the shoreline its only remaining habitats were the smaller outlying islands and skerries furthest from the shore. The great auk could still flourish in such places if there was a good supply of sea-food as fish was its staple diet.

When European fishing vessels began to exploit the Newfoundland fishing grounds their crews soon became aware of the huge numbers of great auks on the outer islands, and this very edible bird quickly became their main source of food in the area. The persecution of great auks began around 1497 and only ended when they had been completely exterminated on the western shores of the Atlantic. The great auk was easy to catch as it was a very submissive, harmless and clumsy bird which was completely defenceless on land as it could not even fly. It was easy to drive aboard ship along

19

2. THE LAST GREAT AUK

gangplanks and sails stretched between ship and shore. Another method used was to herd the great auks into pens and then slaughter them with clubs.

By 1600, fishing vessels from Europe took little meat with them to the Newfoundland waters as the crews relied completely on the great auk for fresh meat. There appear to have been no restrictions on this excessive persecution and far more great auks were killed than were necessary to supply food. On Funk Island, for example, whole skeletons of the bird have been found long after it had been exterminated. They are now museum exhibits.

It is believed that the great auk only laid one egg a year and so reproduced rather slowly. The species rapidly dwindled in numbers in North America and was completely extinct there sometime between 1800 and 1825.

The great auk was extinct in the Faroe Isles by about 1800, in Greenland by 1815, and in the Orkneys by 1812. The last great auks on St. Kilda were killed in 1821.

In 1955 the Icelandic Museum of Natural History obtained a great auk skeleton, one of only 10 such skeletons in existence. The skeleton is composed of bones which Owen Bryant collected in 1908 on Funk Island off Newfoundland, once the home of a huge great auk colony. The species was completely extinct there long before the very last great auks were killed on Eldey in 1844.

On the right is a stuffed great auk bought for the Icelandic Museum of Natural History at an auction at Sotheby's in London on 4 March 1971. It was originally in Count Raben's collection in Aalholm Castle in Nysted, Denmark, and the skin was obtained on the Count's trip to Iceland in 1821. The great auk egg on the stand was bought in the U.S.A. in 1955, but would have originally come from Iceland.

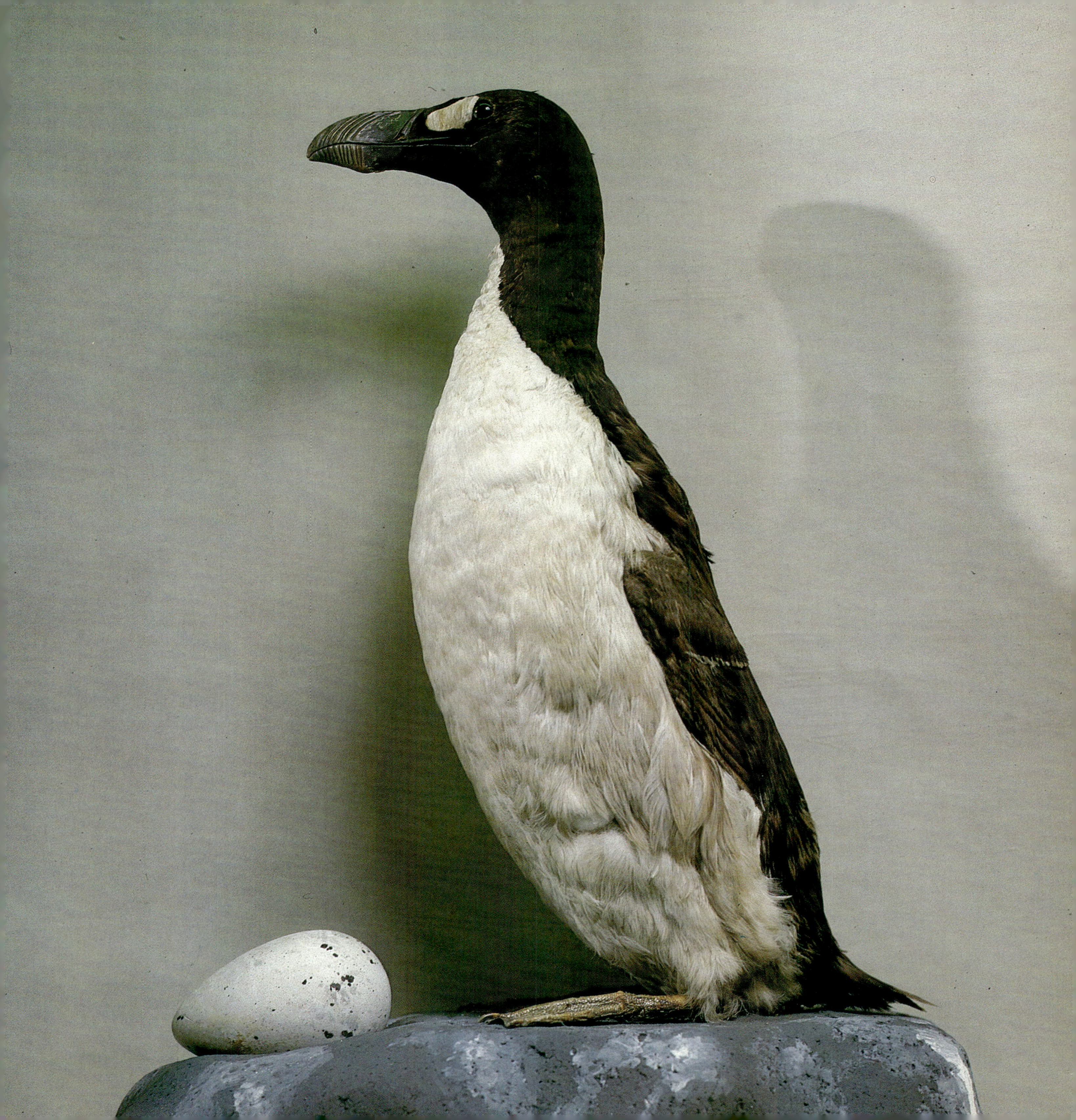

2. THE LAST GREAT AUK

The great auk was probably widely distributed along Iceland's shoreline before the appearance of man, but once human settlement began it retreated to outer skerries, many of which are named after the species. Great auks are believed to have bred on the Geirfuglasker (Great Auk Skerries) of the Vestmannaeyjar (Westman Isles) until around 1800, but its main habitat in Iceland in the 18th century was on the Geirfuglasker off the south-west coast of Reykjanes. The name of the whole group of these skerries is Fuglasker (Bird Skerries). The nearest to land is Eldey, a 77 m high precipitous island formed of volcanic rock which seamen used to call 'the meal sack' as it was covered in white bird droppings. To the south-west of Eldey was the Eldeyjardrangur (Eldey Stack) which has long since collapsed. Further to the south-west of Eldey were the Geirfuglasker, a cluster of skerries which were mostly well above sea-level, but subsided into the ocean in an earthquake around 1830. The largest skerry of the group was said to be a perfect breeding ground for the great auk as part of it sloped down to the sea, thus easily enabling the bird to waddle ashore. The most south-westerly of the Fuglasker was the Geirfugladrangur which would probably have been much higher and steeper than the Geirfuglasker, but the great auk may well have nested there too.

Fowlers were reputed to visit the Geirfuglasker every summer, whenever the weather allowed a boat to sail and land there. The colony was sometimes seriously depleted after these excursions, and they were discontinued for a few years whenever this happened.

In 1628 a dozen men were drowned at the Geirfuglasker, undoubtedly whilst on a fowling expedition. In 1639 3 large boats from Suðurnes and 1 from Grindavík set sail for the Geirfuglasker, but 2 were lost at sea, and the other 2 only returned with great difficulty. In 1732 there was an expedition to the skerry after a 75-year interval; 2 hovels were reputedly found there, along with 3 cudgels and some weather-beaten human skeletons. An-

An old drawing of the Geirfuglasker. The text of the original reads: 'View of the Geirfuglasker from the north-east when approaching from the mainland, showing its two landing-places and the Austur-Rif (East-Reef).' The 2 landing-places had thus been on either side of the Austur-Rif and the drawing portrays 2 rowing-boats at anchor there and 3 men killing birds on the skerry. Sources mention a shelter made of rocks and this appears to be depicted on the drawing. The Geirfuglasker provided the main breeding grounds for the great auk until they sank beneath the ocean during the earthquakes of 1830 (or 1831).

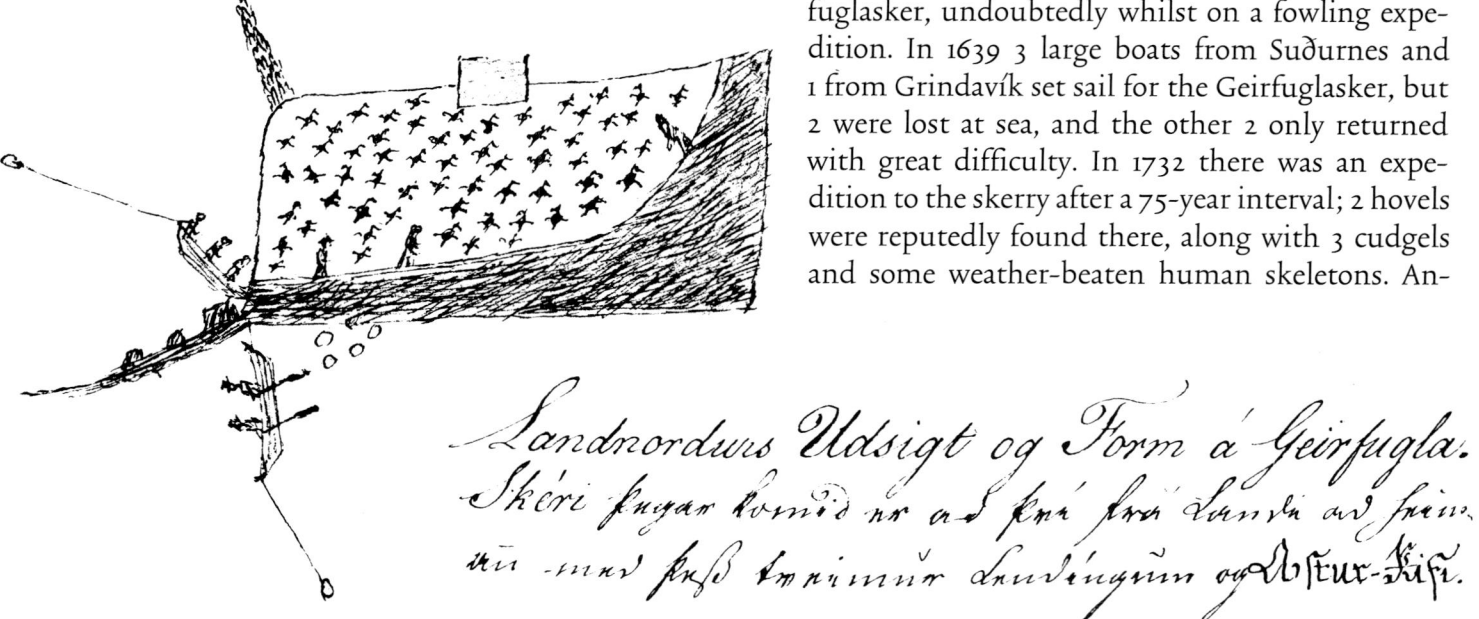

2. THE LAST GREAT AUK

other story relates how 3 men lived on the skerry for 2 weeks before being rescued. They had survived on dried birds and rotten eggs.

Sources indicate that from around 1750 until 1800 there were regular fowling expeditions to the Geirfuglasker, but that they later became far less frequent, probably because of the diminishing catch and the dangers of sailing there. The great auk was sometimes seen on the Reykjanes mainland, however. One was found in Selvogur around 1803, and 2 were killed near Keflavík in 1809.

The outbreak of war between England and Denmark in 1807 brought about a great reduction of the great auk colony on the Fuglasker. In 1808 a British warship, H.M.S. *Salamine*, under the command of Captain John Gilpin, sailed to Thorshavn in the Faroes. The crew pillaged the town and press-ganged a Faroese man, Peter Hansen, into being their guide to Reykjavík, where they duly arrived on 24 July. Once again the crew pillaged the town. On their journey home they anchored off the Geirfuglasker for a whole day and killed large numbers of great auks, trampling on their eggs and young. The warship finally left Icelandic waters on 8 August 1808 and Hansen was repatriated on the way back to Britain.

The war caused famine in the Faroes and in 1813 its government sent a ship to Iceland to procure food and other necessities. The expedition was led by Peter Hansen, and when the Faroese arrived off Reykjanes they were becalmed and used the opportunity to land on the Geirfuglasker. They killed all the great auks they could get hold of, but left many of the dead birds behind when they sailed on with the arrival of a fresh wind. They arrived in Reykjavík on 29 July 1813. In addition to the great auks already salted, there were 24 complete carcasses on deck and they reputedly gave one of them to Bishop Vidalín, who later gave it to a friend in England.

In 1821 a Danish ornithologist, Friedrich Faber, stayed in Iceland studying and writing about Icelandic birds. In the summer of the same year the Danish Count F.C. Raben visited Iceland along with his friend Mörck LL.B. The latter collected plants in Iceland whilst Count Raben intended to add a great auk to his large collection of stuffed birds in Aalholm Castle in Denmark.

Whilst the foundations were being dug in 1944 for Steindór's Printing Works at Tjarnargata 4 in Reykjavík, 76 individual great auk bones were discovered in an ancient kitchen midden. These bones are now preserved in the Icelandic Museum of Natural History, and some of them are pictured here below. At the top is a complete lower-jaw bone, in the middle is a wing-bone, and at the bottom are 2 bones from the spine. Many other great auk bones have been found in ancient kitchen middens (e.g. in the Vestmannaeyjar) and provide clear evidence that there were large numbers of great auks in Iceland when the first settlers arrived.

Raben, Mörck and Faber were thus all very keen to try and get out to the Geirfuglasker and examine the great auk colony. In spite of many attempts they could find neither men nor a boat to take them there, and they eventually had to hire, at great expense, a fishing smack from Keflavík. They sailed to the Geirfuglasker on 29 June 1821, but saw no great auks on the skerry, although there were plenty of gannets and guillemots. They sailed on to the Geirfugladrangur where Count Raben showed a great deal of daring and courage by actually getting onto the rock, though he almost drowned returning to the boat. They returned to Keflavík on 2 July. They had failed to obtain a great auk for Count Raben's collection, but it had been an enlightening expedition nonetheless.

Count Raben must have succeeded in obtaining a great auk skin sometime during his stay in Iceland, however, for the stuffed great auk bought for the Icelandic Museum of Natural History at an auction in London in 1971 was from his collection,

Above can be seen the small reef which extends from the northeast of Eldey. There is a landing-place on a low, flat rock (see dinghy in picture). The last 2 great auks known to exist were killed on the rocky slope at the foot of the cliff-face on the morning of 3 June 1844. To reach the top of Eldey one must move along the ledges of the rock face leading from the slope and then finally climb the sheer cliff to the top.

and according to the information of Count Raben-Levetzau, his descendant, it had been originally obtained on the visit to Iceland in 1821.

After this expedition to the Geirfuglasker and the Geirfugladrangur, the ornithologist Faber was afraid that the Faroese had exterminated the great auk when they had landed there in 1813. His immediate fears were unfounded, however, as a total of 27 great auks were killed in the years 1830–31 and these must have come from the Geirfuglasker or some of the other skerries in the vicinity of Eldey. The Geirfuglasker are known to have disappeared

2. THE LAST GREAT AUK

beneath the sea in the earthquakes of 1830 (or 1831) so it must be assumed that these 27 birds had formed the nucleus of any great auk colony still in existence. A few surviving great auks looked for breeding grounds on other skerries after the earthquakes, and about 10 were killed on these skerries between 1830 and 1841. Their skins were sold to collectors and natural science museums.

After the Geirfuglasker had disappeared a few great auks moved to a small reef extending from Eldey, though as a breeding ground it was much inferior to their original habitat. The reef had a much smaller surface area than the Geirfuglasker and provided very limited breeding possibilities for a flightless bird which could not use Eldey's ledges or flat top for nesting sites. The great auk was also at a great disadvantage on Eldey as it was now near human habitation on the mainland and within easier reach of fowlers. Indeed, almost inevitably, it finally came to pass that the last 2 great auks known to exist anywhere in the world were killed on Eldey on 3 June 1844.

There were 14 men all told, led by Vilhjálmur Hákonarson from Kirkjuvogur, who set out from Hafnir in an eight-oared boat on the evening of 2 June 1844. They arrived off Eldey the following morning. There was a rough sea and heavy breakers round the island, but 3 men, Jón Brandsson, Sigurður Ísleifsson and Ketill Ketilsson, leaped safely onto a flat rock on the reef's landing-place. As they moved up the rocky slope at the foot of the cliffs they immediately saw 2 great auks among some other sea-birds and made a rush for them. The great auks fled precipitately along the rocks above the slope, their heads held high and their short wings stuck out from their sides. They moved remarkably quickly and it would have been difficult to have kept up with them at a walking pace. Jón

Below is an old drawing of adult great auks with ice in the background. The great auk was never really an arctic bird like the various penguins of the Antarctic. The evolutionary histories of all these species are similar, except that penguins are only to be found in the southern hemisphere, whereas the great auk was only to be found around the North Atlantic. Had the great auk still been thriving it would have been very interesting to have compared the behaviour of all these species, especially their ability to adapt and survive in such environments.

soon succeeded in cutting off and seizing one of the birds whilst Sigurður and Ketill chased the other one, Sigurður catching it just as it reached the very edge of a sheer drop of several metres into the sea. Ketill returned to the slope where they had first seen the birds and found an egg lying on the bare rock which he recognised as a great auk's. He picked it up, but as it was broken put it down again. It is unknown if there were any other eggs. All this took but a very short time and the men hurried back to the boat as the breakers were becoming more violent. They wrung the birds' necks and threw the carcasses into the boat. Sigurður and Ketill then jumped into the boat themselves, but Jón, an elderly man, hesitated, and the skipper threatened to hook him in with the boat-hook. Finally a rope was thrown to him and he was dragged aboard through the surf.

The weather was worsening, but everything went smoothly once they had pulled clear of the breakers on Eldey and they reached the mainland safely.

Vilhjálmur Hákonarson set off for Reykjavík the following day, intending to take the birds to Carl F. Siemsen as the expedition had been made at his request. He stopped in Hafnarfjörður on the way, however, and met Christian Hansen to whom he sold the birds for 80 rix-dollars. Hansen then let Müller, a Reykjavík chemist, have them and he preserved the flayed carcasses in spirits. They are now in the Copenhagen Zoological Museum, but what became of the skins is unknown.

It is thanks first and foremost to 2 Englishmen, John Wolley and Professor Alfred Newton of Cambridge, that so much is known about the history and final extinction of the great auk. The 2 men visited Iceland from 21 May to 14 July 1858 and stayed at Kirkjuvogur on the Reykjanes peninsula. They intended to visit Eldey, but unfortunately weather conditions never permitted this. They still made great use of their time before returning to England by collecting and recording information about the history of the great auk in Iceland, including the taking of statements from everyone who took part in the 1844 expedition to Eldey (apart from 2 members who were by then deceased). They also collected a great number of great auk bones which they found in kitchen middens and parts of the coastline which had suffered erosion. Professor Newton published his research in *Ibis*, the journal of the British Ornithologists' Union.

The great auk has thus disappeared from the face of the earth after an evolutionary history of thousands of years. The great auk probably spent most of its life at sea, but every spring it had to seek its breeding grounds on mainlands, islands or skerries, and once ashore it became easy prey for man, and its fate became inevitable.

The tragedy of the great auk is not unique in the history of relations between man and birds. It begins with a primitive people hunting for food and a species is thus only moderately persecuted at first. With increasing industrialisation, however, the species becomes systematically exploited both for food and for commercial trade; and finally, once the species has become increasingly rare, the last surviving birds and their eggs become the targets of collectors.

3 Icelandic birds

Some species of birds is the title of a chapter in this original manuscript by Jón Guðmundsson the Learned (1574–1650) *On the Diverse Natures of Iceland*. This page also marks the beginning of a description of Icelandic bird life as Jón the Learned's ornithological research was amongst the first to deal specifically with Icelandic birds. Although his knowledge is widely blended with superstition and extraordinary flights of fancy, there are still many realistic descriptions to be found in his work. A good example is his description of a water rail: 'The brook-crow or water rail likes to be in the dark and burrows into the banks of streams which are covered in snow, but remain unfrozen. It makes a distinctive zig-zag track; doctors have a lot of faith in the healing powers of its fat.' This old description of the water rail's behaviour is so accurate in essentials that there is no doubt it was based on the observation of the habits of this secretive bird (described in greater detail later, see pp. 144–149).

Further information and knowledge of bird life and bird-hunting in the 16th century can be found in Bishop Oddur Einarsson's *Íslandslýsing* (*Description of Iceland*) from around 1590.

When talking about Icelandic birds one tradi-

3. ICELANDIC BIRDS

tionally means the species which actually breed in Iceland. Some of these species visit their breeding grounds for only 3–5 months a year, but others are residents which remain in or near the country all year round. The migratory birds escape Iceland's harsh winters by flying to more southerly lands. During the summer months, however, both resident and migratory breeding birds dominate the bird life of Iceland.

About 70 species of birds breed annually in Iceland, although over 300 kinds have actually been seen here. Most species are thus vagrants, or winter guests which arrive in the autumn and depart in the spring, or passage migrants which call here in the spring or autumn on their way to and from more northerly breeding grounds. Some of these birds have been known to actually breed here on one or more occasions.

Although there are relatively few species of breeding birds in Iceland compared to the nearest European countries, their huge populations mean that Iceland is teeming with bird life nonetheless. The paucity of Icelandic breeding species is undoubtedly a result of its position in the northern hemisphere and its oceanic weather conditions.

Iceland has very little woodland and a rather limited insect life. Moreover it is too far away for many land-birds from other countries with a more varied bird life to reach Iceland in large enough numbers, or at the right times of the year, to be able to live on insects, though many of them could probably survive well enough in Iceland if necessity demanded it. Thus the country's geographical isolation and climate determine the numbers and kinds of Icelandic breeding birds. Over the last few years some new species have been added to the list of birds which have nested here irregularly, but it is still too early to classify them as breeding birds as they have only nested in Iceland some years and not others. Over the last 70 to 80 years at least 17 species have definitely settled in Iceland and become breeding birds which nest here annually.

After the severity of the last Ice Age, it was probably a very long time before birds became established once more in Iceland. The species which are now considered Icelandic are mostly the same as those found in the nearest European countries, or which have their breeding grounds throughout the northern hemisphere. There are 3 Icelandic species, however, which come directly from North America: the great northern diver, Barrow's goldeneye, and the harlequin. Apart from the harlequin, which also nests in eastern Siberia, none of these birds breed anywhere outside the American continent or Greenland except in Iceland. It thus seems safe to conclude that the vast majority of Icelandic birds originated from Europe and not North America.

Icelandic bird life is dominated by sea-birds, waterfowl, and waders. Compared to nearby countries there are relatively very few passerine birds, for though they make up 60% of the world's total bird species they only provide 17% of all the Icelandic species. This is clearly due to the country's geographical position, natural environment and climate.

Although only one third of Icelandic breeding species are sea-birds, in terms of actual numbers they form the overwhelming majority of all Icelandic birds. Some of the species can be counted in millions, there being an estimated minimum of 13 million breeding pairs of Icelandic sea-birds.

Even though sea-birds are by far the most numerous of Icelandic birds, they can only be found in their most natural environment, and to see large numbers of puffins, fulmars, guillemots and kittiwakes one must be able to get to their breeding grounds. The great black-backed gull, however, can usually be seen along all the shores of Iceland.

The main places of special interest to bird-watchers are marked on the map of Iceland on p. 31.

Iceland's most common land-birds can be seen almost anywhere in the country and include the golden plover, the whimbrel, the redshank, the snipe, the meadow pipit, the snow bunting, the wheatear and the raven. The red-necked phalarope and black-headed gull are common in marshy areas, and the arctic tern, the oystercatcher and the ringed plover are widespread along the beaches. The redwing can be found in woodlands or copses anywhere in Iceland, from the valleys and moors to the cultivated gardens of towns and villages. The

A water rail in search of food. *The pictures above are of a water rail which has come out of its hiding-place and is foraging for food in a pool, perhaps hoping to catch insect larvae or sticklebacks before retreating once more to its hideaway. The water rail is reluctant to fly and there is a popular superstition that this secretive bird disappears into the earth.*

3. ICELANDIC BIRDS

white wagtail is also widespread and often found near human habitation, especially in stone walls or under the roofs of farm outhouses. The number of starlings in Reykjavík and its conurbations has greatly increased over the last few decades. They began to breed regularly in Reykjavík in 1960, and though they increased slowly at first, they have multiplied rapidly since 1965. Starlings have also nested in Höfn in Hornafjörður since 1941 at least.

Geese, whooper swans and several species of duck are to be found on Lake Tjörnin in Reykjavík, and all of them are very tame (see p. 17). Moreover a large number of arctic terns nest on Lake Tjörnin's islet, making Reykjavík most certainly the only capital in the world with such a breeding ground in its town centre! Many shore-birds, including ringed plovers, dunlins, purple sandpipers, mallards, and eider ducks, can be seen in the Reykjavík suburbs of Seltjarnarnes and Álftanes, especially in spring and summer.

One does not have to go far from Reykjavík to find sea-birds in their natural habitat as there are 2 main bird-cliffs on Reykjanes, Hafnaberg and Krísuvíkurberg. One can drive quite close to these cliffs and get to see all the most common Icelandic cliff-birds such as kittiwakes, common guillemots, Brünnich's guillemots, razorbills, puffins, and shags as well as herring gulls and glaucous gulls. The black guillemot haunts the rocks and boulders all along the Reykjanes coast.

The abandoned lighthouse at Garðskagi provides a very good observation post for watching birds along the shore, and there is a good view from the mainland of Eldey, the precipitous island to the south-west of Reykjanes. The island is a bird sanctuary and is believed to have the third largest gannetry in the world (see p. 24 and pp. 38–47).

The main road north from Reykjavík goes through Hvalfjörður where there is a great deal of bird life. There are sea-birds all along the fjord and on nearby Lake Meðalfellsvatn there are whooper swans and great northern divers. On River Bugða, issuing from Lake Meðalfellsvatn, there are harlequins. The black-tailed godwit and many other moorland-birds can be found in the fertile lowlands of Borgarfjörður. The Faxaflói coastline between Borgarfjörður and Snæfellsnes is rich in sea-birds, both on the sandy beaches and on the offshore isles and skerries. Moreover the ebb-tide creates large mud-flats which teem with birds, especially knots, turnstones, sanderlings, dunlins, and ringed plovers. These are sometimes joined by passage migrants such as white-fronted geese and brent geese on their way to Greenland from more southerly countries. There are also considerable numbers of oystercatchers along the Faxaflói coastline.

Continuing along the southern coast of Snæfellsnes one can often see great northern divers, whooper swans, and red-throated divers on the many small lakes in the area. There are large colonies of arctic terns, fulmars, common guillemots and Brünnich's guillemots on Snæfellsnes. In the vicinity of Búðir, Arnarstapi and Hellnar there are large numbers of kittiwakes, especially on Svalþúfa.

Offshore from Grundarfjörður is the island of Melrakkaey, a bird sanctuary and the home of a variety of species. Shags and cormorants breed there, and the glaucous gull nests on the island's even ground, a rather unusual occurrence. There are innumerable islands and skerries in Breiðafjörður and all of them teem with bird life. The grey phalarope breeds on some of them, and the shag and cormorant are widespread. It is also occasionally possible to see a white-tailed eagle flying over the fjord. Its nesting grounds have been declared sanctuaries and it is forbidden to approach their nests anywhere in Iceland.

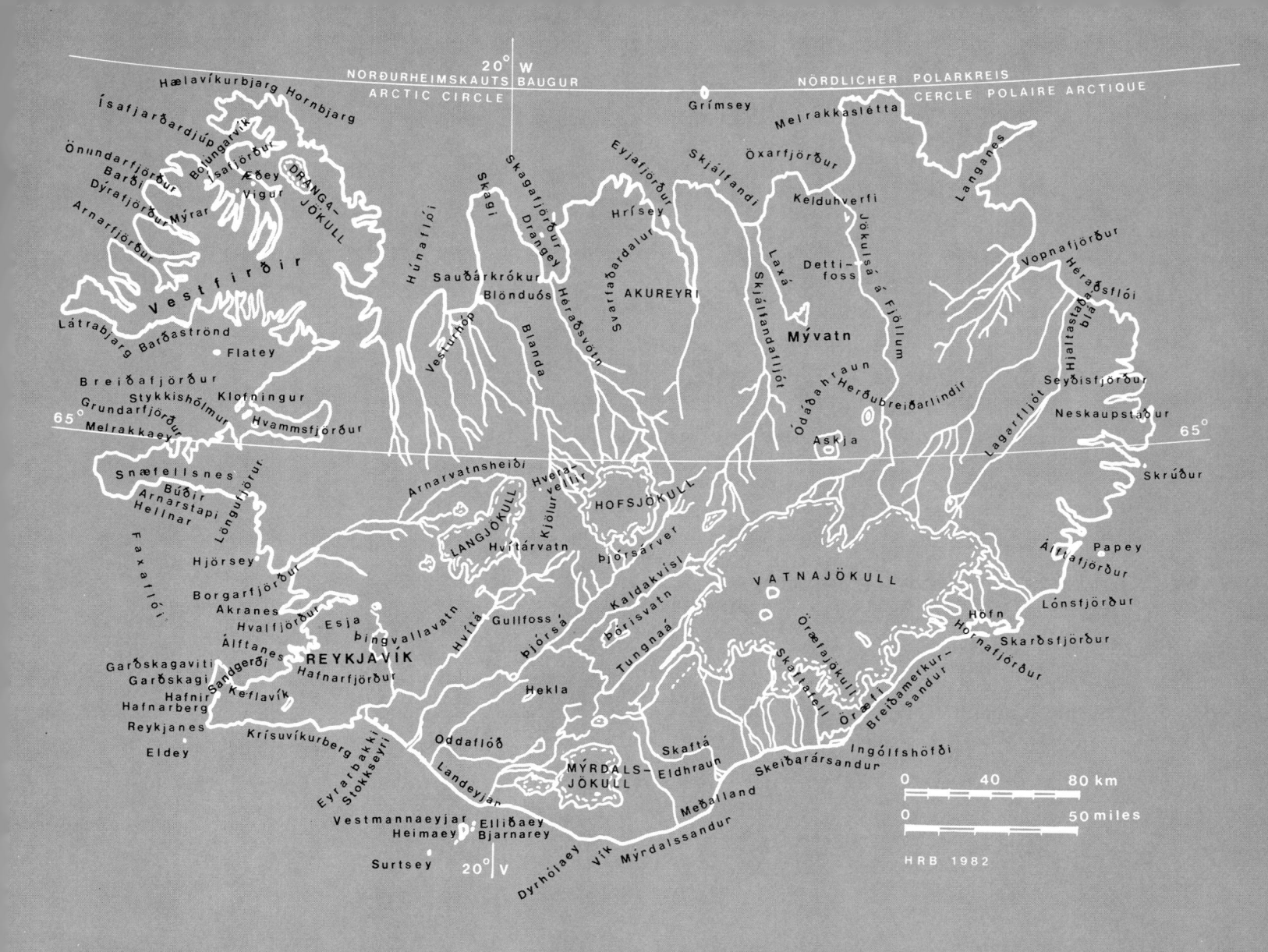

There are many places of interest for bird-watchers in the Vestfirðir, first and foremost Iceland's 3 greatest bird-cliffs, Látrabjarg, Hælavíkurbjarg, and Hornbjarg. Látrabjarg is the largest of the 3 and is considered one of the most magnifi-

This map of Iceland shows some of the most important and interesting places for bird-watchers. More detailed information about the likely habitats of specific species can be found in the main text. This information is not exhaustive, however, and one of the chief delights of bird-watching is to suddenly come across a rarely seen bird where it is least expected.

The Icelandic Museum of Natural History in Reykjavík is the centre of Icelandic ornithological research. Every year it supervises the ringing of a great number of birds. Above are some examples of Icelandic bird-rings, bearing the superscription: MUS. RER. NAT., BOX 5320, REYKJAVÍK, ICELAND. The sizes vary, of course, to suit all kinds of birds. The flat tab with a wire loop attached is a wing-tag. Anyone who finds a ringed or tagged bird should kindly inform the Museum in Reykjavík of the exact date and location of their find. This information provides a lot of valuable data about the life span and movements of species as the Museum keeps a record of where and when these birds were originally ringed or tagged. On the left is a shag chick being ringed on Langey Island in Breiðafjörður.

32

cent bird-cliffs in the world. It stretches for 16 km and in most places is 400–500 m high. It is also the easiest of the 3 cliffs to get to as there is a road right out to the lighthouse on its western edge, the most westerly point in Iceland. From there one can walk eastwards along the cliff-top.

Látrabjarg's ledges are crowded with all the main cliff-birds of Iceland, especially common and Brünnich's guillemots, fulmars, kittiwakes, and razorbills. Landslides and rock falls have formed a rocky, boulder-strewn scree at the foot of the cliff called Stóraurð which provides the breeding ground for the largest single razorbill colony in the world. Stóraurð reaches up the cliff-face somewhat and can be seen from the cliff-top, though the best way to see the razorbill colony is from the sea. The many puffins on top of Látrabjarg are especially tame. They make their burrows in the grass-covered cliff-tops and in the boulders at the foot of the cliff. The multitude of birds on the Vestfirðir cliffs can be quite overwhelming, and indeed the total population of Icelandic cliff-birds can be numbered in tens of millions.

Cliff-birds are also widespread on the sheer rock faces of mountains which are quite a distance from the sea. There is a large glaucous gull colony, for example, on Mt. Barði, between Dýrafjörður and Önundarfjörður.

In many places in the Vestfirðir, as elsewhere in Iceland, farmers have established nesting grounds for eider ducks in order to collect their down. One may not enter these grounds without the farmers' permission. Some of the largest eider duck colonies in Iceland are at Mýrar in Dýrafjörður, and on the islands of Æðey and Vigur in the Ísafjarðardjúp, containing altogether around 2,500–4,500 eider duck pairs. King eiders often come from Greenland to the Vestfirðir and mate with Icelandic eider ducks, but pairs of King eiders have never been known to breed in Iceland.

The low wetlands of the Húnaflói and Skagafjörður basins support a multifarious bird life. The estuary of the River Héraðsvötn is a bird sanctuary where most varieties of marsh-birds occur, including the black-tailed godwit. This area is sometimes partly under water in the spring, and whooper swans, newly arrived in Iceland, gather there whilst waiting for the ice to melt on the Skagi lakes. Barnacle geese also have a short sojourn there when on their way to their breeding grounds in Greenland.

All the commonest Icelandic cliff-birds breed on Drangey island, whose sheer cliffs rise out of the sea in Skagafjörður. Among them are a large number of common and Brünnich's guillemots. There are occasional boat-trips to Drangey from Sauðárkrókur, and the many good vantage points for observing cliff-birds on the island are easy to reach – for those who do not suffer too badly from vertigo.

The bird life in Eyjafjörður is similar to that of Skagafjörður. Common gulls have their nesting sites in the Eyjafjörður basin and in the Svarfaðardalur bird sanctuary. There is a lot of woodland around Akureyri and redwings, redpolls, and other land-birds are common there, as well as such marsh-birds as redshanks, snipes, and ducks. There are many ptarmigans on Hrísey Island, and the gyrfalcon hunts for food there. This majestic bird of prey can be seen over a wide area of north and north-east Iceland as its main breeding grounds are in this part of the country. The gyrfalcon is a completely protected bird, and one must have the permission of the Ministry of Education and Culture to approach its nests.

From Akureyri one can sail or fly to Grímsey, the most northerly habitation in Iceland, and an island with a great deal of bird life. All the main cliff-birds can be found there, and it is the only place in Iceland where the little auk breeds. The little auk is a protected bird, but it is rapidly declining in numbers nonetheless. Only very few breeding pairs remain and there is a danger that they will soon disappear from the island altogether.

The Lake Mývatn area is renowned for its bird life, especially the 14 or 15 species of ducks which breed there, all the Icelandic species apart from the eider which only nests by the sea. The most common of these species are the tufted duck (ca. 3,000 pairs), the scaup (ca. 1,700 pairs), and Barrow's goldeneye (ca. 700 pairs). Other ducks commonly found around Mývatn include the common scoter, the long-tailed duck, the red-breasted merganser, the wigeon, the harlequin, the gadwall and the teal. Mallards and pintails are less in evidence, and the shoveler, the goosander and the pochard are very rare. Slavonian grebes also nest around Mývatn, and the short-eared owl breeds in its marshy areas. Many snipes, red-necked phalaropes and other waders breed around Mývatn too, and gyrfalcons and merlins nest in the nearby mountains.

Many of the duck species found around Lake Mývatn also occur in the extensive marshes inland from Öxarfjörður. At Rauðinúpur on Melrakkaslétta and on Langanes are gannet breeding grounds and colonies of other sea-birds.

Great numbers of greylag geese can be seen inland from Héraðsflói and along the River Lagarfljót. Hallormsstaðir and its surroundings have Iceland's largest woodlands and are thus naturally haunted by many species of land-birds.

The islands of Skrúður and Papey off the Austfirðir are swarming with sea-birds. There are many puffins, a large colony of herring gulls, and a gannetry on Skrúður, but landing conditions on the island make it very difficult to get there unless the sea is very calm.

Many species of waders haunt the extensive mud-flats in Lónsfjörður and Hornafjörður and their surrounding areas.

There are literally thousands of great skuas nesting on the great Breiðamerkur and Skeiðarár sands, and indeed these are the largest great skua breeding grounds in the northern hemisphere. Many arctic skuas and great black-backed gulls also nest among the great skuas. Most of Iceland's commonest cliff-birds can be seen on Ingólfshöfði and its ledges also provide roosting places for gannets, though they have not as yet begun to breed there.

Öræfasveit is the home of quite a few wrens, Iceland's smallest bird, and is, moreover, the best place in Iceland for coming across vagrant birds from continental Europe. The water rail's main breeding ground used to be in Meðalland, below the Eldhraun lava-field, but although there are still many suitable bogs in the area the water rail is rarely seen in Iceland now and no longer has any known nesting sites here.

The first lesser black-backed gull's nest was found near Vík in Mýrdalur in 1929, and the species has flourished since then, now being classified as an Icelandic breeding bird. There are many puffins and cliff-birds on the Dyrhólaey rock, and gannets have frequented the stacks beyond it and have probably also nested there.

All the islands of the Vestmannaeyjar teem with bird life. All the main Icelandic sea-birds can be found there as well as the breeding grounds of Manx shearwaters, storm petrels and Leach's petrels. Gannets nest on 4 of the smaller isles.

There is considerable bird life in the marshes of the southern lowlands in spite of much draining and cultivation. The black-tailed godwit nests

This young white-tailed eagle has a majestic expression, as if aware of its noble descent.

there and white-fronted geese and pink-footed geese occur as passage migrants on the way to and from their breeding grounds. Greylag geese are widespread in the area, but pink-footed geese breed mainly in the Þjórsárver to the south of Hofsjökull glacier.

The snowy owl has bred in the Ódáðahraun lavafields and can sometimes be seen flying over the central highlands, but it is no longer certain that it breeds in Iceland.

Ptarmigans can be found on the inland heaths and moorlands, and whooper swans and great northern divers occur on mountain lakes and sheets of water, swans preferring lakes with some vegetation.

Many Icelandic birds are migratory and seek warmer lands in the winter. A number of them (e.g. the redwing) remain in Iceland all year, however, and are thus really residents. Such small birds as redpolls, snow buntings and wrens are resident Icelandic birds, and when the winters are hard they often seek refuge in towns and villages and willingly accept food from humans who welcome them with pleasure.

Guillemot
(Uria aalge)

Grey Phalarope
(Phalaropus fulicarius)

Shag
(Phalacrocorax aristotelis)

Redpoll
(Acanthis flammea)

Arctic Tern
(Sterna paradisaea)

Snowy Owl
(Nyctea scandiaca)

Great Black-backed Gull
(Larus marinus)

Whooper Swan
(Cygnus cygnus)

Wren
(Troglodytes troglodytes)

Razorbill
(Alca torda)

All the Icelandic birds' eggs shown here are life-size, so one can compare in detail their shapes, colours and dimensions. Cliff-birds' eggs (e.g. guillemots') have a distinctive pear-shape. Conical eggs roll in a narrow circle and are thus less likely to roll off cliff-ledges. Birds which lay pale-coloured eggs usually cover them when they leave the nest. Apart from hiding them from predators, this also keeps them warm, especially if they are covered with grass or down. Dark and speckled eggs are much harder to see against their background so they are much safer from predators when left uncovered.

Gannet
(*Sula bassana*)

Water Rail
(*Rallus aquaticus*)

Harlequin
(*Histrionicus histrionicus*)

Ptarmigan
(*Lagopus mutus*)

Whimbrel
(*Numenius phaeopus*)

Gyrfalcon
(*Falco rusticolus*)

Great Skua
(*Stercorarius skua*)

Little Auk
(*Alle alle*)

Shoveler
(*Anas clypeata*)

Great Northern Diver
(*Gavia immer*)

White-tailed Eagle
(*Haliaeetus albicilla*)

4 Islands and skerries

Hellisey, one of 14 outer isles of the Vestmannaeyjar, is formed of volcanic tuff rock and is part of an ancient circular crater. Above is a view of Hellisey from the north-west, where the cliffs are mostly sheer; Háhaus (122 m) is on the left, Höfði on the right. Just below the cliff-top is a sloping ledge called Flagtir which is crowded with gannets.

4. ISLANDS AND SKERRIES

There are innumerable **islands and skerries** all round the coast of Iceland. Some of the islands are populated, though others, once inhabited, are now deserted. Most of the isles have never been populated but have still been utilised, especially in former times, for sheep-grazing, fowling and egg-collecting. A few skerries support some plant life, but the majority of the smaller ones have little or no vegetation; indeed many of them are under water at high tide. The one thing that most of the isles and skerries do have in common, however, is a flourishing bird life. Their size and shape usually determine which species use them as breeding grounds. Some of the islands have high and sheer bird-cliffs, but as such cliffs are common along the shores of the mainland itself, the birds which nest on them will be examined later. This chapter will deal only with the most characteristic birds of Iceland's offshore isles and skerries: the gannet, the shag, the cormorant, the great and lesser black-backed gulls, the herring gull, glaucous gull and common gull, the little auk, the black guillemot, the Manx shearwater, Leach's petrel, and the storm petrel.

These birds do not keep exclusively to isles and skerries, of course, but seek breeding sites wherever conveniently near to plentiful feeding grounds. Moreover in certain places some of these species can be observed from land, especially along rocky beaches, or where stacks and skerries are very close to shore.

The Vestmannaeyjar are especially interesting for their various species of sea-birds. Only one of the 15 islands, Heimaey, is actually inhabited. Most of the other 14 outer isles are formed of tuff volcanic rock and have grassy tops, even though they rise steeply out of the sea.

Eldey is an island about 14 km south-west of Reykjanes. It is 77 m high, formed of volcanic tuff, and has precipitous cliffs which are difficult to climb. It is grey-coloured from bird droppings and used to be called 'the meal sack' by foreign seamen. The drawing below is from an English travel book of 1835. Eldey is believed to have the third largest gannetry in the world, with an estimated 16,000 breeding pairs. The picture of Eldey overleaf (pp. 40–41) was taken from the air on 15 August 1983 during the gannet breeding season. Eldey is an oblong island lying from south-west to north-east in line with the Reykjanes Ridge and other rifts of this area. The reef on which one can land when the sea is calm extends to the north-east and is on the left of the picture. Above the landing-reef the cliff reaches a height of just over 60 m. The island is about 100 m at its widest, and is just over 200 m long, the surface area of the top being about 10,500 square metres.

The first historically recorded ascent of Eldey was by Hjalti Jónsson and 2 comrades in 1894. They drove a strong iron bolt into the top of the cliff from which a chain-ladder was later attached. Fowlers visited Eldey fairly frequently in the following years, and between 1910 and 1939 there were 21 expeditions to the island, with an average of 3,300 young gannets being killed each trip. Eldey has been protected by law since 1940, and it is forbidden to go there without the permission of the Icelandic Nature Conservation Council. In 1971 some men climbed Eldey illegally; the old bolts were still in place on the cliff, but the chain-ladder had corroded away. On 20 August 1982 a group of 18 had the requisite permission to land on Eldey; this expedition is recorded in greater detail elsewhere (see pp. 45–47).

The Meal-sack and pinnacled Rock.

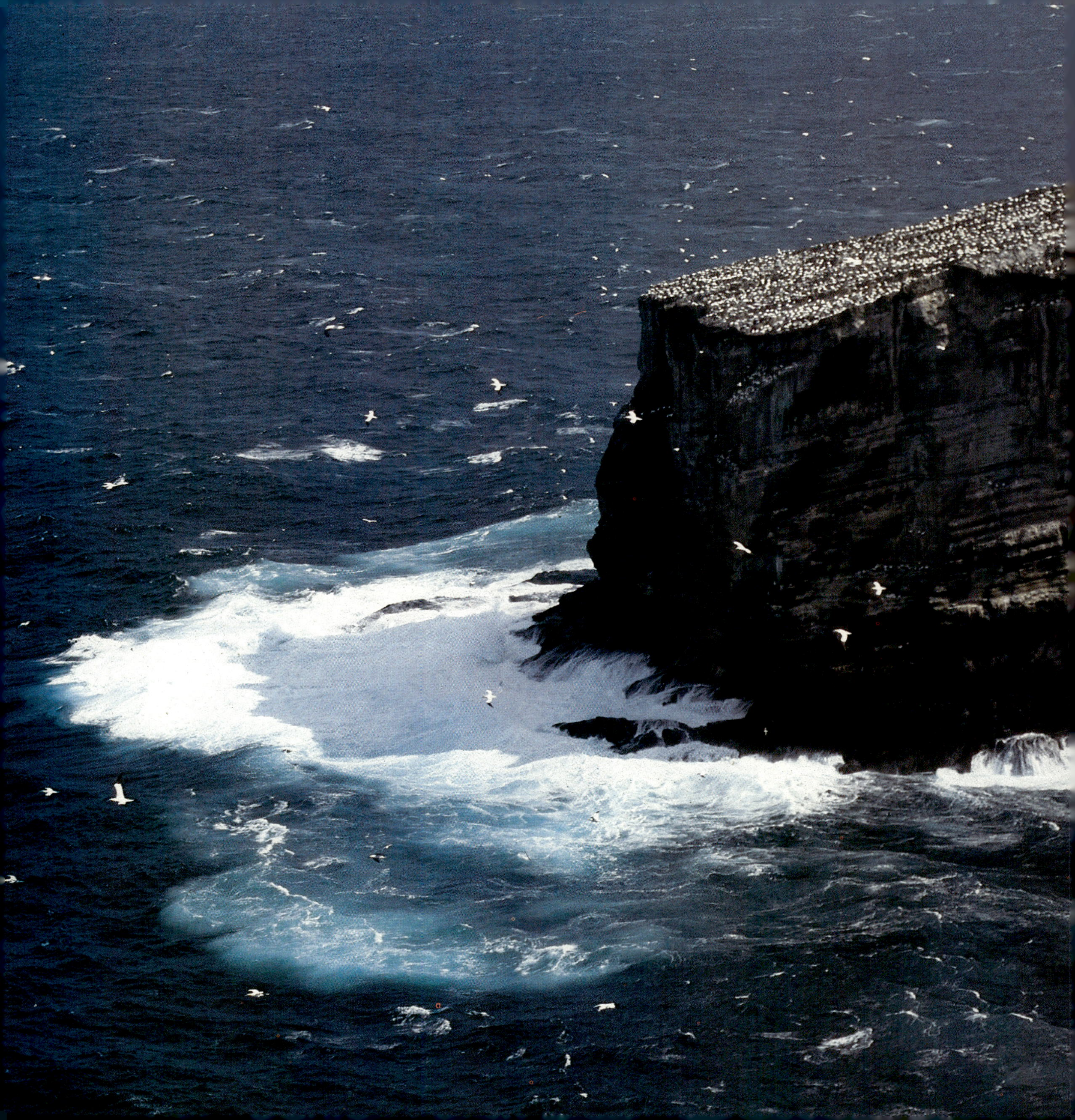

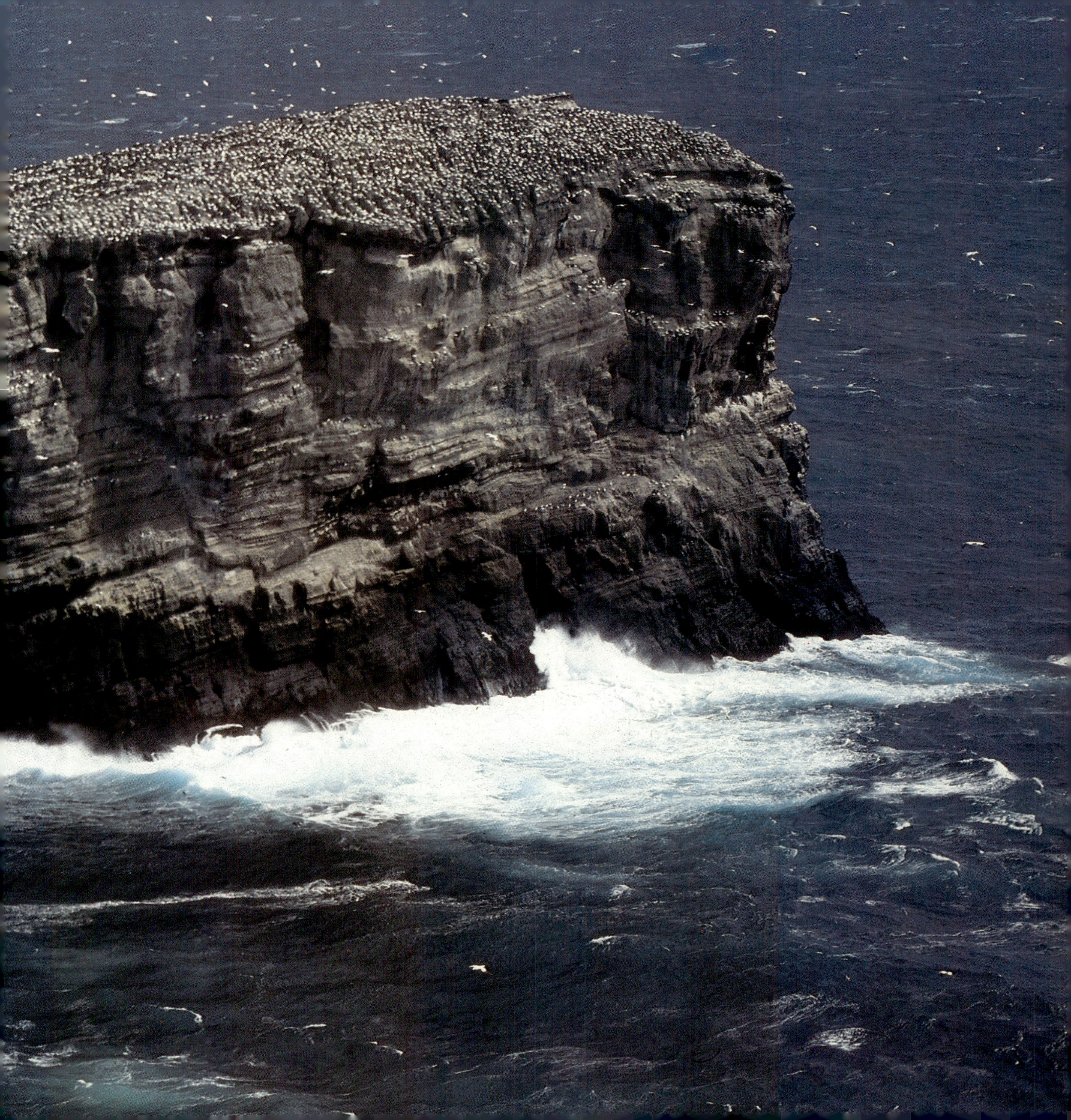

The **GANNET** (Sula bassana) breeds elsewhere in Iceland besides Eldey; it nests on 4 isles of the Vestmannaeyjar, i.e. Geldungur (above), Súlnasker, Brandur, and Hellisey; in the north-east it breeds at Rauðinúpur on Melrakkaslétta and on Langanes; in the east there is a gannetry on the isle of Skrúður. Gannets have also nested on the stacks near Dyrhólaey and have roosted on Ingólfshöfði in the south and on Svörtuloft on Snæfellsnes, though neither place has yet been confirmed as a breeding ground. Gannets used to nest on Drangey and Grímsey, but have abandoned these islands this century. They also used to breed on Súlnastapi by Hælavíkurbjarg, and there were once gannetries on Geirfuglasker and Geirfugladrangur, to the south-west of Eldey, but these were destroyed in an earthquake.

Above are **Súlnasker** (left) and **Geldungur** (right), and below are **Elliðaey** (left) and **Bjarnarey** (right), all outer isles of the Vestmannaeyjar. Súlnasker (Pillar Skerry) is so called because it rests on columns; one can row under it through to the other side. It is about 80 m high with sheer cliffs on all sides, and to climb it one must sometimes haul oneself up on chains fastened into the rock. There is a large gannetry on the slightly grassy top. Geldungur (86 m) is a little bit higher than Súlnasker, but again one has to edge along ledges and sometimes use chains to get up the steep cliffs. On the summit of Geldungur is a gannet colony, and on a sloping ledge below its highest point is one of the largest continuous guillemot aggregations in Iceland (see pictures on pp. 90 & 92). Elliðaey and Bjarnarey also have very high cliffs, but they are much easier to ascend. Manx shearwaters, Leach's petrels and storm petrels breed in burrows on these 2 isles. All 4 islands have many cliff-birds and are often frequented by fowlers, especially for puffins.

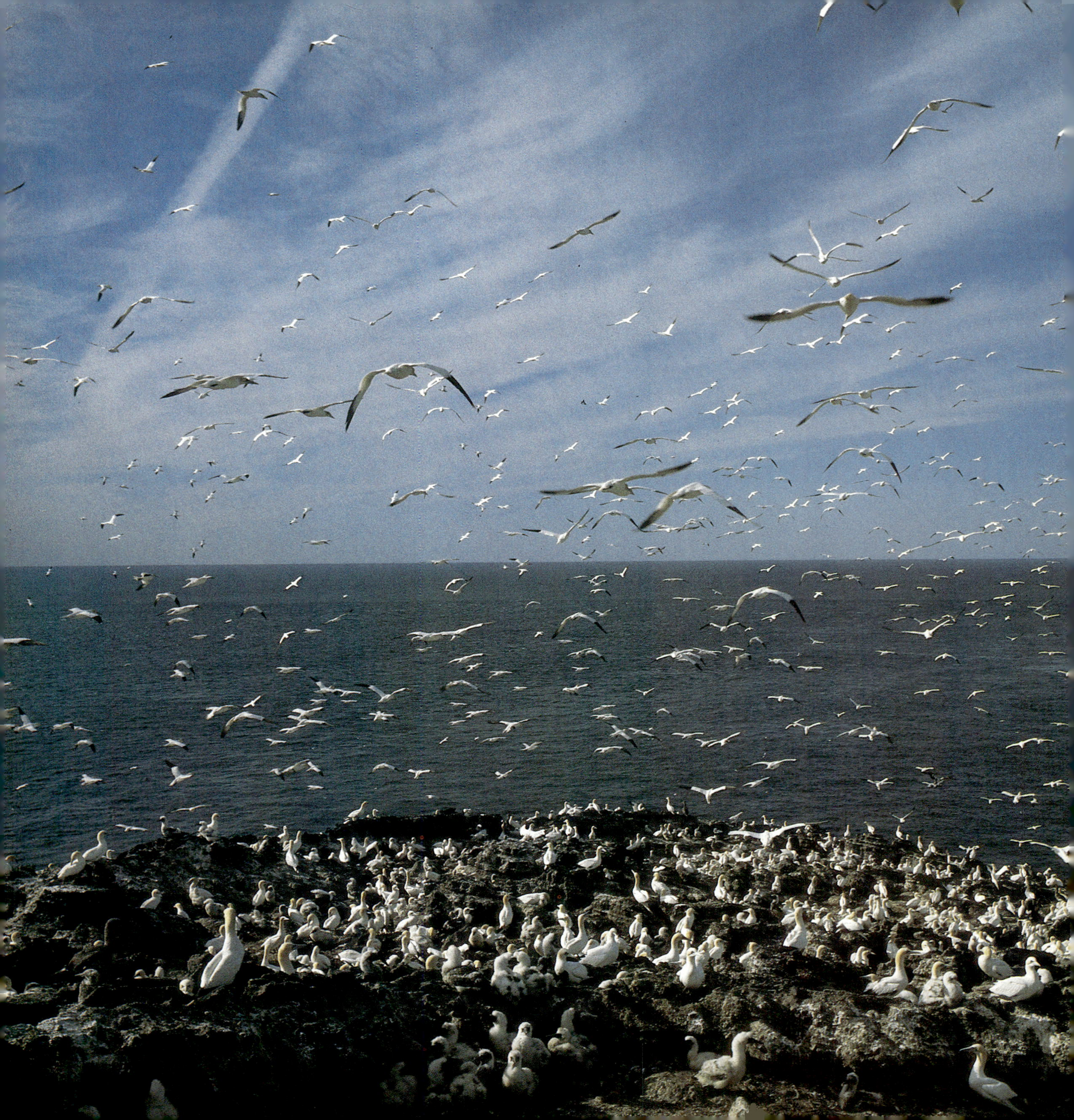

Eldey is the home of the largest gannet colony in Iceland, and the third largest in the world; only St. Kilda and Grassholm in the British Isles have bigger gannetries. On 20 August 1982 a group of 18 ascended Eldey and these pictures were taken on this expedition. The number of gannets on top of Eldey is quite overwhelming. It is only just possible to step between the closely packed nesting-stacks, and even then one is ankle-deep in bird droppings. The treads of one's footwear are soon clogged with it and they become very slippery and smelly. The soles have to be well cleaned if one is to keep one's footing when negotiating the narrow cliff-ledges on the way down. From a distance the sloping summit of Eldey seems much smoother than it really is, and having reached the top one is faced with a very uneven surface; there is a metre-high ridge of tuff rock, with slopes on both sides, running along the entire length of the island. At the very top there is a higher cross-ridge, and at the south-western end a deep fissure.

4. ISLANDS AND SKERRIES

The **GANNET** (*Sula bassana*) is a large, majestic and beautiful bird. In spite of its size, however, it is not as heavy as one might suppose, for although it has many feathers and a huge wing-span it has a proportionately small body. Adult gannets thus weigh between 2.5 and 3.5 kg, though fully grown but flightless young can weigh anything up to 4.5 kg or even more.

The gannet's plumage is mostly white, but with pale buff on the side and crown of the head and on the throat and neck. The extensive wing-tips are black and the legs dark grey. The irises are light grey with a narrow black outer ring. Both sexes have the same colouring which remains constant throughout the year.

A newly hatched gannet chick is blind and almost completely naked, its skin a bluey-black colour, as can be seen on the picture at the bottom of p. 48. The chick is soon covered in white down, however, (see picture at the top of p. 48) which then gives way to a juvenile plumage as it becomes fully fledged (see picture on p. 49). It is then dark brown on the upper-parts, head and neck, but thickly speckled with white, and dirty-white on the under-parts with greyish-brown mottling. The gannet moults every year, gradually becoming lighter in colour until it has attained its full adult plumage when 4 or 5 years old.

The gannet's breeding grounds are on the western and eastern shores of the North Atlantic. As mentioned previously, Eldey has the third largest gannet colony in the world with almost 16,000 of the total 22,000 breeding pairs nesting in Iceland at 8 known nesting areas. Apart from Eldey there are gannet colonies on 4 of the outer isles of the Vestmannaeyjar (i.e. Súlnasker, Geldungur, Hellisey, and Brandur) and also at Rauðinúpur on Melrakkaslétta, on Langanes peninsula, and on the isle of Skrúður, offshore from Fáskrúðsfjörður. Gannets have also nested on the rock-stacks near Dyrhólaey, but it is uncertain as to whether they still do so.

The gannet prefers to breed on the oceanic cliffs of secluded promontories, or in crowded colonies on the summits of precipitous and uninhabited islands which are difficult to ascend (e.g. Eldey, and Súlnasker and Geldungur in the Vestmannaeyjar). The entire plateau of Eldey is packed solid with gannet nests (see pictures on pp. 40–41). The gannet can also breed on sloping slabs of rock or the ledges and buttresses of crags. Its nest is mostly made of various kinds of seaweed which is piled up into a tall stack with a shallow hollow at the top. These stacks are 40–50 cm in diameter at the base, and are usually around 30–40 cm high. In very crowded gannetries the nests are so closely juxtaposed that there is only a very narrow gap between them in which the birds' excreta collects, forming a layer of cess often 10 cm thick. In rainy weather this faecal sludge forms streams on Eldey and Súlnasker which cascade off the cliff-edges. This makes Eldey look greyish from a distance, and foreign seamen used to call the island 'the meal sack.'

The gannet only lays one egg, a small one in relation to the bird's size, and when incubating the egg it covers it with its webbed feet. The main breeding season is in April, but many gannets also breed throughout May, which means that there are often gannet eggs and young at different stages of development within the same colony. The gannet incubates its egg for just over 6 weeks, and the young do not go to sea until 10–11 weeks after they have hatched. The parent birds take it in turns to sit, and they both also take part in the procuring of food and feeding the chick. Once the chick has left the nest and gone to sea, however, the parents have

4. ISLANDS AND SKERRIES

nothing more to do with it. The young gannet thus severs all connection with its parents in one jump, so to speak, as soon as it leaps off the breeding ledge or sill. Moreover the young gannet has to be without the protection of its parents during the fateful days or weeks whilst it is learning the difficult art of plunging headlong into the sea after fish. The last gannet young to go to sea do so in October when the adult birds also finally depart from their breeding grounds. After mid-December, however, they are to be seen once more in the Vestmannaeyjar and south-west Iceland, and they have returned to their breeding grounds by February. It thus seems hardly appropriate to classify fully grown gannets as migratory birds.

The gannet procures food by plunging into the ocean from a height of 45 to 60 m. It usually lets its own weight generate the speed of the dive, and uses its wings to steer with. It enters the water at tremendous speed, but never reaches a greater depth than from 3 to 6 m and is seldom under water for more than 6 seconds. Gannets can also dive for food whilst swimming on the surface of the sea.

The picture above right is of a gannet chick being ringed on Eldey during the expedition of 20 August 1982. About 600 gannet young were ringed in all. Samples of volcanic rock were also collected for geological research, including a comparison with samples from the sub-oceanic Reykjanes Ridge.

The picture on the right is of Eldey at sunset as the expedition members started back for the mainland after a memorable day's visit to the island's magnificent colony of gannets.

Above are 3 gannets and chicks on nesting-stacks on a broad cliff-ledge of Hellisey. The nests are mostly made from seaweed, but sometimes bits of abandoned fishing-nets are used. These are made from artificial materials and can be a danger to chicks if they become entangled in them. Even many adult gannets die at sea in such 'ghost nets'. On the left is a newly hatched gannet chick completely bare of feathers. On the right are 2 well-grown gannet nestlings which have not yet learned to fly. They are moulting and will soon have a speckled plumage.

48

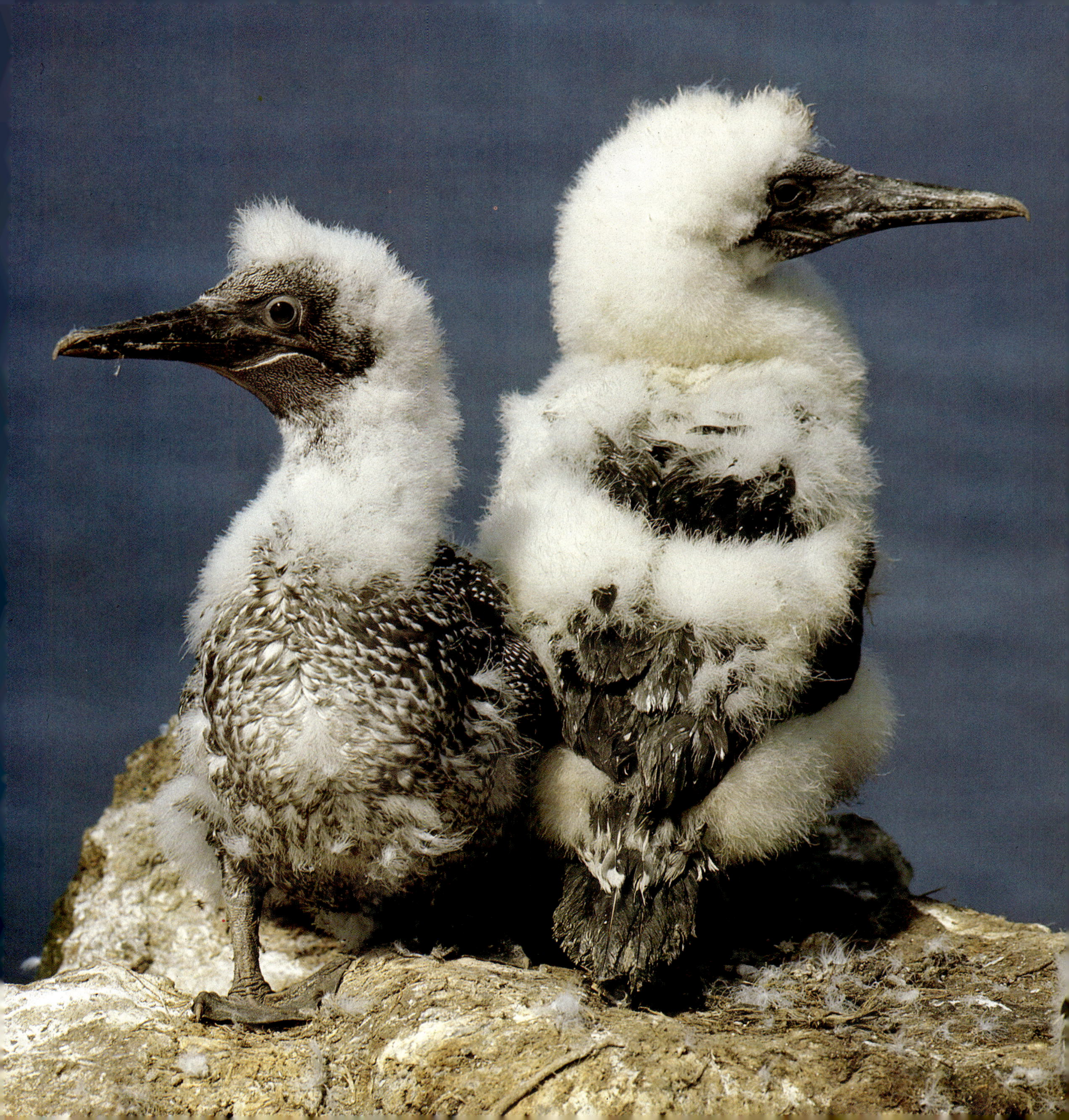

LEACH'S PETREL (*Oceanodroma leucorrhoa*), the **STORM PETREL** (*Hydrobates pelagicus*), and the **MANX SHEARWATER** (*Puffinus puffinus*) are all closely related species belonging to the fulmar family. The life patterns of all 3 birds have many similarities, including a preference for breeding on uninhabited outer islands. Storm petrels prefer to nest under stones, among boulders, or in rocky crevices, but Leach's petrels and Manx shearwaters make nesting burrows in grass or turf; Leach's petrel will also sometimes nest among boulders. A characteristic of all these birds is that whilst breeding they are nocturnal. During the day one would hardly be aware of them in their nesting areas, but at night the darkness suddenly swarms with them as they fly back and forth out to sea. Outside the breeding season these birds mostly live far out at sea, and in winter they seek more southerly parts of the Atlantic, even as far as South Africa; such living habits mean that they are all unfamiliar birds to the public.

Leach's and storm petrels and the Manx shearwater all produce 1 egg per breeding pair. Their eggs are white as they are normally well hidden from predators in deep holes and burrows. The incubation period for the 2 species of petrel is 30–45 days, and for a Manx shearwater 52 days, in all cases the parents taking turns at sitting. The fledging period for a young Leach's petrel is only just over a month, but a Manx shearwater chick is reared in its burrow for over 3 months. The Manx shearwater lives mostly on small pelagic fish whilst the petrels feed on plankton. Leach's and storm petrels are amongst the smallest of sea-birds; the smaller of the 2, the storm petrel, is not much bigger than a snow bunting, or about 15 cm long. Leach's petrel is about 20 cm long and is distinguishable from the storm petrel by, among other things, its forked tail. The storm petrel, on the other hand, has a more distinctive white rump and black square-shaped tail. *The picture on the left (on p. 50) is of a Leach's petrel*, taken at night in the petrels' breeding ground on Elliðaey in the Vestmannaeyjar. The picture at the bottom of p. 53 shows both a storm petrel (left) and a Leach's petrel (right). The picture on this page is of the perfect breeding ground for both kinds of petrel, the so-called Skápar on Elliðaey. These are ledges of stratified lava piled up like huge slabs of stone; storm petrels nest in the deep holes and crevices between the strata whilst Leach's petrels make nesting burrows in the grass slopes on top of Skápar. If one puts one's ear to the cracks and crevices one can often hear a calm purring sound from the sitting birds, not unlike the purring of a contented cat!

Petrels are very light flyers and one can hardly hear them even if they pass close by. They like to fly in the dark, and very low over rough seas as the turbulence of the ocean brings to the surface the plankton on which they live; indeed petrels fly so near to the surface of the sea that, when they dangle their legs, they look as if they are walking on the waves. Seamen have thus called petrels 'St. Peter's bird' after the apostle who intended to walk on water.

The Manx shearwater is the largest of these 3 fulmars and has a length of about 35 cm. It is sooty or browny-black on its upper-parts, but snow-white on its under-parts, and there is a very distinct line where the plumage markings change. Like the petrels, the Manx shearwater is only active at night when breeding. It makes a nesting burrow in grass or turf, just like the puffin, and indeed the 2 birds often share the same breeding ground and it can be difficult to tell their nests apart. Manx shearwater burrows are generally narrower, but this is not always conclusive as it sometimes makes its nest in a side-tunnel from a puffin's burrow. These tunnels are sometimes 1 m long, and at their deepest point there is a wide recess in which the birds collect grass, feathers, tufts of wool, etc., to make a nest for the egg. There is often a short side-tunnel just before the nesting recess where one of the birds can sit if both parents are at home. The Manx shearwater has quite a large breeding ground on Ystiklettur in the Vestmannaeyjar, and also occurs on the islands of Elliðaey, Bjarnarey, Suðurey, and Álsey. Manx shearwaters often collect in flocks in the evenings, and at dusk in late summer many such flocks can be seen on the sea around the Vestmannaeyjar.

The Manx shearwater feeds its chick on regurgitated fish and fish oil, and it soon grows exceedingly fat on such a nutritious diet. In August, however, the parent birds reduce its food supply and thus oblige the chick to learn to fly and fend for itself.

The picture at the top of p. 53 is of a fully grown Manx shearwater chick and was taken on Ystiklettur in the Vestmannaeyjar at the end of August. The young bird has now acquired all the main features of a Manx shearwater.

The picture of a **Leach's petrel** on p. 50 was taken at night at the nesting site on Elliðaey in the Vestmannaeyjar. Above is a **storm petrel** incubating its egg in sand under a large boulder. It was so dark under the rock that a flashlight was used, but this did not disturb the bird, which unconcernedly continued sitting. On the left is a **storm petrel** with an extremely fat chick. At the top of the next page is a fully fledged Manx shearwater ready to leave its nest and go to sea. The picture was taken late in August when the fledgling had moulted almost all of its down and had attained all the main features of an adult Manx shearwater. It has almost the same colouring as an adult except that it is speckled brown on the sides. The picture below, on the right, was taken at night at the Elliðaey nesting grounds and shows both a **storm petrel** (left) and a **Leach's petrel** (right).

52

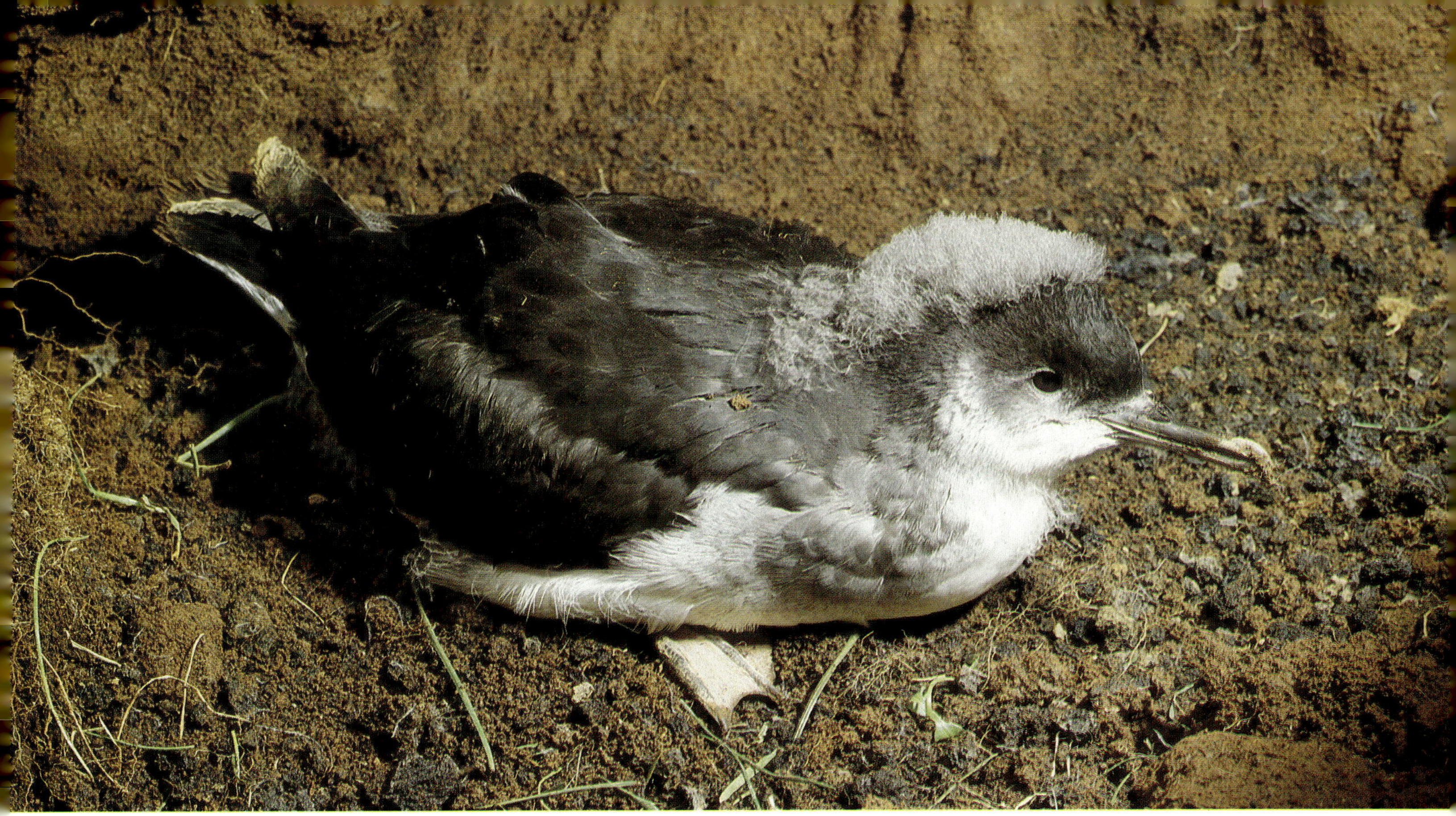

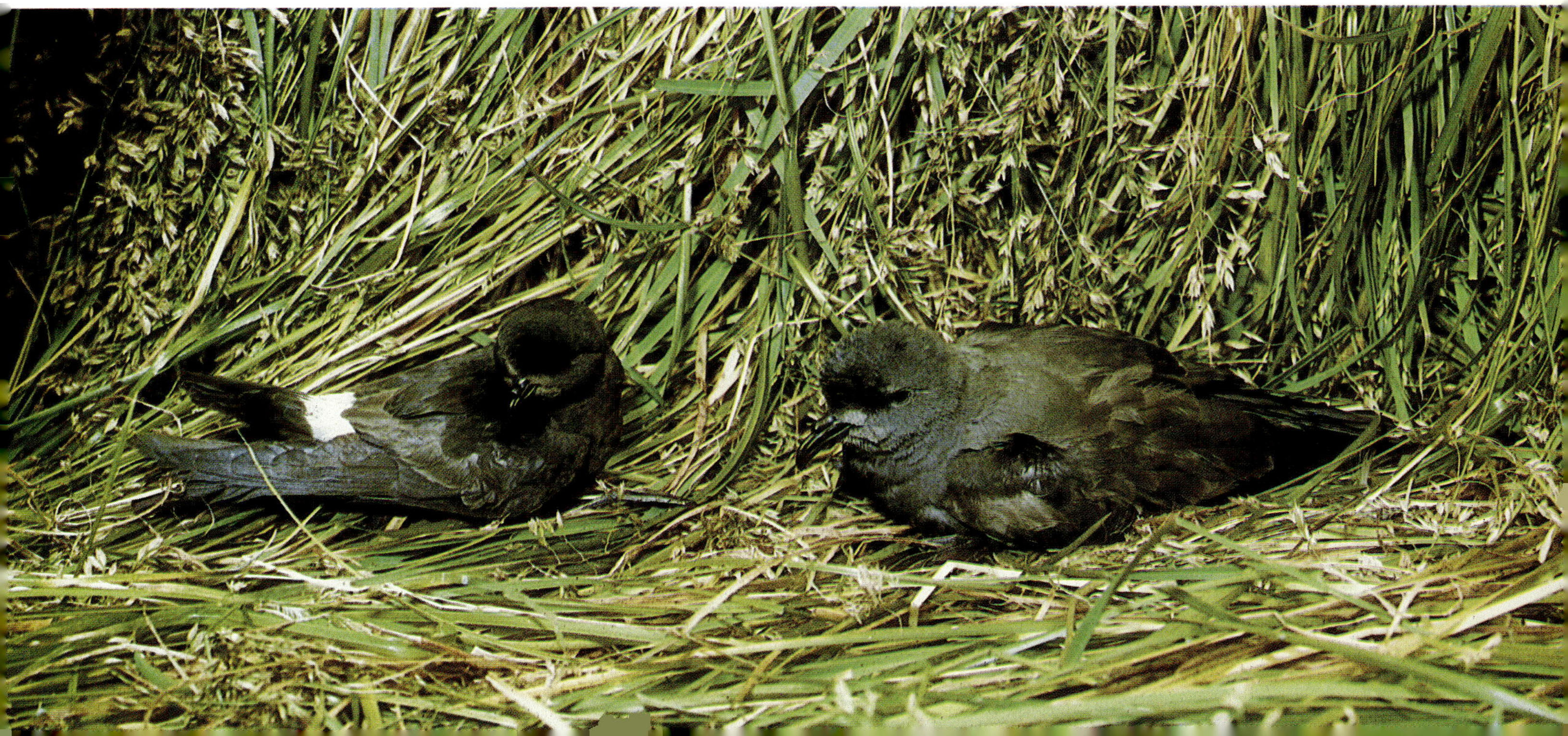

Above is a view of Hellisey from Höfði. Brandur is in the distance, partly obscuring Álsey. All these are outer isles of the Vestmannaeyjar. Even though they are very steep, most of them have grassy summits, often completely riddled with puffin burrows and tunnels. Hellisey's landing-place is in a nook under Höfði, from whence one can walk up the steep tuff rock to the fowlers' cabin on the island. The picture on the right was taken on Langey in Breiðafjörður, where shags breed. In the background are some of Breiðafjörður's innumerable isles and skerries, all teeming with bird life. There is a regular ferry-service from Stykkishólmur to the populated island of Flatey, a very interesting place for the observation of birds. Even though part of the island is a sanctuary during the breeding season, there are still plenty of birds to see outside this area.

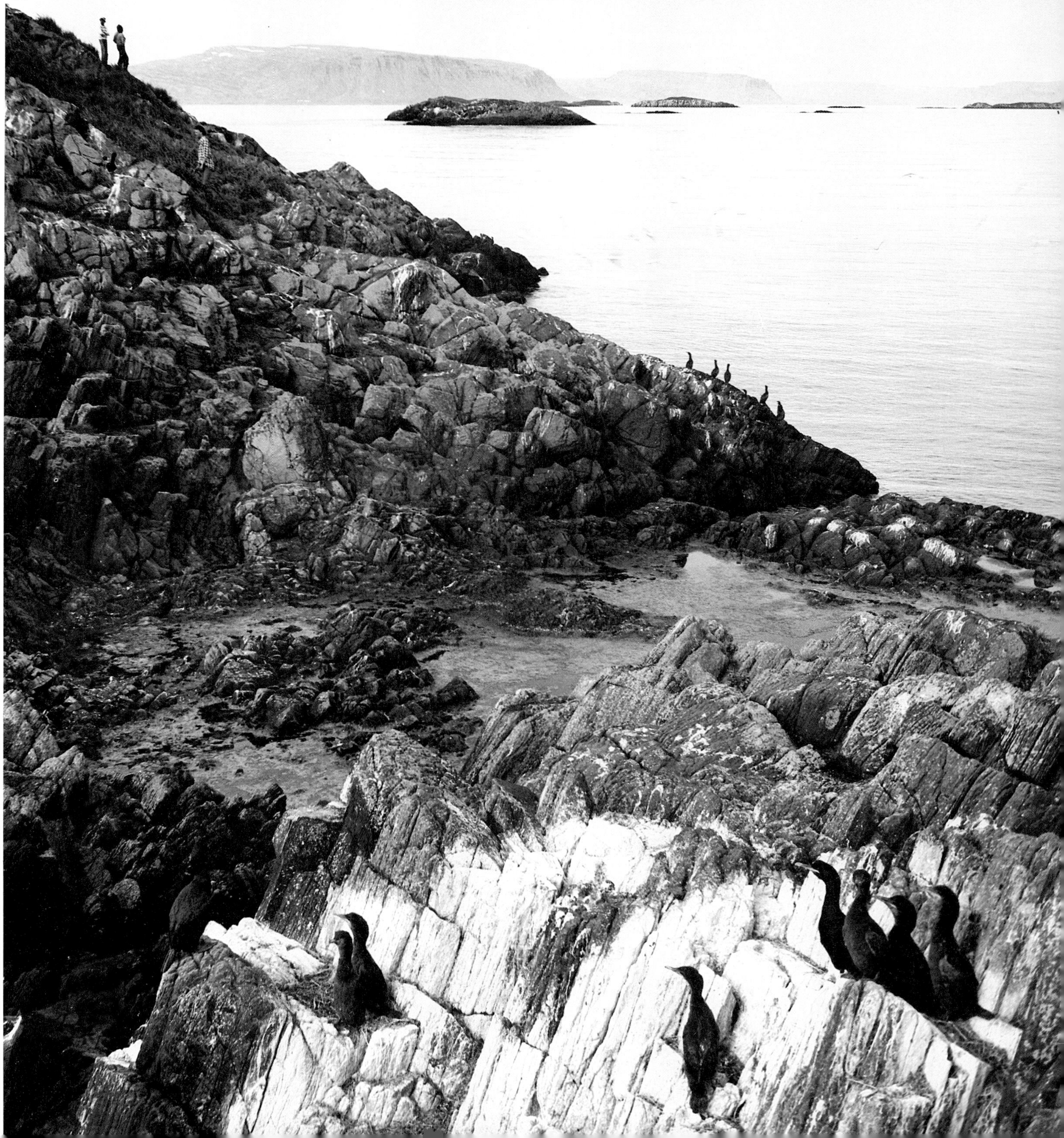

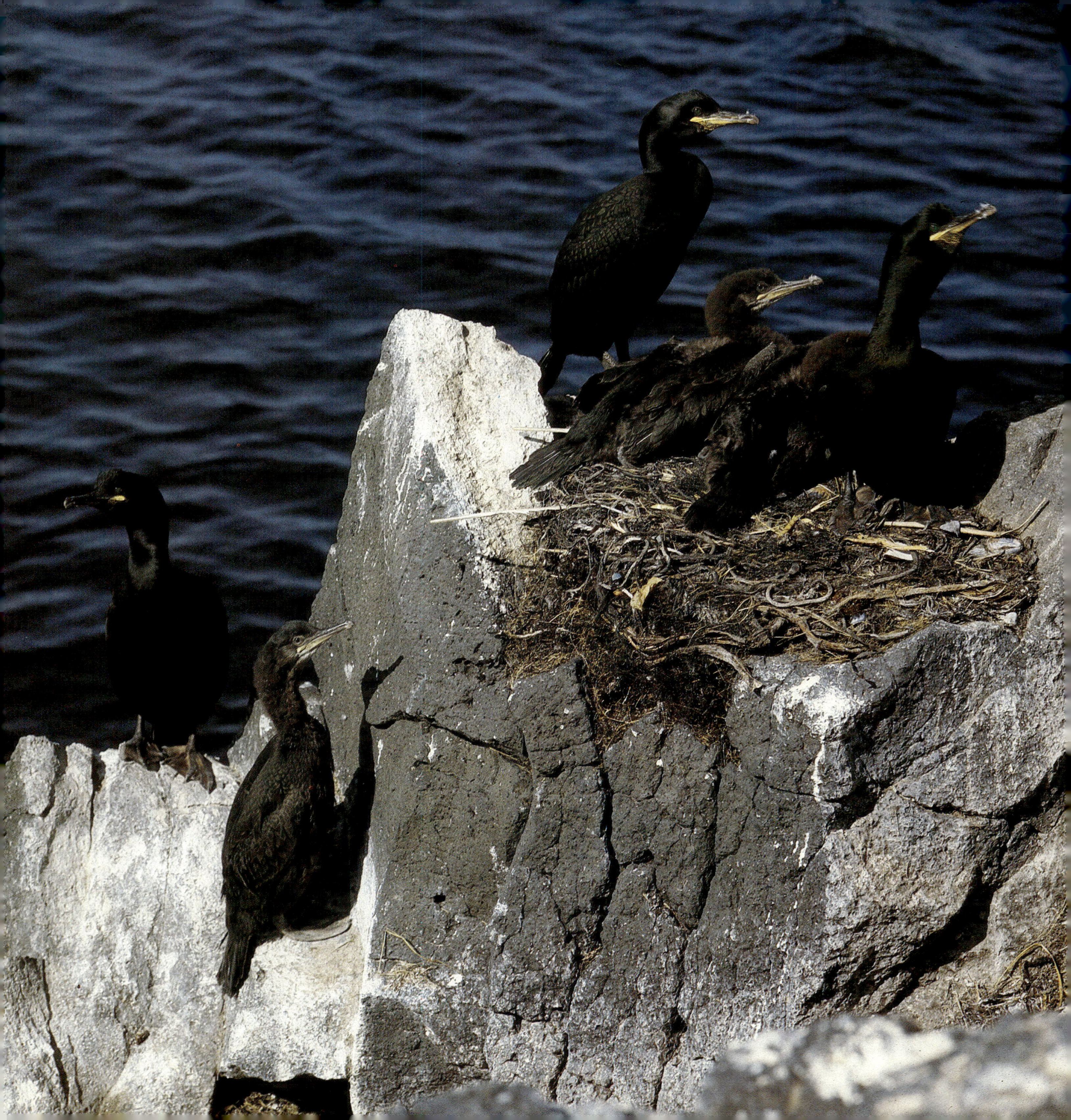

4. ISLANDS AND SKERRIES

The **SHAG** (Phalacrocorax aristotelis) and the **CORMORANT** (Phalacrocorax carbo) are large dark sea-birds with long bills belonging to the cormorant family (Phalacrocoracidae). It can be very difficult to tell them apart at a distance, but the cormorant (91 cm long) is larger than the shag (76 cm long). A notable feature of the shag is that early in spring it has a high recurved crest (see picture on the right) which gradually wears away and has completely disappeared by late summer. The cormorant does not have such a crest, but its plumage has a dull bluish gloss with distinctive white markings on the face, throat, and thighs during the breeding season. The shag, on the other hand, is completely black on the head and neck and has a dull greenish gloss on its body.

Both species breed mainly on isles and skerries, but they do not choose exactly the same kind of nesting site. Cormorants most often nest on the top of rather flat bare skerries. They sometimes breed on grassy isles, but this is normally only when they are establishing a new breeding ground, for once they have nested anywhere for any length of time there is usually very little vegetation left. The colonies which cormorants form on these flat skerries are often dense and crowded. If there are no flat skerries in the vicinity, cormorants will nest on low sea-cliffs or rocky ledges.

The shag prefers a different kind of breeding terrain. It sometimes nests among rocks and boulders along the seashore, but it mostly breeds on sloping cliff-tops of isles and promontories, or else on sloping rocks on the edges of low islands. The shag's breeding grounds thus often form long narrow strips along the shoreline. Shags and cormorants rarely share the same breeding site, but it is not unusual for shags to nest on the borders of a cormorant colony, for example on the highest point of

On the left (p. 56) are adult and young shags by a nest on Melrakkaey in Breiðafjörður. Above is a shag sitting on its nest early in spring on Bjarneyjar in Breiðafjörður. Its crest, a very distinctive feature of the shag, can be clearly seen here. It very gradually wears away and has almost completely disappeared by late summer. Below is a shag family with well-grown chicks.

4. ISLANDS AND SKERRIES

a low skerry. Shags and kittiwakes, however, are often neighbours on rocky islands, the shags on the sloping cliff-tops and the kittiwakes on the sheer cliff-faces.

There are an estimated 7,000 breeding pairs of shags, and 4,000 breeding pairs of cormorants in Iceland. They are well distributed around Faxaflói Bay, but by far their largest breeding grounds are in Breiðafjörður; the shag is more common on the isles and skerries in the north-west of the fjord, whilst the cormorant is more widely distributed over the inner reaches of Breiðafjörður. There are, however, some smaller colonies of shags and cormorants among shoreline boulders or on low sea-cliffs elsewhere in the country; the shag, for example, nests at the foot of Látrabjarg.

Although both the shag and the cormorant are sea-birds they have different feeding habits. Whilst they both live mostly on demersal fish during the winter, the shag feeds mainly on sand eels during the summer.

Both species breed in places which are relatively

4. ISLANDS AND SKERRIES

◁ On the left are cormorants swimming in Breiðafjörður. Cormorants swim so low in the water that they are almost submerged between the neck and shoulders. They are very good swimming birds and especially skillful at diving to catch the demersal fish on which they mostly live. On the right is a young cormorant ▷ demanding food from its parent by pecking at the adult's neck, and, below right, it gets its meal by sticking its head down its parent's throat and feeding on half-digested regurgitated fish.

safe from predatory animals – but not from man. From ancient times both the shag and the cormorant have been considered edible birds in Iceland; in fact the shag was so badly persecuted that it began to decline in numbers. Shags were more persecuted than cormorants mainly because of their behaviour in their nesting grounds. Cormorants are particularly shy birds, and if suddenly disturbed will fly away, even though they leave their eggs and young at risk. Although man may leave the latter untouched during the parents' absence, they may well still die of cold or be gobbled up by opportunist gulls. The shag's reactions are totally different, however, as it is completely unafraid of man. It will steadfastly remain on its nest and prepare to defend itself if approached – and thus becomes easy prey for fowlers. Though man may have disturbed nesting cormorants, and even take their eggs and young, he has not been responsible for any real decline in their numbers due to their precipitate reactions.

There appears to be a slow but gradual increase in the shag and cormorant populations in Breiðafjörður, the shags undoubtedly as they are now much less persecuted, although changes in the quality and supply of their food could also be a contributory factor.

4. ISLANDS AND SKERRIES

60

On the left are a cormorant and its chick in the nest; above is a cormorant in its breeding ground on an isle in Breiðafjörður. The cormorant is a large sea-bird with a dull blue-black gloss. The cheeks and chin are white, but the legs are black. Both sexes have the same plumage. Their young are mostly brown or sooty-brown in colour. The cormorant's nest is a large heap of seaweed, usually on flat, rather bare skerries. It lays its eggs earlier than the shag, as early in the spring as March or April if the climate is good, but normally in late April or early May. Cormorants are very wary of humans and easily disturbed by them. They will immediately abandon their nests if suddenly startled, perhaps leaving their eggs and young to die of cold or be poached by a predatory bird such as the great black-backed gull. It is vitally important, therefore, to take great care in the vicinity of cormorant nesting sites.

4. ISLANDS AND SKERRIES

Gulls are medium-sized or large, stocky swimming-birds with long wings. Most gull species are white with a grey or black back, and some of them have black wing-tips. The tail is often square-shaped. Both sexes have the same plumage, but the male is larger than the female. Gulls are very good flyers, and sit high in the water when swimming. The various species of gulls can be divided into related groups, the largest group consisting of the so-called white-headed gulls. There are 5 species of this group which breed in Iceland; the estimated numbers of their breeding pairs are as follows: the **great black-backed gull** (Larus marinus) 50,000; the **lesser black-backed gull** (Larus fuscus) 15,000; the **herring gull** (Larus argentatus) 5,000; the **glaucous gull** (Larus hyperboreus) 10,000; and the **common gull** (Larus canus) 340.

The **GREAT BLACK-BACKED GULL** is the largest Icelandic gull and common all around the country. Although it is an admittedly fine looking bird, it is far from being popular and often regarded as a pest. This is mostly because it is a bold and inveterate stealer of eggs and young; in spring and summer it often causes panic in eider duck colonies. It sometimes even attacks adult birds, especially if they are weak or sick. Apart from eating both living animals and carrion, the great black-backed gull has a very varied diet and will also hunt

Drangey is a 180 m high island of tuff rock which rises precipitously out of the sea in *Skagafjörður*. The rock-stack on the right, to the south of Drangey, is called Kerling (Old Woman). The island can be ascended at one specific point where there is an iron ladder near the top and chains along the narrower ledges to make the going easier. There are a great many cliff-birds on Drangey and it has always been a centre for fowling and egg-collecting; indeed in former times it was considered the larder of the *Skagafjörður* inhabitants. For a very long time floats were used for fowling in the sea around Drangey; birds would land on these floats and become entangled in snares. This method of fowling was finally banned in 1954.

▽

for small pelagic fish in the ocean such as capelin, herring and sand eels. It breaks eggs with very thick shells (e.g. goose eggs) by flying to an appropriate height and then letting the egg fall to earth. It uses the same method to break shellfish and sea snails. Its most important source of food, however, is the growing amount of all kinds of carrion, fish offal and food leftovers to be found in rubbish dumps, drains, or the refuse from fish-factories. This food supply provides the great black-backed gull with a guaranteed means of subsistence all the year round, and is believed to be the main cause of its increasing population over the last few decades.

The great black-backed gull is not very particular about its nesting site and will breed almost anywhere: on steep and rocky or low and grassy islands; on bare and rocky skerries; and along the coastline from the most extended promontories to inner fjord basins. Nor is it restricted to the coastline as it is widespread far from the sea, even high up in the mountains, though seldom on steep cliffs. The great black-backed gull also nests on the great sands along Iceland's southern shore, and in lava-fields and glacial moraines. Its wide distribution and varying breeding habitats could be a result of its recent large increase in numbers, but may well also be an attempt to evade a growing persecution.

The great-black backed gull is mostly resident in Iceland and is a coastal and shallow-water bird, seldom seen far from land.

The **LESSER BLACK-BACKED GULL** is smaller than the great black-backed gull, although otherwise the 2 species look very much alike. The lesser black-backed gull has a much lighter plumage on its back and wings, and its legs are yellow whilst the great black-backed gull's are pale grey. The 2 species of gulls are not as related as their similar appearance might suggest, however, the lesser black-backed gull being more closely related and similar in size to the herring gull. The lesser black-backed gull is one of the species of birds to have settled in Iceland since 1920. It likes to nest on rather bare gravelly plains or stony hills, and sometimes in lava-fields or on islands. The structure of its nest is similar to that of the great black-backed gull. The lesser black-backed gull lives on fish and many kinds of invertebrates as well as carrion, and it is also a stealer of other birds' eggs and young.

The **HERRING GULL** is a bit bigger than the lesser black-backed gull, but still considerably smaller than the great black-backed gull. Like the lesser black-backed gull it is a relative newcomer to Iceland, first beginning to breed here around 1920. It has also interbred with the glaucous gull in Iceland. It is mostly distributed in the eastern parts of the country, but it also breeds in the south and in the central and eastern parts of the north. The herring gull always nests near the sea, sometimes in crowded colonies, and is for the most part a resident.

The **GLAUCOUS GULL** is the nearest in size to the great black-backed gull and is mostly only found around Breiðafjörður and the Vestfirðir. It is an arctic bird and seldom breeds far from the sea, most often on grassy cliffs but also occasionally on islands. Glaucous gulls from more northerly breeding grounds visit Iceland during the winter, but those which actually breed in Iceland are most probably resident all year.

The **COMMON GULL** is the smallest of the 5 species of large gulls which breed in Iceland; it nests very dispersively, however, and only in very few places. Common gulls breed among other gulls, especially black-headed gulls which are just fractionally smaller than they are.

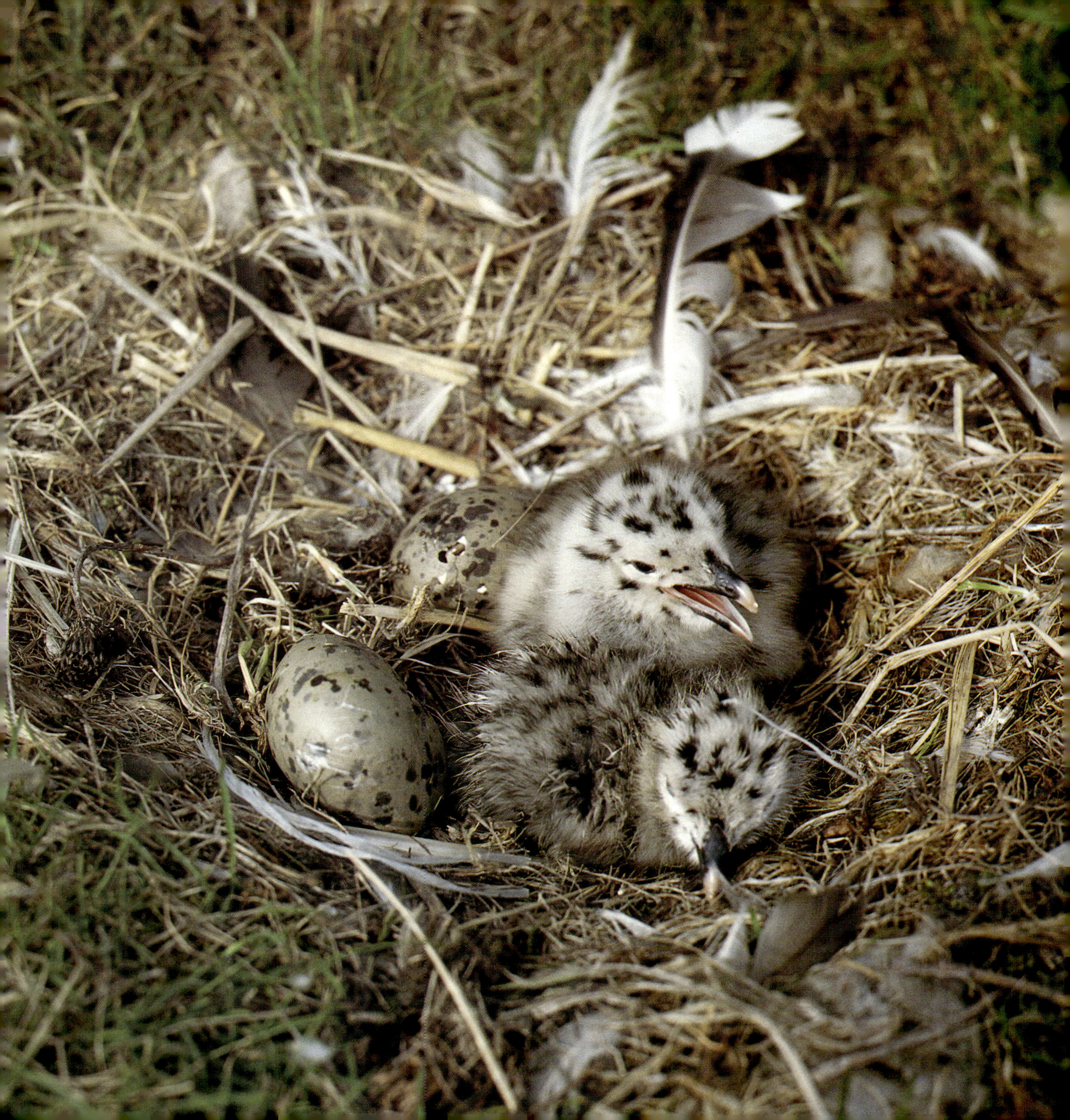

On the left is a **great black-backed gull's nest**. One of the chicks is already dry and lively, but the other is just newly hatched and so still wet. A third chick is using its beak to break through the egg's shell and into this world. Great black-backed gull's nests are usually 25–30 cm in diameter at the top and 7–9 cm deep. They are made out of whatever material is available in the breeding ground, most often grass, moss and feathers. There are usually 3 eggs in a clutch, very seldom fewer, and they are light greenish-grey or slate-grey in colour with dark spots and blotches. Both parents take it in turns to sit, and the incubation period is around 4 weeks. The parents also share in procuring food for the chicks, which are normally fully fledged after 8 weeks. **Above** is a picture of 3 adult great black-backed gulls on a tidal skerry in Breiðafjörður. They seem elegant and relaxed, but keep a sharp eye on everything around them nonetheless.

4. ISLANDS AND SKERRIES

The **great black-backed gull chick** in the picture top left has just left its nest on Flataflaga Island in Breiðafjörður. Great black-backed gull chicks have a light grey down with dark spots on the head, back and wings. This chick fled in panic and tried to hide in some rocks when approached, but shortly after this picture was taken it was ringed with an Icelandic Museum of Natural History ring No. 224014. Below left are 2 well-grown young great black-backed gulls. The great black-backed gull has the reputation of being the greediest of all Icelandic gulls and a great predator in other birds' nesting grounds. It is an infamous stealer of eggs and young and will shrink at nothing. Above is a great black-backed gull which has invaded a cormorant nesting site. If cormorant parents are absent and the eggs or young left unprotected in the nest, the great black-backed gull is quick to seize the chance and eat the eggs, or swallow the young whole. This cormorant is well on guard, however, and will not give way to the gull. The picture on the right clearly shows what a splendid bird the great black-backed gull is. Both sexes have the same appearance, but the female is rather smaller than the male. Great black-backed gulls are black on the back, shoulders and wings, except that the primaries and secondaries have white tips. The rest of the bird is otherwise snow-white, and it has a pale yellow bill with vermilion patches on both sides of the lower mandible.

66

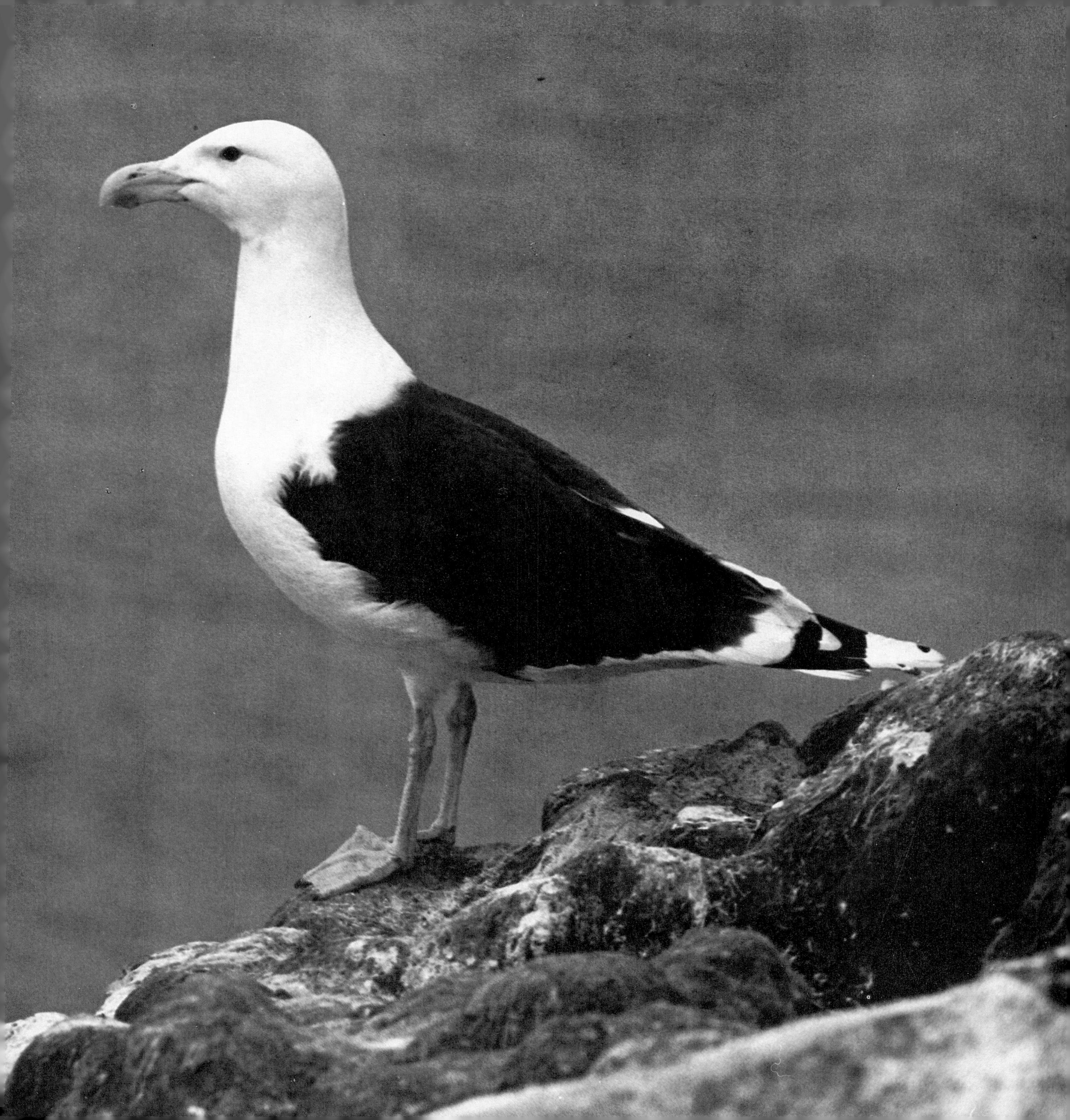

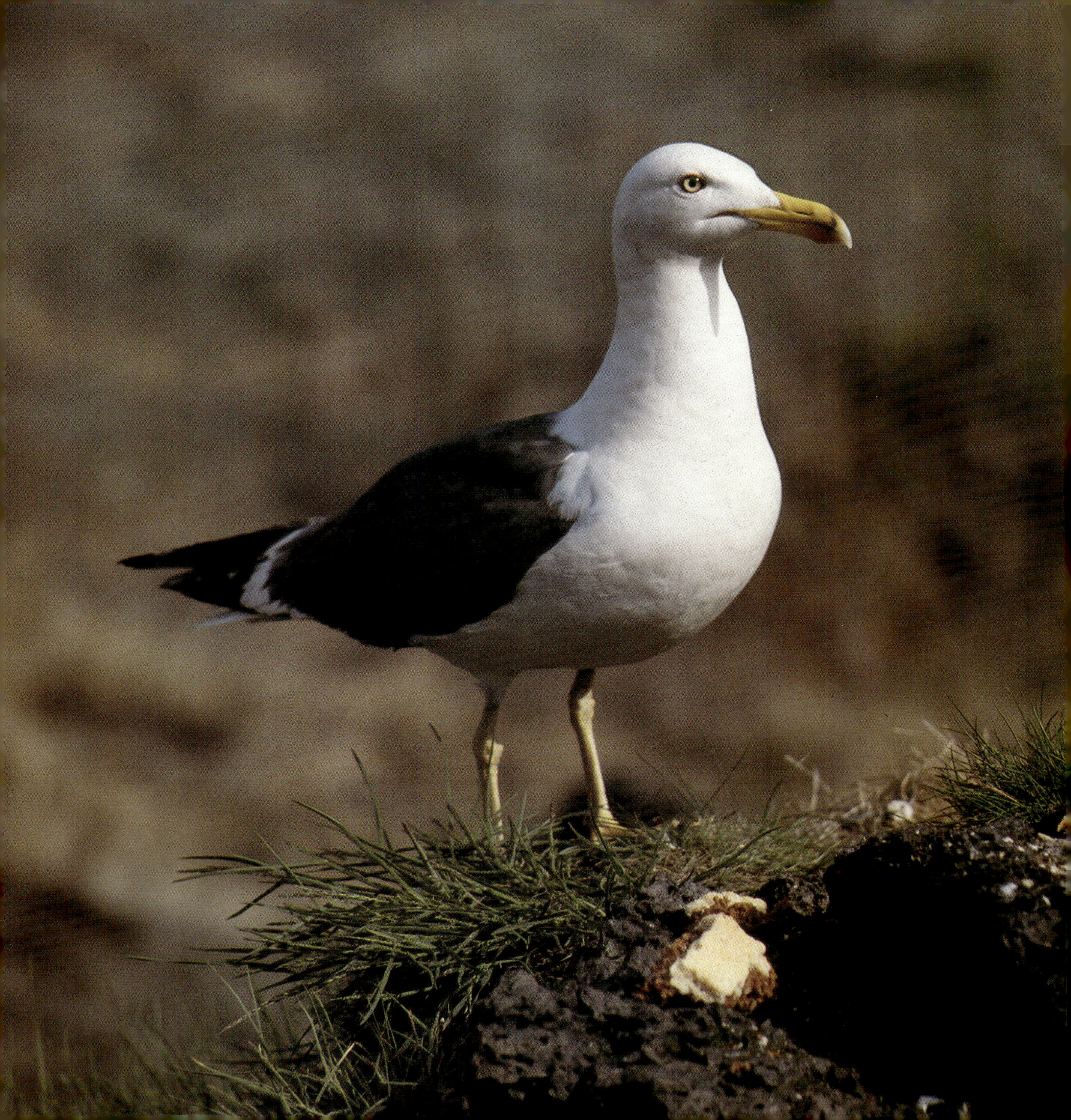

In both these pictures the **lesser black-backed gull** is in its breeding plumage, which is snow-white except for the back, shoulders, and wings which are varying shades of dark grey, but never black, as on a great black-backed gull. The scapulars, primaries, and secondaries have white tips, though when the bird is sitting these white edges are not as distinctive as a great black-backed gull's. The legs and bill are pale yellow, and there are vermilion spots on the lower mandible. The irises are greyish-yellow and the eye-rings reddish. Both sexes have the same appearance, but the male is somewhat larger than the female. In the picture on the left, a lesser black-backed gull is about to feed on some bread near a town dwelling, and above, a lesser black-backed gull arrives at its nest on a moraine near Kvíárjökull in Öræfasveit, to the south of Vatnajökull glacier. The lesser black-backed gull is a migrant in Iceland, usually arriving at its breeding grounds in February, and departing in September or October.

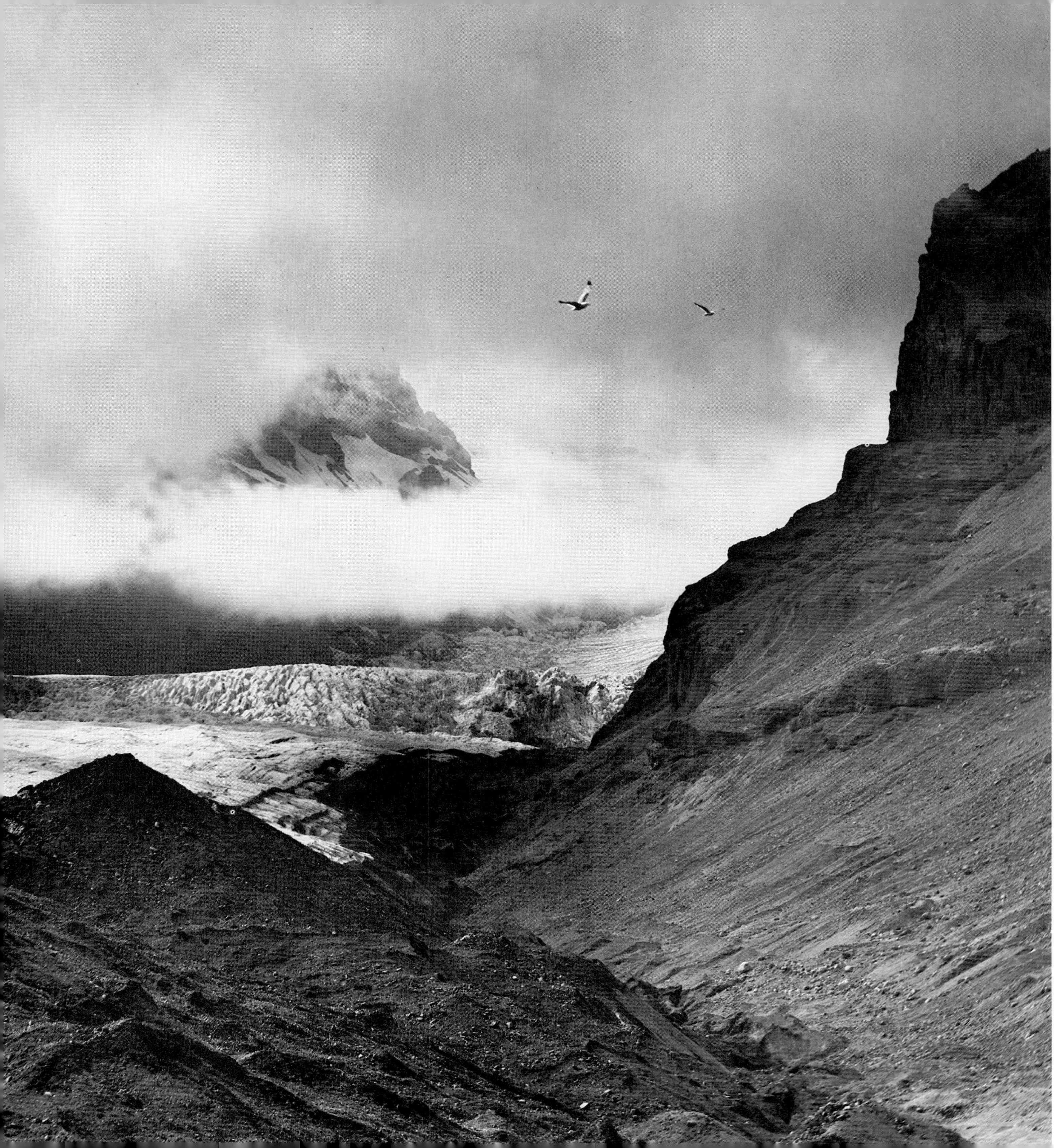

4. ISLANDS AND SKERRIES

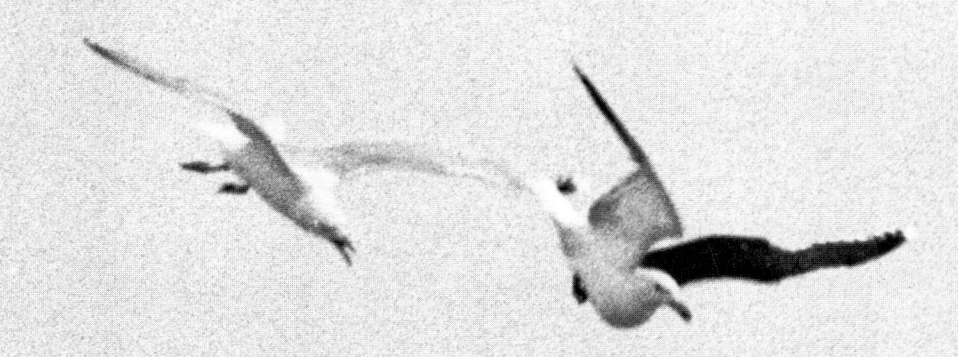

◁ On the left is a pair of lesser black-backed gulls in flight near Kvíárjökull in Öræfasveit where they had their nest on a rather bare moraine (see p. 69). In the background is a view of the glacier from the nesting site.

The Icelandic lesser black-backed gull originates from the same sub-species of lesser black-backed gulls found in the Faroes and Great Britain. These lesser black-backed gulls winter on the shores of France, Spain, and Portugal, and on the west coast of Africa, as far south as Nigeria.

△
Above is a **lesser black-backed gull** chasing away a great black-backed gull. The former had 3 nestlings on a cliff-edge of Ingólfshöfði, and both parents resolutely defended them from the encroachments of other birds, especially the great black-backed gull – and not without reason, for the latter is a sly and determined stealer of young.

The **herring gull** above stands on the highest point of Skrúður Island which has the largest herring gull colony in the country. The herring gull is 1 of the 5 large species of gulls which breeds in Iceland. Although it looks very much like the great black-backed gull, it is a much smaller bird and is light bluish-grey on the back and wings, similar to the glaucous gull, except that the herring gull's wing-tips have a black and white pattern on them, whereas the glaucous gull's have no black on them at all. The herring gull also resembles the common gull, especially as the latter does have a black and white pattern on its wing-tips, but the common gull is much smaller in size and has darker upper-parts. The herring gull has flesh-pink legs and a yellow bill with red spots on the lower mandible.

The **herring gull** above is flying along the summit of Skrúður. On the right is a herring gull's nest on Skrúður containing 2 eggs. Herring gulls usually have a clutch of 3, so breeding may not yet be finished in this nest.

The herring gull is a relative newcomer to Iceland, coming from the south and settling here in or around 1920. The glaucous gull, on the other hand, is an arctic bird and Iceland is the southernmost limit of its range; it is thus in Iceland, where their distribution limits overlap, that the herring gull and glaucous gull have interbred. This phenomenon has been specially researched by an Icelandic ornithologist who has discovered that the herring gull has interbred so much with the glaucous gull that the majority of herring gulls now bear signs of this interbreeding. Glaucous gulls seem to be less effected, though in the western regions of Iceland a large number of them also show some marks of this interbreeding. These 2 species of gulls are clearly so related that interbreeding produces fertile offspring which can then form a new stock of gulls with the blended characteristics of both herring and glaucous gulls.

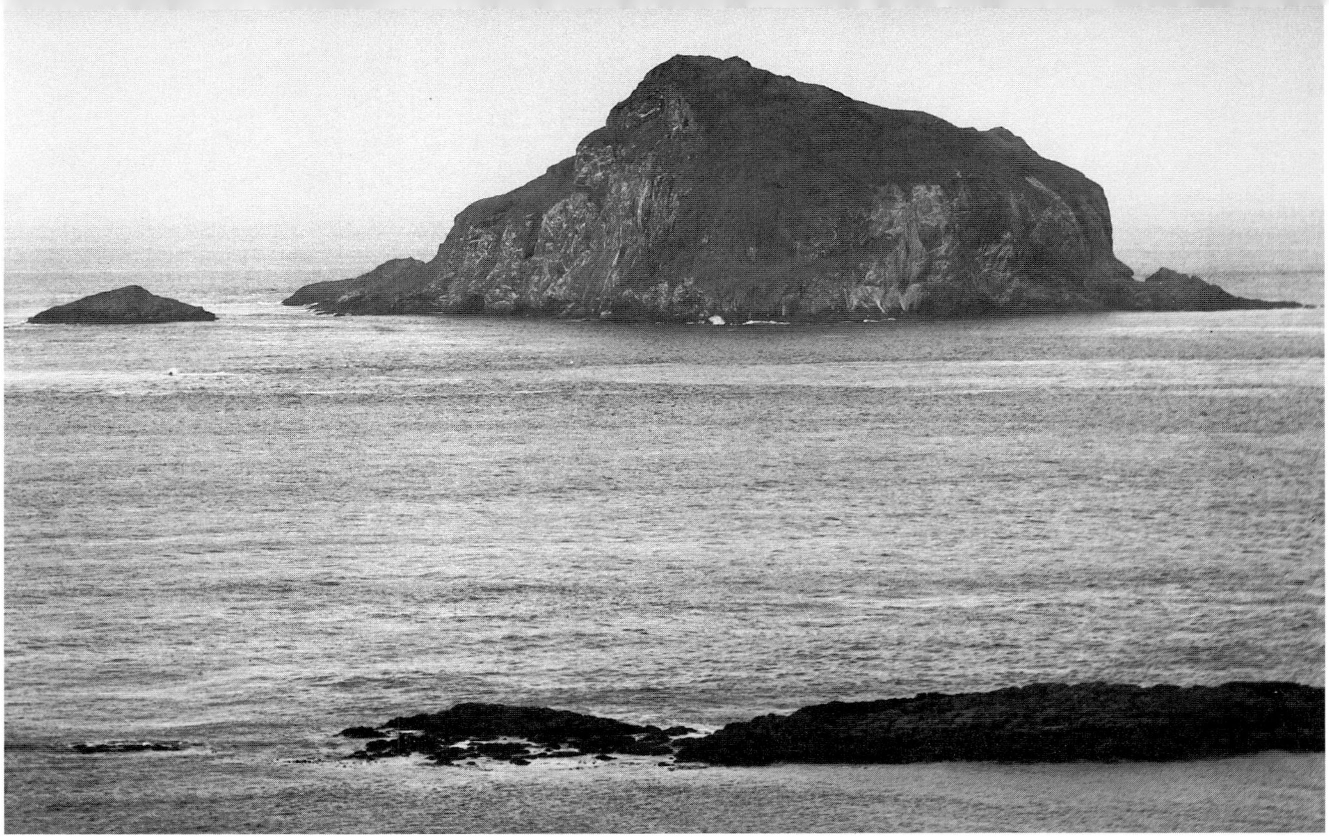

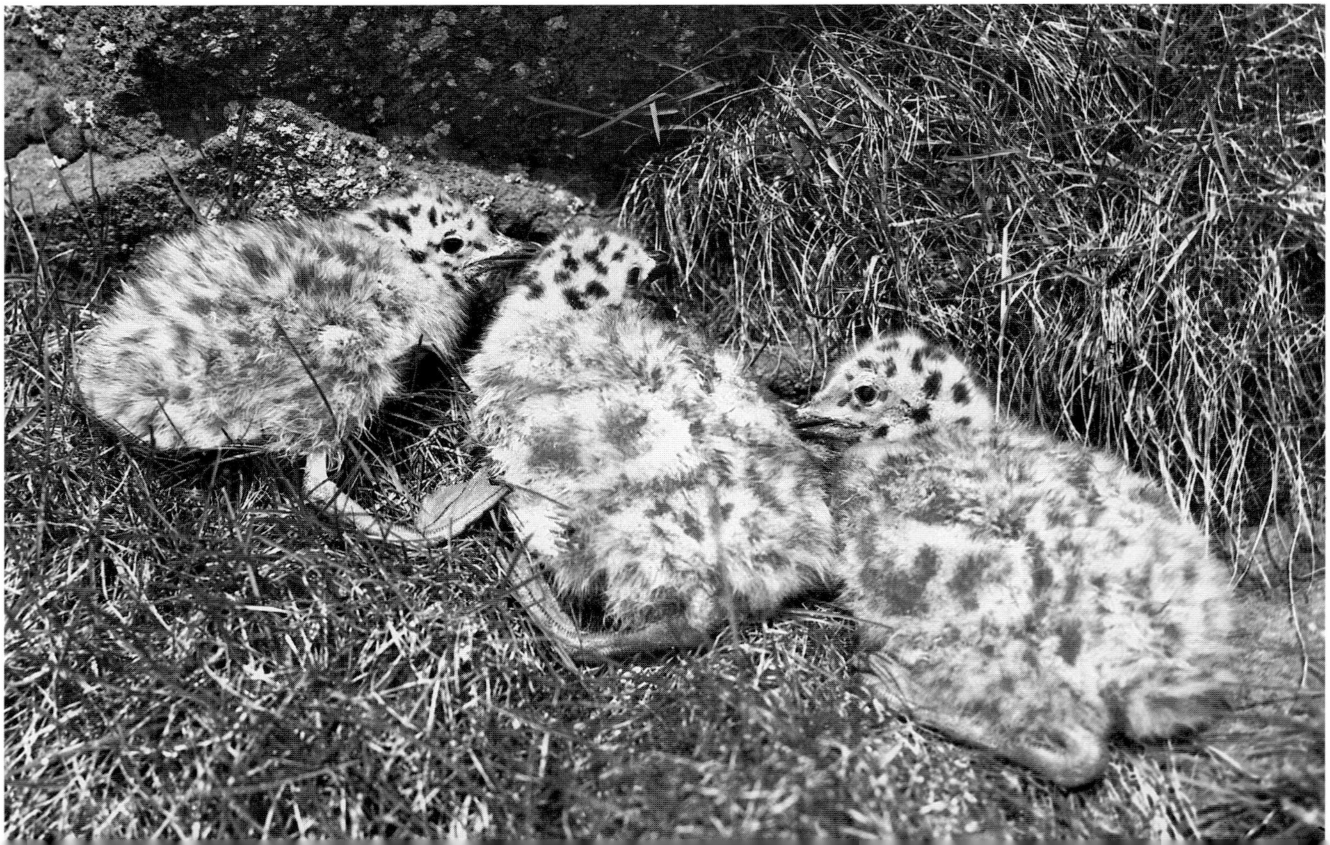

▽ *Above left is a view of Skrúður from the mainland. There is a large colony of herring gulls on the island as well as many other cliff-birds such as kittiwakes and guillemots. Puffins also breed there in large numbers, and it has a fairly large gannetry.*

◁ *Below left are 3 herring gull nestlings on a cliff-edge on Ingólfshöfði. When the parents (see p. 71) give the danger-call the nestlings crouch down motionless, their colouring providing them with superb camouflage.*

△
*Above is a **glaucous gull** nesting near cormorants on Melrakkaey in Breiðafjörður. It is rather unusual for a glaucous gull to nest on such a low island. Glaucous gull breeding grounds on mountainside cliffs are distinguished by the amount of lush grass growing on the ledges which is fertilised by the gulls' droppings. The glaucous gull parents take it in turns to sit on the eggs which are usually 3 in number. The glaucous gull is common all round Iceland during the winter and feeds on more natural foods than the great black-backed gull; it is thus considered much less of a predator. In countries further north than Iceland, however, where there are no great black-backed gulls, the glaucous gull is reputedly a much more infamous stealer of eggs and young. Both the glaucous and herring gulls have a preference for various kinds of molluscs (e.g. mussels), crustaceans (e.g. sand crabs), and small fish (e.g. sand eels).*

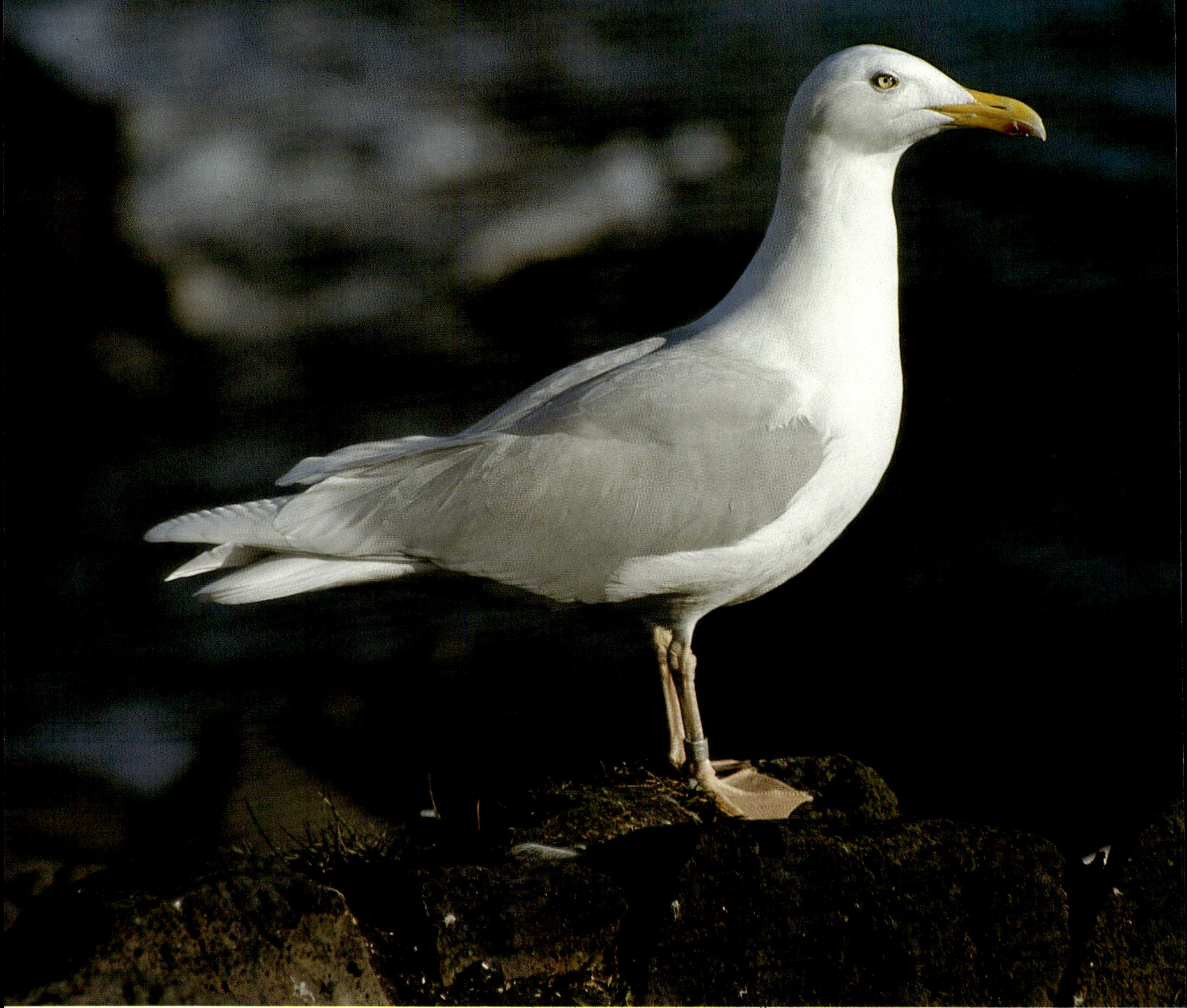

◁ The **glaucous gull**, in its breeding plumage, is light grey on its back, shoulders and wings, but is otherwise completely white, even on the tips of its scapulars and primaries, as can be seen in the picture on the left. The bill is pale yellow, but dark grey at the tip, and with vermilion spots on the lower mandible. The legs are a pinkish colour, the irises a greyish-yellow. Above right is an adult glaucous gull with its young. Young glaucous gulls have off-white under-parts and light grey upper-parts with dull brown speckles and distinctive dark spots on the head and neck. With each successive moult the young bird becomes paler until it attains an adult plumage when fully mature at 4 years of age. Below right is a glaucous gull's nest made in a similar fashion to a great black-backed gull's, i.e. using mostly moss, grass and other materials, almost always including some of the gull's own feathers. There are usually 3 eggs in a clutch, as in this case; glaucous gulls' eggs so closely resemble those of great black-backed gulls that it is often very difficult to tell them apart.

Above is a **common gull** sitting on its nest. Below is a common gull's nest with 1 egg and 2 chicks. Common gulls had become regular winter-visitors by 1920, but have more recently been added to the list of Icelandic breeding birds. The first common gull's nest was found in 1955, though it is likely that the species had nested here before then.

The **LITTLE AUK** (Alle alle) is one of the smallest sea-birds and belongs to the auk family, being closely related to the razorbill. The little auk is of the same size as a redwing, but, apart from its bill, is much more like a puffin in build. It is rather a square-shaped bird as it appears to have no neck and has a black, short and convex bill. The legs are small and the tail is very short. In spring and summer the adult bird is black on the head, neck, back, wings and tail, apart from a narrow white wing-bar. The remaining under-parts are all white with a very distinctive dividing line between the black and white colouring on the neck and breast. Both sexes have the same appearance.

The little auk is an arctic and oceanic bird and is a common breeder in the area between Greenland and Novaya Zemlya. As far as is known it has only nested on Grímsey and Langanes in Iceland, and indeed Iceland is at the southern limit of its

78

breeding range. Only very few little auks still nest on Grímsey, and the bird is thus strongly protected by law; it is forbidden to approach its nests without the permission of the Ministry of Education and Culture. In fact in 1983 there were only 2 pairs on Grímsey, so that within the next few years the little auk may well disappear from Iceland as a breeding bird. Foreign egg and bird collectors have sometimes been blamed for this. Human interference might well have accelerated the decline in little auk numbers, but the main reason is undoubtedly the changing and warmer climate.

The little auk feeds on plankton and various kinds of pelagic crustaceans. Its favourite nesting ground is amongst large boulders under cliffs. Bottom left are a few little auks on Grímsey where they have their nests in holes and crevices between the boulders. The nests themselves are made of little or nothing. Little auks lay 1 egg on the bare earth late in May or in June, and both parents share the incubating which takes about 24 days. They feed the chick on regurgitated food which they collect in a gular pouch. It is quite charming to observe life in a little auk colony as it is not a shy bird if one is careful enough to avoid any sudden movements. Even though a little auk is very busy collecting food, it will always have time, as in the picture top left, to rest among its comrades on the edge of a rock. The bird on the far left has just returned from the sea, its gular pouch bulging with food. It pauses for a little while before squeezing between the rocks to feed its ever-hungry chick. The continuous twittering of the young can be heard from within the rocks as they constantly demand more to eat and so keep their parents busy. The little auk has such small wings that it has to fly with very rapid wing-beats.

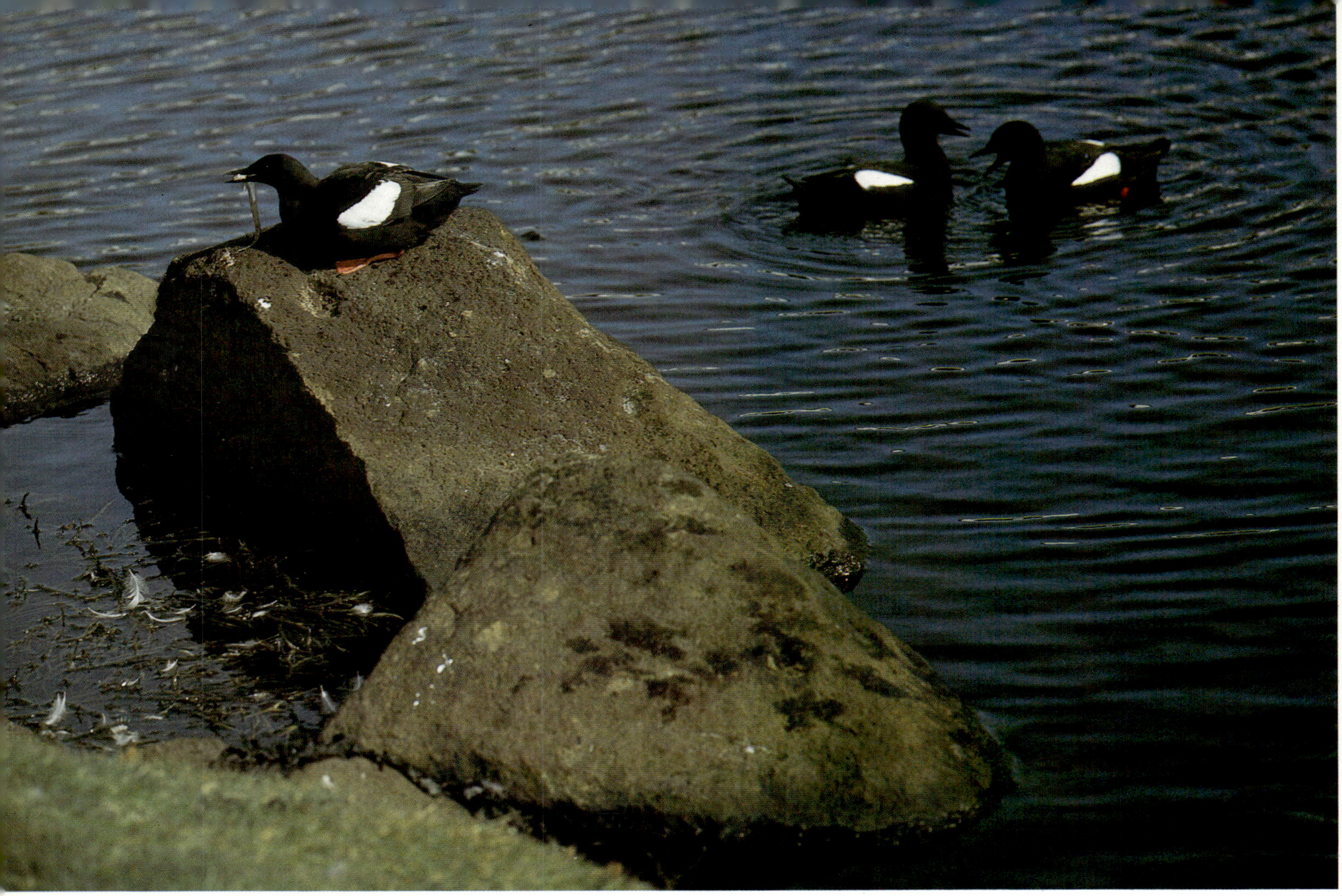

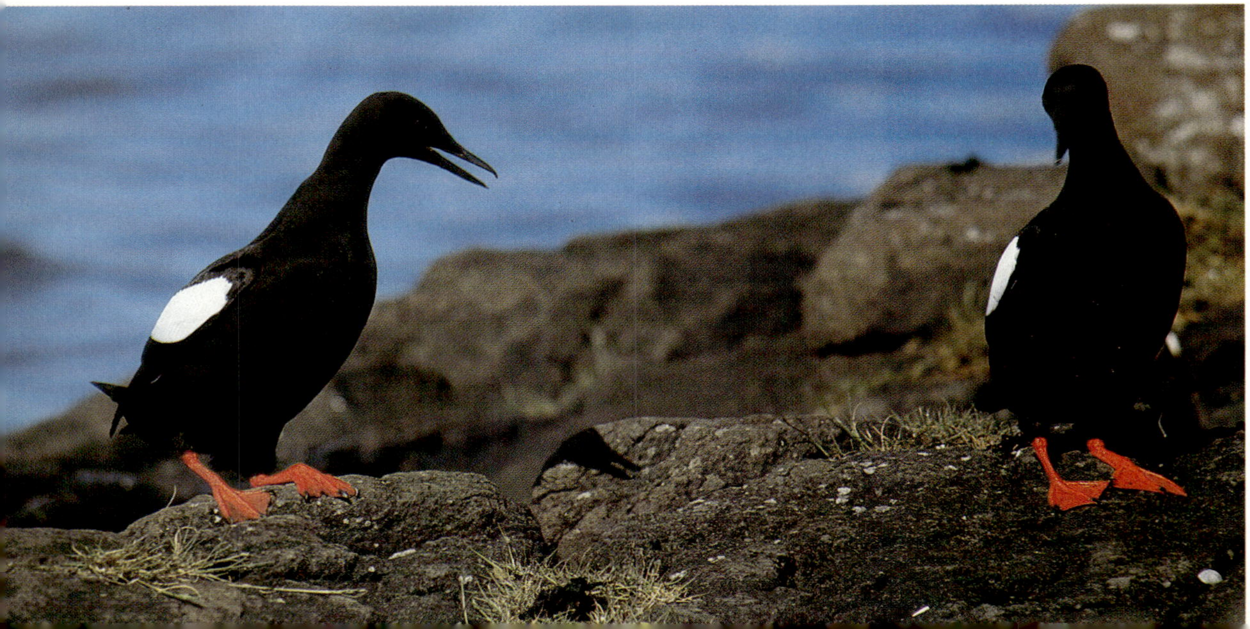

The **BLACK GUILLEMOT** (Cepphus grylle) is a member of the auk family. It is a much bigger bird than the little auk, but a bit smaller than the puffin and much smaller than a common guillemot. The black guillemot is easily recognisable in the summer as, apart from a large white wing-patch, it is completely black and has very distinctive bright red legs. It is a coastal bird, seldom going far out to sea, and is mostly a resident in Iceland, breeding all round the country, its usual nesting sites being in holes between boulders or in crevices in rocks. The black guillemot's favourite food is butterfish, which dwell up to 15 m below the surface of the sea, but it also feeds on sea scorpions, young plaice, sand eels, crustaceans and worms. Above is a black guillemot just returning from the sea with a butterfish in its bill, and above left is another coming ashore with food for its young. The other black guillemots in the pictures are either conversing tête-à-tête or enjoying a rest. The black guillemot is an entertaining, sociable and intelligent bird wherever it can live undisturbed and in peace.

81

4. ISLANDS AND SKERRIES

The **black guillemot** in the picture on the left has arrived at its nesting hole in a stone wall with a newly caught fish in its bill. An adult will frequently strut about for quite a while with its catch in its bill before entering the nesting hole. Once it has fed its young it will come back out immediately, and after a short rest will go out to sea again to search for more food.

The black guillemot's breeding season does not begin until May, and it never nests in large colonies like puffins or other auks, but often only in a few pairs among some boulders or in a stone wall; sometimes a pair will even breed entirely alone. The black guillemot usually lays 2 eggs, rarely only 1, and as there is hardly a nest to speak of, the eggs rest on bare rock or gravel. The eggs are often so well hidden in holes and crevices that it is either only just possible to get a glimpse of them, or they cannot be seen at all. It is also frequently impossible to actually reach the eggs without first clearing away stones and rocks.

The incubation period lasts 4 weeks, and both parents take it in turns to sit and later collect food for the young whilst they are still in the nest. The young finally leave the nest about a week before they are fully fledged.

The black guillemot had always been considered a resident bird, but in recent years black guillemots ringed in Iceland have been recovered abroad, and the indications are that about one fourth of young Icelandic black guillemots visit Greenland outside the breeding season.

There is no information as to the exact number of black guillemots breeding in Iceland; indeed their nesting sites are so widely distributed all around the country's islands and coastline that it is difficult to count the birds with any reasonable accuracy. It has been estimated, however, that the number of black guillemot pairs breeding in Iceland can be reckoned in tens of thousands.

A **Kittiwake** on a cliff attends to its 3 chicks. Kittiwakes lay 1–3 eggs and the incubation period is 21–24 days. The chicks are fully fledged after 4–5 weeks. Kittiwakes do not carry food for their young, but swallow it and regurgitate it for them later.

5 Cliff-birds

5. CLIFF-BIRDS

The **KITTIWAKE** (*Rissa tridactyla*) is considered one of the gull family (Laridae), but as certain features distinguish it from the genus **Larus** it is classified as belonging to a special genus, **Rissa**. Among other things it has smaller legs than a genuine gull, and only 3 toes not 4. Above is a large group of kittiwakes on the sands of Básavík on Grímsey. On the left is a kittiwake in a nesting site on Hafnaberg cliff, Reykjanes. On the right are kittiwakes on a bird-cliff on Melrakkaey in Breiðafjörður. In all these pictures the kittiwake is in its breeding plumage, which is snow-white except for a light bluish-grey on the back, shoulders, and wings. The tips of the 5 outermost primaries are more or less black. The bill is greenish-yellow and the corners of the mouth a yellowy-red. The legs are black. There is no difference in colouring between the sexes, but the male is often slightly larger than the female. All the main Icelandic kittiwake breeding grounds are on promontories or oceanic islands. It is a very gregarious bird, often nesting in large crowded colonies; huge numbers of them can be found on all of Iceland's main bird-cliffs. In many places it nests only with its own species, especially on low cliffs such as on the rocky islands and skerries of Breiðafjörður, as in the picture on the right.

84

5. CLIFF-BIRDS

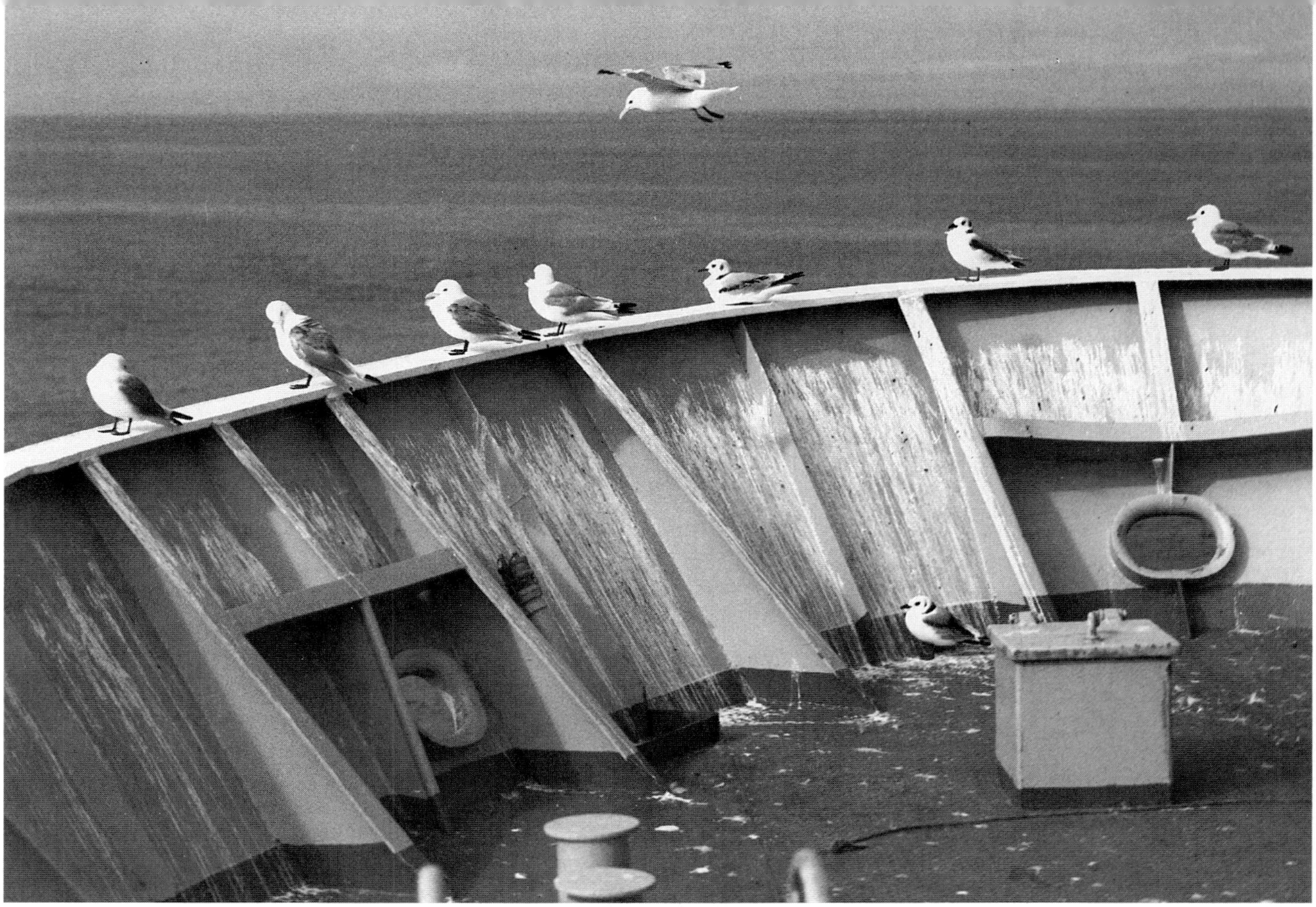

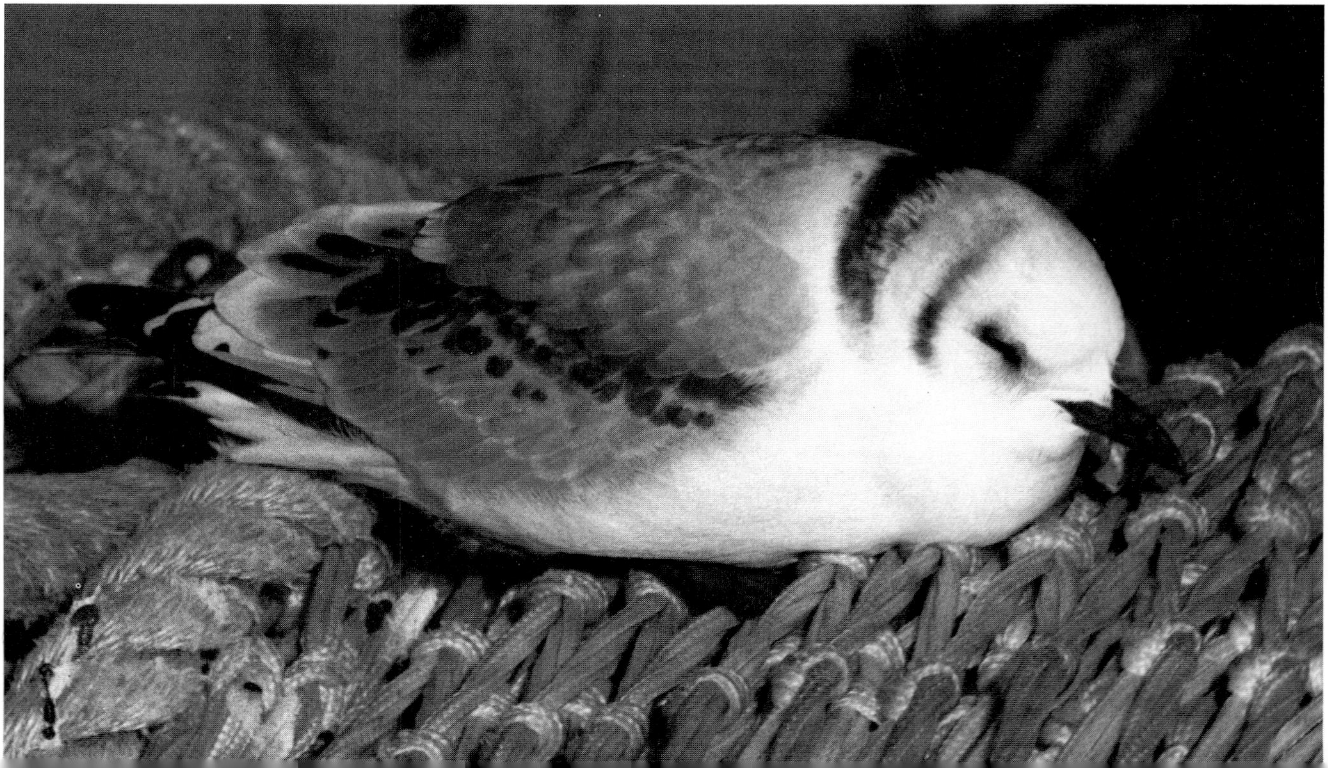

The **kittiwake** is much more of an oceanic bird than any other gull. During the summer it is one of the most numerous sea-birds around the coasts of Iceland, but in winter, outside the breeding season, it travels great distances out to sea, and along with the fulmar is one of the commonest birds of the North Atlantic. It is very familiar to seamen as it often resolutely follows ships, especially as it feeds, like the fulmar, on the waste from fishing vessels. Kittiwakes also like to rest on ships' decks while far out at sea. Above left is a group of adult and immature kittiwakes on the bows of a trawler in the fishing grounds off the north-west of Iceland. Bottom left is a young kittiwake fast asleep on a net-drum aboard a stern-trawler, totally undisturbed by the strong working-lights of the after-deck. Immature kittiwakes are dark around the eyes and have blackish ear-spots and a dark rear half-collar. The tail-feathers have black tips forming a black band round the end. The wing-tips are also mostly black, and there is a distinctive dark diagonal band across the wing. The bill is black and the legs are brown. They keep this plumage until they are fully mature at 2 years of age. Above is a kittiwake chick on the lower cliff-face of Hornbjarg. Kittiwake chicks have white under-parts, head, and neck, but pale greyish-brown upper-parts.

Hornbjarg is one of Iceland's 3 largest bird-cliffs. Overleaf is ▷ a view of the cliff from the sea during the summer. The cliff's highest peak is the 534 m Kálfatindur. The enormous numbers of birds on Hornbjarg meant that it was formerly a popular cliff for fowlers and egg-collectors.

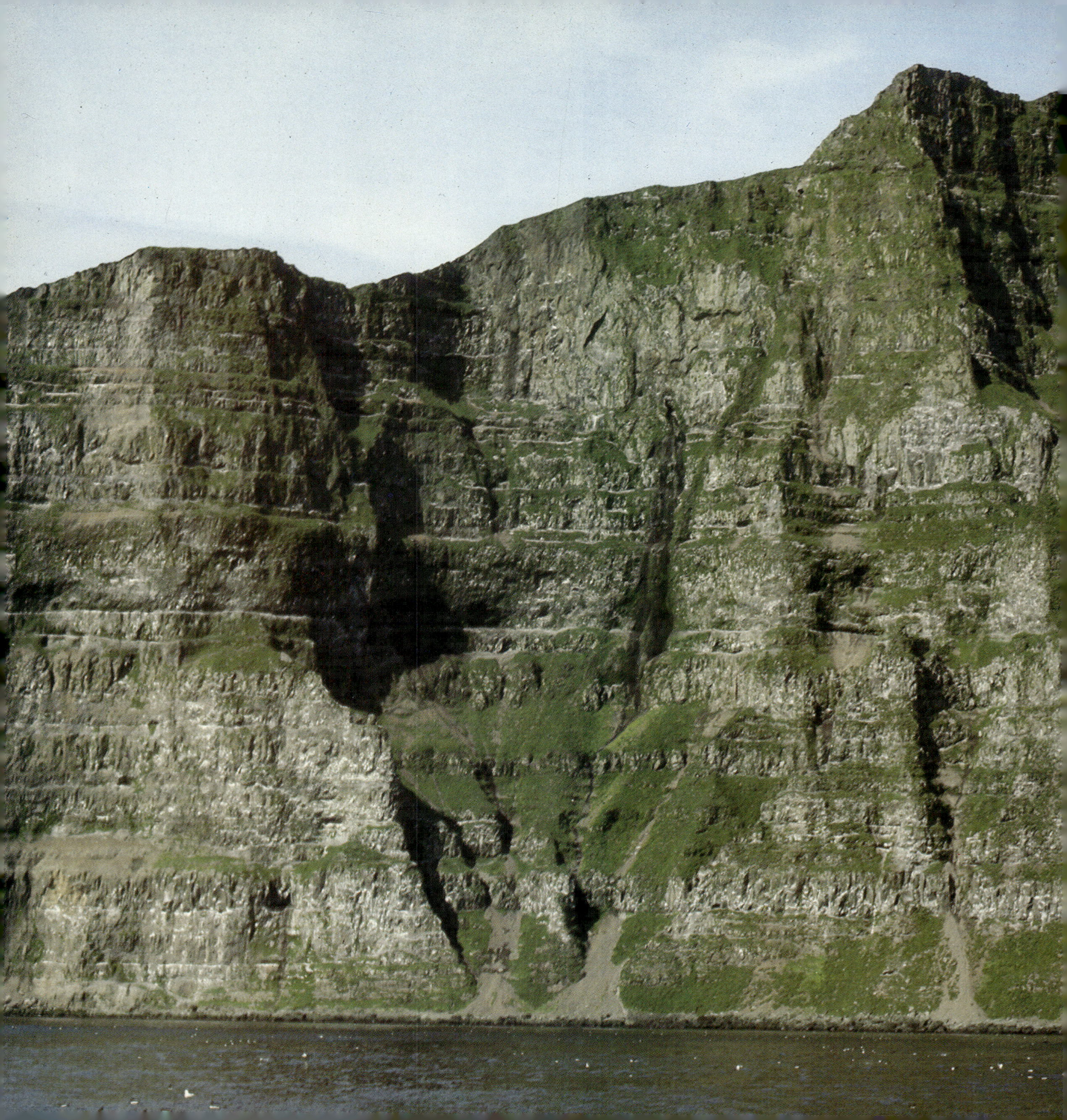

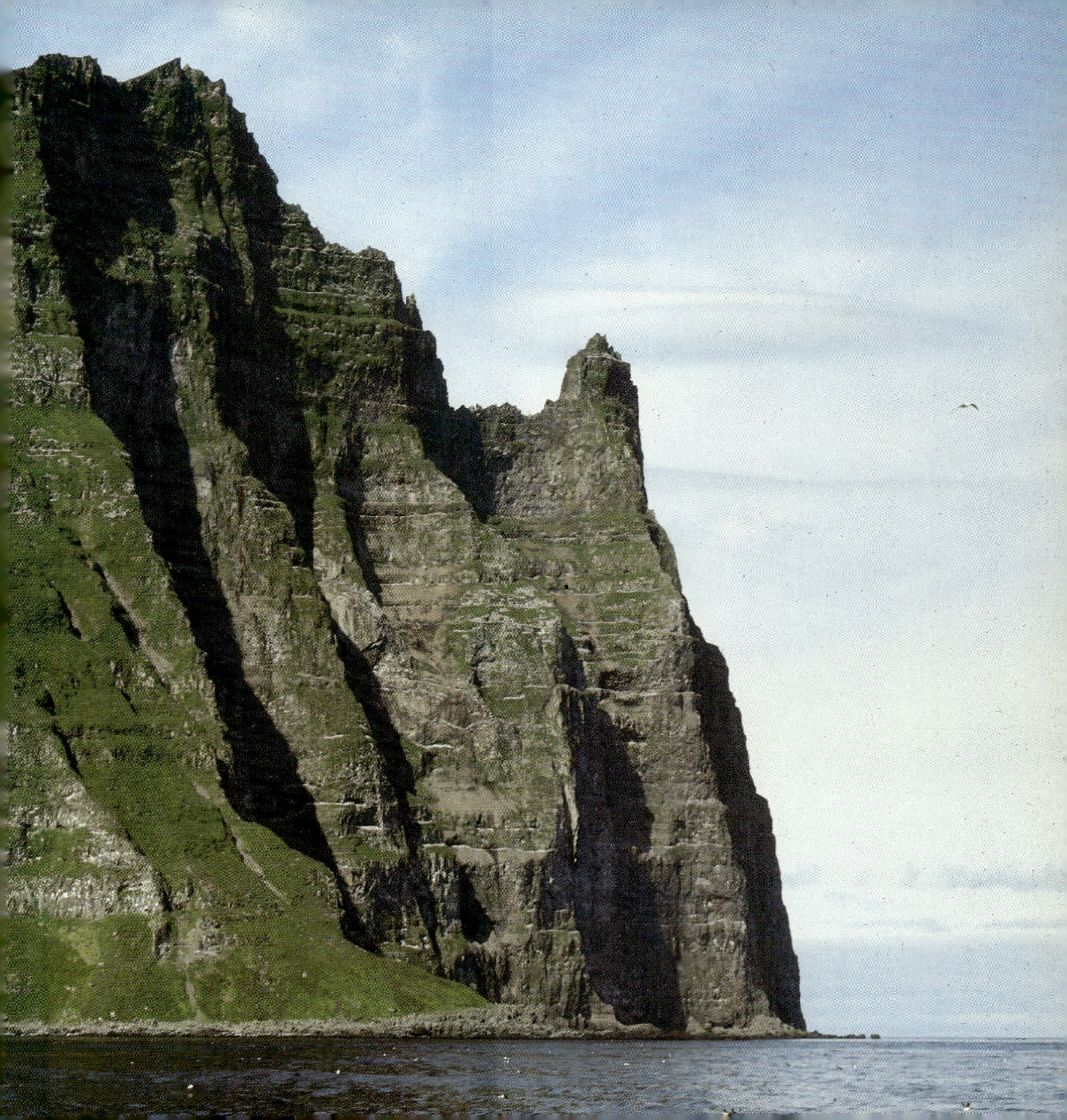

5. CLIFF-BIRDS

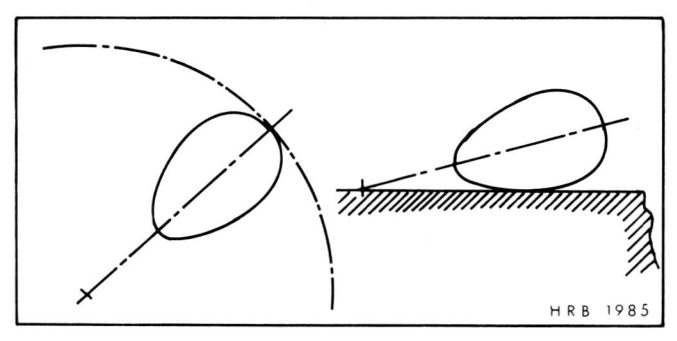

The **eggs** *of some cliff-birds, such as the guillemot, are noticeably pear-shaped. Such eggs roll in a narrow circle if disturbed, so there is less danger of their rolling off cliff-ledges. The different shapes of Icelandic birds' eggs can be studied in detail on pp. 36–37.*

The **GUILLEMOT** (Uria aalge) *is a member of the auk family (Alcidae) which also includes Brünnich's guillemot and the razorbill. The guillemot has dark brown upper-parts and white under-parts, whereas the razorbill has black upper-parts; the guillemot can also be distinguished from the razorbill by its thinner neck and slender pointed bill. Above left are 3 adult guillemots, 2 of which are of the so-called bridled form which have a white eye-ring and a white line extending backwards from it; this is a variant form of guillemot and not another species. In the foreground of the picture, taken in the so-called Kofabæli on Hellisey in the Vestmannaeyjar, is a guillemot chick. The bottom left picture was taken on Geldungur, also in the Vestmannaeyjar, where Iceland's largest continuous guillemot aggregation can be found. The guillemot is a common breeder on Icelandic bird-cliffs and there are an estimated 1,600,000 pairs in the country. Both common and Brünnich's guillemots (see pp. 93 & 94) nest on steep towering cliffs, and the common guillemot also likes such precipitous stacks as Geldungur. Guillemots have little or no nest to speak of, except perhaps for congealed droppings. It lays 1 egg, like most auks, usually in May or early June. The incubation period is about a month.*

90

5. CLIFF-BIRDS

Cliff-birds breed in mixed crowded colonies on cliff-faces. Some of these species have very definite preferences for certain parts of a cliff, so there is sometimes competition for good nesting sites. The puffin looks for a place where it can make a deep nesting burrow in grass or turf, and is thus usually found on the grassy sloping edges of cliff-tops. The fulmar prefers rather broad ledges where there is some vegetation, usually just under the cliff-top, though sometimes further down the cliff as well. Common and Brünnich's guillemots mix rather seldom on bird-cliffs. The common guillemot prefers broad ledges or buttresses for a nesting site, whereas Brünnich's guillemot likes narrow sills. On high cliffs the kittiwake often nests below all other species, usually in the middle or lowest parts of the cliff; indeed they can breed so low down on a cliff that they sometimes risk having their nests and eggs washed away by spray from the sea. Kittiwake nesting sites on tiny rocky ledges and sills are unsuitable for most other birds, so it usually has no rivals for a breeding ground, though it occasionally has to compete with common and Brünnich's guillemots, especially the latter. There is rarely any competition between kittiwakes and fulmars. The kittiwake makes a tidy nest out of grass, moss, and seaweed, cementing all these materials together with excreta, mud, or wet sea-vegetation which has adhesive qualities. This gives the nest additional strength and helps to secure it to the cliff-face. The razorbill often chooses rather broad ledges, holes or crevices on the upper-parts of cliffs, though the largest razorbill colonies are to be found among boulders at the foot of cliffs, as for example at Látrabjarg.

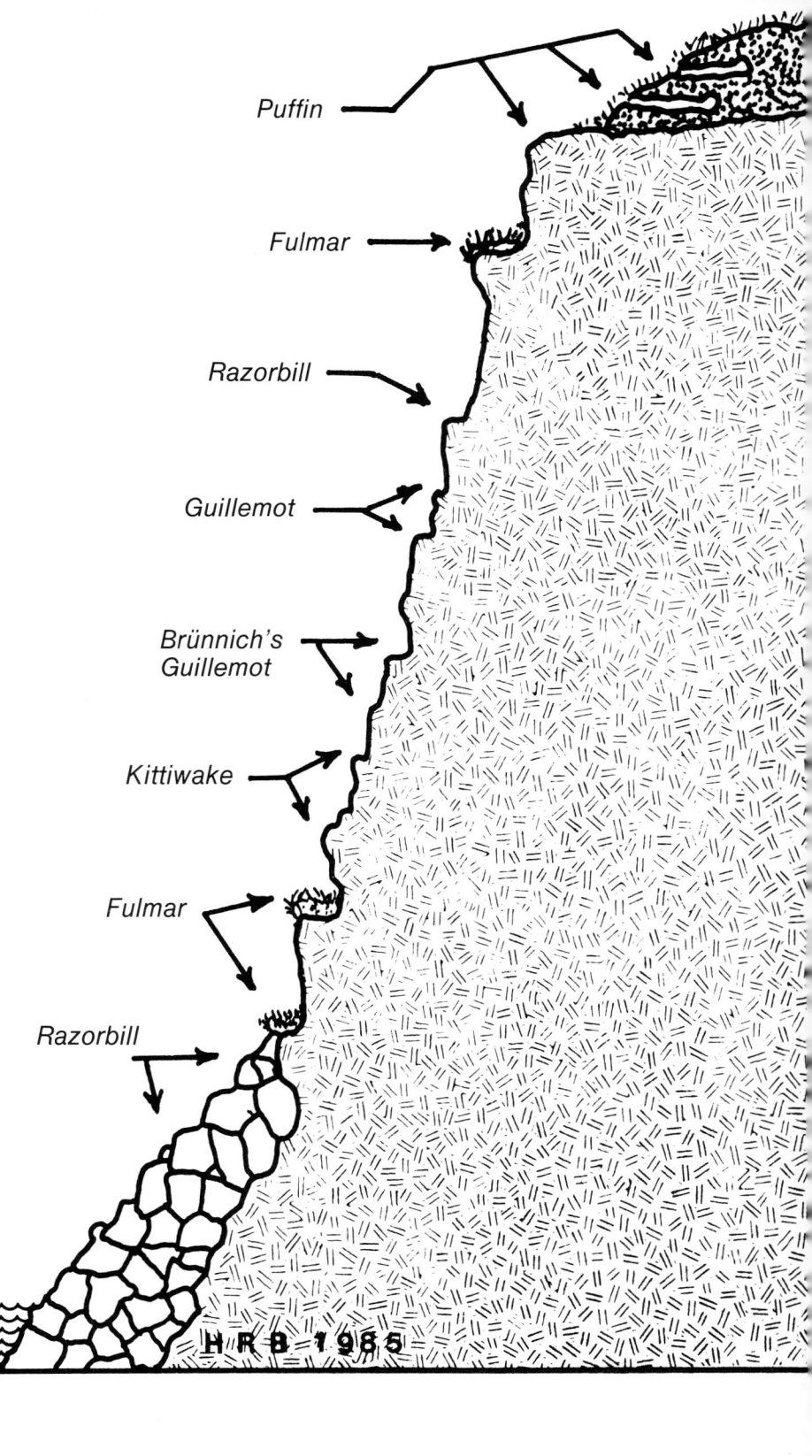

5. CLIFF-BIRDS

There is a **guillemot colony** on a broad ledge of Svalþúfa, a low cliff on the southern coast of Snæfellsnes. The good view of the cliff, above left, is only a short walk from the main road. Below left is a view of a Látrabjarg guillemot colony, viewed from the foot of the cliff. Above is a view of Heimaey in the Vestmannaeyjar, with the guillemot colony on the summit of Geldungur in the foreground.

Both guillemot parents take part in incubating the egg, and once the chick has hatched one of the parents will protect it whilst the other hunts for fish fry for food. When 3 weeks old the half-grown but still not fully fledged chick is urged by its parents to leap off the cliff and into the sea, waving its little wing-stumps rapidly to reduce the speed of its fall. In the sea the male parent teaches it how to catch fish. The parents thus ensure that their young know where the feeding grounds are as they would probably be incapable of providing it with enough food themselves, particularly if they had to travel long distances to do so.

Guillemots were often hunted and eaten in Iceland in earlier days, and auk eggs have always been considered a tasty meal. There have been many fatal accidents when men have been lowered down cliffs to collect birds and eggs, especially as a result of rock falls.

92

5. CLIFF-BIRDS

BRÜNNICH'S GUILLEMOT (*Uria lomvia*) is very similar to the common guillemot, but is easily distinguished from it by the conspicuous pale line along the basal sides of its much shorter bill. The Brünnich's guillemots pictured here are nesting on Látrabjarg.

Both species of guillemots have similar life patterns as far as breeding is concerned, but as Brünnich's guillemot is an arctic bird it is more widely distributed in the north of Iceland, especially on the cliffs of Látrabjarg, Hælavíkurbjarg, Hornbjarg, Drangey, and Grímsey. Common guillemots, on the other hand, are proportionately more numerous on the southern cliffs of Iceland. The Brünnich's guillemot population in Iceland is estimated at around 2 million breeding pairs, slightly more than the 1.6 million pairs of common guillemots.

5. CLIFF-BIRDS

The **FULMAR** (Fulmarus glacialis) is a little bigger than a kittiwake, but is a much stockier bird with a stout bull-neck. Its bill is thick and yellow with distinctive 'tubed' nostrils. It is mostly white except for grey shoulders, back and wings, the shades of grey varying from bird to bird. There is little difference in colouring between the sexes.

The fulmar is a maritime bird and a powerful flyer with a lot of stamina. It breeds on sea-cliffs and rocky islands in northern lands. Around 1750 the fulmar was recorded as breeding in Iceland only on Grímsey, and in 1780, to a lesser extent, in the Vestmannaeyjar. Its population has increased tremendously since then, and it is now very common and widely distributed all over the country. No exact figures are available, but the fulmar population in Iceland is generally estimated at several million breeding pairs. The fulmar has especially benefitted from Iceland's growing fishing industry as it feeds on waste from fishing vessels. It also hunts for marine food itself, including plankton, crustaceans, cuttle-fish, etc., and is also greedy for all kinds of fat, particularly liver-fat and blubber.

The fulmar lays only 1 egg which is white and not pear-shaped like that of an auk as it has different nesting sites, often on broad ledges, or hollows in earth and grass. Fulmar parents share the incubating and then feed the newly hatched chick for 2 months, first of all on half-digested oil. The fulmar is famous for ejecting oil at an intruder, and birds have even died as a result of this as the oil clots their feathers together, and it is impossible to remove it.

◁ On the left are adult Brünnich's guillemots on a cliff-ledge with a chick and egg. The distinctive white line on the basal part of the bill is clearly visible.

On the right are fulmars flying over the ocean 'in step', both ▷ birds having their wings in virtually the same position. The picture was taken from a trawler in the fishing grounds off the north-west of Iceland.

94

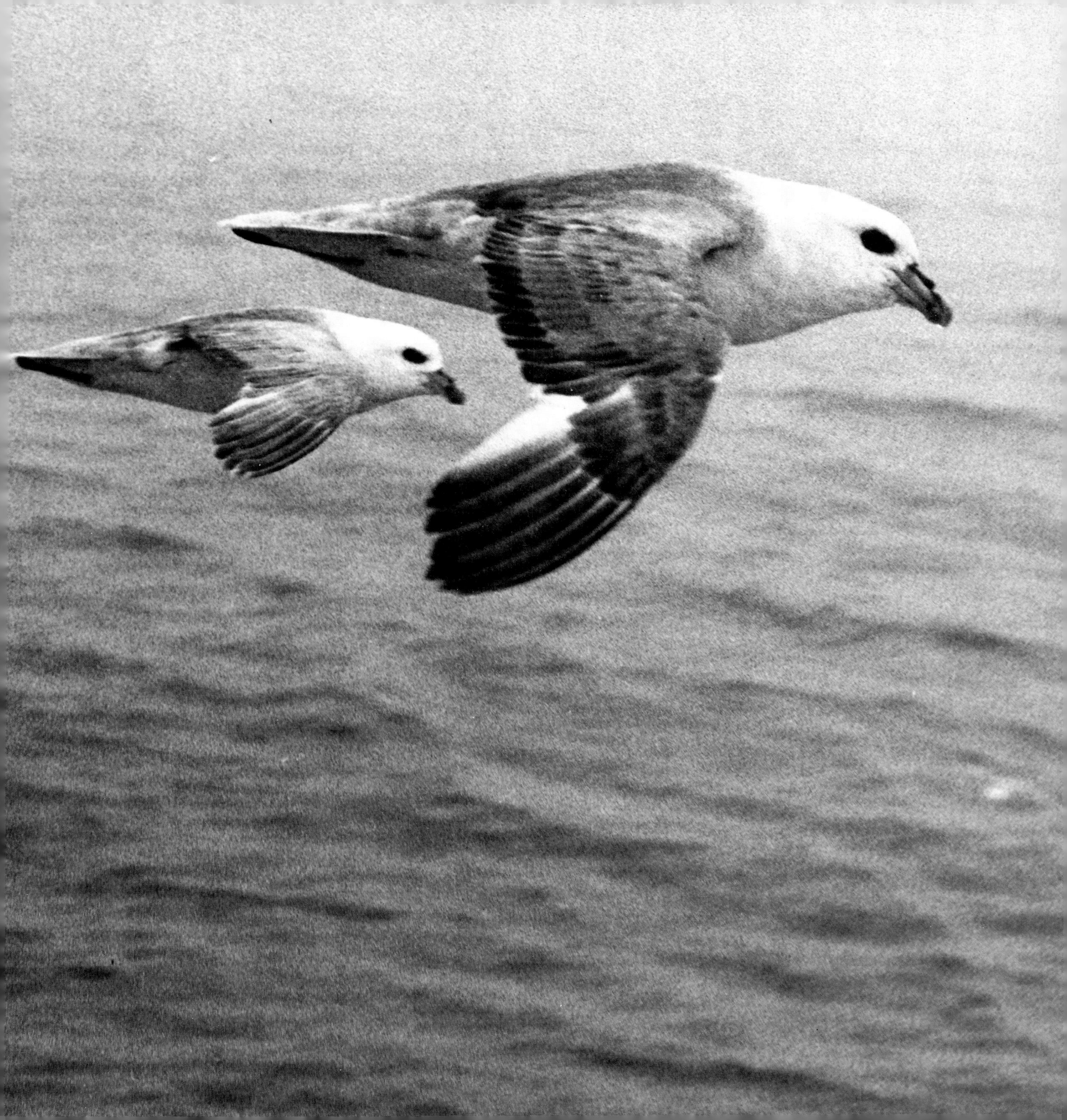

5. CLIFF-BIRDS

Above is a two-storey fulmar home on Hellisey in the Vestmannaeyjar: 2 nests, 1 above the other, in a fulmar's choice nesting site surrounded by vegetation. Above left are fulmars swimming near Drangey in Skagafjörður. The fulmar is a good and vigorous swimmer and dives to catch its food. It is not very agile on land and just shuffles on its tarsi as it can hardly walk. In the air the fulmar has no restrictions, however, and glides nimbly and lightly in between brisk wing-beats. It can also fly very swiftly, keeping up with fast-sailing vessels, even against the wind. On the left is a group of fulmars and kittiwakes following a stern-trawler at sea. As an oceanic bird, the fulmar is much admired by seamen. On the right are a fulmar and chick in a nest on Grímsey.

96

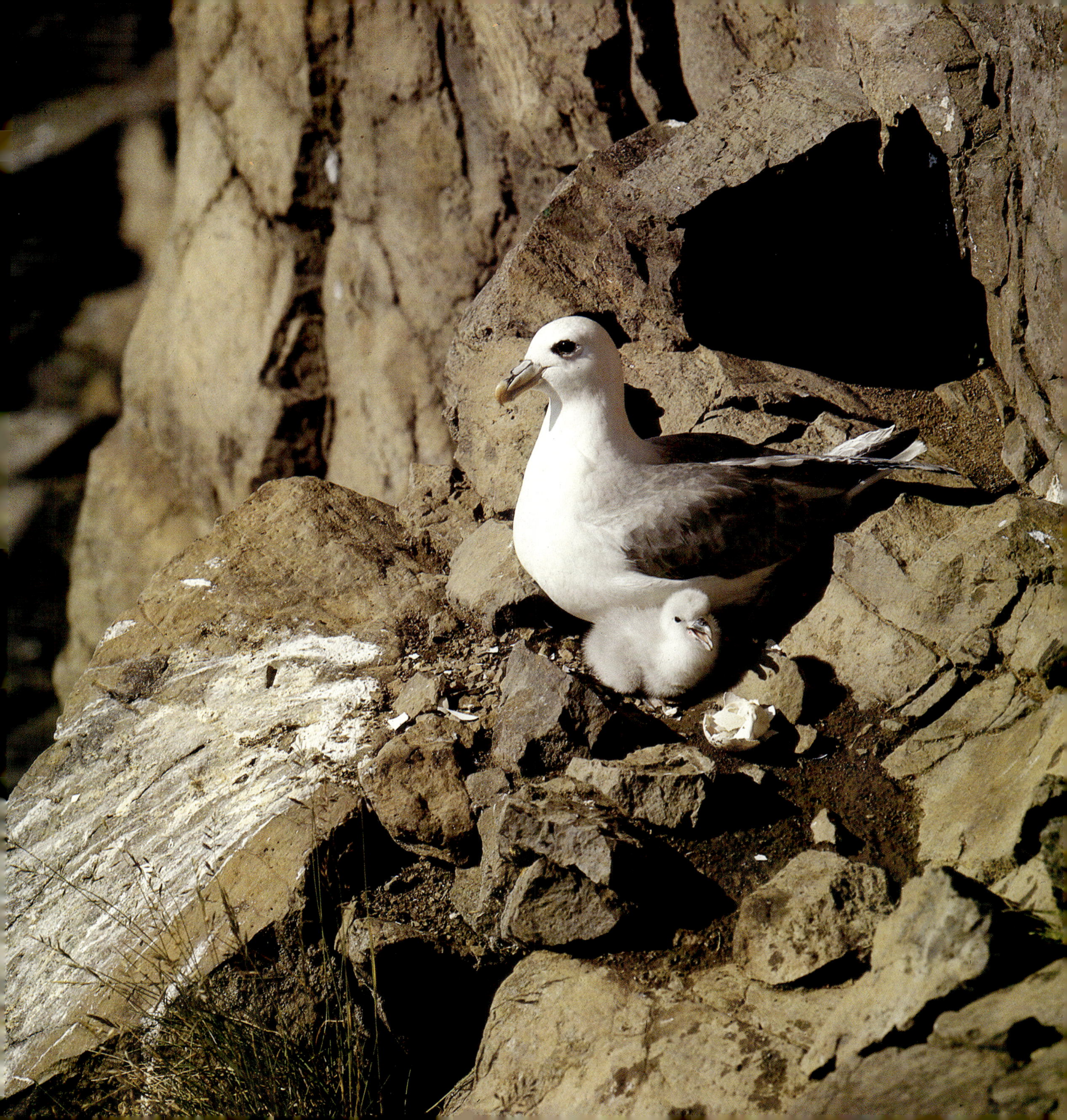

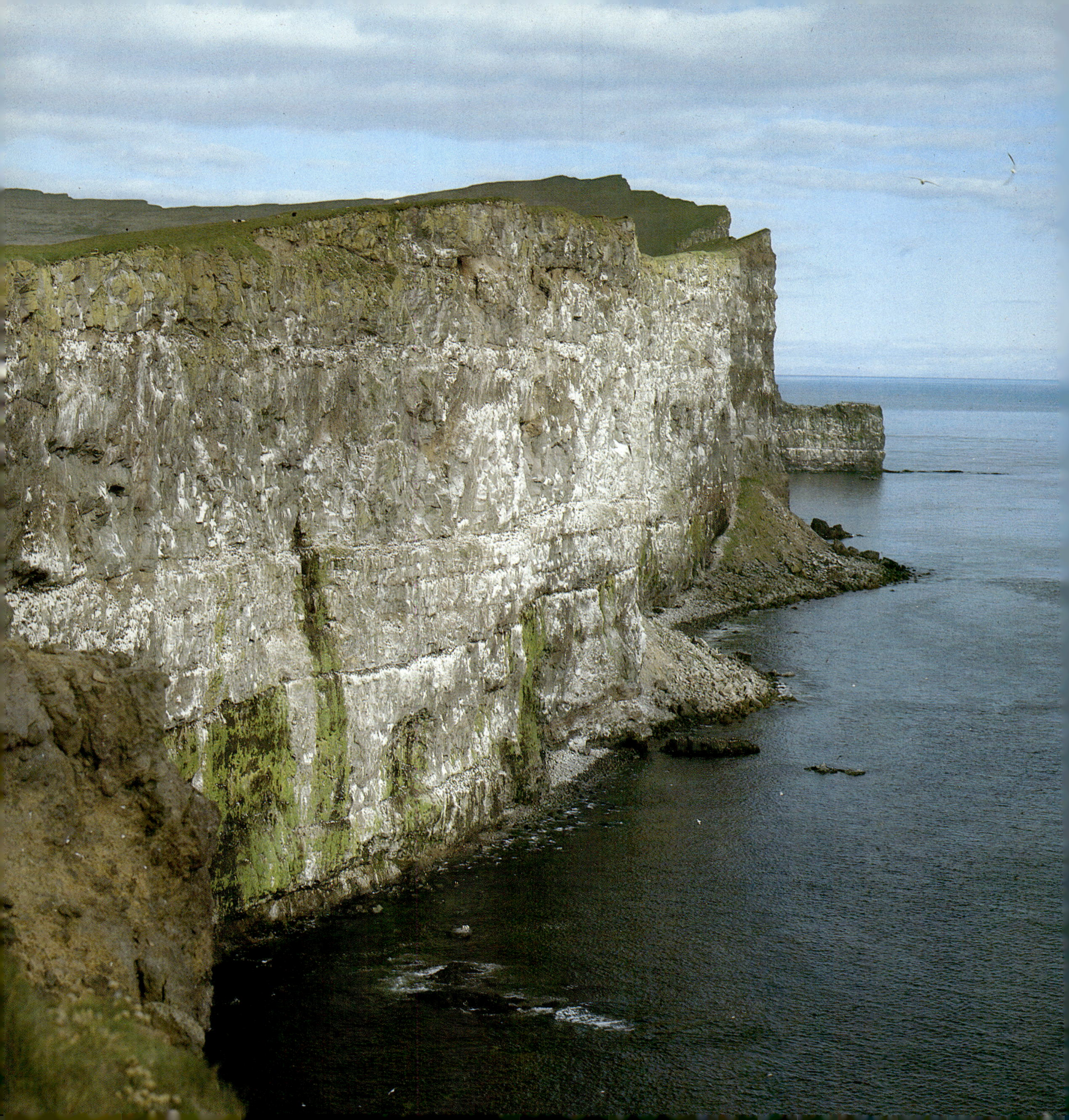

Látrabjarg is the largest bird-cliff in Iceland, and considered one of the most magnificent in the world. The picture on the left only shows the most westerly part of the cliff. The rocky extension jutting out from the main cliff and forming a smaller independent crag is called Barðið. The highest point of Látrabjarg is the 444 m Heiðnukinnarhorn in the outer reaches of Djúpidalur. Parts of the cliff sometimes collapse, creating mounds of bouldered rubble at its foot. On the left can be seen 2 such screes. The one furthest away is called Hrútanefjaurð, formed by a rock fall in 1921, and which once reached half-way up the cliff before the sea eroded part of it. The nearer rocks crashed from the cliff in 1950. Above is a picture taken in Stóraurð, at the foot of Látrabjarg. This is the largest stretch of all, formed by a rock fall in the 19th century, and the home of what is believed to be the largest razorbill colony in the world.

The razorbill is a cliff-bird and sea-bird like the common and Brünnich's guillemots which it resembles. Its life pattern is also similar to these other auks. The razorbill is a good swimmer and expert diver. Its small wings mean that it has to use frequent wing-beats when flying, but it can reach high speeds nonetheless. The razorbill was often hunted for food in Iceland, just like the 2 species of guillemots.

5. CLIFF-BIRDS

5. CLIFF-BIRDS

The **RAZORBILL** (Alca torda) has black upper-parts and white under-parts, very like Brünnich's guillemot, but is more easily identifiable by its distinctive laterally compressed bill with white transverse stripes. It has a rather large head and a very thick neck. Razorbills are very sociable birds, often sitting upright or lying on their bellies on cliff-ledges among guillemots and puffins. On the left are 2 razorbills high up on Látrabjarg. Above are razorbills on the edge of a cliff on Grímsey. The one coming in to land has been hunting out at sea and has food for its young in its bill. The pictures on the right are of razorbills and puffins together on Látrabjarg. The razorbill only lays 1 egg, which is not quite as pear-shaped as a guillemot's. The incubation period is about 4 weeks, and both parents take it in turns to sit. After 3 weeks feeding, the still not fully fledged chick, accompanied by its parents, is obliged to leap off the cliff or clamber over the boulders to go to sea where it is taught how to dive and catch food. After about a further 4 weeks it is fully fledged and self-supporting. The razorbill population in Iceland is estimated at a few hundred thousand breeding pairs.

5. CLIFF-BIRDS

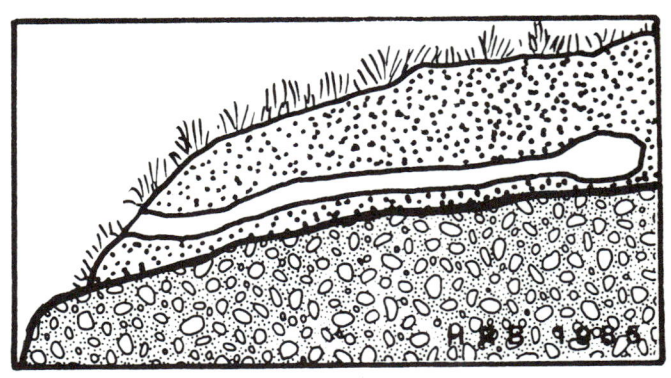

The **PUFFIN** (Fratercula arctica) is in many ways a remarkable bird. Its distinctive appearance, especially its bill, makes it the most easily recognisable of all Icelandic birds. In its breeding plumage the puffin has black upper-parts and a broad black neck-band. It is also black on the head and nape, but the sides of its head and its chin are ash-grey. Its under-parts are white. The bill is laterally compressed and very thin, the part near the base greyish-blue and the front part red with raised white transverse furrows. The basal ridge is yellow or yellowish-green and the corners of the mouth are bordered with a hard wrinkled reddish-yellow skin. There is similarly coloured hard skin around the eyes. The legs are red.

The puffin breeds in burrows which it usually digs itself. Above is a cross-section of such a burrow. Above left is a crowded puffin colony on Skrúður Island, and below left is a puffin colony on Ingólfshöfði. Below is a puffin chick, and on the right an adult puffin in its splendid breeding plumage on the cliff-edge of Látrabjarg.

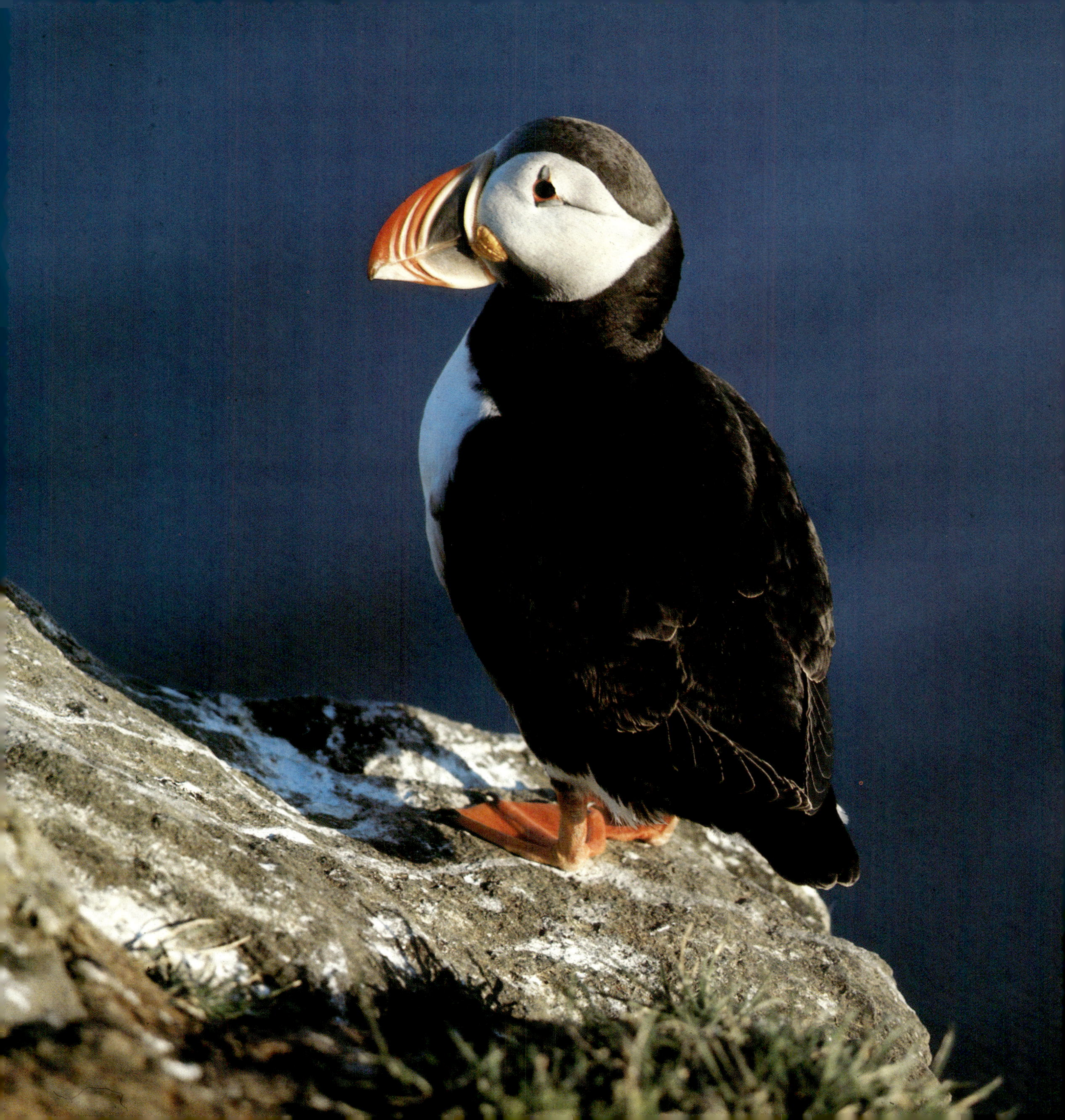

5. CLIFF-BIRDS

5. CLIFF-BIRDS

In its splendid breeding plumage the puffin is a very distinctive bird. In the autumn it sheds the hard skin on the basal ridge of the bill and around the eyes and also the colourful sheath of its bill, which is thus much less spectacular in the winter. On these 2 pages all the puffins are in their summer plumage. It is an extremely sociable bird, and can look very wise as it sits on the cliff-edge, apparently speculating on the meaning of life. Above left are 3 thoughtful puffins on the isle of Brandur in the Vestmannaeyjar. Above are 3 puffins on Hellisey, the one on the far right on the way to its burrow with food for its young. Above right is an evening gathering of puffins on Melrakkaey in Breiðafjörður. Below left is a large group of puffins at sea near Melrakkaey, and on the right is a puffin with its bill full of small fish. It is quite astonishing how many fish a puffin can hold in its bill, and it can add to its collection without losing a single one of the others. A characteristic of the puffin is that it likes to strut about for a while with a lot of food in its bill, before eventually returning to the burrow and feeding its young.

5. CLIFF-BIRDS

The bird-cliffs of Grímsey (above left), and Þórðarberg and Skrúðshellir on the isle of Skrúður (below left) are the nesting areas for enormous numbers of cliff-birds, especially kittiwakes. Above Þórðarberg is a steep grassy slope reaching up under Skrúðskollur, the summit of Skrúður, and the nesting area of one of the largest puffin colonies in Iceland (see top left picture on p. 102). The slope is consequently riddled with puffin burrows. The puffin above is clearly enjoying a rest in the flowery surroundings of the cliff-edge of Látrabjarg near to its breeding ground. The young puffin pictured top right on p. 107 is walking in the sands of Ingólfshöfði. Below right is a puffin in colourful surroundings on a rocky ledge of Látrabjarg.

The puffin is considered the most common of all Icelandic breeding birds with an estimated population of 8–10 million. Its breeding sites are on offshore islands, oceanic cliffs, and steep mountainsides near the sea. Large puffin colonies are widespread on low grassy islands, but the largest colonies of all are on the high sea-cliffs of uninhabited islands. The puffin makes its burrow on the slopes of the cliff-top, or on the grass-covered ledges of the cliff-face itself. The length and shape of the burrow varies according to the depth of the soil and other local conditions. On low grassy isles with a spongy topsoil, the burrow is sometimes 1.5 m long. The opening is almost round, and on average 15 cm in diameter. Just inside the entrance the burrow slopes downwards and generally becomes bow-shaped, sometimes having quite sharp bends. There are tens of thousands of puffins in the larger colonies, and the underground breeding area can be such a maze of tunnels and burrows that

106

the ground can subside under the weight of a man.

The puffin is a migratory bird in Iceland. It begins to arrive in April, and the main breeding season starts on or shortly after 20 May, and continues into the first half of June. Puffins lay only 1 egg, which is well protected in a wide recess at the bottom of the burrow. The incubation period is about 6 weeks, and the fledging period 6–7 weeks. Both parents take part in sitting, and later in the feeding of the chick, chiefly on sand eels and fish fry. In the first half of August the parents gradually stop feeding their young, so that they are obliged to abandon the burrow, the departure usually taking place at night. From 20 August onwards this exodus of young puffins increases, and by mid-September all the puffins have left their breeding grounds and gone to sea.

6 Shore-birds

The **EIDER** or **EIDER DUCK** (*Somateria mollissima*) is a shore-bird belonging to the waterfowl family. A stout bird with a long head, it is one of the largest Icelandic ducks. The sexes differ greatly in their plumage; the duck is not very colourful to look at, being mainly brown and mottled and barred with black. The drake, however, is much more splendid in appearance, and is white on its head, neck, and back, but black on its belly and crown. The eider is 3 years coming to full maturity, but it is believed it can live for up to 20 or 30 years.

The eider is mostly a sea-bird, both in and outside the breeding season, and in the autumn, when they are most numerous, there must be at least half a million of them in Iceland. The eider eats only marine organisms, mostly mussels and other molluscs, but its diet can vary according to circumstances and the time of year; a duck and its chicks frequenting shallow waters will feed mostly on sand hoppers. As the winter progresses, eiders will feed on capelin, and will later congregate at the capelin's spawning grounds to eat its roe. Eiders will also gather in fishing harbours to feed on fish waste.

The eider is a sociable bird, and large and small groups of them can be seen along many parts of the coast. The drakes begin to leave the nesting sites and gather in groups in June, and by July most of them have already lost their breeding plumage and resemble the duck in appearance. In September and October the eiders begin to form pairs, although breeding does not generally start until the following May.

Eider breeding grounds are nearly always near the sea, preferably on grassy isles or by estuaries, though they can also be by inland lakes if they are not too far from the coast. The eider's sociability is most noticeable in the breeding grounds, for hundreds, if not thousands, of nests can be crowded together in a very small area. The nest is rather simple, and preferably sited in the shelter of a windbreak, such as a tussock or stone. The bottom of the nest is packed with seaweed, grass, and moss, and then lined with the duck's own dark grey down. There are usually 3–4 eggs, though there can be as many as 10. Only the duck sits, but the drake remains near the nest during the early stages of incubation. The eider duck is well camouflaged and

6. SHORE-BIRDS

remains perfectly still on the nest, sometimes crouching down if approached. The chicks hatch after about 3 weeks in June, and the duck then leads them to the sea, sometimes a difficult journey. As soon as the chicks are in the water, however, they start to swim briskly and to dive after food, though they always keep close to their mother, who defends them as best she can. Nonetheless great black-backed gulls and other birds eat many eider chicks, often sweeping them up off the sea. Great black-backed gulls will also feed on eider eggs if they find an undefended nest.

Throughout history the eider has been utilised by man and still is to this day. In earlier times its flesh and eggs were considered more valuable than its down, but now the eider is a protected bird, and its down is the only produce which matters. Eider-farming involves the care and protection of eider nesting sites and the harvesting of the down which the duck moults. Each duck provides about 17 g of pure down every year, adding up to a national total of an estimated 2000 kg per annum, and providing earnings for around 250–270 eider breeding ground owners.

Above right is a crowded and superintended eider nesting site at Mýrar in Dýrafjörður on 4 June. On the right is a sitting eider duck. The drake is by the nest, but leaves the incubating entirely to the duck.

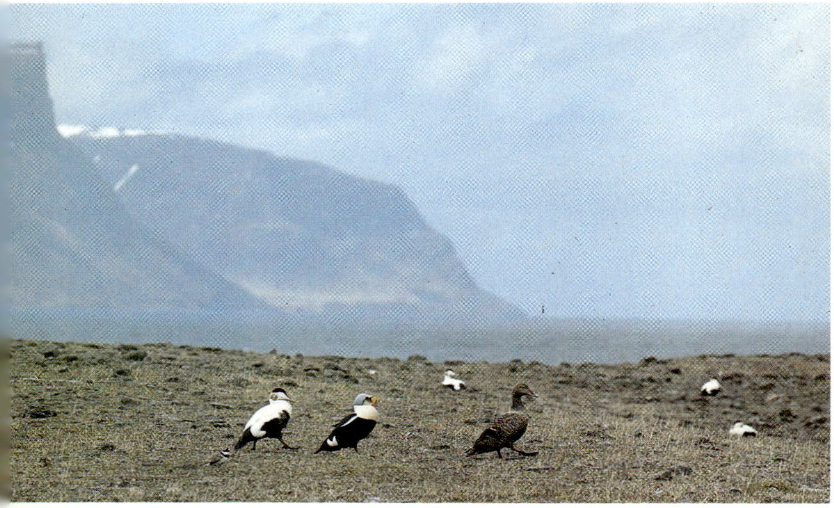
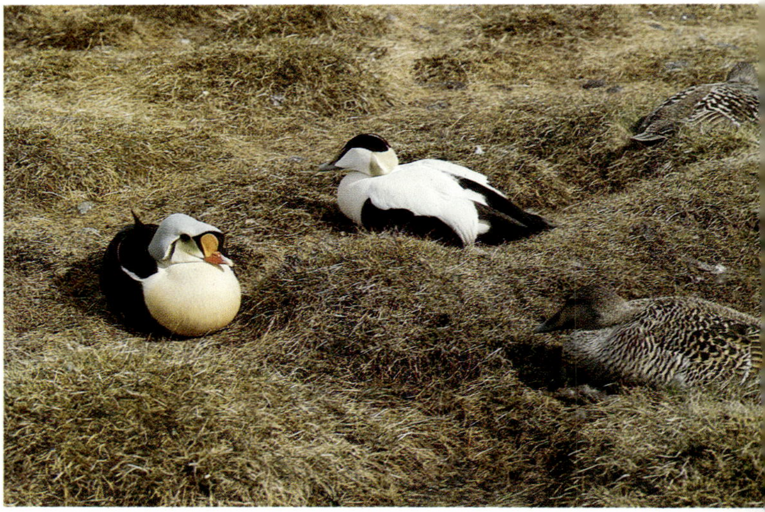
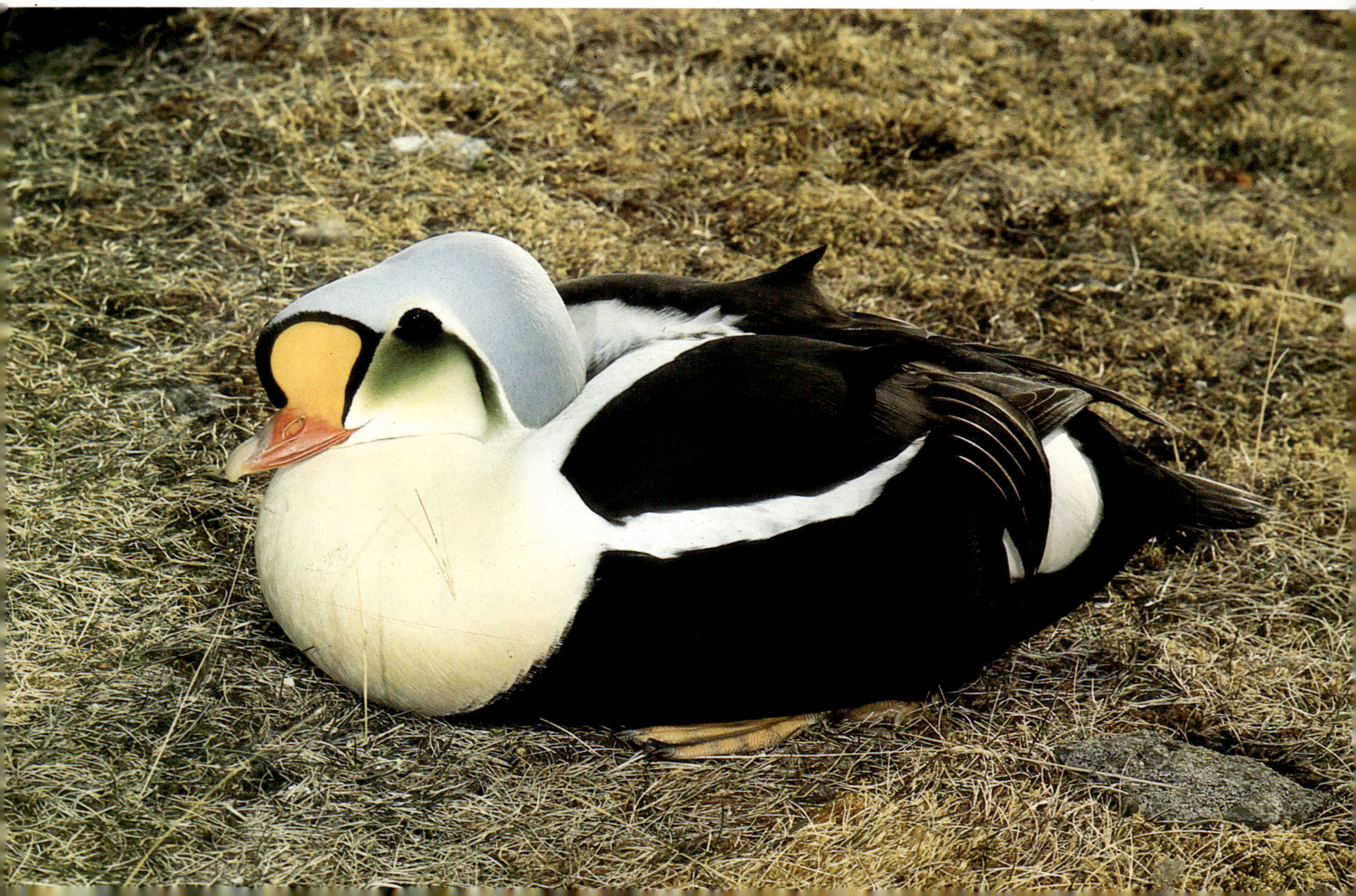

6. SHORE-BIRDS

The **KING EIDER** (*Somateria spectabilis*) *is slightly smaller than the eider. The drake is easily identifiable by its colourful bill and distinctive orange shield on its forehead.* King eider drakes often come to Iceland from Greenland, one of their main breeding grounds, and occasionally mate with Icelandic eider ducks, particularly in the Vestfirðir. On the left is a King eider drake in its splendid plumage. An eider duck at the Mýrar colony in Dýrafjörður was accompanied by both an eider drake and this resplendent King eider. Both followed her on her walks, and both sat resolutely by the nest whilst she was incubating, as can be seen top left. It is well known that King eider drakes and eider ducks can interbreed, and the resulting hybrid can have distinctive features of both species, as can be seen in the picture above. This singular hybrid (a drake) was with eider ducks and drakes both at sea and in the eider colony on Æðey in Ísafjarðardjúp. It was paired with an eider duck, and at least one of their young had probably reached the sea with the duck. Pairs of King eiders have never been known to breed in Iceland, although female King eiders have been seen here.

6. SHORE-BIRDS

Eider nests are preferably sited in the shelter of tussocks or stones (above left). The eider-farmer collects the down from the nests in the protected breeding grounds (above). The down is only sparingly collected whilst the duck and her chicks are still in the nest (below left) and the remainder taken once they have left for the sea. Below is an eider duck and her 3 chicks, one of which is an albino, an occasional occurrence. Eider young are grey-brown or dark brown with paler under-parts. The eider is a peaceful bird and can be very tame whilst nesting, the same duck often returning year after year to the same nest, and apparently seeming to appreciate the local farmers' care and protection.

The **RINGED PLOVER** (Charadrius hiaticula) is a shore-bird, its main habitat being sands and mud-flats by the sea or lakes. It feeds on insects, sand hoppers, other small crustaceans, and worms, which it finds and draws out of the mud with its bill, as in the picture above. The ringed plover is a small plump bird, similar to a golden plover in build, and easily recognisable by the broad black band across its white breast, reminiscent of a black bib. Its upper-parts are pale brown with a white collar and white forehead. There is a broad black stripe across the front of the crown from eye to eye. The bill is yellow with a black tip (see picture p. 115). Both sexes have the same colouring, but the female is not so dark on the head and breast.

The ringed plover breeds all round Iceland. It is so unbelievably quick and nimble that when it is running about it is almost impossible to see its legs move! It is an expert at enticing uninvited guests away from the nest by feigning injury, usually a broken wing. It limps for a few paces, waits until the intruder approaches, and then limps a bit further, this performance being repeated again and again until the intruder has been drawn far enough away from its nest and young. Once the danger has thus been averted, it suddenly flies off and disappears.

6. SHORE-BIRDS

Above is a ringed plover foraging for food on the beach. It is quick on its feet, and once the tide is out can always find something tasty in the sand or mud under the seaweed. It roots about in the mud with its bill, and is very quick to pounce as soon as it feels something move.

On the left is a ringed plover's nest with 3 eggs. Its nest is very simple, often just a slight depression in sand or gravel. The eggs have such good protective shape and colouring that they can be very difficult to find. On the right is a ringed plover about to sit in its nest. There are usually 4 eggs, laid in June, and the incubation period is just over 3 weeks, both parents taking turns to sit. The parents also feed the chicks when first hatched, but they soon learn to find their own food. The chicks are so well camouflaged that it is almost impossible to see them when they crouch down and keep perfectly still. They are fully fledged 4 weeks after hatching. The ringed plover is a migratory bird, arriving in Iceland late in April, soon after the golden plover, and usually leaving the country again by mid-October.

6. SHORE-BIRDS

6. SHORE-BIRDS

The **OYSTERCATCHER** (*Haematopus ostralegus*) is a large stocky black and white shore-bird with a very distinctive long and reddish-yellow bill.

'Its red bill is just like a knife which it uses to split open shellfish,' says Jón the Learned in his book *On the Diverse Natures of Iceland* (see picture p. 27). The oystercatcher's bill is certainly long and red, and is used with great dexterity in obtaining all kinds of food along the seashore. It breaks open shellfish by sticking its bill into the slightly ajar bivalve, and then with very precise blows loosens the suction muscles so that the shell opens up completely. The oystercatcher is as common on shingly beaches as mud-flats, and is just as adroit at digging up lugworms as the ringed plover. If the beaches are too sandy to support any life, as in many places on Iceland's southern coast, it will move further inland, where it can feed on earth-worms and insects. Later in the summer, after haymaking, it often gathers in groups in the homefields like the golden plover.

The oystercatcher is a noisy bird, and not every-one likes its song. It is most vociferous in spring, and on fine days the bays and fjords can resound with its call. There are even such events as oyster-catcher concerts. These begin when 2 oyster-catchers face each other, stretch out their heads and necks, their bills pointing straight down, and start to utter a high sharp tone, best transcribed as 'blee-blee-blee'. These notes are repeated constantly and

Above left is an oystercatcher chick breaking out of its shell one evening. On the left, dawn the following day, the newly hatched chick begins to orientate itself. At the end of its bill can be seen the egg-tooth with which it breaks out of the egg, and which gradually wears away.

6. SHORE-BIRDS

Above is an oystercatcher breaking open a mussel with its bill. It sticks its bill between the shells and tears the muscles which hold them together. On the right is an oystercatcher pair taking a stroll, and below is an oystercatcher sitting on its eggs.

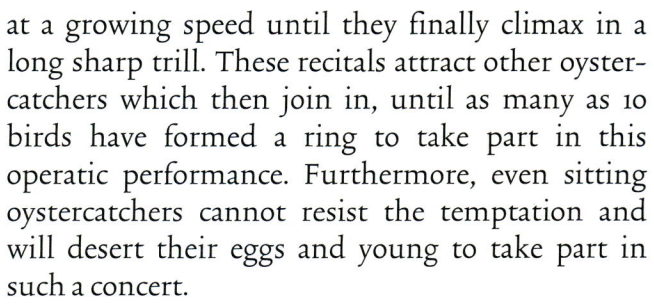

at a growing speed until they finally climax in a long sharp trill. These recitals attract other oystercatchers which then join in, until as many as 10 birds have formed a ring to take part in this operatic performance. Furthermore, even sitting oystercatchers cannot resist the temptation and will desert their eggs and young to take part in such a concert.

The oystercatcher is a southern species, but since around 1920, when the climate began to become warmer, its numbers have greatly increased in Iceland. It is now a common breeding bird in southern and western Iceland, and even a resident, as quite a number remain in the country all year. The migrating oystercatchers winter in Great Britain. It occurs much less in northern and eastern Iceland, however, and the birds in these areas are always migratory.

An oystercatcher bathing in a freshwater pool. The oystercatcher mainly haunts the mud-flats and shingle of the seashore, but it can also be found further inland by rivers and lakes, sometimes quite far from the sea. Its breeding grounds are preferably by the shore, just above the spring high-tide level, in fine gravel or shell-strewn beaches. It also breeds on the gravel banks of rivers or on slightly grassy and stony hills near lakes. The oystercatcher normally lays 3 eggs early in May. The nest, if any, is very simple, merely a hollow in sand or gravel. The incubation period lasts about a month and the parents feed the chicks for the first 7–10 days, or until they have learnt to support themselves.

6. SHORE-BIRDS

The **GREY PHALAROPE** (*Phalaropus fulicarius*) is closely related to the red-necked phalarope and similar in build and habits, though slightly larger in size. The grey phalarope is an arctic bird and breeds so dispersively in Iceland that its exact numbers are unknown, though there are probably not many more than 100 birds all told. It breeds mostly in coastal areas and on small islands, but as it is a rarely seen bird its nests are difficult to find. It has also abandoned known nesting sites in Iceland in recent years, possibly because of the warmer climate and human interference. The grey phalarope is a good swimming-bird and often darts its head under water to seize food in the shallows. It also spins in circles on the water, like the red-necked phalarope, to stir up food to the surface. It is a very nimble flyer. Like the red-necked phalarope, the male grey phalarope takes the role of housewife and incubates the eggs and tends the young until they go to sea. The male has accordingly duller colouring than the female. Grey phalaropes feed mostly on small marine animals such as sand hoppers and other small crustaceans.

The grey phalarope is migratory and arrives in Iceland rather late, not before 20 May. Nesting begins early in June and by the end of July all grey phalaropes have generally left their breeding grounds and gone to coastal waters, where they remain until late in September when they finally leave the country. The Icelandic grey phalarope is believed to winter on the open sea in the far south of the Atlantic.

A grey phalarope foraging on the seashore for such small creatures as sand hoppers and annelids.

Above is a female **GREY PHALAROPE** foraging for food, 23 June. In summer the grey phalarope is reddish-brown on its under-parts, looking almost black on its belly. It has a white face, a dark crown, and a striped back like the snipe. The bill is yellow with a black tip. On the left is a male grey phalarope swimming. Its colours are similar to the female's, but, as with the white cheek-patch for example, they are not as pure or bright. – The grey phalarope's behaviour greatly resembles that of the red-necked phalarope (see pp. 161–3) as far as courting, incubating eggs, and tending young are concerned. It is the female which woos the male, whilst it is the latter which chooses the nesting site, usually on the seashore, not too far above the spring high-tide level. The male prepares the nesting hollow by pressing down the grass or shore-vegetation, and then invites the female to lay its eggs there. It usually lays 4 eggs, and once they are laid the female departs and leaves the male to incubate them, the incubation period lasting about 18 days (see picture on the right).

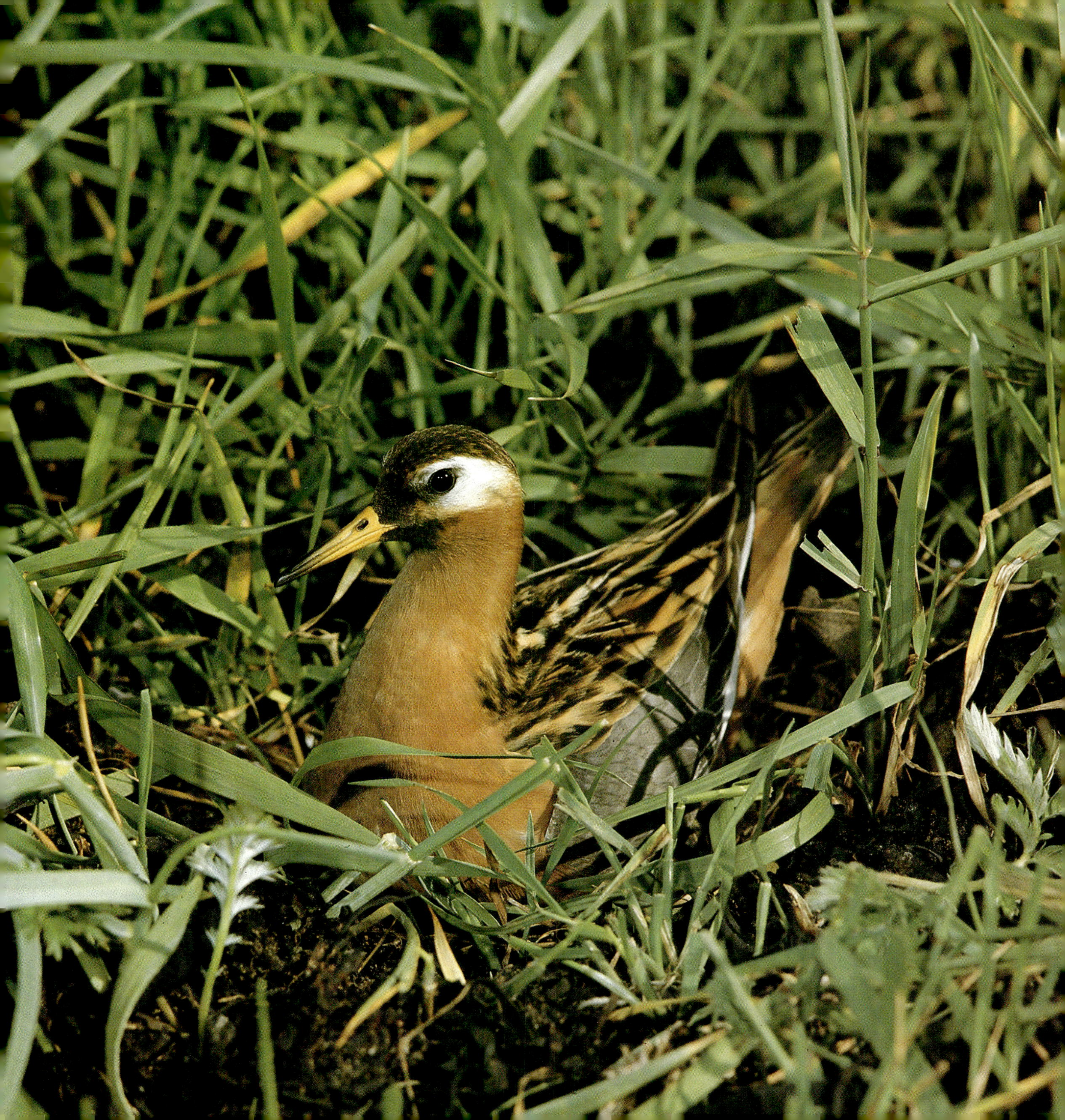

The **GREAT SKUA** (*Stercorarius skua*) is a stocky bird with a short square-shaped tail. The central tail-feathers are only fractionally longer than the others, and do not form a long projection like the arctic skua's. The great skua is closely related to the arctic skua, but is not very similar in appearance. Adult great skuas weigh 1200–1600 g, or up to four times the weight of an arctic skua, which is generally 350–450 g. The wings are broader and stubbier than an arctic skua's, and it is a heavier flyer. Nonetheless it can be very agile and fast in the air when necessary, especially when chasing other birds or defending its eggs and young – as anyone who has trespassed on its nesting site will know. It will often furiously attack both man and beast, and can give quite a hard blow with its feet.

Both sexes have the same colouring, but the female is usually just a little bit bigger and heavier than the male. The great skua's breeding plumage is dark brown on the upper-parts, head, and throat, but light brown on the under-parts. There

Above are great skuas flying over their main breeding grounds along the great sands of the south coast. On the right is a great skua in flight near the Jökulsá river on the gravel plains of Breiðamerkursandur.

are yellow streaks on the nape, and some skuas' heads and chins are mottled with white. There is often a varyingly discernible white ring around the eyes. The back, shoulders, and wing-coverts are mottled with rust or grey.

The tail-feathers are dark brown, and white at the base. The wings are also dark brown and have a distinctive white patch at the base of the primaries which is especially noticeable in flight (see picture on p. 123). The legs are black, and so is the bill, which has a slight greenish gloss. There is very little difference between the summer and winter plumage except that during the winter the yellowish streaks on the nape disappear.

There are believed to be 4–6 kinds of great skuas in the southern hemisphere, but there is only 1 in

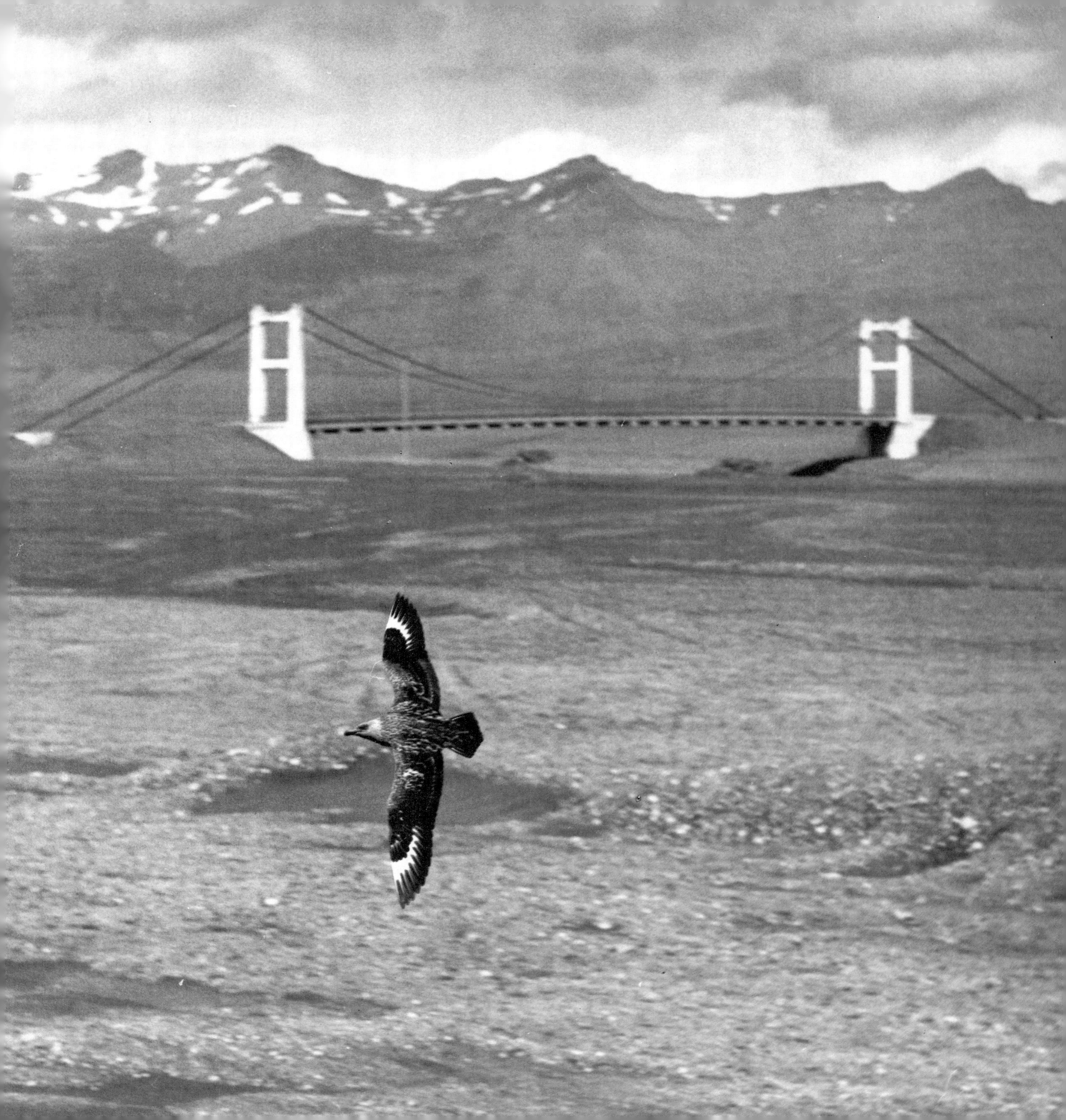

6. SHORE-BIRDS

the North Atlantic, and its range extends right up to the Arctic Circle. This species mainly breeds in Iceland, the Shetlands, the Orkneys, and the Faroes. About half of the population breeds in Iceland. These great skua colonies are thus isolated from the species in the Antarctic, and the reason for this extraordinary distribution has long been a mystery. One theory is that at one time in ages past, some Antarctic great skuas were blown into the far north of the Atlantic where they settled on islands with conditions similar to those of their breeding grounds in the southern hemisphere.

There are an estimated 6,000 breeding pairs of great skuas in Iceland, though apart from a few scattered nesting sites, its distribution is limited to the great sands of the south coast. The great skua is a large distinctive bird, and is extremely fierce and aggressive at its nesting site. Some of its breeding grounds on the great sands south of the Vatnajökull and Eyjafjallajökull glaciers seem devoid of vegetation at first glance, but a closer look reveals small patches of grass and turf here and there, where the great skua almost inevitably prefers to nest; indeed it probably plays a large part in the creation of such spots of greenery. The nests are seldom close to each other as great skua pairs insist on large individual breeding territories. The great skua, like the arctic skua, winters at sea, though it is often nearer to land than the arctic skua.

Top left is a great skua on the Breiðamerkursandur; in the background is a glacial lagoon next to the Fjallsjökull tongue of the great Vatnajökull glacier. Centre left is a great skua at its nesting site on the sands of the southern coast. Bottom left is a great skua's nest with 2 eggs. Above is a great skua sitting. The great skua mostly remains at sea during the winter, and begins to return to its breeding grounds in the second half of March. It usually lays its eggs in the latter part of May, much earlier than the arctic skua, but later than the great black-backed gull. These 3 species often share the same breeding grounds over a wide area of Iceland's south-coast sands. The great skua's nest is not an elaborate affair. It is 23–30 cm in diameter and 4.5–8 cm deep. It is sometimes unlined, but the skua usually surrounds its eggs with moss and some of its own feathers. There are almost always 2 eggs, brown or olive-green in colour, with dull purple or dark brown spots and blotches.

The incubation period is 28 days and both parents take part in sitting, foraging for food, and feeding the chicks. The chicks become fully fledged after 6–7 weeks, in August, when the great skua then departs from its breeding grounds.

Great skuas often obtain food piratically by chasing other birds, especially gannets and certain kinds of gulls, and forcing them to release their catch, or even disgorge it. It cannot dive under water, but will seize fish on the surface. The great skua also steals the eggs and young of various species, and will also kill adult birds, e.g. ducks and fulmars. It exhausts ducks whilst they are swimming, or else seizes them as they re-surface from a dive. It also eats carrion and fish offal.

Above is an arctic tern on its nest, and on the left an arctic tern's nest; this is often a very simple affair, just a shallow depression which is sometimes loosely lined with straw, moss, small stones, or bits of shells. There are 1–3 eggs, usually 2 and only very occasionally 3, and they are pale grey or greyish-green or greyish-brown with dark spots and blotches, which sometimes form large patches or even a ring around the middle or thicker end of the egg. The incubation period takes about 3 weeks, and the young are fully fledged when 3–4 weeks old. Both sexes sit and provide food for the young, which leave the nest shortly after they have hatched.

6. SHORE-BIRDS

The **ARCTIC TERN** (*Sterna paradisaea*) is a rather small bird, the adult only weighing 100–120 g. It always seems much bigger than it really is because of its many feathers and long wings and tail. There is no difference in colouring between the sexes, but the male is just a little bigger than the female. In its summer plumage an adult arctic tern is light grey with a black cap from its forehead to its nape. It is darker on the back, shoulders, and wings, and palest on the chin; it is almost white on the cheeks, beneath the black cap, and white on the rump. The upper and under tail-coverts are white and so are the tail-feathers, except for the outer ones at the sides which are more or less grey. The outer primaries are almost black at the edges, but are paler further in, and the innermost secondaries are pure white. The bill is blood-red, the tip of the upper mandible being dark grey. The legs are very red and the feet dark brown.

The arctic tern is totally migratory and has usually arrived in Iceland by mid-May. Icelanders look forward to its coming and give it a special welcome as it is a harbinger of spring. It is also one of the delights of Reykjavík as it breeds on a small

6. SHORE-BIRDS

On the left is an arctic tern arriving at its nest and, above, it arranges the eggs before sitting on them. Arctic tern chicks have yellow-brown or light grey upper-parts heavily mottled with dark spots and streaks (see picture on the right). They are white on the breast and belly, but dark grey around the throat, chin, and bill. The bill is light pink with a black tip, and the legs are pink with grey or dark grey feet.

island on Lake Tjörnin, thus making Reykjavík almost certainly the only capital in the world to have a ternery in its town centre! The arctic tern also deserves a warm welcome as no Icelandic bird has travelled so far to get here. Indeed its spring and autumn migrations are one of the wonders of the world and have been carefully researched through the study of ringed birds. The arctic tern, as its name suggests, has its breeding grounds in all the countries within the Arctic Circle as well as in nearby lands in the northern parts of the Atlantic and Pacific Oceans. In the autumn the arctic terns on the east and west coasts of the north Atlantic travel down the west coasts of Europe and Africa until they reach the Antarctic Ocean. It is notable that

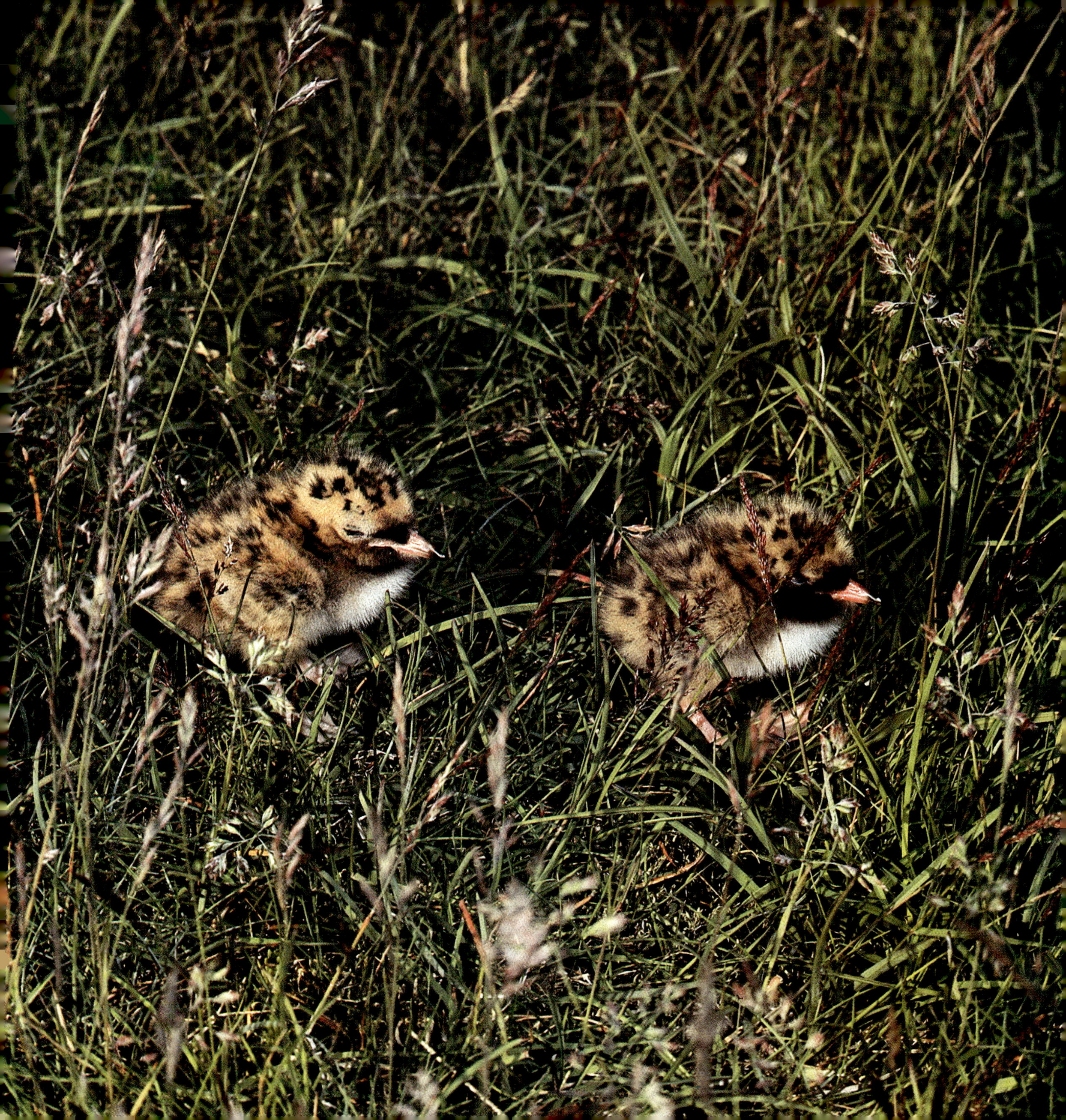

6. SHORE-BIRDS

The arctic tern's short legs are clearly visible in this picture.

the arctic terns of east-coast North America first cross the Atlantic to Europe before turning south, instead of just travelling due south along the east coasts of North and South America. They do this in order to follow oceanic currents rich in food supplies on their long journey. Whilst their northern breeding grounds are in the depths of winter, the arctic tern enjoys the warm weather and bountiful food supplies of the southern hemisphere; when autumn returns there, however, it makes the long journey back to its northern home and arrives there early in summer. The arctic tern thus enjoys a never-ending summer, but it has to make extraordinary efforts to do so. On its spring and autumn journeys the arctic tern flies much greater distances than any other migratory bird in the world. A young arctic tern ringed in Greenland in June was found the following October on the east coast of South Africa, having covered 18,000 km.

The arctic tern is a very common bird in Iceland with an estimated population of a few hundred thousand breeding pairs. It haunts the coastline, and breeds in small and large colonies on the beaches, or on isles and skerries just offshore. It also nests much further inland by rivers and lakes. The smallest colonies can have between a dozen and several hundred breeding pairs, but in the larger colonies there can be 5,000 pairs or more.

Black-headed gulls have occasionally succeeded in breeding in the midst of a ternery, and this can lead to clashes over nesting sites in which the black-headed gull is usually in a better position as it begins nesting earlier. However, it has never totally evicted the arctic tern from any of its traditional breeding grounds. It is common for arctic terns to breed among eider ducks on isles and skerries. This is generally considered beneficial as terns will defend the site from such predators as the great black-backed gull. Most people are aware of how aggressive terns can be during the breeding season if an uninvited guest approaches their nests. They will harass any intruder, be it bird, beast, or man, and try to drive him out of the nesting area, using their sharp bills unsparingly.

The arctic tern's choice of nesting ground is variable, though it normally avoids areas with a lot of vegetation as it cannot perch in such places because of its very short legs. Near the sea it breeds on grassy plains, or on moors with very stunted growth, or on slightly grassy and stony hills, or on sand or shingle beaches, or piles of seaweed. Wherever there is enough space, the nesting areas are generally well spread out, and even in more crowded terneries there are seldom less than 2 m between nests.

The arctic tern's main breeding season is in the first half of June, though weather conditions can influence exactly when it begins. The first terns begin to leave Iceland in mid-July, but the main exodus is not until August, and by the beginning of September the breeding grounds are empty and deserted.

Barring sickness and accident, an arctic tern can have quite a long life span. A tern chick ringed at Grímsstaðir by Lake Mývatn was found 21 years later in Nigeria. Many arctic terns return year after year to the very same place where they were originally ringed, and apart from providing data as to the bird's age, it also gives evidence of the arctic tern's loyalty to a specific place, and its extraordinary accuracy in finding its way.

The arctic tern feeds mostly on small fish and fish fry, various kinds of plankton, insects and their larvae, and earthworms. Its favourite saltwater fish are sand eels, capelin, small herrings, and coalfish fry; its preferred freshwater fish are sticklebacks, and trout and salmon fry whenever it can get them.

Wherever the arctic tern and the black guillemot are neighbours, the former often steals food from the latter. The black guillemot can obtain food much deeper under water than the tern can as it can dive deep and is an expert swimmer, using its wings for propulsion. An arctic tern will sometimes lie in wait for a black guillemot returning from the sea with a fish in its bill, and thanks to its superior flying skills, can often succeed in robbing the black guillemot of its catch before it can reach its nest and young. The arctic tern then flies home to feed its own chicks with the pirated meal!

The arctic tern is a very agile flyer and can hover in the air like a helicopter, especially when locating small fish or other prey under water. It will then draw in its wings and swoop down to snatch its prey off the surface in its bill, often without even settling on the water. If no other method will suffice, it will also dive under water to seize its food. It sometimes catches insects in flight. The arctic tern can swim, but does so very rarely, seldom even sitting on the water except to bathe. It will also hover, as shown here, when it intends to steal a fish from another bird, in this case a black guillemot. It watches the black guillemot whilst it is under water, and as soon as it surfaces, swoops down and 'buzzes' it, forcing it to dive once more in panic. The arctic tern continues to do this until the black guillemot eventually tires and releases its fish, which the tern is quick to seize and take to its own young. To hover in the air the tern must beat its wings at an incredible speed and spread out its tail, bending it downwards. It can remain stationary in the air whether it is windy or calm, but it must always face the wind.

6. SHORE-BIRDS

An arctic tern stealing food from a black guillemot.
These pictures were taken in Björnsvogur on Æðey, where arctic terns and black guillemots are neighbours. The black guillemot usually dives under water to find food, something an arctic tern will hardly ever do. However, it can sometimes steal the black guillemot's catch before it can reach its nesting hole. Above is a black guillemot swimming with a butterfish in its bill. Top left is a black guillemot coming ashore with a small fish. On the left is a black guillemot with a sea scorpion. Below is an arctic tern following a black guillemot ashore in the hope of stealing its catch. To try and shake off the tern, the black guillemot returned to the bay and dived under water with its catch. The arctic tern, however, using its aerobatic skills to hover in the air like a helicopter (see p. 131), followed the black guillemot's movements under water. When the latter re-surfaced the tern dived down and 'buzzed' it, forcing it to submerge once more. When the black guillemot finally tired of swimming under water it released its fish, which the tern was quick to seize.

The struggle for life can thus be a hard one in the world of birds. The black guillemot shook its head, had a short swim to recover its equanimity, and then flew out to sea once more to hunt for food, undoubtedly hoping to avoid the arctic tern next time.

132

The **great northern diver** is originally an American species. It is a large and magnificent bird which breeds by lowland and mountain lakes full of fish. Its distinctive long wailing cries can be heard echoing around the mountains on a calm summer's day.

7 Marshland-birds

7. MARSHLAND-BIRDS

1 A great northern diver swims to its nest on the end of a low headland.

2 It crawls slowly into the nest.

3 It turns over and re-arranges the eggs before sitting on them.

4 The bird is now incubating in peace and quiet.

5 The sitting bird calls to its mate out on the lake.

6 The mate swims quickly to the nest.

7. MARSHLAND-BIRDS

The **GREAT NORTHERN DIVER** (Gavia immer) is one of the largest and most impressive of Icelandic birds. Its main breeding grounds are in the northern part of the American continent, and apart from Iceland, it has also nested in Greenland and on Bear Island near Svalbard.

The great northern diver is widely distributed in Iceland, but nests very dispersively, preferring large deep and trout-filled lakes in the remoter moors and mountains. It rarely nests by lakes where there is no fish, or where there is a lot of vegetation, or a teeming bird life. Apart from the larger lakes, therefore, there is usually only 1 breeding pair to any sheet of water.

Great northern divers always breed by a lake or on a small island. Its nest is wide, 37–47 cm in diameter, but shallow, only 4–10 cm deep, and loosely lined with bits of grass and moss which the bird tears up from around the nest. The nest is often wet and always near enough to the lake for the bird to slide easily straight into the water, often forming a worn pathway between the nest and the lake. It lays 2 eggs, seldom only 1, and they are seaweed brown or green with a few dark brown spots. The incubation period is 30 days, and the fledging period 45 days. The parents both share the incubating and procuring of food for the young, which leave the nest 1–2 days after they have hatched. Great northern divers begin to arrive at their nesting sites as soon as the ice melts on the lakes, and they lay their eggs late in May or early in June. In late August or in September they go out to sea once more, wintering off the coasts of Iceland and Western Europe. There are a maximum of about 300 pairs of great northern divers in Iceland.

Above is a great northern diver coming into its nest from out the water. It re-arranges the eggs before sitting on them. On the right is a great northern diver which has settled on its eggs. In its summer plumage the great northern diver is a splendid bird. Its head and neck are black with a slightly bluish gloss, especially on the neck. Just under its chin it has a row of black and white stripes on its throat. Its under-parts are white, and its upper-parts are black, but chequered with large white square-shaped patches, especially high up on the back and on the shoulders. The bill is black, though paler at its tip, and the irises are wine-red. The legs are positioned well back on the body, which is very good for swimming, but means that it is virtually incapable of walking on land. There is no difference in colouring between the sexes. The great northern diver weighs about 4 kg and lives mostly on trout whilst on freshwater lakes; during the winter it also feeds on various kinds of oceanic fish, shellfish, and molluscs.

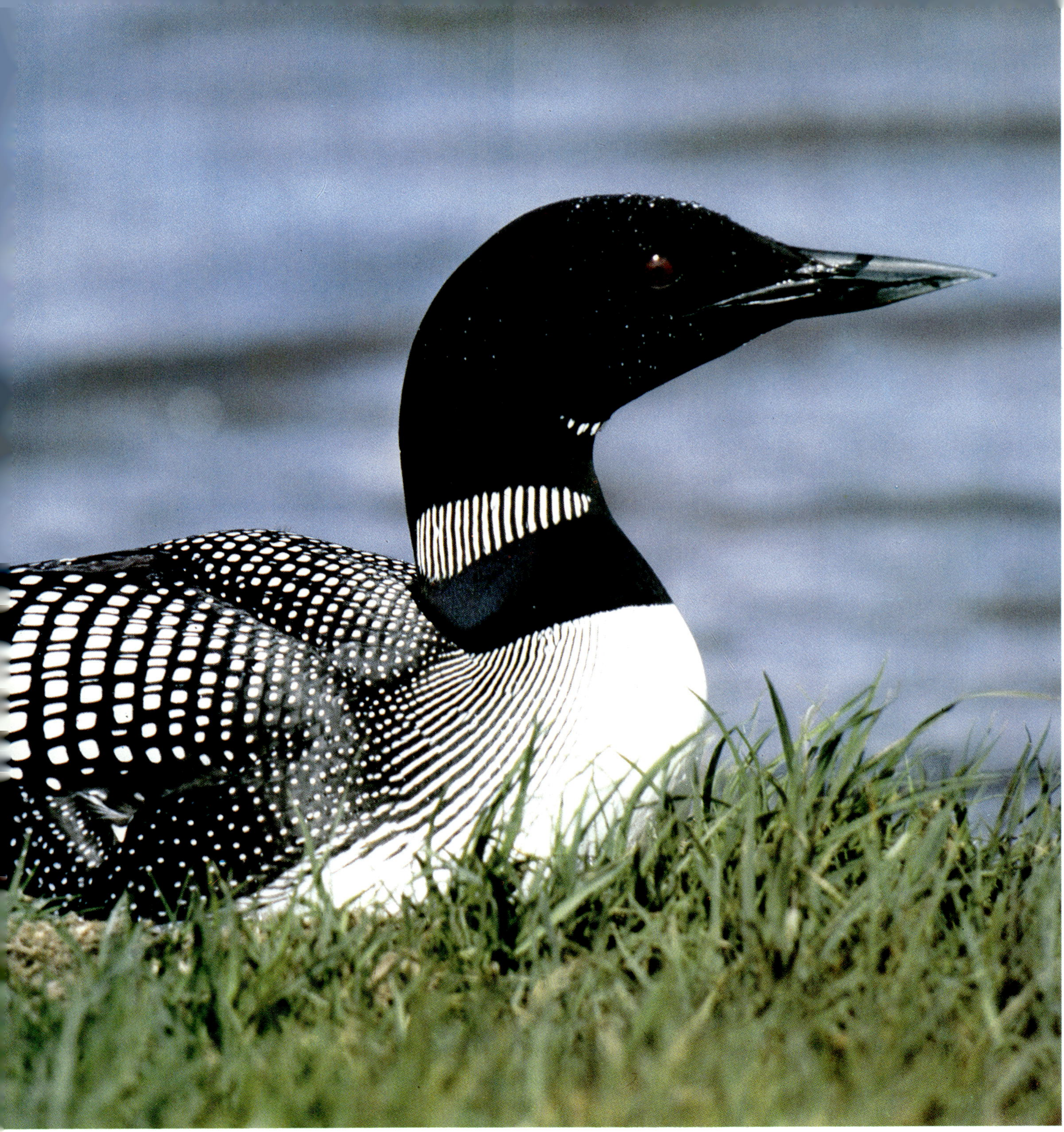

The **RED-THROATED DIVER** (*Gavia stellata*) is closely related to the great northern diver and very similar to it in build and behaviour. The red-throated diver is only half the size of the great northern diver, however, and weighs less than 2 kg.

In its summer plumage the red-throated diver is white on its under-parts, and very dark brown on its upper-parts. There are small white spots on the wing-coverts and upper-back, and often also on the lower-back, rump, and upper tail-coverts. Its chin, cheeks, and sides of the neck are ash-grey and it has a dark red patch on its throat. It is dark grey on the top of its head, and the nape is black with long white stripes. The bill is black, as are the outer sides of the legs, but the inner sides of the legs and the webbed feet are pale grey. There is no difference in the colouring between the sexes, but the female is usually a bit smaller than the male.

Above are 4 red-throated divers on Fjallsjökull lagoon. The glacial tongue in the background is from Vatnajökull. On the right is a red-throated diver on its nest by a lowland lake surrounded by rushes. There is usually only 1 pair of red-throated divers to a lake, but they are also known to breed in colonies.

The red-throated diver breeds in northern countries all round the world. It is distributed all over Iceland, especially in the lowlands, and nests mostly by lakes and ponds, and occasionally by calm rivers. Unlike the great northern diver, it often nests by small lakes surrounded by rushes and which have no fish. In such cases it has to find its food in nearby lakes, or even out at sea, and is prepared to fly long distances to do so. Red-throated divers and great northern divers seldom breed by the same lake.

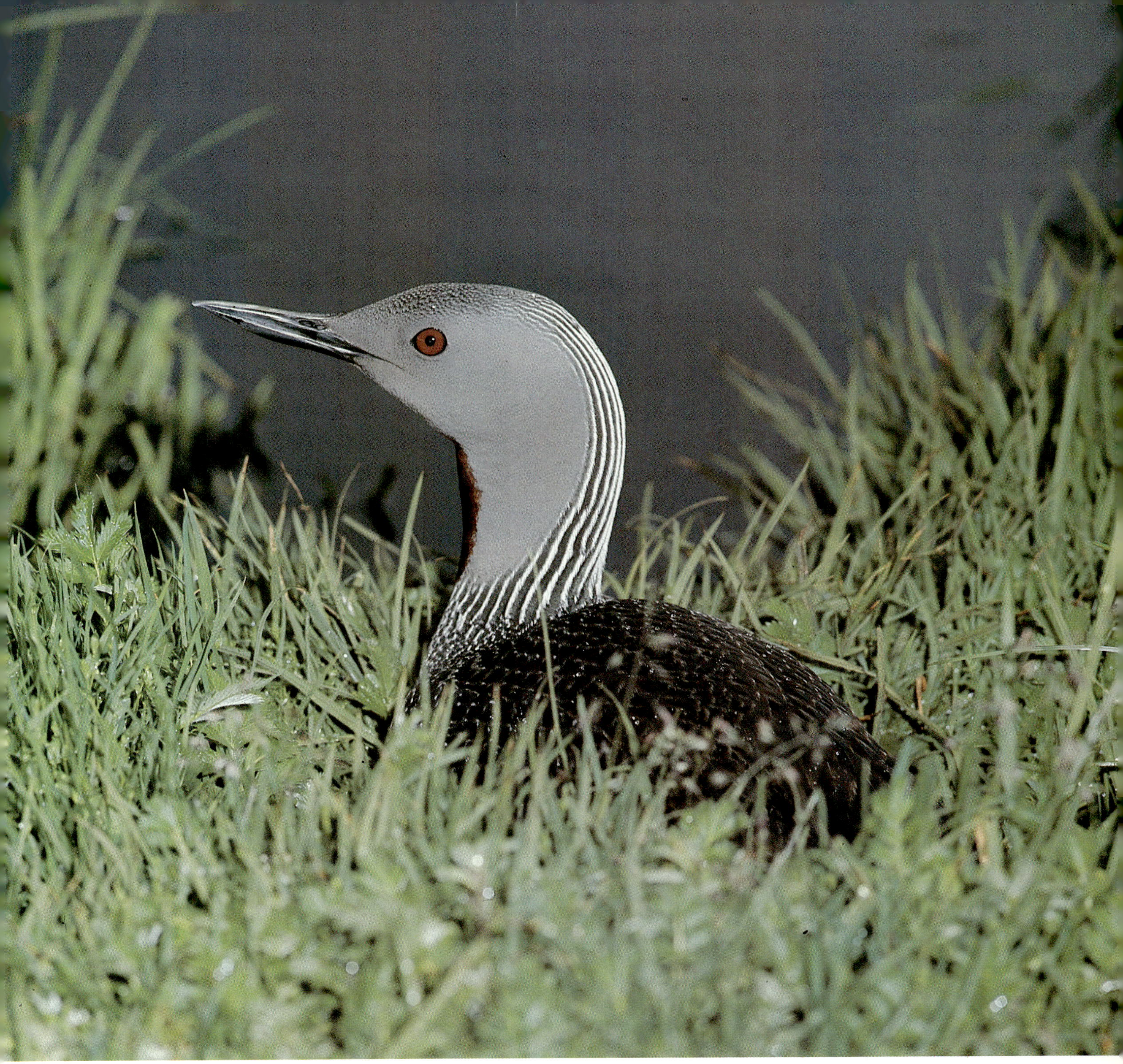

Above is a red-throated diver swimming on a small lake. The position of its legs, far back on its body, is clearly visible. Like the great northern diver, it is thus a good swimmer, but has difficulties in walking. On the left are a chick and an egg in a red-throated diver's nest. Below left is a red-throated diver swimming with its young on a lake surrounded by rushes.

Red-throated divers make their nests on the banks of lakes, and like the great northern diver's, they are always so near the water that the bird can slide directly into the lake on a well-worn pathway. The nest is also similar to the great northern diver's, except that it is smaller, 27–28 cm in diameter and 4–5.5 cm deep. Red-throated divers lay 2 eggs, rarely only 1, late in May or early in June. They are much smaller than great northern divers' eggs, but have the same colouring. The incubation period is 26 days, and the parents share the sitting, tending, and feeding of the young. The red-throated diver is mostly migratory in Iceland, and winters on the coasts of Western Europe. Like the great northern diver, it feeds a lot on trout, as well as on various kinds of oceanic fish.

7. MARSHLAND-BIRDS

The **SLAVONIAN GREBE** (*Podiceps auritus*) is a small bird weighing only 500–600 g. In the summer it keeps to freshwater lakes, but in the winter it is usually at sea along the coastline. It breeds by fertile lakes and ponds, chiefly in the lowlands and valleys where there is plenty of wildlife. It is most common, however, at its highest breeding ground around Lake Mývatn, 277 m above sea-level, where there are about 250 breeding pairs. It is also quite common in other places in the north-east and Skagafjörður, but it now rarely breeds elsewhere in the country. The total population of Slavonian grebes in Iceland is estimated at 500 pairs. Both its nest and nesting site are rather unusual as it is the only Icelandic bird which has a floating nest. It is made out of rotting marsh vegetation, and often situated in thick swathes of sedge or rushes. The base of the nest is attached to surrounding plants so that it does not get swept away and can rise or fall with any change in the water-level. Slavonian grebes generally breed in single pairs in thick, well-grown expanses of sedge, though a few pairs will occasionally breed together, and indeed the Slavonian grebe seems to be, on the whole, a rather sociable bird.

On the right is a Slavonian grebe entering its floating nest; its mate is swimming in the background. Below is a pair of Slavonian grebes swimming on Lake Mývatn.

A *Slavonian grebe* on its nest amongst sedge on Lake Mývatn. It is a splendid bird in its colourful summer plumage with its silky gloss and its very distinctive reddish-yellow head-tufts and bright red eyes. Both sexes have the same plumage, but the female is often just a little smaller than the male.

7. MARSHLAND-BIRDS

Pictured top right is a Slavonian grebe arriving at its nest among rushes on Lake Mývatn. Before leaving the nest, the bird had covered its eggs to hide them and keep them warm. In the middle picture the Slavonian grebe has entered its floating nest. It removes the covering before sitting on its eggs. Below right the sitting bird has called to its mate, which has swum to the nest and is preparing to take over, whilst the other bird slides into the water. The parents share the incubating and tending of their young.

The Slavonian grebe is an unusual and attractive bird. The upper-parts are black and speckled with grey. The under-parts are a silky, glossy white; its flanks are dull red and streaked with dark grey. It is black on its head, nape, and neck, but is dull red on its throat and sides of the neck. There are dull red stripes between its eyes and bill, and pointed backwards from its eyes are the very conspicuous reddish-yellow head-tufts. The chin, cheeks, and top of its throat are black, forming a sort of black collar. Its bill is black, but has a pale tip. The irises are light red or pink.

The Slavonian grebe is mostly migratory in Iceland. It arrives at its breeding grounds in April, as soon as the ice has melted on the lakes. It lays its eggs in June, usually 4–5, but sometimes 3 or 6, and at first they are pale blue or bluish-green in colour, with a transparent milky-white, soft, and uneven calcious layer on the outside. They soon become stained yellow or brown, however, because of the dampness and decaying vegetation in the nest. The incubation period is 24–25 days, and the young are fully fledged after 4–6 weeks. When the chicks are very small the parents will often swim with them on their backs.

The Slavonian grebe departs from its breeding grounds in late September or in October. A few of them remain off the south-west coast of Iceland all winter, but many of them winter off the coasts of Western Europe.

Whilst at their nesting sites, Slavonian grebes feed chiefly on sticklebacks, crustaceans, and various kinds of water insects, such as water beetles and midge larvae; but when at sea during the winter, they live mostly on small fish and crustaceans.

7. MARSHLAND-BIRDS

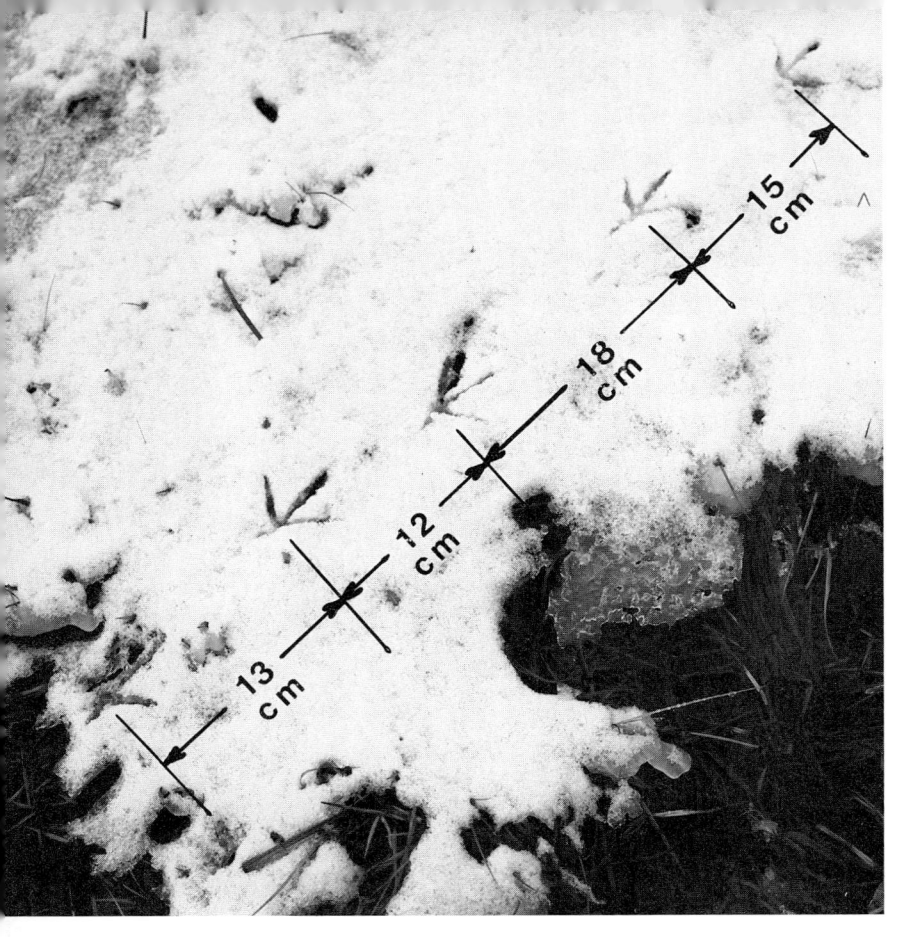

After years of searching for a water rail all over Iceland, these clear tracks in the snow raised new hopes. The fresh layer of snow on wet growth by a small lake was so thin that the tracks went right through it. There could be no doubt that a water rail had recently been there. The tracks went from the lakeside to some withered grass, where this secretive bird, as was its wont, could disappear from the sight of man. The distance between the prints in the snow showed that, although it is small, the water rail can take long strides when it runs. A hide was set up, and the waiting began – with excellent results. Every day for a week it was possible to observe and record on film the various habits of this rarely seen bird. On the right is a water rail looking for food in boggy marshland which warm underground water keeps unfrozen during the winter.

The **WATER RAIL** (*Rallus aquaticus*) is one of the rarest and most mysterious birds living in Iceland. It is rather small and lean with olive-brown upperparts streaked with black, and ash-grey underparts. Its flanks are very distinctively barred black and white; its bill is long and red. Although the water rail is rarely seen, even when there are many of them, it is much more often heard. It has an extraordinary voice and an amazing range of calls. It calls to its young with a gentle yelp, and to its mate with a harsh and longlasting 'gep... gep... gep', followed by 'krui... krui... krui', constantly repeated in runs and interspersed with an incredible mixture of squealing, screeching, twittering, shrieking, groaning, grunting, and whistling sounds. It is a piercing song, and can be heard for several hundred metres. Quite the opposite to most birds, the water rail is thus amazingly noisy in its nesting grounds and draws attention to itself. Its nest is well hidden in thickets, however, and impossible to see from the outside. The water rail is very secretive and remains out of sight more than any other Icelandic bird. It does not like to fly, and is mostly active at twilight and at night. It occurs mostly in bogs and marshes full of dense and high vegetation, where it can slip with great dexterity between narrow streams, rivulets, and brooks, and it seems to like nothing better than to be in a dark hole in the earth. It can be no great surprise, therefore, that it has been the source of many folk tales and superstitions. It was once believed to be half a worm and to be able to crawl underground when in danger; it was also once thought to be totally flightless. Very little is known about its behaviour, numbers, or distribution in Iceland, though it seems certain that, earlier this century, it was a far more common bird than it is now.

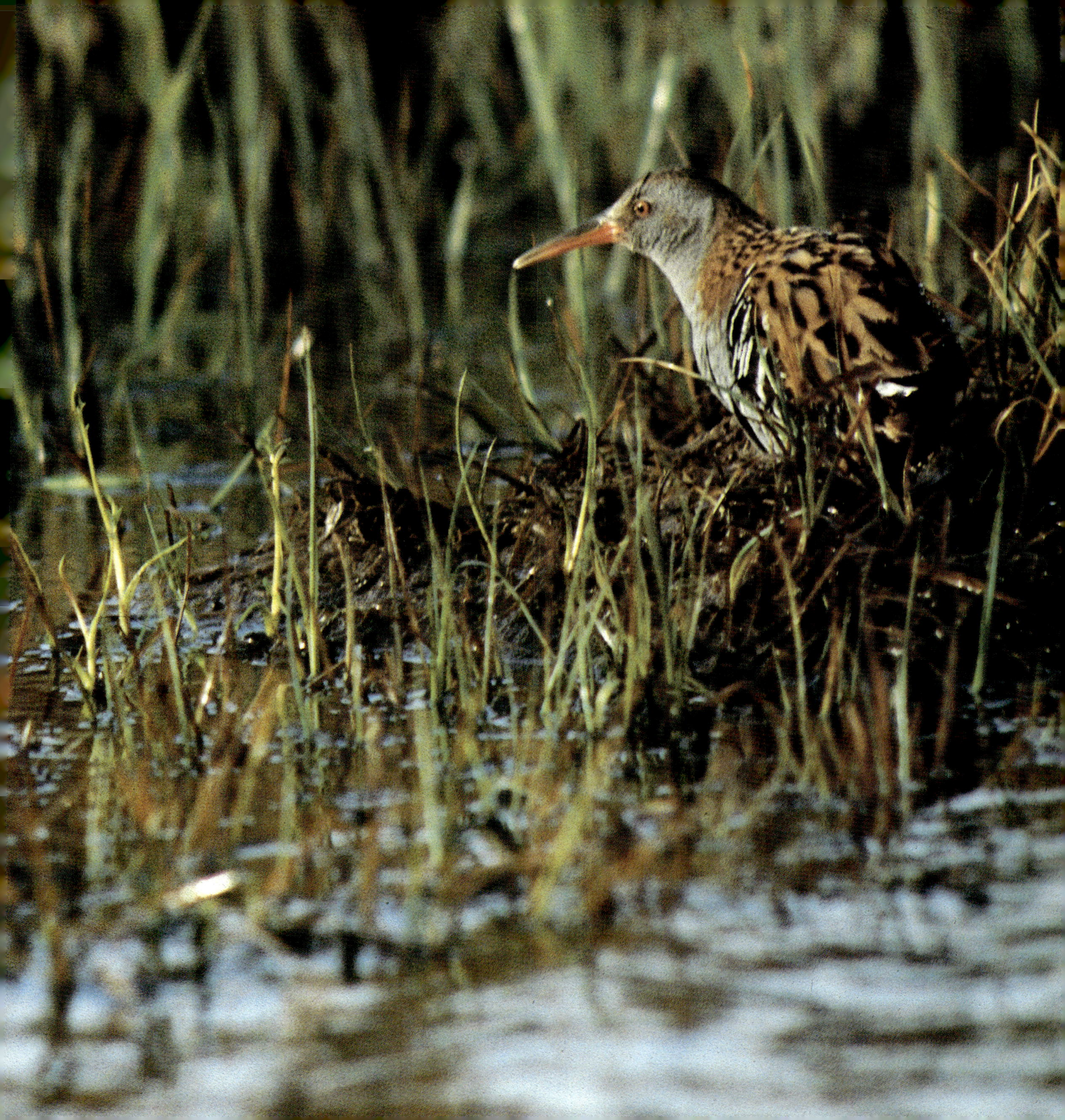

The **water rail** likes to live secretly, and remains so well hidden that, for a long time, little was known of its habits and behaviour. It has declined in numbers in Iceland over the last few decades, mostly because of the draining and cultivation of bogs, its choice habitat, but also because of the appearance of the mink in Icelandic wildlife. The mink slips through dense undergrowth and lava holes just like the water rail, and as the latter is a reluctant flyer, it has become easy prey. The water rail has thus a very doubtful future in Iceland, and it is not unlikely to disappear from the country altogether. Traces of water rails can be chiefly found in the winter near unfrozen springs with plenty of hiding places in nearby holes and vegetation. The pictures on these 2 pages show a water rail in exactly such a place. Above left it is coming out of its hideout, a wide pipe open at both ends and choked with vegetation. It runs down to an unfrozen pool where it forages, among other things, for worms and small eels. The drawing shows the water rail's gait as it slips nimbly and unseen through the dense high sedge of the bogland.

147

7. MARSHLAND-BIRDS

On the right is a picture of the water rail's typical habitat, the fertile boglands between the sands and lava of the south coast of Iceland below Eldhraun. Its favourite nesting sites are on small isles thick with vegetation in the middle of shallow lakes or ponds. But it is many years now since the water rail has nested in this area. This is not a result of drainage or cultivation, but of drifting sands which, from around 1950 until recently, periodically interrupted or even blocked the natural outflow to the River Eldvatn, causing a corresponding rise in the water-level of the surrounding boglands. The water rail is very sensitive to such changes in the water-level as it always breeds close to water, but does not make a floating nest like the Slavonian grebe does (see pp. 141–3). Consequently, if the water-level rose during the breeding season, all the water rail's nests, eggs, and young would be destroyed. The water-level in this area is much more stable now as the sands have been irrigated and have begun to support vegetation, which prevents further drifting. The water rail was also threatened by the mink, which has plagued these boglands, as elsewhere in the country. Nonetheless there is still a great variety of bird life in the area, including a large number of red-necked phalaropes.

On the left is a water rail, which during the winter (in November) used an incoming water-pipe to get into a fish-breeding plant, where it proceeded to feed itself on fish fry, much to the owner's annoyance. The picture is taken indoors. This rarely seen bird was soon forgiven, however, and after being allowed to eat the fish fry it had damaged, it was released once more near the spot where it had got into the plant.

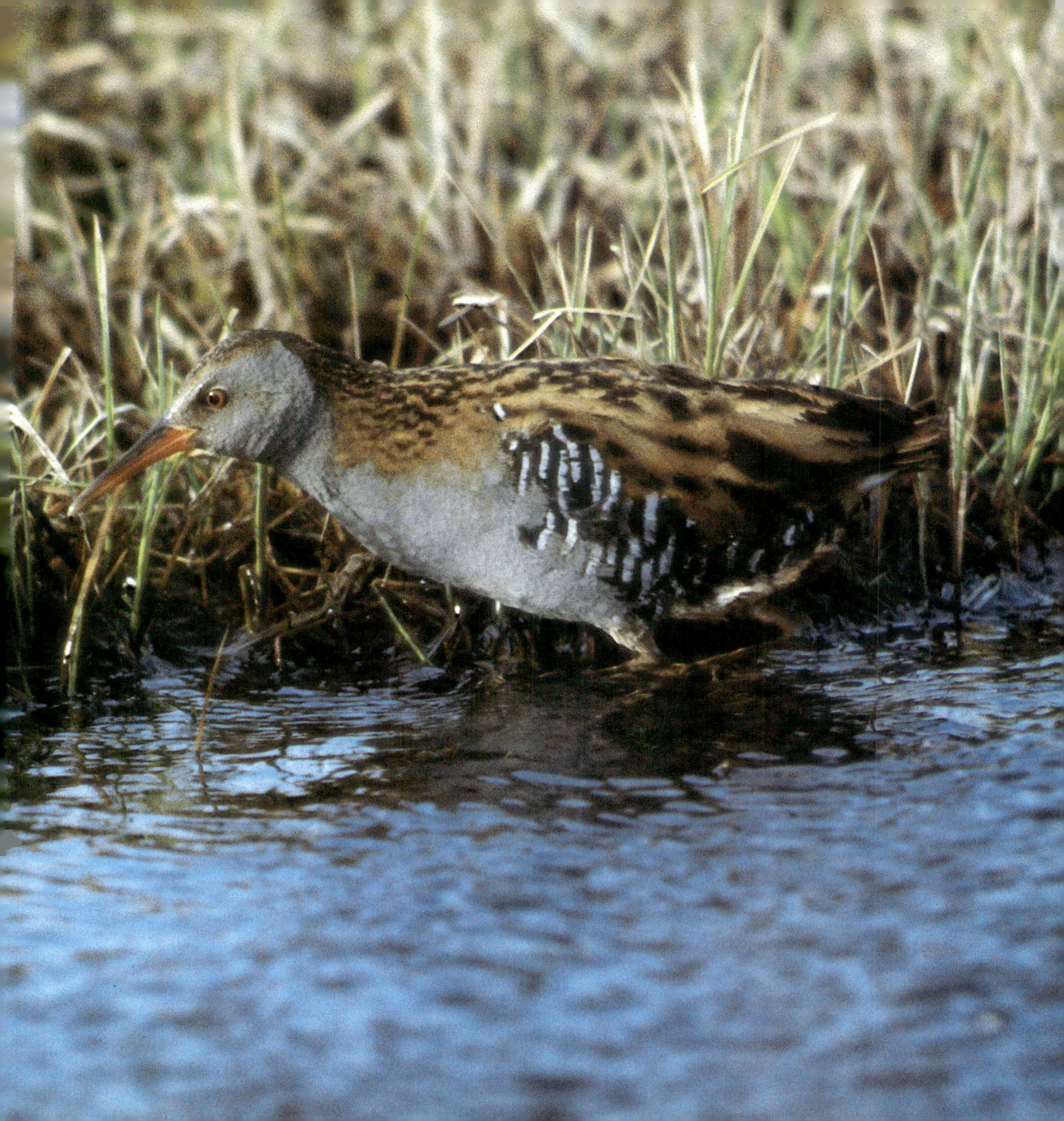

The Icelandic whooper swan is considered by many to be the most beautiful of all Icelandic birds. Its pure white plumage is an integral part of its majestic appearance, whether seen on deep blue mountain lakes in bright sunshine, or flying in flocks across the sky. The song of the whooper swan is also renowned for its beauty. Whooper swans are common all over Iceland, both in the highlands and lowlands, and in October there are an estimated 10,000–11,000 swans in the country. About 18% of these are reckoned to be immature birds, so that the total of adult whooper swans is around 8,600. They nest on small islands, or on lakes or ponds, chiefly on the highland moors.

Above is a whooper swan coming in to land on a lake. Above right is a herd of swans in Neslandavík, Lake Mývatn, at the end of May. Herds of swans often gather there, mostly non-breeding birds. On the far right is a pair of whooper swans swimming near their nest. Bottom right is a whooper swan coming to its nest and preparing to sit on its eggs. Only the pen incubates the eggs, but the cob is always on guard nearby. A whooper swan's nest is made of piled up aquatic vegetation and moss, but its inside is lined with such delicate materials as greyish-white down and feathers.

The picture overleaf (pp. 152–3) is of a whooper swan pair with 4 cygnets on a lowland lake full of vegetation.

The **WHOOPER SWAN** (*Cygnus cygnus*) is the largest Icelandic bird, being 152 cm long. The cob weighs 8–10 kg, but the pen is a bit lighter. An adult swan is usually completely white, though it can sometimes be yellowish on the head and neck, and even rust-coloured on the under-parts during the breeding season because of the bog iron-ore. The legs are black, as is the front part of the bill, which is light yellow at its base. There is no difference in colouring between the sexes. Whooper swans are mostly migratory in Iceland, but a few hundred of them are residents, haunting freshwater rivers and lakes during the winter, as long as they remain relatively free of ice. When the weather worsens, they move to the coast and dwell in shallow bays and firths where there are large ebb-tides and plenty of eelgrass, their favourite food at this time of year. The migratory swans leave the country late in the autumn and winter mainly in the British Isles. They return to their nesting sites as soon as the ice melts on the lakes, though the actual breeding season does not start until the latter part of May. Whooper swans nest dispersively, and there is usually only 1 breeding pair per lake or tract of sedge, though there can be more nests by larger lakes with plenty of vegetation. They lay 3–5 white eggs, seldom 6; the incubation period is 35–40 days.

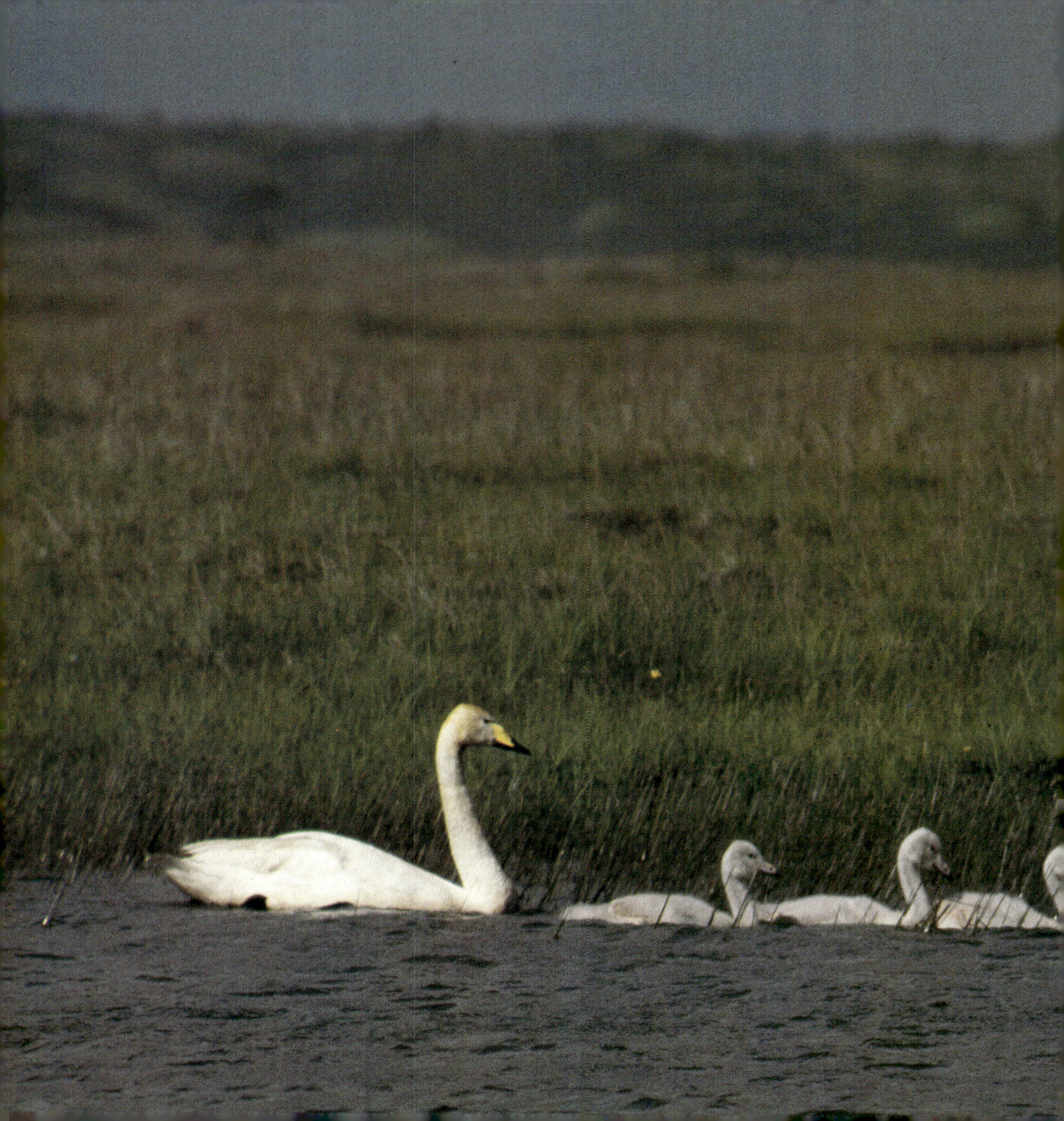

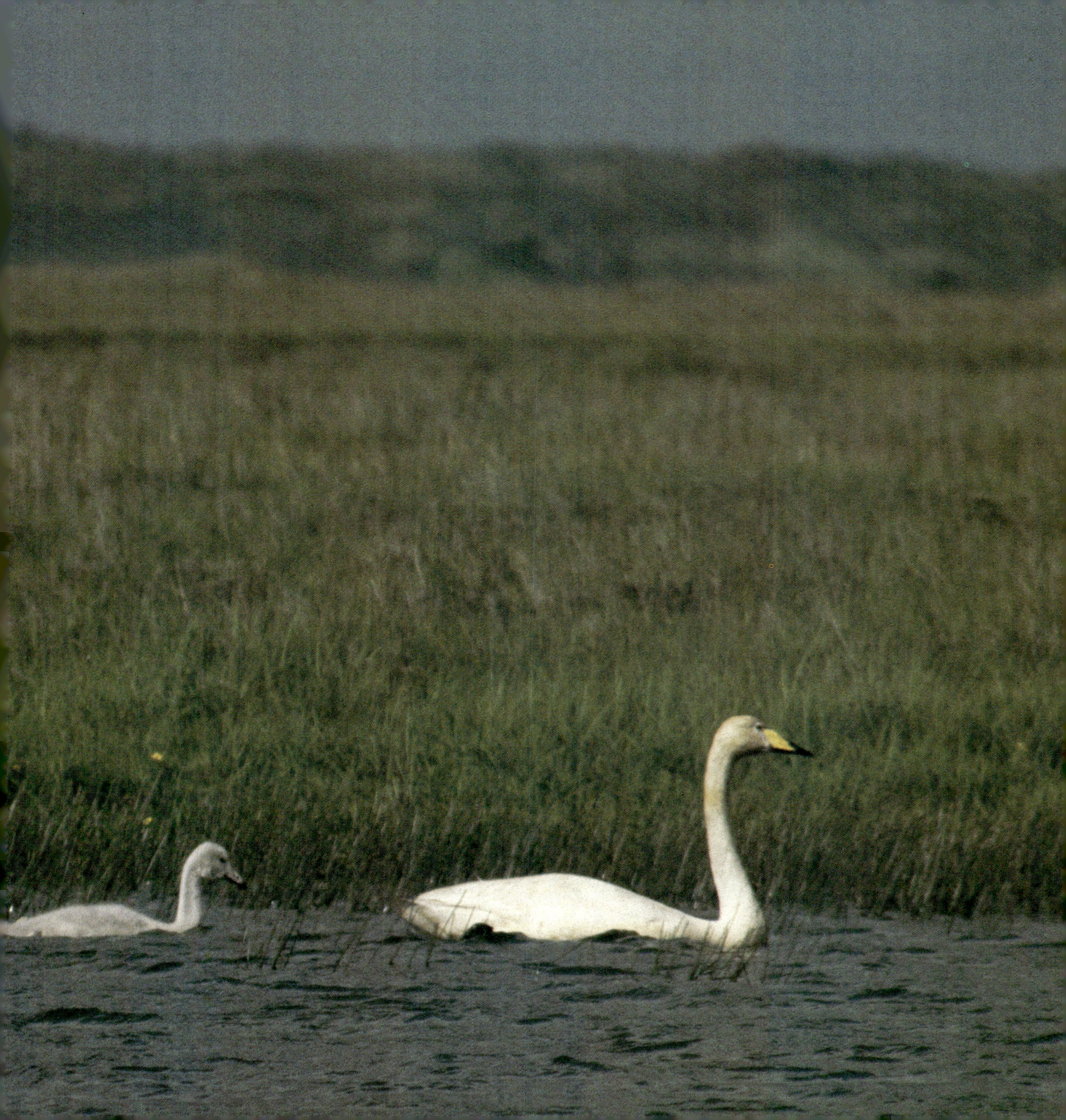

Above are whooper swans flying over the wetlands of Skagafjörður in spring (21 May). On the right is a whooper swan on water. On the left are uncovered eggs in a swan's nest, but bottom left is the same nest after the swan has covered the eggs before leaving the nest for a while. If the eggs are covered they keep warm, and are better hidden from predators.

Below is a hide raised on a pylon made out of aluminium poles. From this hide it was possible to observe and photograph the behaviour of the whooper swans in the nest which can be seen on the far left of the picture. The whole strip of vegetation out on the lake was completely afloat, but with great care it was possible to walk over most of it. The pylon rested on long supports lying across the top of the floating vegetation.

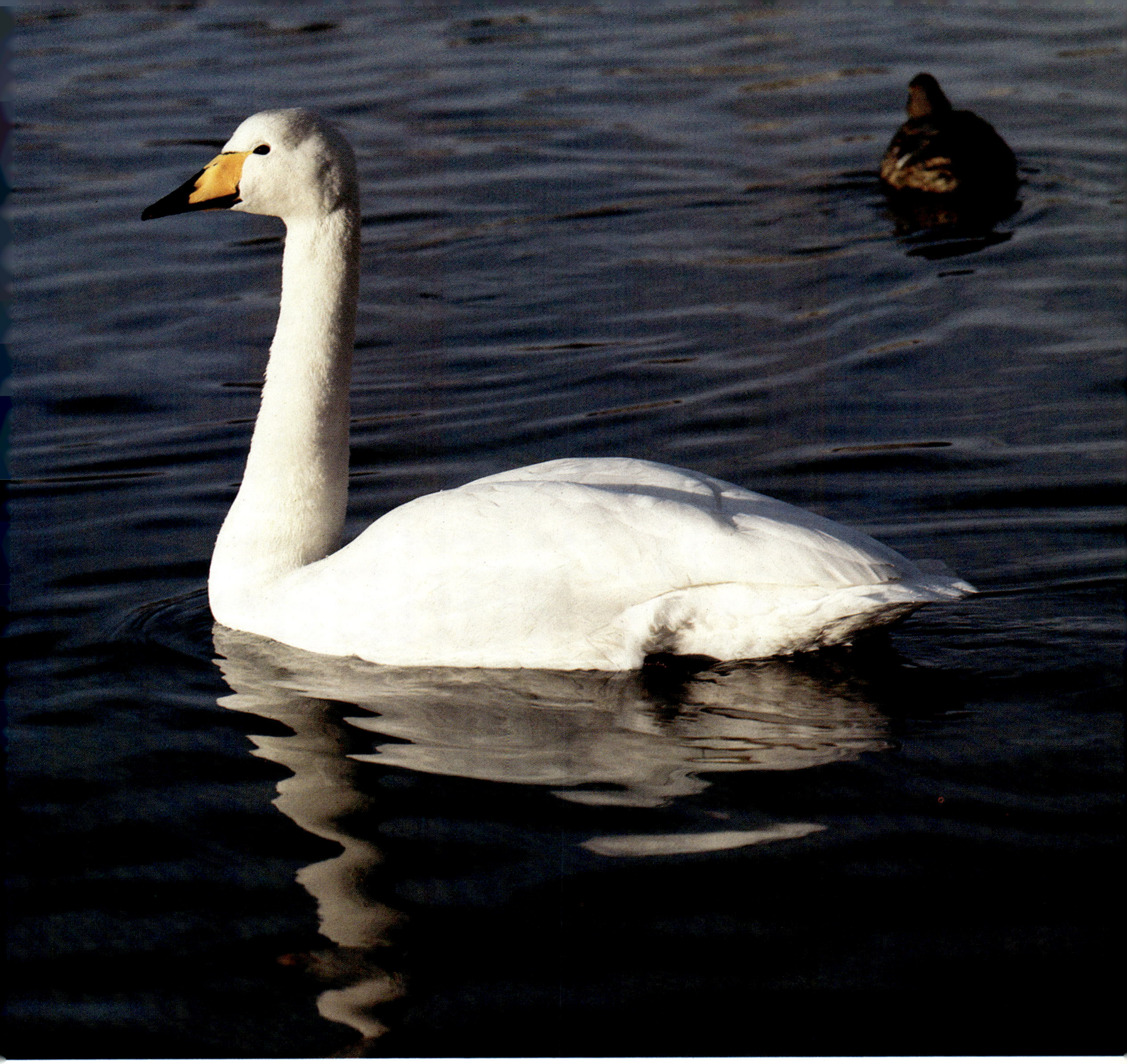

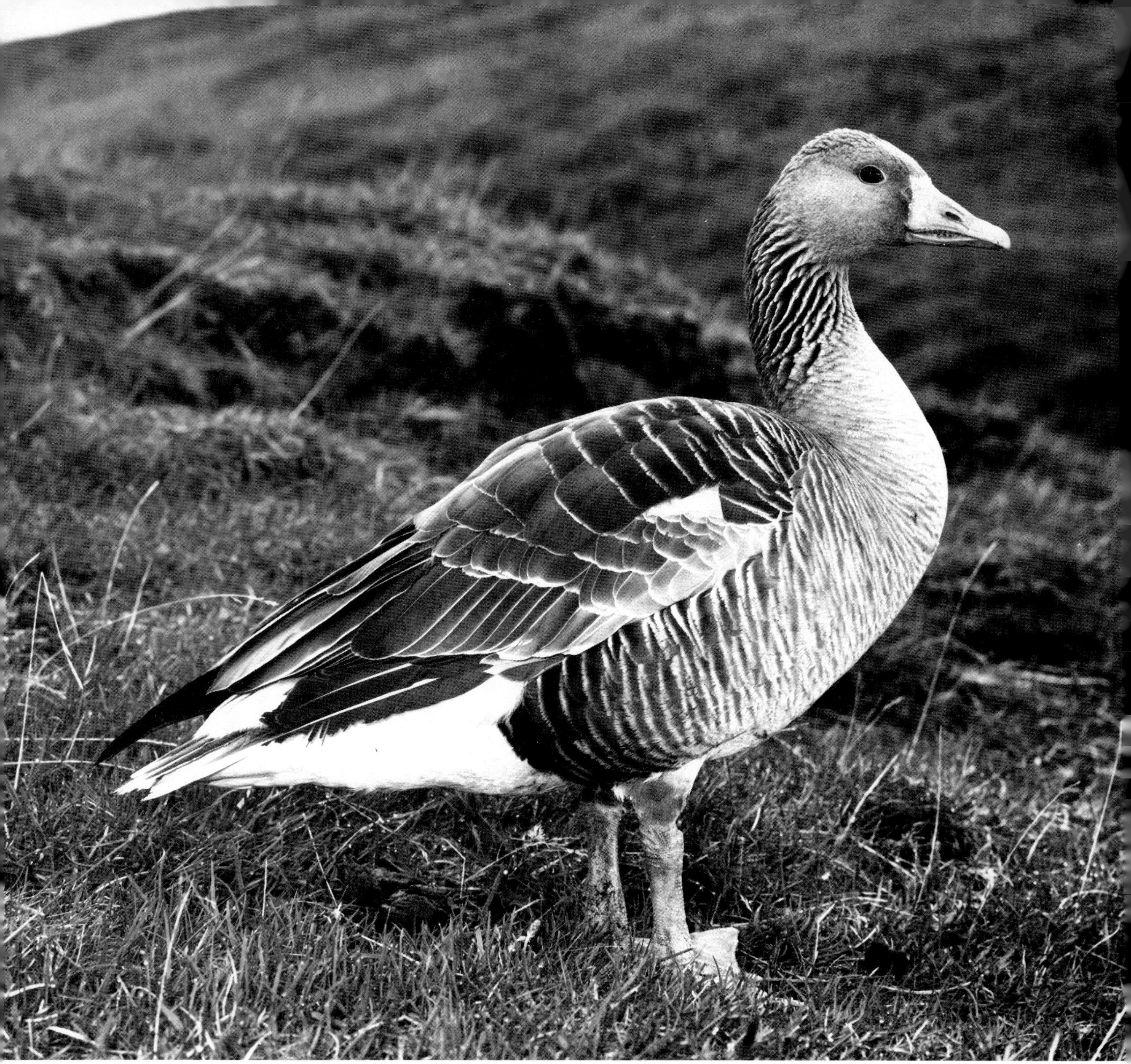

The **GREYLAG GOOSE** (*Anser anser*) is 1 of the 2 species of geese which commonly breeds in Iceland, the other being the pink-footed goose. Both species are migratory and winter in Scotland and northern England.

The greylag goose arrives in Iceland early in the spring, usually in April, and often collects in groups on farmlands before continuing on to their breeding grounds. Large gaggles of geese in flight can be a very impressive sight, as in the picture above. Greylag geese nearly always breed in the lowlands in uncultivated and remote areas. Its nesting sites are on isles in rivers, or in lakeland areas near large rivers, and preferably where there is a lot of vegetation, as the latter provides them and their young with both food and shelter. The nest is usually made out of grass, and is repaired and used year after year. Greylag geese also remain faithful to their mates for life. The nest is lined with down and feathers, which are also used to cover the eggs. Only the goose incubates the eggs, but the gander remains resolutely on guard near the nest (picture on the left). There are usually 4–6 white eggs in a clutch, and they are mostly laid in early May, the goslings hatching out about a month later. They only remain in the nest for 1–2 days before the mother takes them to where there is plenty of grass to eat and where they can hide themselves. The mother often leads the way, the goslings follow her, and the gander brings up the rear. Whilst the goslings are small, they do not try to flee from danger, but crouch down and keep perfectly still. This is usually sufficient, as their colouring provides them with perfect camouflage, and they are very difficult to see against their background.

1

2

A GREYLAG gosling hatching. Goose eggs are white, but they often become stained in the nest. (1) Towards the end of the incubation period (35–40 days) the gosling becomes active. Its head is in the broader end of the egg, its legs in the middle, and its tail in the narrower end. There is an air-pocket in the broader end of the egg, and the embryo itself is enclosed in a thin membrane. The gosling's first act is to puncture this membrane and take its first breath of air. At the same time it begins to chirp, giving the first indication that it is beginning to hatch. On top of its bill is a hard egg-tooth with which it can chip at the egg-shell by nodding its head. This takes a lot of effort for such a small and weak creature, but at last a tiny hole appears in the shell. This is gradually enlarged into a long crack as the gosling slowly turns in an anti-clockwise direction (as seen from the broader end) whilst it chips away at the shell. (2) Once the crack reaches half-way round the egg, the gosling pushes with his feet in the narrow end until the top splits open. (3) The gosling then stretches out fully, kicking and pushing until the top of the egg falls off altogether. (4) It raises its head and opens its eyes. (5) The gosling finally crawls out of the egg. It still needs a lot of rest after all its exertions. (6) When the gosling first emerges out of the egg it is wet

5

6

3

4

and ugly, its downy featers enclosed in a sheath. The friction from its mother's brooding soon causes this to drop off as the gosling dries. (7) The wet ugly thing now becomes a soft, yellow-green and plump little gosling. It will just sit or lie at first until it can gather enough strength to stand up. (8) Once on its feet it soon becomes very sprightly. In picture No. 7 the gosling's egg-tooth is clearly discernible on its bill. This quickly wears away as it is of no further use once the gosling has hatched.

8

7

Above is a greylag goose family in a hurry. Below is a greylag goose swimming. The greylag goose is a large bird, weighing 3–4 kg. The gander is slightly larger than the goose, but both sexes are otherwise very similar in appearance.

Geese feed mainly on plants and can cause considerable damage in spring as they uproot far more plants than they actually eat. They especially like to settle on fields where the grass is just beginning to grow, but as they are very wary and nervous of humans, scarecrows are often fairly effective in keeping them off cultivated land.

At the end of July and the beginning of August, adult geese moult all their flight-feathers at the same time, and for about a week they cannot fly. During this most dangerous period of their lives, geese seek haunts which will provide them with some kind of defence, and where they can hide easily, or dive under water, if any danger is at hand. Extensive and impassable bogs and marshes, large rivers and estuaries, and the shallows around isles are thus often their habitat at this time of year. Once the geese can fly again they eat as much as they can to fatten themselves and store up energy for the long autumn flight ahead of them to their winter quarters. They leave the country in September or early October. It is believed that geese maintain their family groups whilst migrating, and that the young do not leave their parents until they return to the breeding grounds the following year. Greylag geese become fully mature at 2 years of age, when they find themselves a mate and choose a nesting site, often in the vicinity of where they themselves were brought up. The greylag goose population has increased considerably over the last few decades, and there are now an estimated 90,000 of them in Iceland.

The greylag goose is a protected bird during its breeding season and when it is moulting, but between 20 August and 15 March it is a game bird in Iceland. As mentioned earlier, the greylag goose is a very shy and wary bird, but it is easy to tame nonetheless. Man has exploited this fact for centuries, domestic geese being derived from the greylag.

7. MARSHLAND-BIRDS

The **RED-NECKED PHALAROPE** (Phalaropus lobatus) is a small bird, about 18 cm long. It is only a bit smaller than a grey phalarope, and behaves in a similar way. The red-necked phalarope is a very attractive bird in its summer plumage, as can be seen in the picture on the right. It is white on its underparts and throat, and dark on the head, and has a very distinctive bright red neck-collar. There is little difference in the colouring of the sexes, though the male's plumage is usually slightly duller than the female's.

The red-necked phalarope is widespread over all the wet areas of Iceland, both in the lowlands and the highlands. It is a migratory species, like those of North-West Europe, and winters in the South Atlantic, especially on the coast of Africa. It arrives on the shores of Iceland late in April or early in May, and moves to its breeding grounds in mid-May, its nesting sites generally being in fertile bogs and wetlands near pools and small lakes. The red-necked phalarope is a good swimmer, very quick in its movements, and constantly nodding its head whilst on water. It feeds on various small creatures, especially midges, flies and their larvae, and small crustaceans. It is very easy to get to know its habits and behaviour as it is not at all a shy bird and will quite unconcernedly allow an observer to come within a very short distance of it.

Red-necked phalaropes usually have well hidden nests in high-grown grass or brushwood, and always near wet land. They lay 4 eggs in June, greyish or yellowish-green in colour with dark blotches (see picture on the right). Only the male incubates the eggs and tends the young. The incubation period is 2–3 weeks, and during the 3–4 week fledging period the male looks after the chicks very conscientiously, teaching them how to hide, swim, fly, and fend for themselves. Red-necked phalaropes move to the coast in the late summer and begin their winter migration in August or September. It is a long flight for such small birds as their winter quarters are in the South Atlantic.

7. MARSHLAND-BIRDS

7. MARSHLAND-BIRDS

On the right is a **red-necked phalarope** on its nest, which was well hidden in the high marsh-vegetation of Þjórsárver in the central highlands of Iceland. It is the male of the species which incubates the eggs and then tends the young. The female abandons 'house and home' as soon as it has laid its eggs, and then just wanders about with other birds of its sex. After the breeding season, red-necked phalaropes congregate around the coast of Iceland, where they feed mainly on sand hoppers and small crustaceans, the females often arriving well before the males and young. In the marshlands they feed mostly on midges and their larvae. The red-necked phalarope is well known for its spinning rapidly on water in order to stir up edible larvae and other titbits in the shallows, stabbing its bill into the water every now and again to seize its prey. The series of pictures on the far left were taken in one sequence with an automatic camera taking 6 shots per second; the bird span round so fast that it had completed a whole circle within a second. Above left are red-necked phalaropes in their summer plumage and in their typical habitat, a lakeside with plenty of vegetation. Bottom left is a red-necked phalarope at the end of July when it has begun to change into its winter plumage; it will then become white on the head, neck, and under-parts, with a dark grey patch on its cheeks, and its upper-parts will be dark grey and streaked.

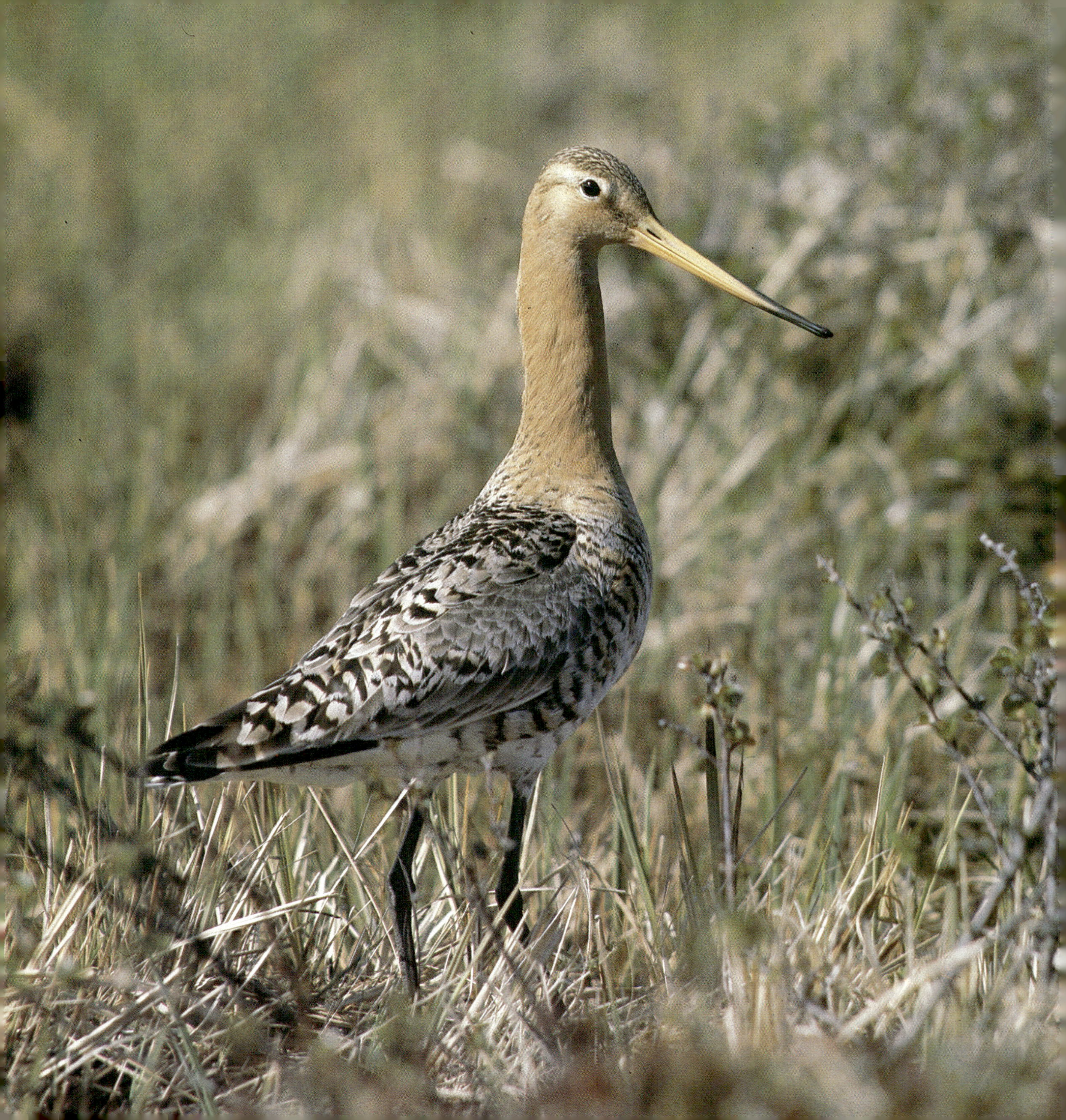

7. MARSHLAND-BIRDS

The **BLACK-TAILED GODWIT** (Limosa limosa) is a marshland-bird, very like a whimbrel in build, but a little smaller and thinner. It has very long legs and bill, though the latter is not bent like a whimbrel's, but straight, or even a little upturned. The black tailed-godwit can also be easily distinguished from the whimbrel as it is a more colourful bird. In its breeding plumage, as in the pictures here, it is chestnut on its head, neck, and breast, and grey or dark grey on its upper-parts and mottled yellowy-red; its belly is dirty-white, and its flanks are barred with black. It has a black band at the end of its white tail, and has a broad white wing-bar, which is very conspicuous in flight. Its bill is yellow with a darker tip

At the beginning of the century the black-tailed godwit only bred in the southern lowlands of Iceland, and rarely occurred elsewhere in the country. Nowadays it breeds all over Iceland, almost certainly as a result of the warmer climate since around 1920. In fact, it is really quite amazing that it should breed here at all as it is a southern species and does not even breed in Britain or Scandinavia, Iceland being its northernmost breeding ground. The Icelandic black-tailed godwit is thus classified as a separate sub-species, *Limosa limosa islandica*, its main distinguishing features being a shorter bill and stronger red colouring than the main species.

The black-tailed godwit is migratory in Iceland, arriving in the country in April or May and laying its eggs in late May or early June. The incubation period is 24 days, and the fledging period around a month. Its nesting sites are on dry land, often in brushwood close to bogs and marshes. It feeds mostly on insect larvae, earthworms, and water snails. In September it departs for its winter home on the coasts of Western Europe, and as far south as north-west Africa.

On the left is a black-tailed godwit in its breeding plumage. Above, it is on its way into thick brushwood where it has its nest. Once the bird had sat on its eggs it could not be seen. Below is the nest with 4 rather long olive-green eggs with dark speckles.

The black-headed gull is a rather beautiful and stately bird in its summer plumage. Its distinctive feature is the dark brown hood it sports in the spring; in winter its head is white. It is the smallest bird belonging to the gull family in Iceland, though it is not much smaller than the kittiwake or common gull. Black-headed, common, and lesser black-backed gulls feed more on insects than other kinds of gulls, although the black-headed gull will also feed on eggs and young like the larger gulls do. Black-headed gulls' eggs are very edible, but only the first clutch should be taken from the nest as the black-headed gull pair will then breed again.

7. MARSHLAND-BIRDS

The **BLACK-HEADED GULL** *(Larus ridibundus)* is a rather small gull, 38 cm long and weighing 280–320 g, which has only settled in Iceland since the beginning of this century. In its breeding plumage it is coffee-brown, or almost black, all over its head down to the nape and throat, thus forming a black hood. It is light grey on its back and wings, but otherwise white, apart from the black tips of its 7 outermost primaries. Its bill and legs are red.

The black-headed gull is a lake and shore-bird which lives on insects, larvae, snails, earthworms and, almost inevitably, fish offal. Its nesting sites are usually on flat ground near water, and nowadays it breeds all over Iceland, both along the shore and by inland lakes, and in small groups or larger colonies, sometimes in the neighbourhood of arctic terns. It is mostly migratory, but a good many black-headed gulls remain along the coastline all year round, especially in the north and south-west. The ones which do migrate winter on the shores of Europe. Its breeding season begins in late May, and it usually lays 3 greenish eggs speckled dark brown. The parents share the incubating, which takes 16–18 days. The young become fully fledged after 3–4 weeks, the parents feeding them during this time on various insects, larvae, and worms.

The black-headed gull is a lively and noisy bird which is quick to drive away uninvited guests from its nesting site, just like the arctic tern. It resembles a common gull in colouring, except for its hood, which is its distinctive feature. Common gulls are a little bigger than black-headed gulls, and sometimes breed among them. Ducks and waders also nest in black-headed gull and arctic tern colonies, probably to enjoy their protection.

The black-headed gull is a fine flyer, using fairly rapid wingbeats like the arctic tern. It is also an expert glider. The black edging to its wings is more conspicuous in flight (see picture above). Below is a black-headed gull arriving at its nest, which is usually a large pile of rushes in high grass next to a lake. It lays 3 greenish eggs speckled dark brown.

Above is a black-headed gull's nest with 2 eggs and a chick in high rushes next to a lake. On the right are black-headed gulls swimming on a small lake full of rushes.

168

Above is a **short-eared owl** in flight. Its wings are rather long, and the dark barring and carpal patches are clearly visible. It has distinctive bright yellow eyes in its flat round face. It is a southern species, and a relative newcomer to Iceland, feeding mainly on mice and rats, and on smaller birds and young. It is an expert flyer, often flying very low over the ground when hunting, quickly changing direction as it looks for prey. It often hunts during the day, but like other owls, it has extremely good eye-sight in the dark. Owls can hardly move their eyes and thus have to turn their heads to look around them, and are well known for their ability to turn their heads through 180 degrees to see directly behind them. They also have binocular vision, which makes it easier for them to judge distances, an important factor when hunting, especially when swooping silently onto their prey from behind. As well as its excellent vision, an owl can use its superb hearing to find its prey.

7. MARSHLAND-BIRDS

The **SHORT-EARED OWL** (*Asio flammeus*) is the only owl which is definitely known to breed in Iceland. The snowy owl bred in the Ódáðahraun until 1945, and again in 1957 and around 1974, but no definite nesting sites have been recorded since then, although it has been seen on the wing. The short-eared owl is a medium-sized bird, 35–40 cm long, considerably smaller than the snowy owl. It has yellowish upper-parts mottled with dark brown and barred on the tail. Its under-parts are a lighter yellow streaked with dark brown. It has a pale face, rusty-yellow at the edges. It has black rings round the eyes and bright yellow irises. Its bill is black.

The short-eared owl's main breeding grounds are in more southerly countries, but it began to breed in Iceland in 1912; before then it had only been a vagrant here. It now breeds all over Iceland, although there are very few of them and they nest very dispersively. It breeds in boggy areas, often making its nest on dry ground near lakes or fens, and it is usually well hidden in birch thickets or heather. The short-eared owl lays 6–8 eggs over a period of days, the incubation period being 26–30 days. Only the female sits, and as she starts to do so before all the eggs are laid, there are often owlets of varying ages in the same nest. This sometimes means that the bigger owlets seize more than their fair share of the food, and the younger owlets do not get enough to eat, especially when food is in short supply. Whilst the female remains in the nest brooding and feeding the owlets, the male hunts for prey, mostly mice and rats and, in the summer, lots of smaller birds and other birds' young. As soon as they are able to, short-eared owlets crawl out of the nest, even though they are not fully fledged. The parents continue to feed them in the brushwood until they can fend for themselves. Icelandic short-eared owls are mainly migratory.

Above is a short-eared owl with 6 owlets in its nest, 5 of which are sticking their heads out from under her wing, where she broods them whilst they are very small. The difference in size among the owlets is clearly visible, and is caused by the female incubating her first eggs before all the others are laid. Pictured below is the biggest owlet sticking its head out from under its mother's right wing. On the right is a facial portrait of a short-eared owl, its famous expression always seen as symbolising great wisdom.

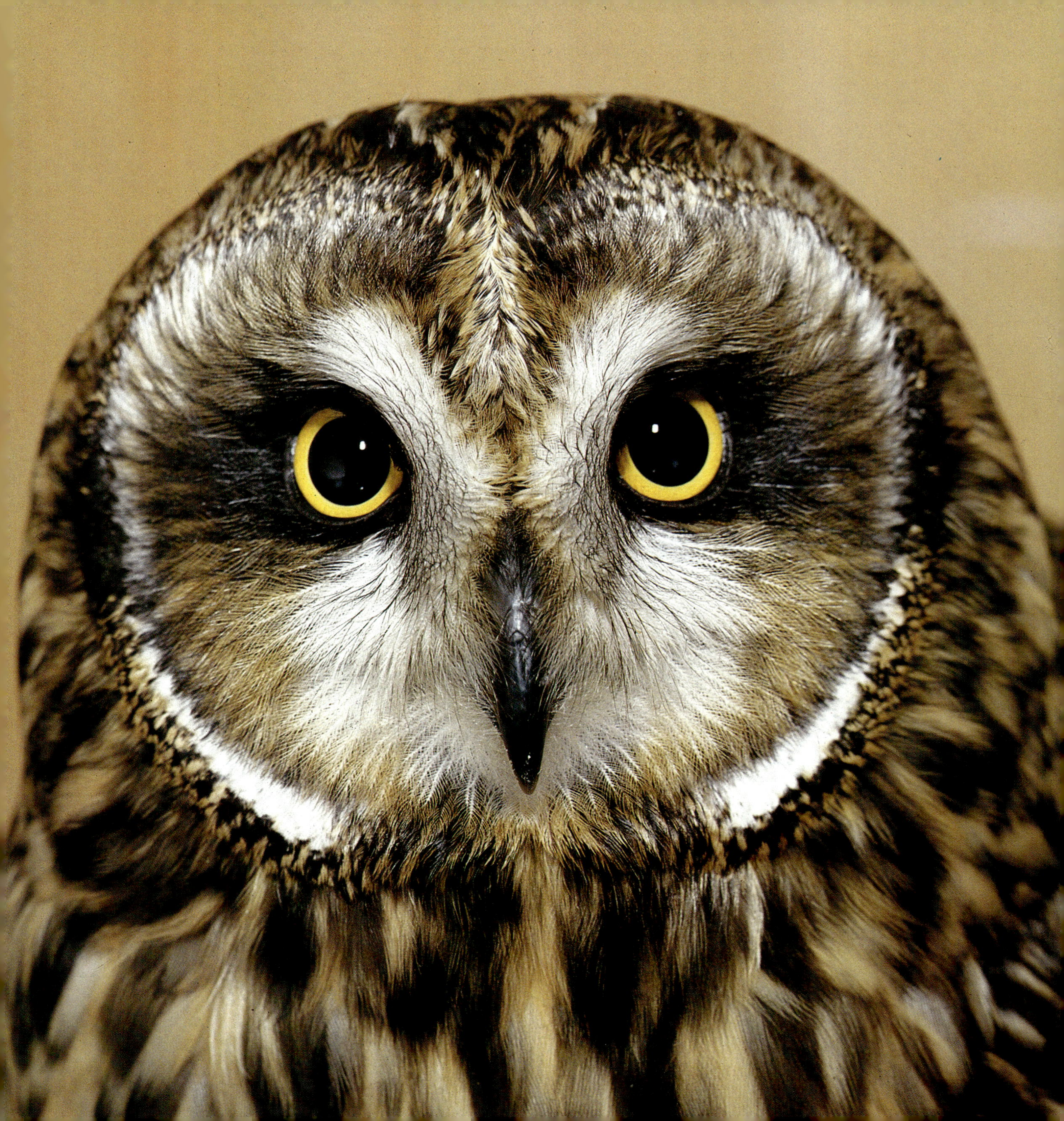

Life in a short-eared owl's nest

1 Downy short-eared owlets in the nest, which is often on a dry patch of land in boggy areas. Owlets in the same nest often vary in size.

2 A short-eared owl on its way through thick brushwood to its nest and young.

3 The short-eared owl brooding its young; the biggest owlet sits by its mother's side.

6 A short-eared owl with prey (a duckling) in its bill. The male hunts and brings the prey into the brushwood.

7 The female tears it into pieces which she feeds one at a time to her young.

8 The mother has almost finished feeding the young on the prey (duckling).

172

7. MARSHLAND-BIRDS

The 2 largest owlets feeding on prey, which the mother has torn into portions for them. On the right (5) are 2 short-eared owlets.
Under the short-eared owl's right wing is an owlet with the foot of a passerine bird in its bill. On the right (10) is an owlet learning how to feed itself.

Lake Mývatn has long been famous throughout the world for its multifarious bird life and its beautiful and varied landscape. In the background of this old drawing of Lake Mývatn is the explosive crater Hverfjall, which was formed in a huge eruption about 2,500 years ago.

8 Ducks

Ducks, geese, and swans are very conspicuous birds. They all belong to the waterfowl family (*Anatidae*), along with a few other related species. This is the best represented family of birds in the country as no fewer than 19 species of *Anatidae* breed in Iceland, if the pochard is included; this is a very rare bird and its nests are seldom found. Moreover there are 3 species of geese which are passage migrants in the spring and autumn, the brent goose, white-fronted goose, and barnacle goose (which has recently started to breed in Iceland). There are a further 3 species of ducks which are regular visitors: the King eider, the common goldeneye, and the American wigeon. This chapter will deal with the 14 species of ducks which add so much colour and life to Icelandic lakes and marshes during the summer. (The eider duck was considered as a shore-bird in Chapter 6.) These 14 species are divided by appearance and behaviour into 2 separate groups: surface-feeding ducks and diving ducks.

There are 6 species of **surface-feeding** or **dabbling ducks** which breed in Iceland: the **mallard**, the **teal**, the **gadwall**, the **wigeon**, the **pintail**, and the **shoveler**.

The **diving ducks** which breed on Icelandic lakes and rivers are the **scaup**, the **tufted duck**, **Barrow's goldeneye**, the **common scoter**, the **long-tailed duck**, the **harlequin**, the **red-breasted merganser**, and the **goosander**.

Surface-feeding ducks are so called because they forage for food on or just under the surface of the water, either by dabbling with their bills, or by upending themselves, 'half diving', leaving their hindquarters sticking up in the air (see picture on p. 182). Surface-feeding ducks are mostly vegetarian except during the breeding season, when they will feed a lot on animal matter, mostly midges and their larvae. Diving ducks find their food largely by diving, and live on several kinds of small animals including midge larvae, insects, crabs, water snails, and *Lepidurus arcticus*. Diving ducks only occasionally

The **TEAL** (*Anas crecca*) is the smallest Icelandic duck, being 36 cm long and weighing only around 340 g. Pictured above is a teal drake in its breeding plumage; the body is grey, the head chestnut brown with a curving green eye-patch. There is a distinctive horizontal white stripe above the wing. The under-rump is black with a yellowish-white patch on either side of the base of the tail. Both sexes have a bright green speculum on the back of the wing. The duck is speckled brown and buff with lighter under-parts; it is rather like the mallard duck, only much smaller.

The teal breeds in the lowlands, preferably on lakes and ponds with thick and high vegetation. It lays 6–10 white eggs between mid-May and early June. Only the duck incubates them and they hatch after 3–4 weeks. The fledging period is about 4 weeks. The teal population is not very large, and it is thus not a very conspicuous bird in Iceland. Some teals are resident, but most are migratory, wintering chiefly in the British Isles.

eat vegetable matter. The **fish-eating** ducks, the goosander and the red-breasted merganser, live almost exclusively on fish, which other diving ducks seldom eat. Diving ducks patter along the surface of the water before taking off, but surface-feeding ducks can launch themselves straight into the air.

The **MALLARD** (Anas platyrhynchos) is one of the largest species of ducks in Iceland. It is about 58 cm long, and the drake weighs around 1200 g. It is common all over the country and easily adapts to the close proximity of man, as can be seen in the picture above of a group of mallards and a pintail on Lake Tjörnin in Reykjavík during the winter. The picture also clearly reveals why the mallard is sometimes referred to as the 'green-headed duck' in Icelandic, as the green glossy head and white neck-ring are distinctive features of the drake. The breast is dark brown, the under-parts dark grey, the tail white, and the bill yellow. On the left are 2 mallard ducklings swimming. On the right hand page is a mallard drake swimming and a duck promenading. The duck is not as colourful as the drake, and is speckled brown and buff and has a greenish bill. Both sexes have orange legs. Like other surface-feeding ducks, it prefers lakes and ponds with plenty of sedge and rushes. The Icelandic mallard is mostly resident and winters around the coast on inlets and lagoons which do not freeze and which are shallow enough for it to reach the bottom with its bill when upending. Mallards return to their nesting grounds in late April or early May, as soon as the lakes and ponds are free of ice and plant life has begun to flourish once more. They lay their 8–12 white eggs in May. Only the duck incubates them and they hatch after about 4 weeks. The ducklings become fully fledged about 5 weeks old. The mallard population in Iceland is estimated at about 5,000 breeding pairs.

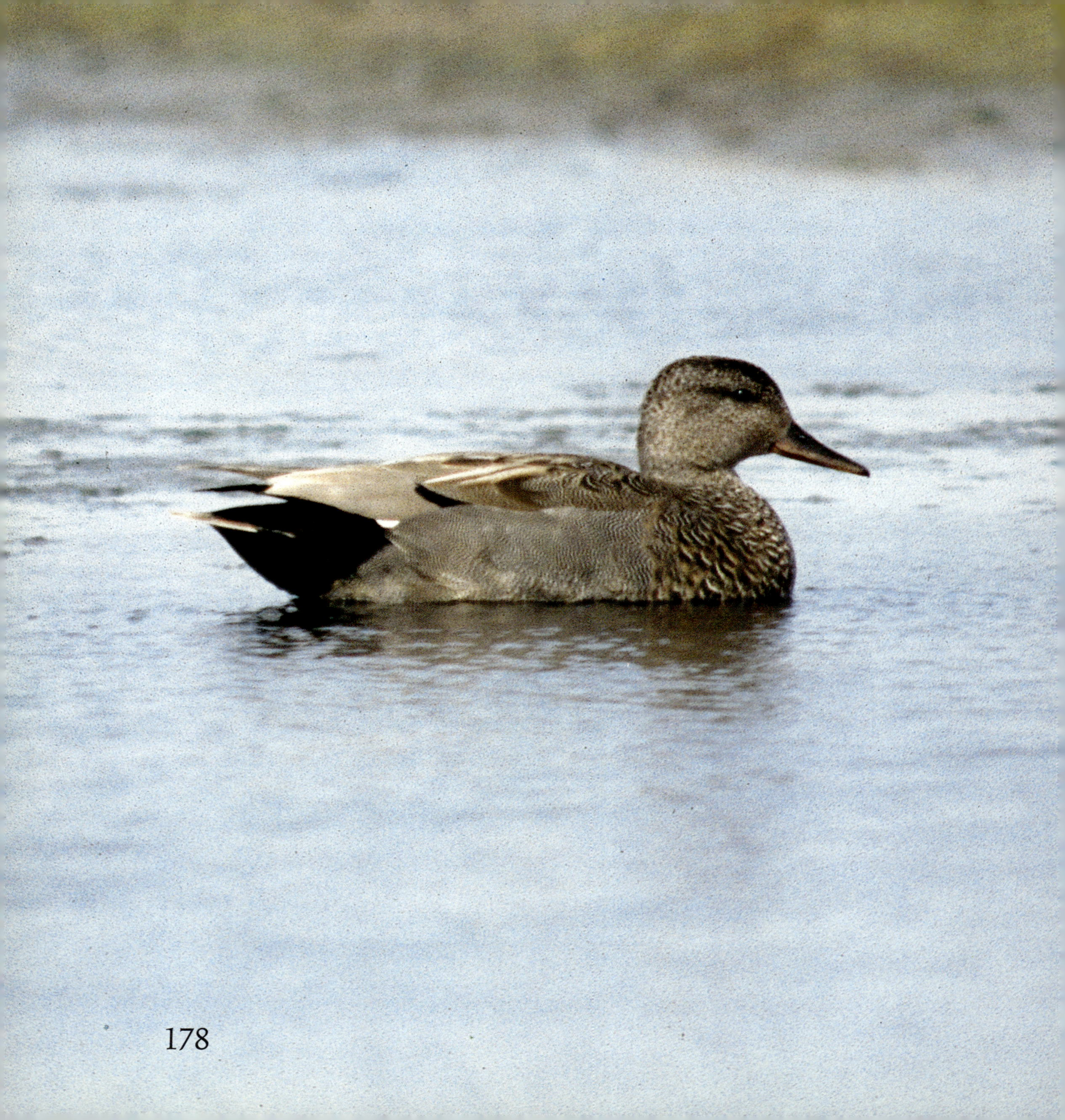

8. DUCKS

The **GADWALL** (*Anas strepera*) is smaller than the mallard, being about 51 cm long and weighing around 800 g. Pictured on the left is the drake; above is a gadwall pair; below is a gadwall drake. On the right are 6 gadwall ducklings in a nest in a thicket by Lake Mývatn; they are just about to leave the nest with their mother. The gadwall drake is grey coloured with reddish-brown wing-coverts and black tail-coverts. On the water it is easily distinguishable by its black rear parts which make a stark contrast with its greyish body. The duck is very similar to the mallard duck. The gadwall is very rare in Iceland, and is almost exclusively found in the lake Mývatn region, though it also breeds in a few other places. There are believed to be less than 300 gadwall pairs in Iceland, most of which are migratory, wintering largely in Ireland. Some gadwalls are resident, however, and spend the winter on Lake Mývatn, although they are also occasionally seen in south-western Iceland.

8. DUCKS

The **WIGEON** (*Anas penelope*) is a medium-sized duck, about 46 cm long and weighing 700–800 g. On the left is a duck incubating; below is a duck with 2 ducklings, and on the right is a drake in its summer plumage. The head is chestnut brown and the forehead yellow. The body is grey and the breast pinkish. The duck has lightly spotted greyish-brown upper-parts, breast and flanks. Wigeon ducklings have dark brown upper-parts, reddish-brown cheeks, and yellow-white front and upper-parts, as can be seen in the picture below. The wigeon is a common breeding bird in the lowlands and there are also large numbers of them around Lake Mývatn and its surrounding areas. It prefers shallow lakes and ponds with plenty of sedge and rushes.

A few hundred wigeons are resident and spend the winter along the coast of south-west Iceland. Recoveries of wigeons ringed in Iceland have revealed that large numbers of the migratory birds winter in the British Isles, and that a number of younger wigeons go to the east coast of North America. The wigeon population in Iceland is probably a little less than 5,000 breeding pairs.

8. DUCKS

Above is a flock of wigeons on the wing. The top left picture shows a wigeon pair swimming, and in the bottom picture, taken a moment later, they have just upended, the characteristic method by which surface-feeding ducks forage for food in shallow water. All surface-feeding ducks live on vegetable matter, including seeds, which they obtain either on land or on, or just under, the surface of the water. Like other surface-feeding ducks, however, the wigeon feeds on animal matter when breeding, especially midges and their larvae. Animal food is a much richer source of energy than plant food and is thus a vital part of the ducks' diet when their eggs are developing and while they are bringing up their young. Pictured below is a wigeon duck with 5 ducklings on lake Mývatn.

The **PINTAIL** (*Anas acuta*) is a conspicuously slim and long-necked surface-feeding duck with a long and pointed tail. It is rather large, about 56 cm long. The total pintail population in Iceland is not reckoned to be much more than 500 pairs. It nests very dispersively all over the country and is consequently not very common in any particular area. It likes to haunt sedge-grown fens full of puddles, as in the picture above. On the right are a pintail drake and a mallard duck; related species of ducks can interbreed. Bottom right is a pintail drake which has begun to moult, during which time it will often preen itself thoroughly.

The drake is brown on the head and nape, and its back, flanks, rump, and tail are pale grey. It has characteristic white bands from the white breast up both sides of the long and thin neck. The duck is similar to the mallard duck, but much slimmer in build and with a thinner neck and more pointed tail.

Like other surface-feeding ducks, the pintail lives mostly on vegetable matter, such as aquatic plants, seeds, and berries, but it will also feed on water insects such as midges and their larvae. The majority of pintails in Iceland are migratory and their main winter quarters are in the British Isles. A few resident birds can often be seen in south-west Iceland during the winter. The pintails return to their nesting sites in late April, and lay their 6–9 eggs between late May and mid-June. Only the duck incubates them, but the drake is attentive when they are hatching and helps to tend the young, which become fledged after 4–5 weeks. Most of the pintails leave for their winter quarters in September or October.

8. DUCKS

Above is a pintail drake in its spring plumage. It is slim in build with a distinctively long and thin neck which has white bands on its sides from its breast up to its coffee-brown head. The long and spear-like tail is also conspicuous and only one other Icelandic duck can rival it, the long-tailed duck, one of the species of diving ducks.

8. DUCKS

The **SHOVELER** (Anas clypeata) is a very rare breeding bird in Iceland and there are probably considerably fewer than 100 pairs in the country all told. It breeds mostly in northern Iceland in the wetland areas of Aðaldalur, Kelduhverfi, and Lake Mývatn.

On the right is a shoveler duck in flight over a typical nesting habitat. Shovelers like to breed on marshes and lakes full of vegetation not too far from the sea. Below right is a shoveler drake on Lake Mývatn.

The shoveler is 51 cm long and thus a bit smaller than the mallard. It is easily distinguishable from other ducks by its large spatulate bill and, in flight, its sky-blue shoulders. The shoveler drake is mostly black and white on its upper-parts, and has a green head, white breast, and chestnut belly and flanks.

The shoveler is a relative newcomer to Iceland. The first confirmed shoveler nest was not discovered until 1931, and a second nest was found in 1933. It has continued to breed in Iceland since then, but is a shy and wary bird and still rarely seen. It is mostly a freshwater bird and feeds on small animals. The large spatulate bill is full of thin brush-like lamellae which it uses like a sieve when foraging for food in the water. The shoveler also catches midges and other insects, and sometimes feeds on vegetable matter.

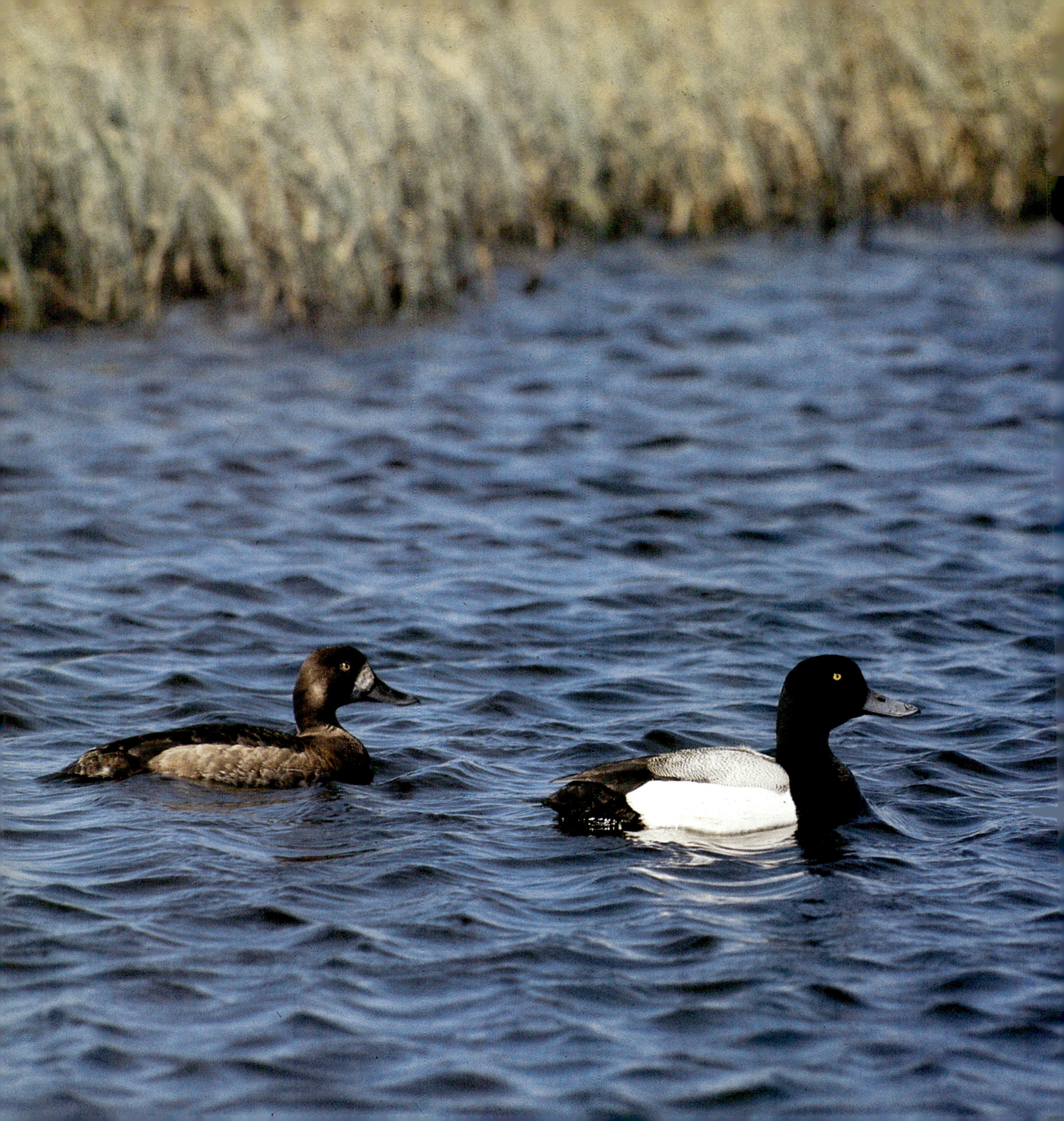

The **SCAUP** (*Aythya marila*) is very common in Iceland, with an estimated 9,000–10,000 pairs distributed over most parts of the country. It is a medium-sized, stocky, short-legged duck, about 48 cm long and weighing around 1000 g. From a distance the scaup drake looks black at both ends and white in the middle, but a closer view will reveal that it has a pale grey back, a feature which helps to distinguish it from the tufted duck drake, which has a black back and a drooping crest on the back of its head. The belly and flanks of both these drakes are white. The scaup duck has a dark brown head and a very distinctive white patch around the base of the bill; it has reddish-brown upper-parts, paler towards the front and darker towards the rear. It has a reddish-brown breast, but paler flanks and a whitish belly.

Pictured on the left is a scaup pair, and above is a tufted duck with 6 ducklings. Both these pictures were taken at Lake Mývatn where most of the scaups in Iceland can be found. Like most other diving ducks, the scaup lives on animal food, on small shellfish, snails, midges and their larvae, and fish fry. The scaup will dive for food to a depth of 3–4 m. It eats few plants, and then preferably eelgrass in bays and inlets. The scaup is a migratory bird and arrives in Iceland in March and April. It nests on islets or the banks of lakes where there is plenty of vegetation. It usually lays 8–10 eggs in late May or early June, and they hatch after about 4 weeks. Only the duck incubates them and as soon as the ducklings have hatched she leads them straight to the water. The young are immediately able to swim and dive, and are fully fledged after 5–6 weeks.

Above is a scaup pair on Lake Mývatn. In very calm weather myriads of midges are visible above the smooth surface of the lake. On the left is a scaup pair on the shore of Lake Mývatn. In both these pictures the distinctive feature of the female, the white patch at the base of the bill, is clearly visible. In the beginning of September the scaups leave their nesting sites for the coast, and a short while later they depart for their winter quarters in Western Europe, especially the British Isles.

The **TUFTED DUCK** (*Aythya fuligula*) is closely related to the scaup and greatly resembles it, though the tufted duck is a slightly smaller bird, about 43 cm long and weighing around 700 g. The 2 species can be compared in the picture above which shows both scaup and tufted duck pairs. From left to right: the female tufted duck, the scaup duck, the male tufted duck, the scaup drake. The similarities between the species are clearly visible, but one distinguishing feature is the scaup duck's white patch at the base of the bill.

The tufted duck may also sometimes have such a patch, but it is never so big or so distinct. The tufted duck is also usually darker than the scaup duck. There is a greater difference between the 2 drakes. The scaup drake's back is grey, whereas the male tufted duck's is black, and the latter's drooping black crest on the back of the neck is usually clearly discernible.

Both these closely related diving ducks are inland waterbirds in the summer, but when resident they haunt bays and firths along the coast during the winter. Most birds of both species are migrant, however. Both species nest on river banks, islets, or lakes full of vegetation, and it is quite common for them to share nesting sites.

The tufted duck, just like the scaup, lives mostly on animal food, chiefly midge larvae, water snails, and various kinds of insects. The tufted duck is an expert diver and is believed to forage for food down to a depth of 6 m, where it can usually find plenty to eat in the muddy bottoms of lakes.

Pictured above is a female tufted duck in its nest in the fertile surroundings of Lake Mývatn. Traces of a crest can be seen on its nape. On the left is a tufted duck's nest with 5 eggs, one of which is hatching. – The tufted duck likes a well hidden nesting site among rushes or in birch thickets. The nest itself is made out of grass, feathers, and down. The tufted duck usually lays 5–8 (sometimes 6–10) greyish-green eggs in June. Only the duck incubates them and they hatch after about 4 weeks. Just as with the scaup, the duck then immediately leads her young to the water, and they begin to swim and dive as soon as they are afloat. They are quick to learn how to catch food and practice all day long. If there is any danger in the vicinity their mother's alarm call will send them scurrying into cover in the rushes by the side of the water. – The tufted duck has only recently settled in Iceland, first being seen here in 1895. It has since then become widely distributed in the lowlands and has even become one of the most numerous duck species in the country, its population approaching 10,000 pairs, half of which are around Lake Mývatn. It is a general belief that several species of ducks have declined in numbers in Iceland in recent years, and several possible explanations for this have been put forward: human persecution; the drainage of wetlands (both in Iceland and in the ducks' more southerly winter quarters), an improving climate, the increase in gull populations, and the introduction of the mink into Icelandic wildlife. On the other hand the increase in the shoveler and tufted duck populations has also been linked to the general amelioration of the climate over the same period of time. It must be borne in mind, however, that duck populations fluctuate considerably and that they are extremely mobile between areas and countries, and even between continents.

Above is a flock of tufted ducks in flight, and on the right is a tufted duck pair swimming on Lake Mývatn in May.

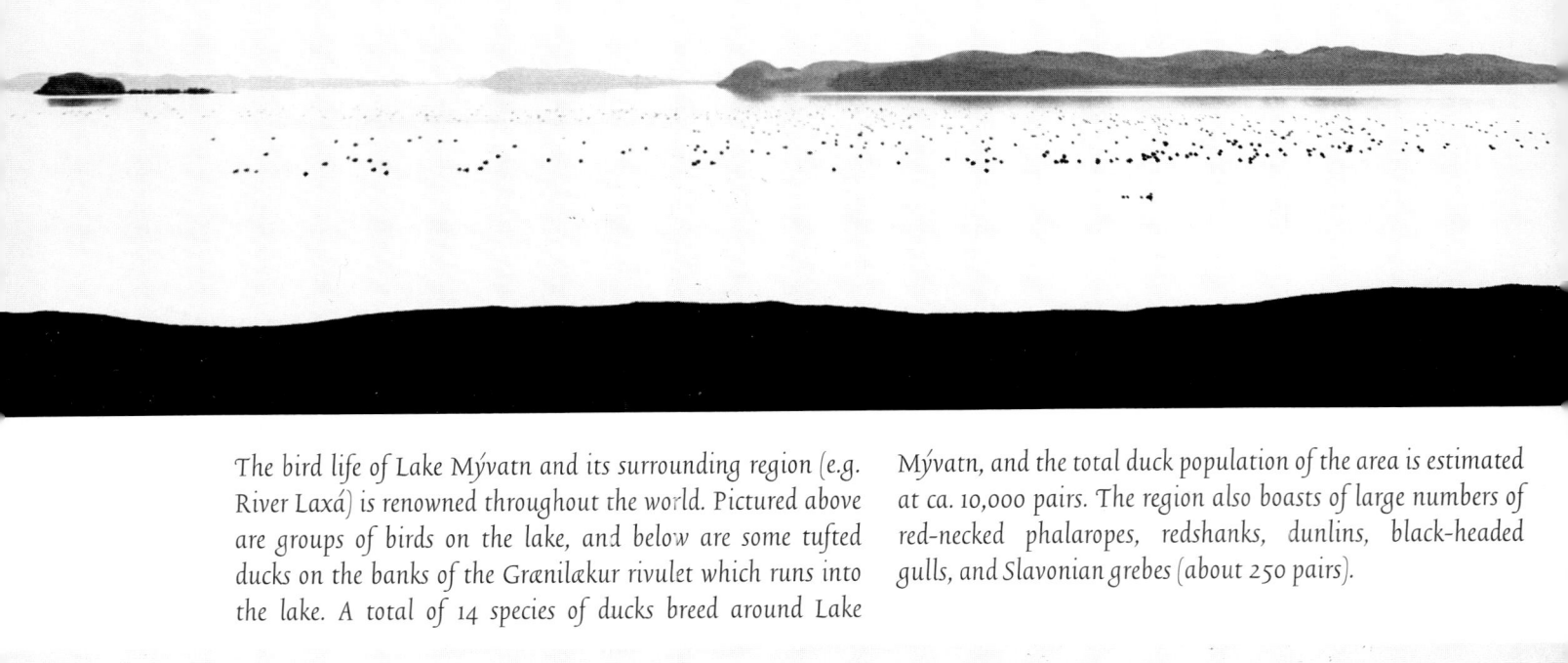

The bird life of Lake Mývatn and its surrounding region (e.g. River Laxá) is renowned throughout the world. Pictured above are groups of birds on the lake, and below are some tufted ducks on the banks of the Grænilækur rivulet which runs into the lake. A total of 14 species of ducks breed around Lake Mývatn, and the total duck population of the area is estimated at ca. 10,000 pairs. The region also boasts of large numbers of red-necked phalaropes, redshanks, dunlins, black-headed gulls, and Slavonian grebes (about 250 pairs).

BARROW'S GOLDENEYE (*Bucephala islandica*) is one of the largest species of Icelandic ducks; it is 40–53 cm long, only a little smaller than the mallard. The drake weighs about 1200 g and is quite a lot bigger than the duck which only weighs around 800 g. Above is a pair of Barrow's goldeneyes at the edge of the ice in Lake Mývatn in spring (16 May). Barrow's goldeneyes are probably mainly resident in Iceland, though some of them may also visit the American continent during the winter. They occur almost exclusively on fresh water, even in winter, especially on Lake Mývatn and River Laxá, and to a lesser extent on the rivers and lakes in southern Iceland.

The main breeding grounds of Barrow's goldeneye are in the northern parts of North America. It is considered a very rare breeding bird in Western Greenland, and Iceland is the only place where it breeds in Europe. It occurs as a vagrant in continental Europe and the Faroes, probably from Iceland. The Barrow's goldeneye population in Iceland of around 800 pairs seems to have remained quite stable. Barrow's goldeneyes nest in holes and crevices in the lava, in ready-prepared boxes, and even in outhouses or the stone walls of buildings; in Icelandic it has thus been called 'the house-duck'.

The Barrow's goldeneye drake is a splendid bird in its spring plumage, as can be seen in the picture above. It is a rather stocky bird with a very high forehead and a mane on the back of its neck. Its head is black with a white crescent-shaped patch between the eye and the base of the bill.

The **Barrow's goldeneye drake** has black upper-parts and white breast and under-parts and a white ring around its neck. When sitting, its boldly barred black and white scapulars are very conspicuous. Its head is black with a white crescent-shaped patch between the eye and the base of the bill.

(1) The pictures below are of a Barrow's goldeneye pair mating. The first picture shows precopulatory behaviour.

(2) The pair are now mating. Only the head of the duck is above water; the drake grips her nape with his bill.

The **Barrow's goldeneye duck** has a dark brown head, but is otherwise mostly ash-grey apart from a white band around the neck, and a white lower breast and upper-belly. The bill is black, the legs yellow, and the eyes pale yellow. The eggs of the Barrow's goldeneye are bluish-green and its down pale grey.

(3) Mating has reached its climax. The drake keeps his balance by holding onto the duck's mane.

(4) Mating completed, the drake releases the duck.

Pictured above is a group of Barrow's goldeneyes by Kálfaströnd on Lake Mývatn in late July. Mount Vindbelgur is in the background.

Below are drakes washing and preening themselves, rolling and cavorting in the water.

Above is a Barrow's goldeneye duck with 9 ducklings on a stream which flows into the River Laxá. Barrow's goldeneye ducklings are brownish-grey on their upper-parts and white on the chin and sides of the neck. The body is speckled with white. Pictured on the right is a young drake. In its immature plumage the drake resembles the duck, although it is larger and has a white breast and traces of a pale crescent-shaped patch in front of the eye. The pictures below are of a Barrow's goldeneye duck diving. The first picture (on the left) was taken just before it was about to dive; in the next picture only the hindquarters are still above water; in the third picture there are merely air bubbles where the duck has submerged.

8. DUCKS

The **COMMON SCOTER** (Melanitta nigra) is quite a large duck, about 48 cm long and weighing around 1000 g. It is thus similar in size to the scaup, though it actually looks bigger. The common scoter drake is the only Icelandic one to have an entirely black plumage. The bill is also black, but it has a bright orange patch on the upper mandible and there is also a large knob at its base. The duck has reddish-brown upper-parts and lighter brown cheeks, neck, and belly. Immature common scoters resemble the duck, but their colouring is paler. The ducklings are dark reddish-brown and pale grey on the belly, chin, and cheeks.

Pictured on the left is a common scoter drake on a pool near Lake Mývatn. On the right is a duck on its nest, also by Lake Mývatn. Below are 3 common scoter ducklings. On the picture overleaf (pp. 200–201) is a common scoter duck trailed by 27 ducklings. They are not all her own offspring, however. Common scoter ducklings have a habit of collecting in groups and then sometimes attaching themselves to a single duck. This duck certainly looks nothing but proud to have such a large retinue! – The common scoter population in Iceland is not very large, probably around 300 pairs all told, of which the majority, about 200 pairs, nest in the Lake Mývatn area. Like other diving ducks, it chooses a nesting site near inland lakes with a plentiful food supply; it is believed to have the same diet as the scaup. The common scoter prefers to build its nest in hidden places in brushwood or other thick vegetation, as in the picture on the right. It lays 7–10 eggs which only the duck incubates, and they hatch after about 4 weeks. The common scoter is a migratory bird in Iceland and winters on the shores of mainland Europe.

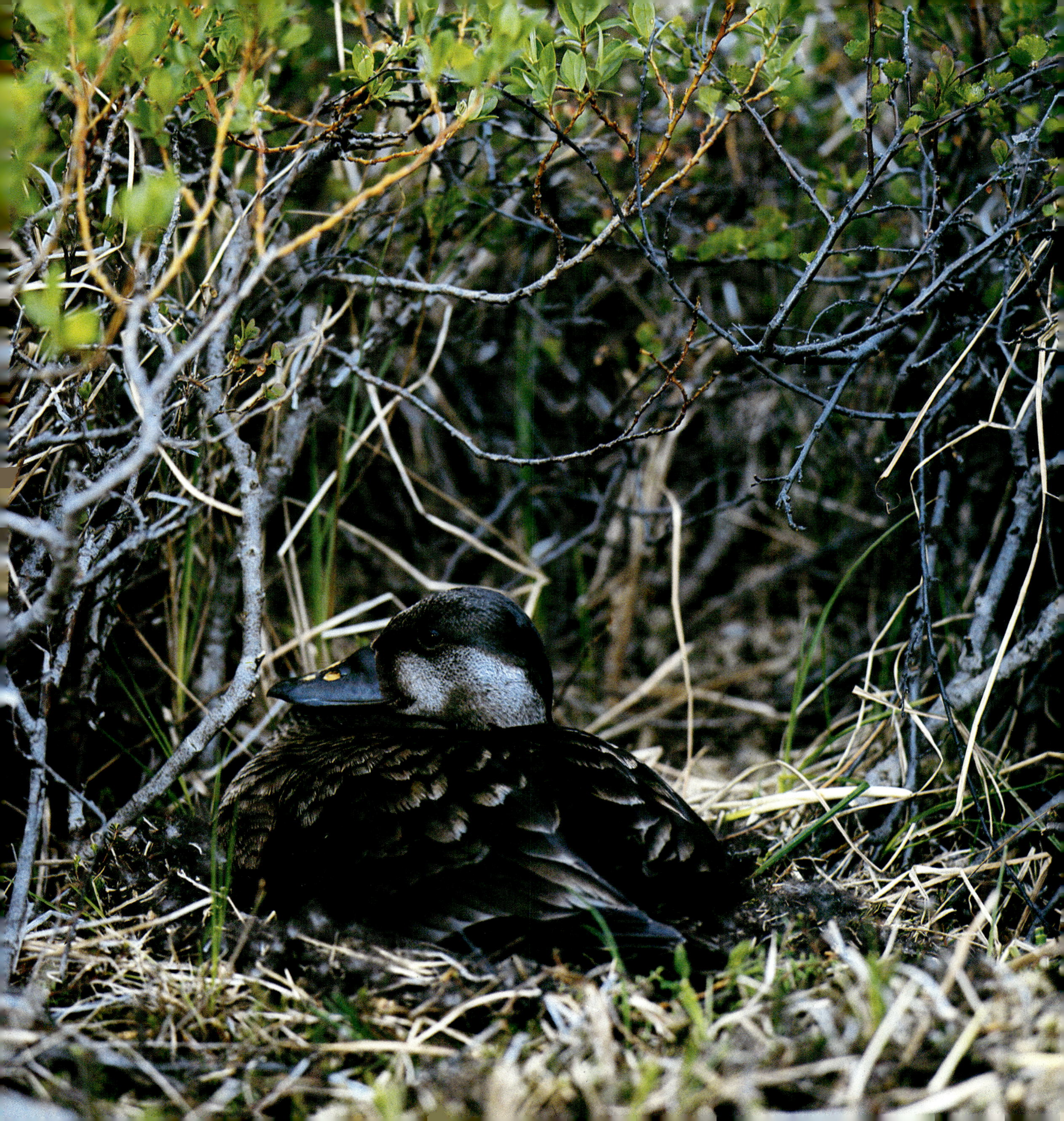

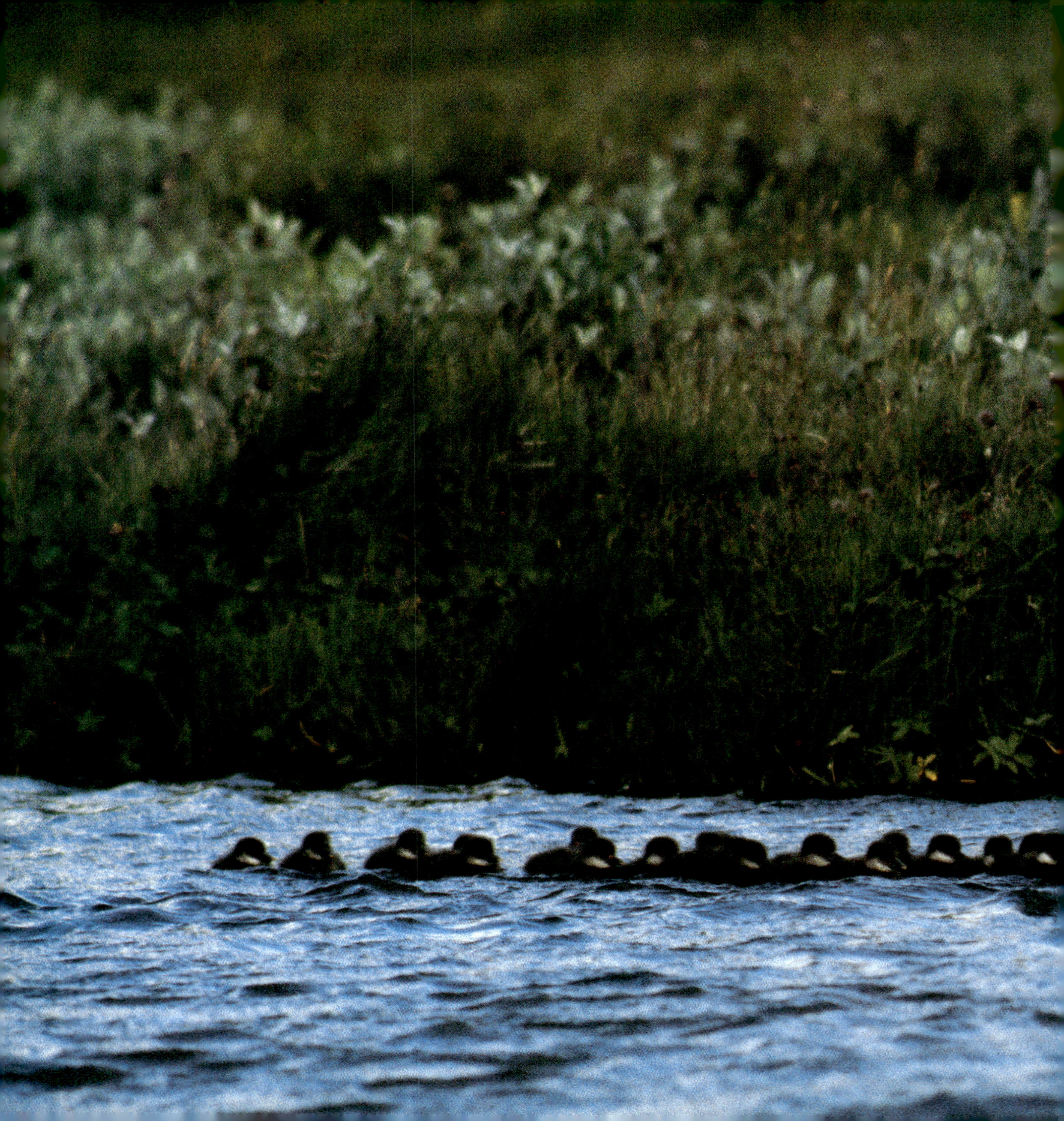

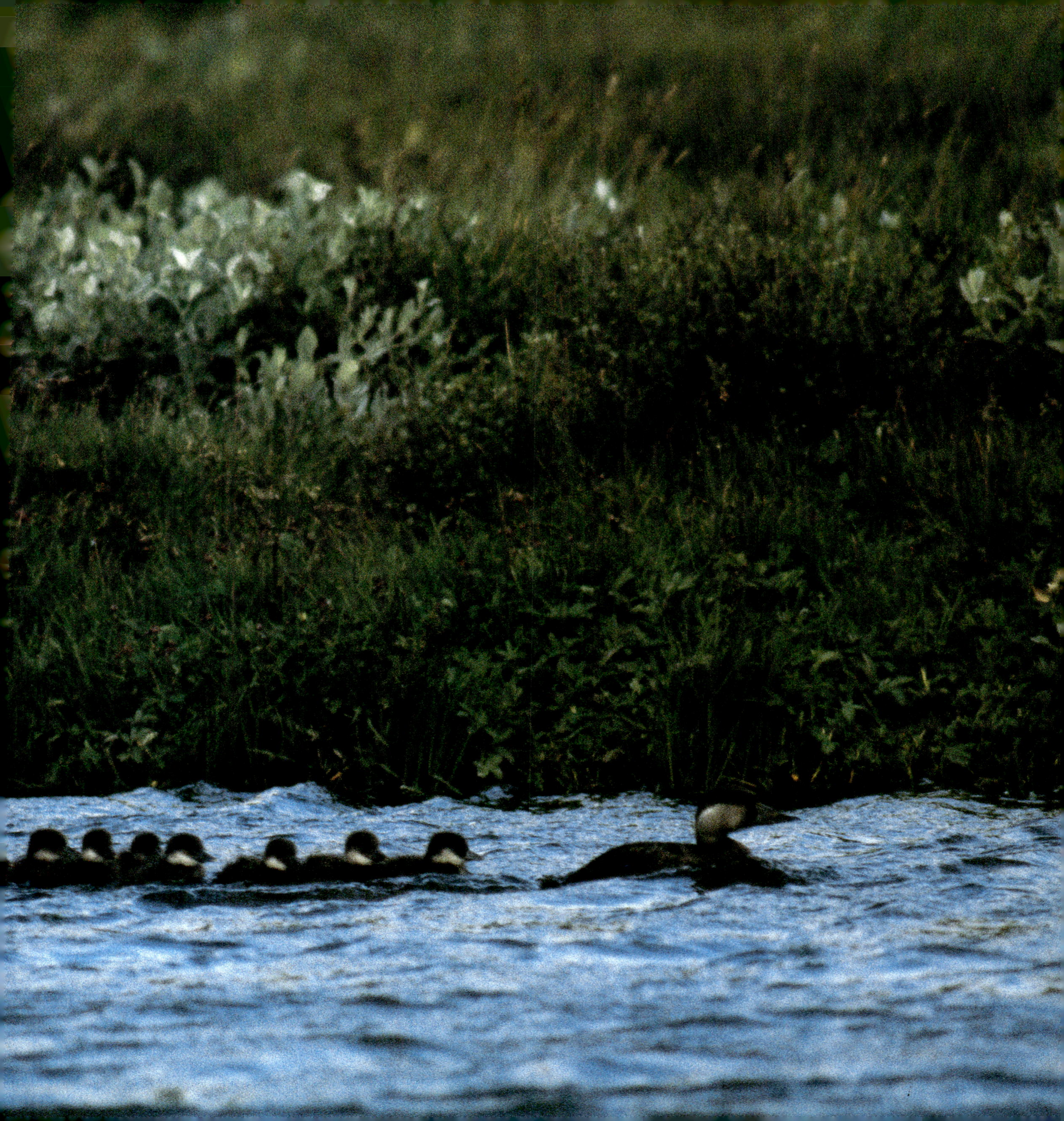

8. DUCKS

The **LONG-TAILED DUCK** (Clangula hyemalis) is a rather small short-billed diving duck. The drake is 53 cm long if its very distinctive long spear-like tail is included. The duck is 41 cm long, and both sexes generally weigh around 700 g. The long-tailed duck is the only diving duck which has an almost completely white body and uniformly dark wings. All other ducks have a speculum on the wing. In its summer plumage the drake, as pictured on the left, is dark brown on its upper-parts and white on its belly. It has a white patch around the eye. The duck has dark brown upper-parts and white under-parts. On the right is a duck coming to its nest, and in the bottom picture of this page is a duck with 7 ducklings on a sedge-grown lake near Mývatn. – The long-tailed duck is a common breeding bird in the central highlands and northern lowlands of Iceland. Its population is estimated at between 1,000 and 3,000 pairs. Icelandic long-tailed ducks are mostly resident; they spend the summer on inland lakes and waters and move to the coast in the autumn, where they spend the winters. The decline in long-tailed duck numbers over the last 60 years has been attributed to the warmer climate in Iceland, as the long-tailed duck is a very hardy arctic bird and a common breeder in Arctic countries.

8. DUCKS

8. DUCKS

The **HARLEQUIN** (Histrionicus histrionicus) is rather small, 39–45 cm long and weighing less than 700 g. In its summer plumage the drake is a particularly striking bird. It is dark bluish-grey with a navy-blue breast, chestnut flanks, and conspicuous white streaks and spots on its head, neck, and breast. The duck is dark brown with whitish patches on the cheeks.

The distribution of the harlequin is rather irregular, and outside Iceland it breeds in Greenland, north-east Canada, the west coast of North America, and north-east Siberia. In Iceland it is distributed all over the country, including the central highlands, though its population is not very large, probably less than 3,000 pairs.

Icelandic harlequins are mostly resident and winter all round the coastline, especially where it is steep and rocky or where the sea is usually rough. It keeps in small groups and seems to like nothing better than to be in the surf, expertly diving between the breakers before they reach the shore. In Icelandic the harlequin is thus sometimes referred to as the 'surf-duck' or 'surf-dove'. Its main winter habitats are the south and west coasts of the Reykjanes peninsula. In April the harlequins move into the bays and firths and gather in groups in river estuaries. In late April or early May they begin their sometimes long journey up the rivers to their breeding grounds. Their largest nesting areas are where fast-flowing rivers issue from lakes rich in vegetation and animal life, e.g. River Laxá, especially as harlequins live mostly on animal food like most diving ducks. On the rivers they feed mostly on gnat larvae and pupae. Their favourite nesting sites are on islands with thick vegetation. The harlequin usually lays 6–7 eggs, and the incubation period is around 30 days. As soon as the ducklings are dry, the duck takes them to a calmer stretch of the river where it is easier for them to find food. The ducklings become fully fledged when 2 months old. When the duck has finished laying all her eggs and has begun to incubate them, usually in early July, the drake departs for the coast where it moults its flight-feathers and attains its eclipse plumage. The harlequin ducks remain on the rivers with their young until they are fully fledged. In late September they then all depart for the coast, where the family units finally appear to break up. The ducks do not moult until they have arrived at the coast.

    Anyone familiar with harlequins will know how effortlessly and agilely they can swim and dive in turbulent currents and cataracts. They often rest on rocks jutting just above swirling eddies and whirlpools. They are quick in their movements and can walk more swiftly and easily on land than most other ducks. They swim high and easily in the water, constantly jerking their heads. They are seldom or rarely seen in the company of other species of ducks. When taking off from a river they will fly low, following every bend in the river.

The **RED-BREASTED MERGANSER** (*Mergus serrator*) is 1 of the 2 Icelandic fish-eating ducks, the other being the goosander (see pp. 210–213). They are physically quite different from other ducks, being lean and rakish in build and with long narrow bills which have sharply serrated edges. The red-breasted merganser is about 58 cm long and weighs around 1000 g like the common scoter and the scaup. It can be distinguished from the goosander by its slightly smaller size, different plumage, and wispy double crest on its nape. The exact size of the red-breasted merganser population is unknown, but estimated at a few thousand breeding pairs. Above is a red-breasted merganser pair on Lake Mývatn. On the left are 2 red-breasted merganser pairs on Grænilækur near Mývatn on 31 May; the drakes are fighting. Bottom left is a drake on Lake Mývatn. The red-breasted merganser drake has a broad whitish collar separating its blackish-green head from its brown breast. Its flanks are grey and there are 2 narrow black lines across the white wing-patch. The duck has brownish-grey upper-parts, a chestnut head and neck, and the distinctive crest.

The red-breasted merganser is distributed all round Iceland, mostly on the coast, but also on inland lakes.

Above is a red-breasted merganser duck and a duckling on a pool near Lake Mývatn. On the right is a red-breasted merganser nest with 9 eggs. Bottom right is a duck in its nest in a deep hole. Red-breasted mergansers make their nests in narrow holes and crevices or in dense thickets. They are also known to nest in puffin burrows and outhouses. The down in the nest is ash-grey and there are often 9–12 brown or greyish eggs. The red-breasted merganser is both resident and migratory, the resident birds often wintering along the coast of western and southern Iceland. Its natural diet is fish, but it will also feed on various invertebrates. The red-breasted merganser has its enemies among sportsmen who believe it spoils the fishing in rivers and lakes. The truth is, however, that on lake Mývatn it lives almost exclusively on sticklebacks. There has been little research done on its feeding habits elsewhere in the country, though presumably it must occasionally take trout and salmon fry.

Above is a red-breasted merganser duck, and on the left a young drake. On the right is a red-breasted merganser duckling. The red-breasted merganser is a very shy, rather silent bird which is not very sociable. In the winter it feeds in the shallow waters of bays, firths, and estuaries during the day, but with the twilight it flies out to sea, returning to land early the following morning. When foraging for food it often swims with its bill and part of its head under water. It is a good diver, and when submerged propels itself with its feet, hardly using its wings at all. It is usually under water for 20–25 seconds, but can remain below the surface for up to 2 minutes. On average it is reckoned that a red-breasted merganser eats around 300 g of fish per day.

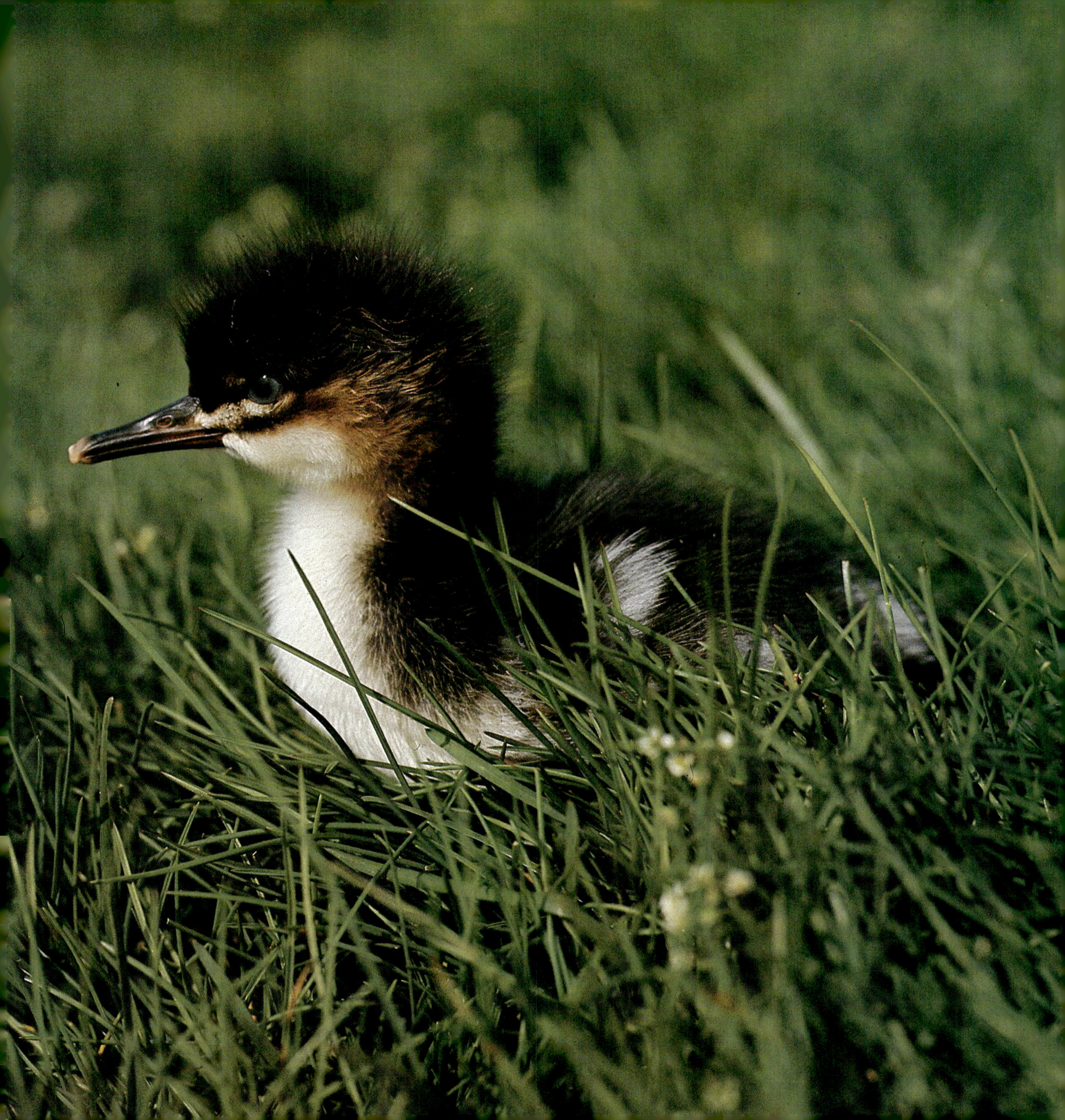

8. DUCKS

The **GOOSANDER** (Mergus merganser) is by far the largest of all Icelandic diving ducks, about 66 cm long and weighing 1500–2000 g. It is slim and streamlined in appearance like the other fish-eating duck, the red-breasted merganser.

The goosander nests dispersively in Iceland along fishing rivers and inland lakes. It is a resident bird, though it has a small population, estimated at only a few hundred pairs. During the summer it is chiefly on lowland lakes near rivers where there is a plentiful supply of fish, its principal diet. The mouth of the goosander is so wide that it can swallow quite large fish whole. It will also feed on lower forms of life, however. In other countries it nests high up in trees, but in Iceland it nests in holes, burrows, crevices and small caves, or else under tussocks, in thickets, among angelicas, or in any other suitable hiding place.

On the left is a goosander nest in a cavity formed between the outer turf and inner wooden wall of an old disused Icelandic 'turf-house' by Lake Mývatn. There was a narrow gap at the top through which the bird could slip in and out. It was just possible to slide a camera and flashlight through the same gap to photograph the eggs. There were 8 of them on 26 May, one of which had just been laid. The duck did not begin to incubate them continuously until 29 May. Pictured on the right (p. 211) is the goosander duck in the nest on 24 June. On 30 June the eggs began to hatch. On 1 July the duck went to the lake for a bathe, and that same night she led the ducklings from the nest to the water. The incubation period for this goosander was thus 31 days from when she first began sitting continuously, and 2 more days passed before she took the ducklings to the water.

There are usually reckoned to be 7–12 eggs in a goosander clutch, and they hatch after about 30 days. Only the duck sits, but during the earlier part of the incubation period the drake remains near the nest. It then disappears to a remote place to moult its feathers. After leading the ducklings to the water, the duck remains with them until they are fully fledged, when they all depart for the coast.

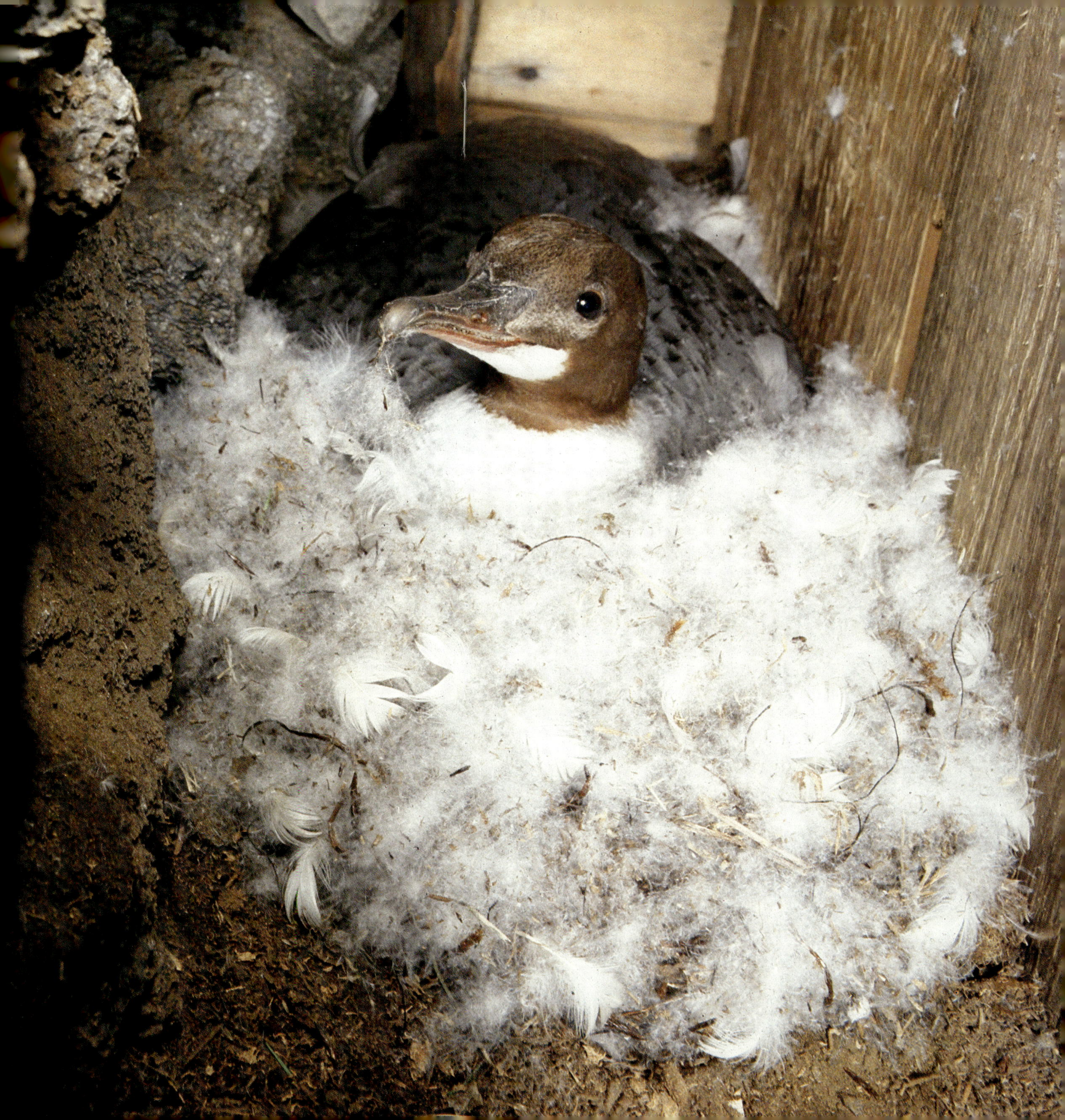

Above is a goosander drake on Lake Mývatn. On the left is a goosander duck on Grænilækur, Lake Mývatn. On the right is a duck on the banks of Grænilækur.

The goosander drake is a large and splendid bird. It has creamy-white under-parts, a black back, and greenish-black head. Its bill is long, narrow and red. Unlike the smaller red-breasted merganser drake, it does not have a crest on its nape. The ducks of both species are very alike, however, and both have a crest on the nape; the goosander duck also has a white chin-patch and a sharper division between its reddish-brown head and its white and bluish-grey under-parts, as is clearly visible in the picture on the right.

It is estimated that the diet of both species is 75% to 90% fish. The red-breasted merganser feeds mostly on sticklebacks, but the goosander readily eats trout and salmon fry. As the goosander population is so small and scattered, however, it provides no real threat to the sport of fishermen.

Diving ducks have developed superb diving skills which are as important to them as the ability to fly as they chiefly forage for food under water. For a bird to survive in and on water, however, it is vitally important that it never allows its feathers to become completely waterlogged. In the downy feathers under the outer contour and flight-feathers air pockets are formed which provide essential insulation. If these downy feathers get wet they stick together and the protective layer of air will disappear. Moreover if a bird's feathers become completely waterlogged it becomes too heavy to be able to fly. If a bird lands in oil-polluted water its feathers will stick together, which will not only prevent it from taking off, but also allow cold water to seep through to the skin, and the bird will consequently die of exposure. Birds which dive, like the diving ducks, have a high specific gravity and their wings can be pressed very close to the body. When swimming, birds use their feet alternately backwards and forwards, but when diving they use both feet simultaneously. Diving ducks kick their legs upwards and outwards when they dive. When submerging they have to use a lot of energy as they are light in weight and have to overcome hydrostatic pressure. Conversely, of course, they can float back to the surface as easily as a cork. When swimming under water, a large amount of the air between the feathers and the body is expelled as the feathers are pressed tightly against the body. When a bird has dived a few times, it must renew this air-supply. It does so by lifting its wings out of the water and extending its outermost feathers. A diving bird can hold its breath under water for quite a while, but it is not usually submerged for more than a minute. Most diving ducks prefer to dive in shallow waters, 4–6 m deep; eider ducks, however, can dive to a depth of 20 m.

A golden plover, sitting motionless in its nest on a heather moor, blends so well with its background that it is hardly visible.

9 Moorland-birds

The **GOLDEN PLOVER** (Pluvialis apricaria) is a common breeding bird in Iceland, especially on moors, highland heaths, and stony hills where there is some vegetation. The golden plover is about 28 cm long. It has dark upper-parts streaked with gold and dark under-parts and cheeks, the 2 sets of colours divided by an S-shaped white line running from the neck down through the flanks. Both sexes have similar colouring. – The golden plover lives chiefly on earthworms, midges, insect larvae, and snails, though in the summer it will also feed on plants, particularly berries towards the autumn. The golden plover is a migratory bird in Iceland, wintering in the British Isles or mainland Western Europe. It usually returns to Iceland early in April, sojourning along the coast at first, but soon moving inland to its breeding grounds on moors, bogs, and heaths. – The golden plover's nest is little more than a depression in heather or grass lined with blades of grass or leaves. In the second half of May it usually lays 4 greyish or brownish-yellow eggs, speckled dark brown. Both parents share the incubating and the eggs hatch after about 3 weeks. As soon as the chicks have hatched they are on the move and can quickly fend for themselves. If any danger threatens they hide immediately in surroundings where their colouring will act as protective camouflage (see picture on p. 217).

Golden plover parents keep a sharp look-out when protecting their young, and are especially skillful at enticing unwanted guests away from their nest. The chicks are fully fledged a month after hatching. In late July the golden plover moves back to the coast, and at the end of summer both adult and immature birds fly south to their winter quarters.

A characteristic habit of the golden plover is that when running about it will suddenly come to a dead stop, and remaining completely motionless, closely observe its surroundings, preferably from a tussock or stone. It will then set off briskly once more, and after a short run come once again to an abrupt stop to look around; this sequence is repeated again and again. It is very quick on its feet and an agile flyer, migrating in flocks in the spring and autumn.

'The plover has come...'

'The plover has come, bid farewell to the snow! Its song will dismiss all boredom and gloom...' are the opening lines of Páll Ólafsson's poem on the golden plover, the harbinger of spring. Newly arrived from more southerly countries, the golden plover's plaintive chirp captures the hearts of people in more northerly parts of the world, for it announces that spring and summer are not far off and that the flowers will soon be blooming again. The arrival of the golden plover has thus become symbolic for Icelanders as marking the beginning of spring, and Icelandic poets have been inspired by it for centuries; indeed it has become renowned as the 'poets' bird'. A typical poem on the plover is recorded below. The golden plover has become an integral part of Icelandic folklore, and it is a completely protected bird in this country. Tradition has it that the golden plover is very sensitive to any changes in atmospheric conditions, and that it is possible to forecast the weather from its behaviour.

Pictured on the right is a golden plover observing its surroundings from a small tussock. Below is a golden plover singing its melancholy song of spring. Bottom right is a golden plover chick crouching motionless in the heather, a protective measure which has saved many a plover chick in times of danger.

The plover has come, bid farewell to the snow!
Its song will dismiss all boredom and gloom.
It tells me the whimbrel is soon to follow,
The sun will start shining, and the flowers bloom.
It stirs up my conscience to how lazy I've been,
For I sleep too long and do little but mope.
It tells me to arise and shake off my spleen,
And to meet the new summer with heart full of hope.

(PÁLL ÓLAFSSON)

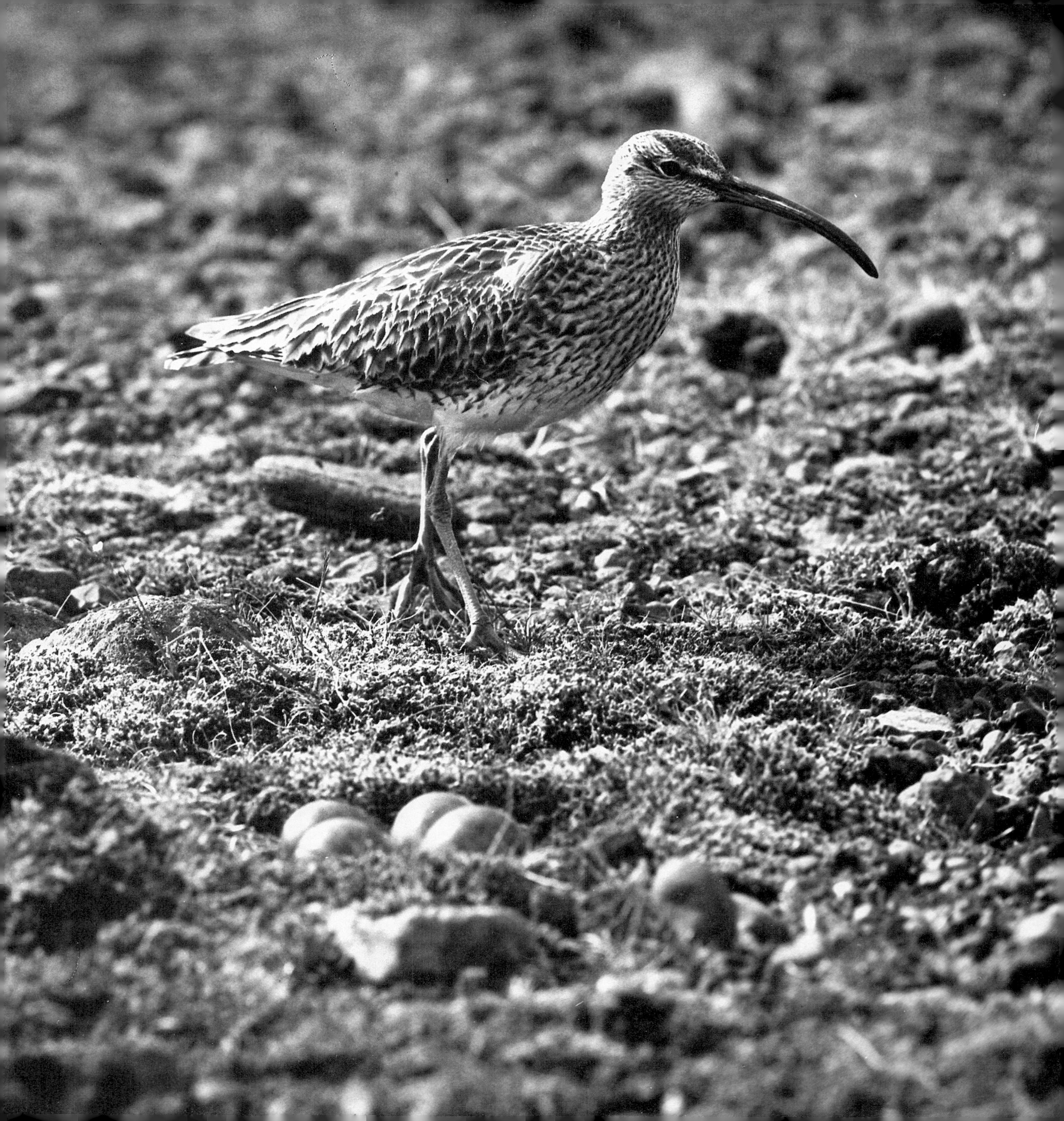

The **WHIMBREL** (Numenius phaeopus) is one of the commonest moorland-birds in Iceland and familiar to almost everyone in the country, especially as it is a characteristic feature of all Iceland's bogs and moors. It is not its plumage which attracts attention, however, but its shape, particularly its long curved bill (proportionally longer than any other Icelandic bird's) and its distinct and easily recognisable shrill call.

Adult whimbrels usually weigh 400–500 g, but they can weigh considerably less in a cold and windy spring. Both sexes have the same colouring, and there is no difference between the summer and winter plumage, even though the whimbrel moults twice a year. The whimbrel is distributed all over Iceland, especially in the lowlands and valleys, but it will also breed on highland heaths or near the sea. Its nesting sites can vary considerably, though it usually breeds on moorlands near bogs and marshes. Its nest is often on a reasonably dry tussock of moss, in dry grass, in heather, in brushwood, or even on a rather bare stretch of sand, as in the picture on the left; the whimbrel is strolling near its nest. The whimbrel's nest is a rather large but shallow depression loosely lined with withered grass and leaves and sometimes some of the bird's own feathers. The nest is always in the open and never hidden in grass, thickets, or other vegetation. The whimbrel usually lays 4 pear-shaped eggs, which are rather broad compared with their length. The eggs are brownish-green or pale brown with dark brown spots. Both parents share the sitting and, later, the tending of the young. The incubation period is 27–28 days, and the chicks leave the nest as soon as they are completely dry; they are immediately able to fend for themselves and are fully fledged at 5–6 weeks of age.

The whimbrel is completely migratory in Iceland. It has usually settled in the country between late April and mid-May, and its breeding season is from late May until mid-June, though this can be delayed by unfavourable weather conditions. From mid-July onwards the whimbrels begin to prepare themselves for their departure. The first signs of this are when they begin to fly about restlessly in small flocks. As the summer passes they gradually leave their breeding grounds, first in the north, and the flocks of whimbrels grow larger and larger and they often fly in formation. During the nights in August, especially around midnight, a distinctive departure call can be heard from flocks of whimbrels on the wing as they leave Iceland and embark on their long and dangerous journey over the open seas. A few birds linger on, especially in the south, but they have all departed by the end of September. The whimbrels from Iceland and other northern lands winter chiefly in West Africa.

The whimbrel's diet consists mostly of insects, especially beetles, and when foraging on beaches, sea snails and other invertebrates. During late summer, however, it is particularly fond of berries (crowberries, bilberries, and whortleberries) and haunts the heaths where such berries are abundant. The whimbrel cannot be called a shy bird, but it is nonetheless a wary one. It is often difficult to find its nest, for the whimbrel has usually sneaked away from it long before it can be found, and only draws attention to itself when at a safe distance from the nest. It is even more difficult to get a whimbrel to return to its nest once disturbed, even if one is a long way off and well concealed. If someone does find a nest containing eggs and young, the parent bird will sometimes try to divert the intruder by injury-feigning, trailing its outstretched tail along the ground. Whimbrels will often perch on such high points as cairns and

One bright spring day, usually early in May, the first whimbrels arrive in the bogs and moors of Iceland. They are rather silent and downcast at first, but they quickly become more lively and the sharp trill of the whimbrels begins to resound across the country's moors and valleys. For centuries Icelanders have rejoiced at the arrival of this harbinger of summer. The breeding season begins in late May and continues until mid-June. On the left is a whimbrel settling in its nest with 4 eggs. Below is a whimbrel sitting. Top right, a whimbrel is in flight, and below right is a whimbrel strolling in its nesting area.

9. MOORLAND-BIRDS

fence-posts and there give vent to their shrill calls. There are few birds which defend their nesting sites as tenaciously as they do, and if a predatory bird enters one of their breeding grounds it will be quickly and noisily attacked by a whole flock of whimbrels which will try to drive away the uninvited guest. White-tailed eagles, gyrfalcons, merlins, ravens, short-eared owls, great black-backed gulls, and arctic skuas can always expect a hostile reception from them.

The golden plover and the whimbrel are very dissimilar birds indeed, but are nonetheless the 2 species which, above all others, are the most truly characteristic of Iceland. Both birds are very common all over the country, and both play an important part in bringing life and music to the wide open spaces of the countryside. Iceland's bogs, moors, and heaths would never be the same without the harsh trill of the whimbrel and the plaintive cry of the golder plover.

The **REDSHANK** (Tringa totanus) is a rather small bird, about 28 cm in length, with a long neck and long legs. When seen in flight it is rather pale and its long legs stick out conspicuously beyond its tail. On the ground it is most easily identifiable by its bright orange legs, as can be seen above in the picture of an adult redshank foraging for food. Pictured on the right is a well-grown redshank chick. The redshank's bill is long and straight and coloured red except for its black tip. Both sexes have the same plumage.

The redshank is widespread in Iceland. It is a wader and its choice habitats are shallow ponds or lakeside and bogland mud-banks, particularly in the lowlands. The redshank feeds on various small animals, water and land insects and their larvae, water and sea snails, and earthworms. The majority of redshanks in Iceland are migratory; they begin to arrive in the country in March, and start laying their eggs in mid-May. The nest is very simple, merely a depression made in withered grass. They usually lay 4 eggs, and the incubation period is about 24 days. The chicks leave the nest as soon as they are dry, and are fully fledged when 25–30 days old. The parents take great care of them during this fledging period, teaching them how to forage for food, and giving the alarm should any danger be in the vicinity. The redshank is a very shy bird, noisy and quick in its movements. Its call is high and shrill. Some redshanks are resident and winter along the south-west coast of Iceland. The migratory redshanks winter in the British Isles.

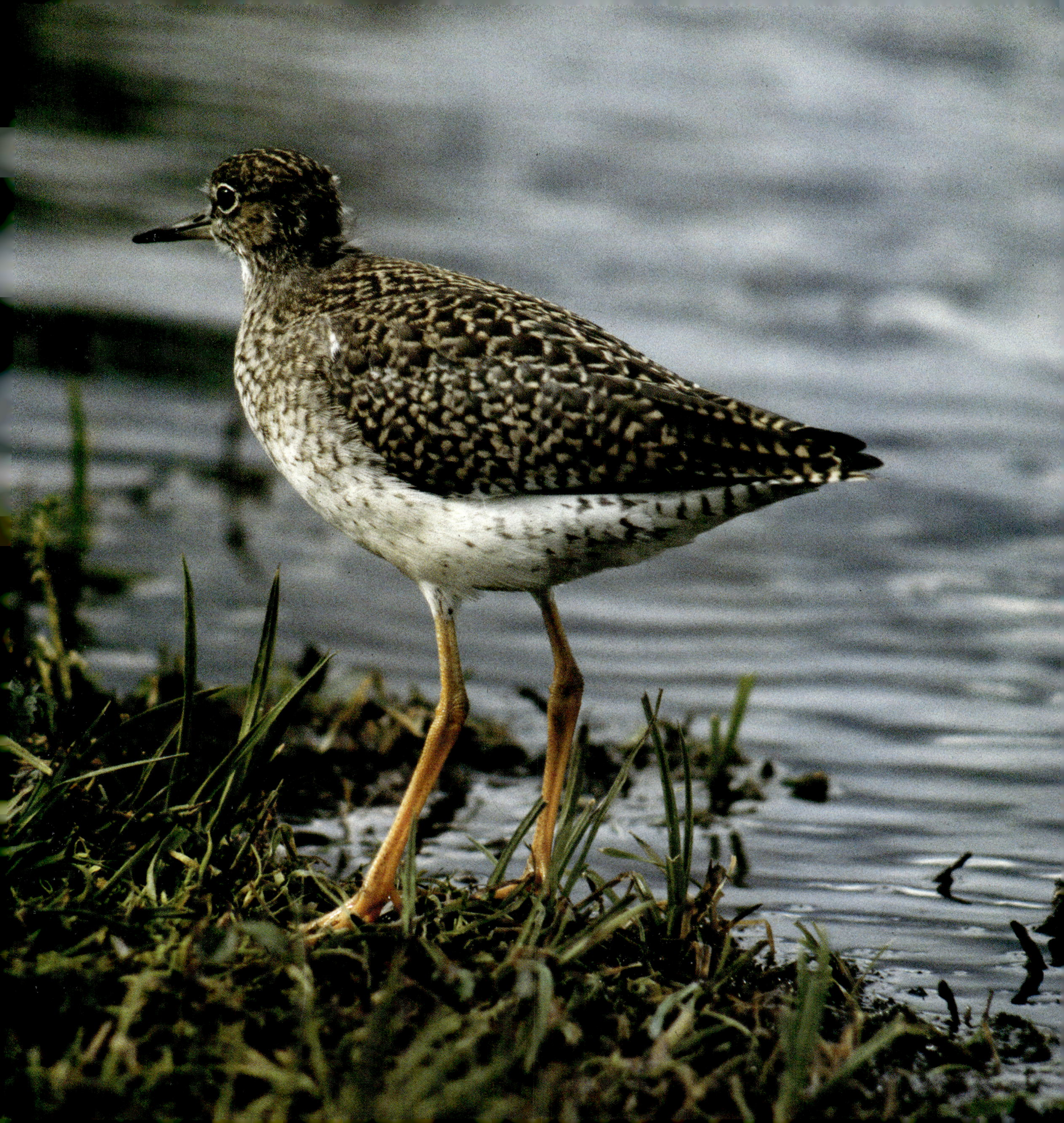

Above is a redshank looking for food in wetlands. On the right are 2 redshanks on a shallow lake. The redshank is a typical wader and loves to haunt shallow ponds and boggy fens in which it can wade and forage for food in the mud. It is very conspicuous in the lowlands all over the country as it is a lively bird and always on the move. It is also noisy and suspicious; if surprised it will dramatically shoot up into the air, screaming and fussing.

9. MOORLAND-BIRDS

The **dunlin** is a wetland and moorland-bird and a common breeder in Iceland. It feeds on worms, insects and their larvae, sand hoppers and other crustaceans. The dunlin is a migratory bird, arriving in Iceland in April or May. There are also passage-migrant dunlins which sojourn in Iceland in the spring and autumn on their way to and from their breeding grounds in Greenland. Most of these dunlins winter on the coast of Morocco.

9. MOORLAND-BIRDS

The **DUNLIN** (Calidris alpina) is a small quiet and mild bird, about 18 cm long. It is most easily recognised in the summer by the large black patch on the lower part of its breast. Otherwise it has yellowish-brown upper-parts barred with black, whilst its flanks, under-rump, and under tail-coverts are white. Its bill is quite long and black, and just a little bent at the very tip. Its legs are black. The dunlin breeds chiefly in boglands. The nest is often well hidden in a dry place in high grass, as in the picture on the left. It usually lays 4 eggs late in May or early in June. Both parents take turns in sitting, and the eggs hatch after 18–20 days. The chicks are fully fledged when about 24 days old. Above is a dunlin in its summer plumage. Below is a dunlin in its resting position, standing on one leg, in the middle of a pool. Pictured on the right is a dunlin foraging for food on the sandy shore of Lake Mývatn.

9. MOORLAND-BIRDS

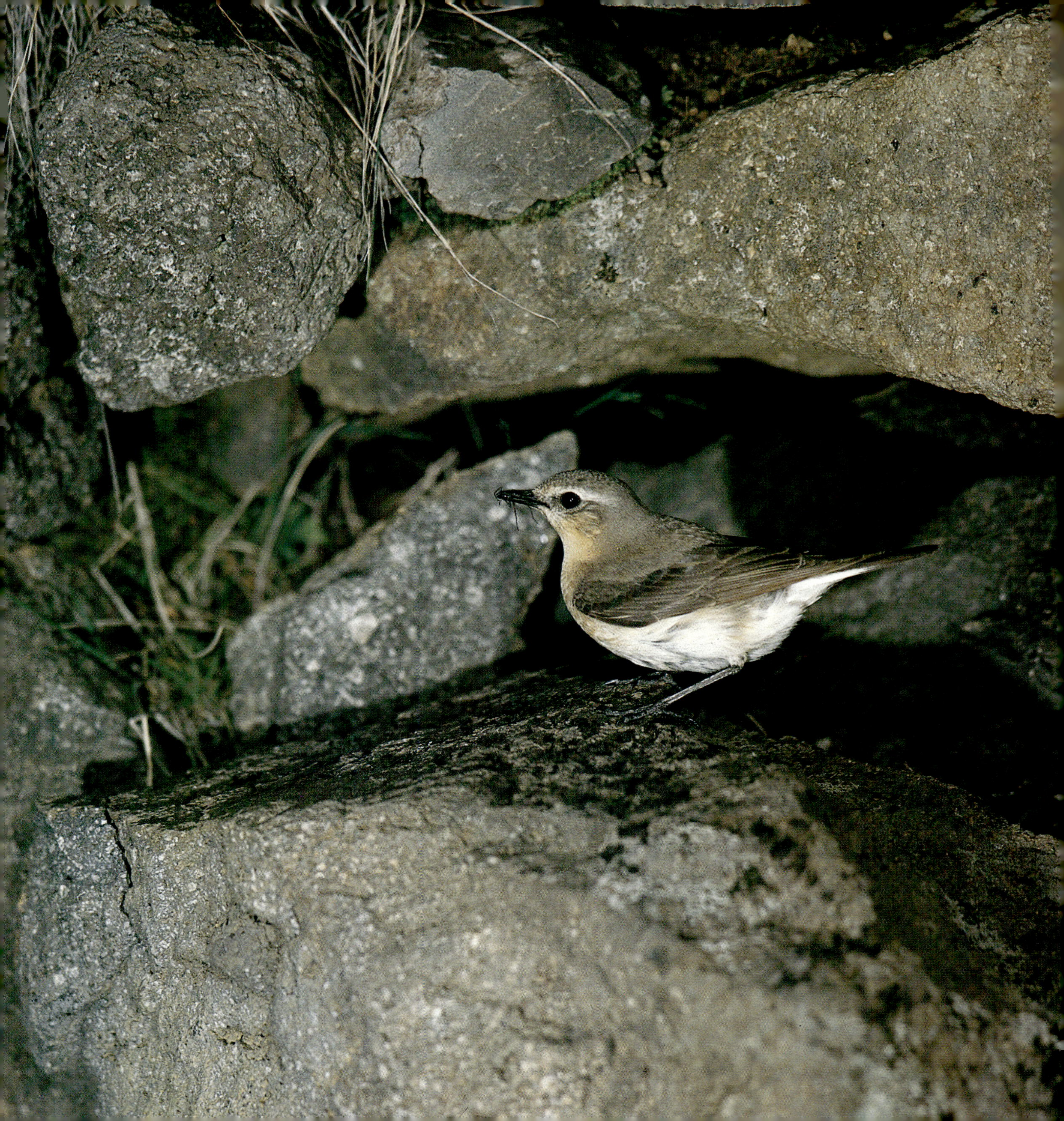

9. MOORLAND-BIRDS

The **WHEATEAR** (Oenanthe oenanthe) is a medium-sized passerine bird, about 15 cm long. The rump and sides of its tail are snow-white on both sexes. In its summer plumage the male is a beautiful bird. It is blue-grey on its head and back, and has black ear-coverts and wings, and a white supercilium, as can be seen in the picture on the right. The female is brown on its back and wings (see picture on the left). The wheatear is a lively bird which seldom keeps still for very long. It is shy and wary and likes to perch on high spots, although it always flies low over the ground. If startled it will bow down low and wag its tail rapidly and vehemently, uttering short sharp cries which sound like a stone being patted. Its choice habitat is stony and barren land where it makes its nest in holes and crevices between rocks and stones. When near human habitation it will nest in stone walls. The female pictured on the left is sitting in front of the entrance to such a nest in a wall. It has insects in its bill and is on the way to feed its young. The wheatear lays 6–8 pale blue-green eggs.

During the summer the wheatear is distributed over an area stretching from the Mediterranean to Greenland. It is astonishing how this small bird, originally a southern species, has managed to adapt to natural conditions in more northerly regions. The wheatear feeds on insects, and it is important that there is a good supply of them when its eggs are being produced and when the chicks are being reared. The young must have enough to eat to ensure they will grow quickly and become fully fledged before the northern winter arrives. In the autumn the wheatears from Iceland and Greenland have a long flight ahead of them to their winter quarters in Africa – and they make the same journey back in the spring. This long flight, part of which is over the open sea, has meant that these wheatears have developed longer wings than those in mainland Europe. The wheatears in Iceland, Greenland, Canada, and the Faroes are thus classified as a special sub-species (Oenanthe oenanthe leucorrha).

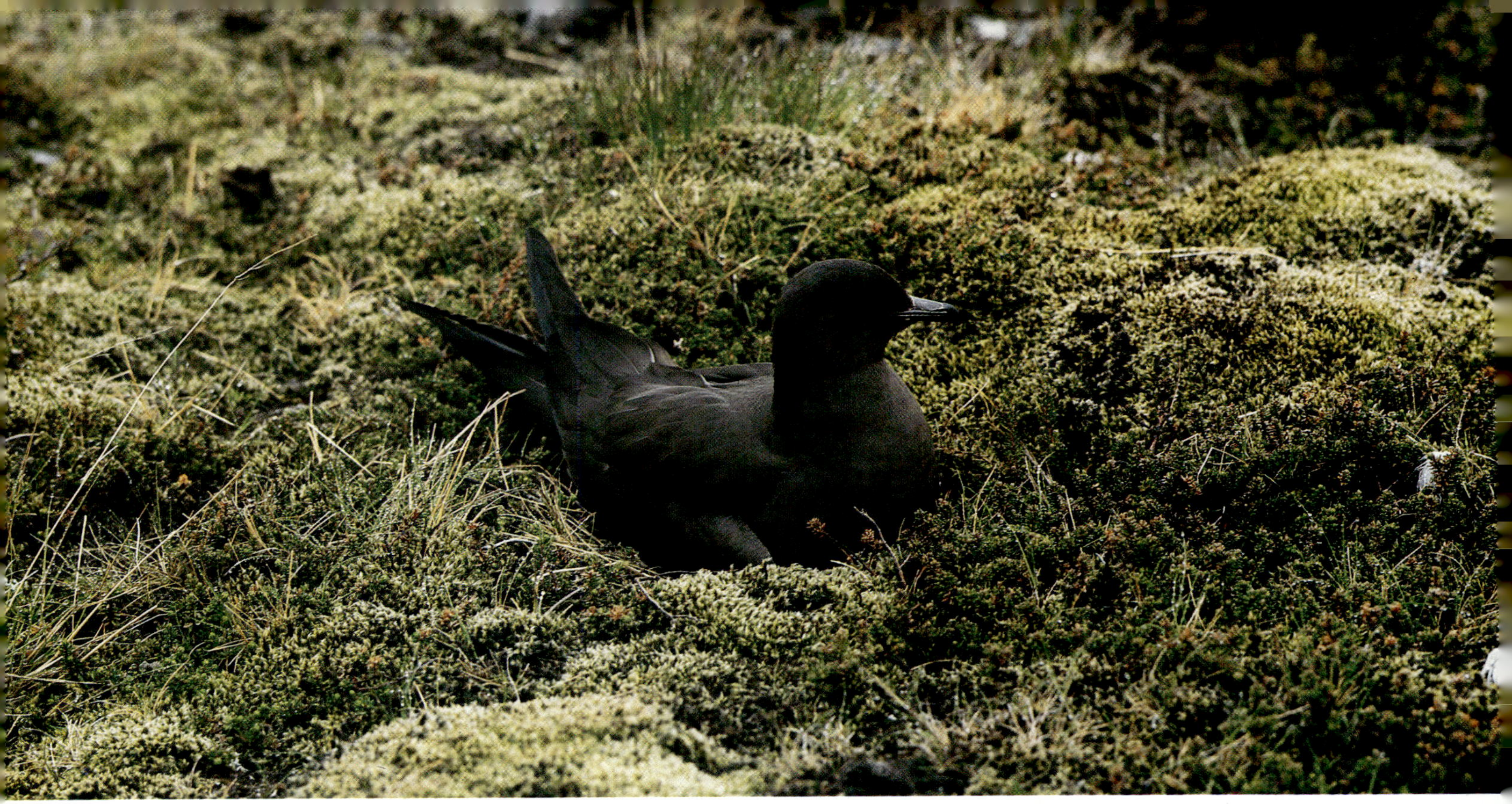

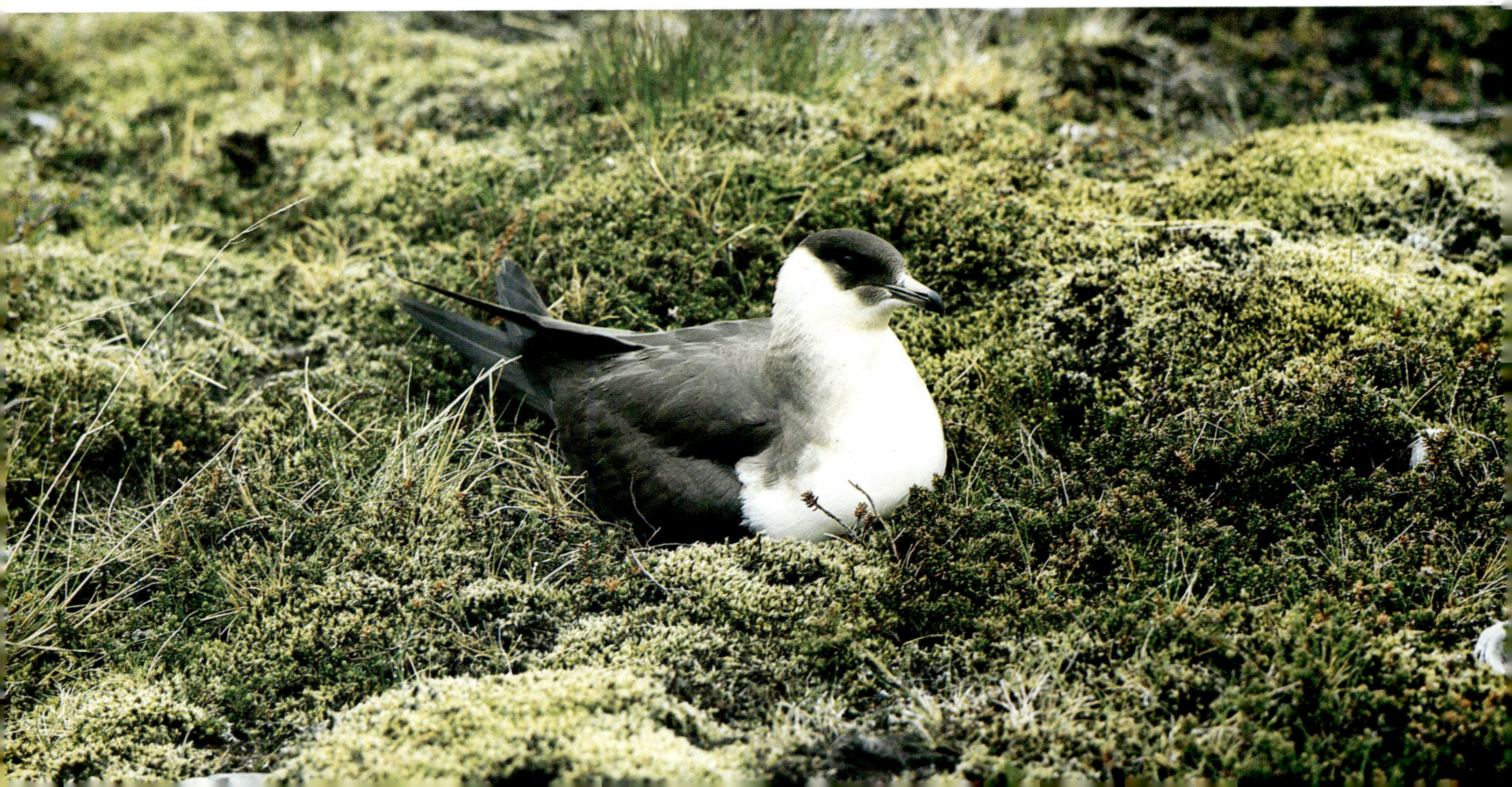

9. MOORLAND-BIRDS

The **ARCTIC SKUA** (Stercorarius parasiticus) is a medium-sized bird, similar in build to a gull. It belongs to the skua family (Stercorariidae) like the great skua (Stercorarius skua). Skuas, gulls, and terns all belong to the sub-order Lari. The arctic skua is a slender and agile bird, its main distinctive feature being its tail. The 2 central tail-feathers are much longer than the others and form a long trailing projection. Adult arctic skuas are of the same size as small gulls and weigh 350–450 g.

Arctic skuas occur in 2 forms of plumage which bear no relation to either sex or age. The **dark form** (pictured above left) is uniformly blackish-brown in its summer plumage, but with paler under-parts. It has a black cap on its head which reaches down to its eyes and nape, but which is often rather indiscernible. The **light form,** in its summer plumage (pictured bottom left), has white under-parts and a white, or yellow-white, neck-band. Its under-rump, flanks, and under tail-coverts are greyish-brown. Its upper-parts are the same as those of the dark form of arctic skua, including the black cap. In the 2 pictures on the left are a pair of birds, one of each form. The pictures were taken at the same nest. Immature arctic skuas do not attain an adult plumage until they are 3–4 years old. It is estimated that 20%–30% of all Icelandic arctic skuas are of the dark form.

The arctic skua is common all over Iceland, though especially in the lowlands and valleys. It breeds on moors, bogs, and sands, e.g. the sands on the southern coast of Iceland. Its nest is very inelaborate, simply a shallow depression, sometimes without any lining at all. It mainly lays its eggs at the end of May or beginning of June. There are nearly always 2 eggs, and they are greyish-green or brownish-green in colour with dark brown speckles, as can be seen in the picture above right. The incubation period is reckoned to be just under 4 weeks, and the young are fully fledged at 3–5 weeks of age. Both parents share the sitting, as in the pictures on the left. They also both forage for food for the young, which actually leave the nest shortly after they have hatched.

The arctic skua is a completely migratory bird in Iceland. It arrives in spring between mid-April and mid-May, usually before the arctic tern. It leaves the country relatively early, or about the same time as the arctic tern, in late August, though a few birds linger on into the first week of September. Outside the breeding season the arctic skua is an oceanic bird, and the Icelandic arctic skua is believed to winter in the southern part of the Atlantic. The arctic skua's diet is as variable as its methods of procuring it. It often robs other birds of their food by chasing them until they either drop their catch from their bills, or even disgorge what they have already eaten. In Iceland it is often arctic terns, kittiwakes, puffins, and fulmars which are subjected to such harassment. The arctic skua also steals the eggs and young of various other species, and kills smaller birds such as passerines and small waders. It also feeds on carrion and waste, such as fish offal, and is partial to spiders and insects and their larvae. It also feeds a little on plants, including crowberries and bilberries.

10 Town and farm birds

The raven at the window
Calls to those inside:
'Give me a bite, dear fellow!
My bill is open wide!'

The **RAVEN** (*Corvus corax*) has from time immemorial had a special place in the world of birds and man, and was revered in ancient religions and mythologies as being the most prudent and intelligent of all birds. There are certainly very few birds which figure so prominently in so many kinds of stories in so many cultures.

Ravens can fly great distances over a very wide area and were thus commonly reputed to learn many things and to be the bearers of news wherever they went. In the biblical account of the Flood, a raven was one of the birds released by Noah from the Ark to fly round the world and report if the waters were receding and land becoming visible once more. According to Nordic mythology, Odin had 2 ravens called Huginn and Muninn which would fly all round the world before settling on his shoulders and telling him all that they had seen and heard.

Although the raven was greatly esteemed by the Vikings, its close proximity before a battle was considered an ill-omen as it settled on the bodies of the fallen. This association with death may well ex-

Icelandic folk tales relate how ravens, at their autumn assembly, decide on which farms they will settle. These ravens were called farm-ravers, and the farm folk would often give them food, especially as 'God rewards those who favour the raven.'

plain why the raven was credited with the gift of prophecy in the Norse world. Men believed it was possible to foretell the future by interpreting the raven's various calls.

Ravens are commonly mentioned in Icelandic folklore. They are said to hold assemblies every spring and autumn. At the spring assembly they agree on how they will behave themselves during the summer, and at the autumn assembly they divide up into pairs, a male and a female, each pair claiming a particular farm as its own domain for the winter. These ravens are called farm-ravens or home-ravens.

People claim to have noticed how 2 ravens stay at every farmstead over the winter, living off the leftovers thrown out from the house. If any other ravens appear on the scene, the home-ravens will harass them until they leave.

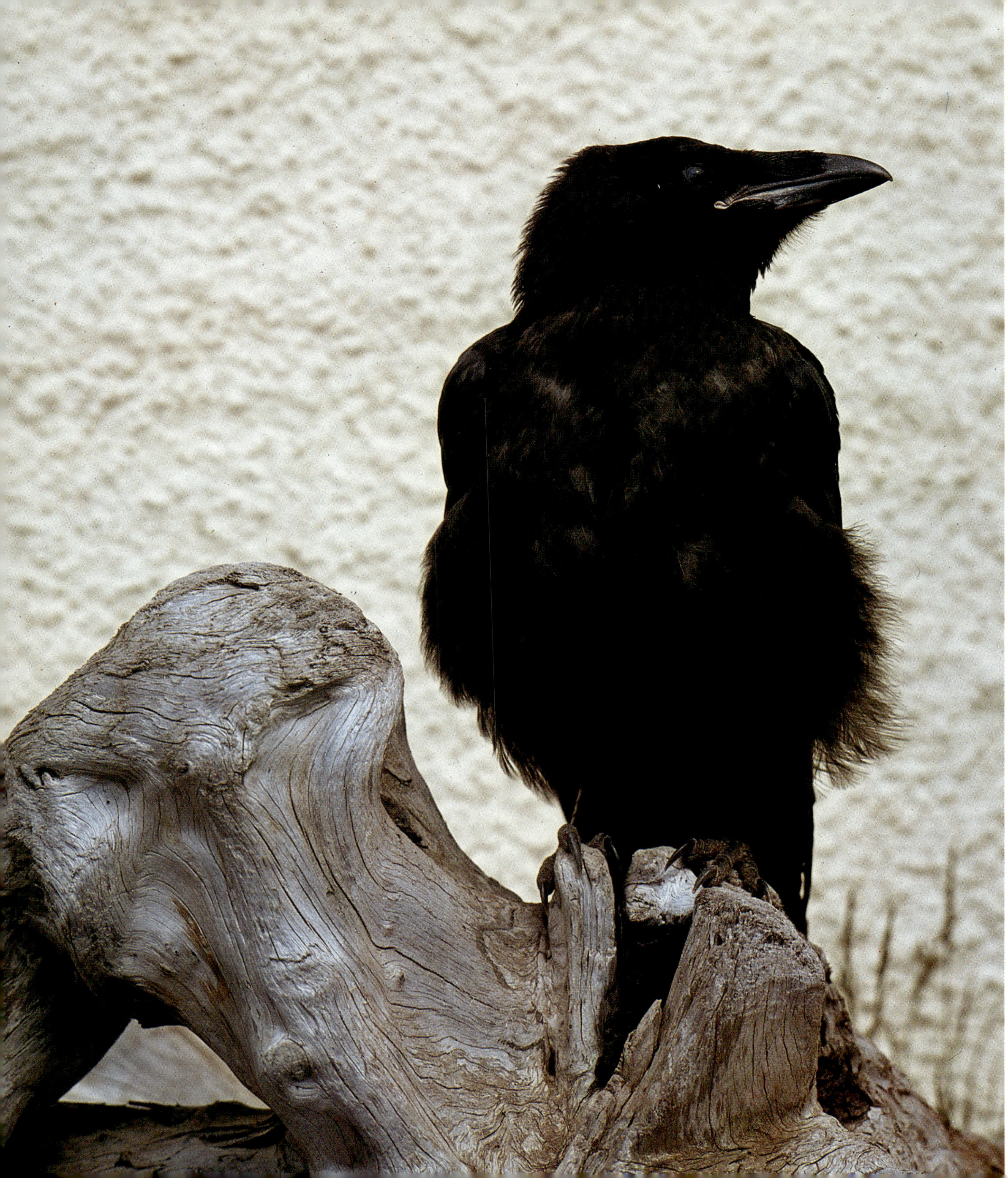

10. TOWN AND FARM BIRDS

Everyone in Iceland can recognise the raven, it is so common all over the country. It is the largest of the passerine family of birds, being 63–71 cm long. It has a large, powerful, and distinctively down-curved bill, and long wings and tail. It is a glossy black all over, iridescent in bright sunshine. It is said that the raven will eat anything it finds, dead or alive. Its stomach certainly seems able to cope with whatever it can get into its massive bill. On the left is a young home-raven, its expression clearly indicating that it is very much the king of the castle! On the right are raven chicks in a typical raven's nest, which is made out of various things including brushwood and fish-bones.

The raven is a monogamous bird, remaining faithful to its mate for life. If one of the pair should die, however, another raven will come and take its place, thus ensuring that a pair of ravens can always maintain their position on a farmstead and its neighbourhood.

Farm-ravens are said to be creatures of habit, always leaving the farm at twilight for their nocturnal roosting place, and returning at dawn the following day to check if anything edible has been thrown out overnight. It is thus considered very unnatural to see or hear a raven at night, and usually means that the bird is possessed by an evil spirit. Such ravens are called night-ravens, as indeed is the name in Icelandic for guests who arrive or leave very late!

On many farmsteads food is specifically left out for the home-ravens. There is a folk tale concerning a farmer's daughter in northern Iceland who always gave some of her meal to the home-ravens. One day the ravens refused to touch the food she put out of the window, and she was so surprised that she went outside to investigate. The ravens approached her, but still would not touch the food. They continued to behave strangely and slowly

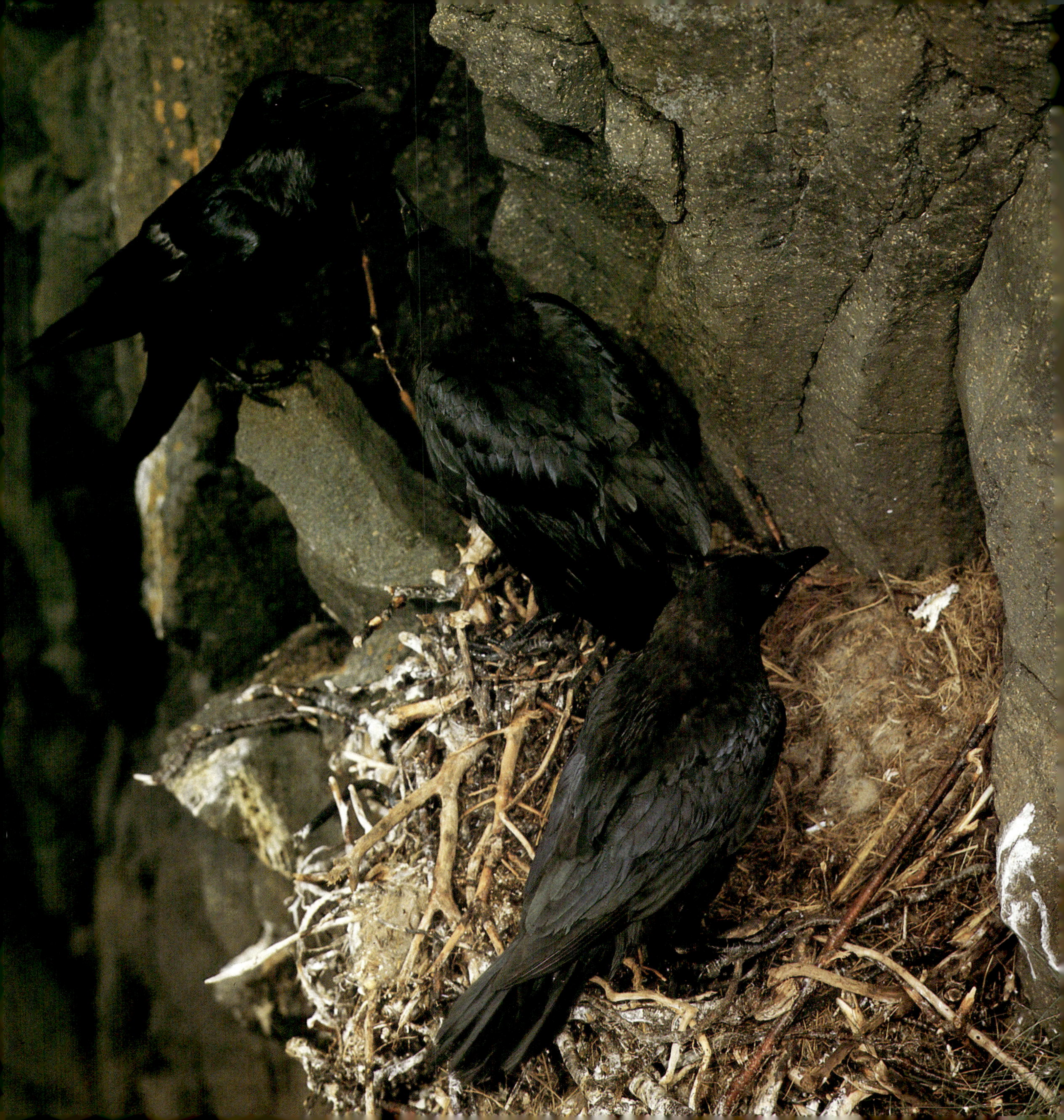

10. TOWN AND FARM BIRDS

enticed the girl out into the homefield. All of a sudden she heard a roar from the mountainside above the farm, and turning round saw a landslide crash down onto the farmhouse. Everyone inside was killed, but the girl was completely unharmed; the ravens had rewarded her for the food she had always given them.

Icelandic folk tales describe many methods of learning how to understand the raven's calls so as to gain a lot of interesting knowledge. Even without learning the raven's language, it was still possible to benefit from their intelligence and foresight through a careful interpretation of their flight, the way in which they cawed, and their general body movements and behaviour.

Thus if one has just set off on a journey and a raven flies ahead of one on the right-hand side of the road, this is said to signify a successful and happy day. If the raven flies towards one, or high in the air above one, on leaving home, however, this is said to signify that things will go badly that day and it is advisable to return home and say one's prayers instead!

If one or more ravens fly over the forecourt of a farm, or settle on the farm's midden and caw for a long time, this forbodes the death of a low-class person or an acquaintance of the onlookers. If it caws at the farm window, this foretells the death of a relative or neighbour of those who are sitting inside.

If a raven canters backwards and forwards on top of a house, or limps, changes its calls, caws into the air, bends its head and neck, shakes its wings or

On the left is an adult raven and 2 young in the nest, and on the right are the same young alone in the nest. They were fully grown and flew from the nest with their parents the day after this picture was taken.

ruffles its feathers, then men are in danger at sea or on a river.

If someone sees a flock of ravens gather and begin noisily cawing at him, this means that fish or something edible will be, or already has been, washed ashore on his land. Ravens are always jealous of anyone who has food and will ask them for something to eat. It is often said that 'God rewards those who favour the raven', especially by giving it food.

One such story is of a man who, riding on his way home from Búðir to Staðarstaður on Snæfellsnes, found a lumpsucker fish which he put into his bag. When he passed the fishing-station there were 2 ravens sitting on one of the huts, and one of them seemed to ask him for a bite to eat. The man replied that he had nothing, as he had forgotten about the fish he had found. The raven reminded him that he had something in his bag. The man duly found the fish, and gave a piece of it to the ravens. He then asked them if the men from his farm would have a good catch that day, and the ravens replied that they would catch 2 very large halibuts. The man rode on home and told his family the whole story, but they only laughed at him for his stupidity. The man remained undaunted and left for the fishing-station in the evening with 2 pack-horses to fetch the catch – and learned that his men had indeed caught 2 very large halibuts that day! Thus the existence of the folk tradition which says that God rewards those who are kind to the raven.

According to other ancient stories, blind men who give food to the ravens will get back their sight. This belief could well be related to the fact that when ravens settle on a carcass they pick out the eyes first of all before eating the viscera and other soft parts of the body.

A lot of the raven's behaviour attracts attention. There is often a glint in its eye which seems to suggest an ancient wisdom – but with a mocking sense of humour behind it. When a raven examines something, it has a comical way of nodding or cocking its head whilst hopping and waddling from side to side, movements which often bring a smile to the lips of an observer. The raven can also be a determined thief, however, if given the opportunity.

The raven sometimes seems clumsy and heavy in the air, but in fact it is a very agile flyer, especially when it is in a good mood, when it will sometimes give an extraordinary display of aerobatics, twisting and rolling in all directions. The raven's caw is not considered very attractive, but it is quite variable, and the raven can also, like the parrot, give a very good imitation of human speech.

Thus in spite of its appearance and behaviour, man has an affectionate regard for this black, droll sage of the world of birds.

On the right is a raven feeding two well-grown young in the nest; they are almost fully fledged, at which time they can weigh even more than their parents.

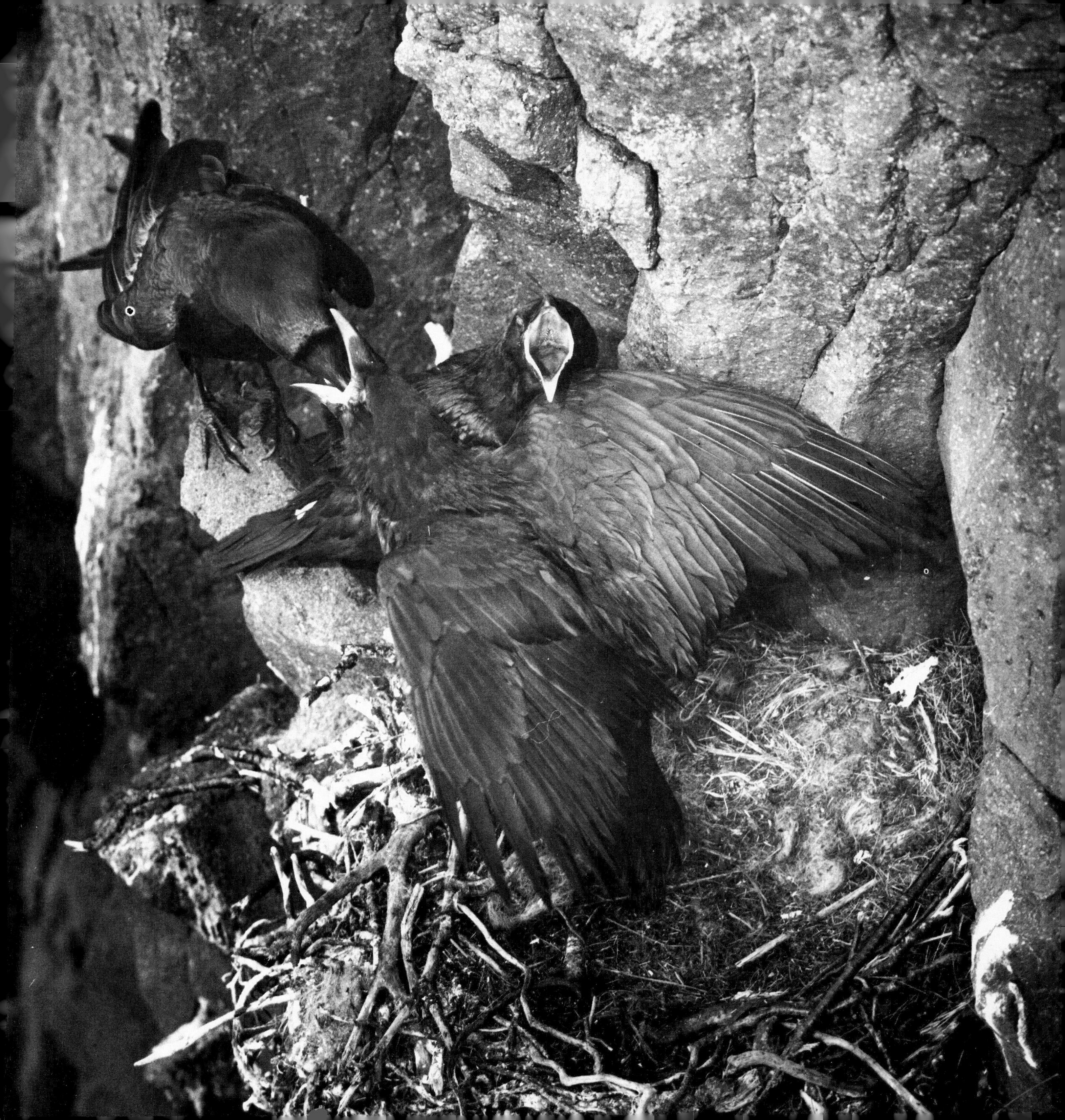

The **WHITE WAGTAIL** (*Moticilla alba*) is more attached to places of human habitation than any other Icelandic bird. Most of Iceland's farms have one or more white wagtail pairs as summer residents, and they are common in towns and villages all over the country.

The white wagtail is a small bird, about 18 cm long. It is easily recognised by its bluish-grey, black and white plumage, and its long, constantly twitching tail. It is a very meek but lively bird, constantly on the go from morning to night. It does not hop like many other passerines, but trots forwards, constantly wagging its tail and bobbing its head backwards and forwards. The white wagtail has a very distinctive undulating flight: it shoots upwards with rapid wing-beats and then pulls in its wings tightly and glides in a downward curve until it reverts to flapping its wings to ascend once more.

The white wagtail makes its nest out of grass and then lines it with hair. It lays 5–7 light grey or light blue eggs, speckled dark grey or brown, often symmetrically over the whole egg. It nests in or on houses or other buildings, and very often under bridges over rivers or streams. It will also nest in fissures in rocks near rivers, lakes, or the sea. Pictured above is a white wagtail which has found a cosy nesting site under the roof of a barn. On the right is a pair of white wagtails bringing food to their young in a nest they had made in a gap between the stones of a farm outhouse wall. The male waits outside, its bill full of insects, whilst the female feeds the chicks.

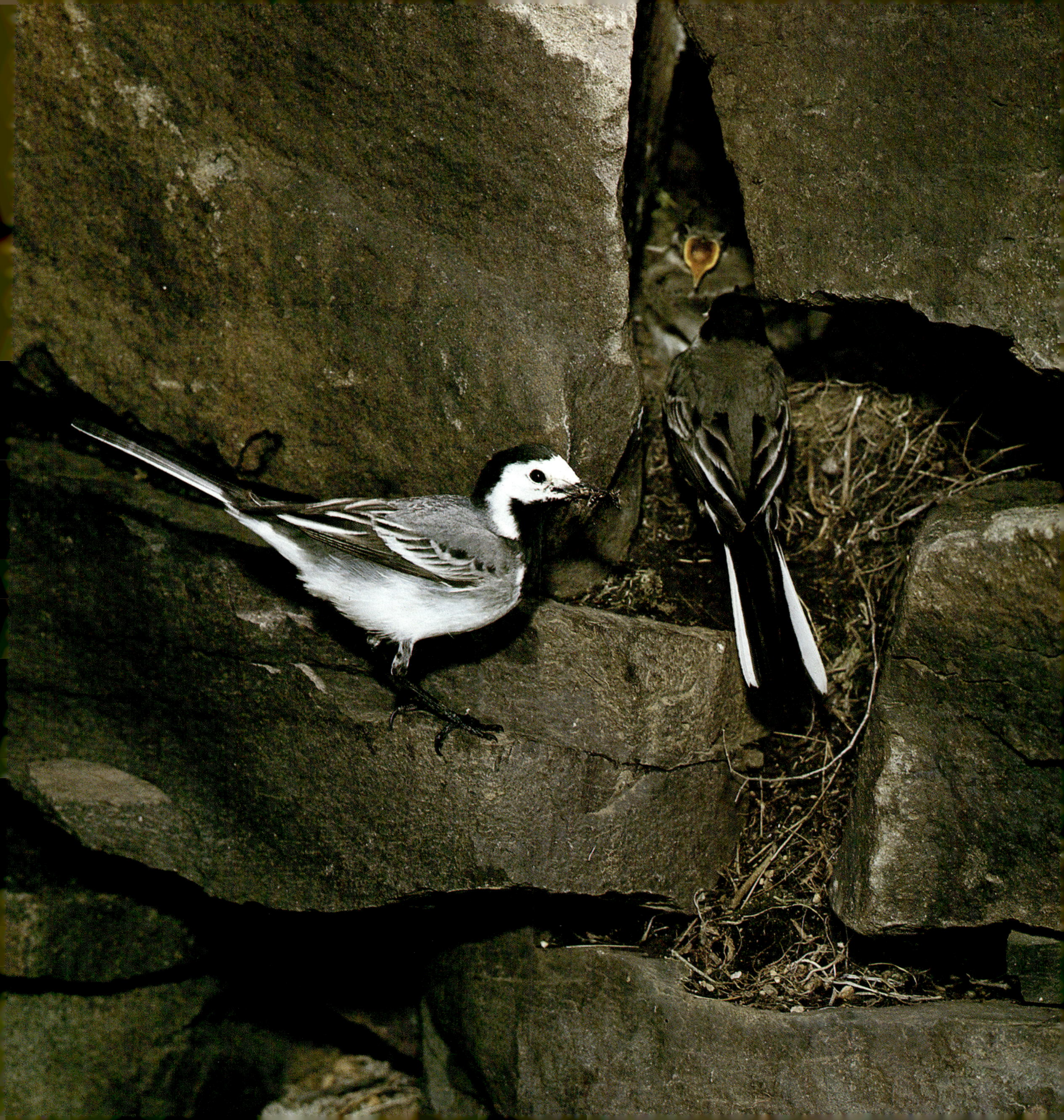

10. TOWN AND FARM BIRDS

The white wagtail is migratory in Iceland, leaving the country between late August and mid-September for its winter quarters which are chiefly on the coast of West Africa. It arrives in Iceland in the spring, in late April or early May, and immediately begins to make its nest. The picture above was taken 23 May. The white wagtail is collecting strands of hair with which to line the nest. Above left are 6 red gaping maws of white wagtail chicks. When a chick is hungry it opens its bill, and the bright red opening, bordered with orange, helps guide the parents when feeding them. When the chick has had enough, it closes its mouth. Thus the chicks which have their bills open the longest receive the most food. It is a very demanding task for the parents to provide 6 chicks with enough to eat, and both of them are constantly busy bringing insects to the nest come rain (as in this picture) or shine. It is perhaps possible to see a sign of tiredness in the female bird which, dripping wet, has just finished feeding the chicks and is about to set off again to collect more insects as all 6 mouths are still open and demanding. In the lower left picture the rain has abated and the stones of the wall, in which the nest is situated, have begun to dry. The adult bird sometimes remains a little in the nest to see if any excreta needs to be removed, but it usually flies off immediately it has filled the ever-hungry mouths with larvae and worms.

10. TOWN AND FARM BIRDS

On the right, both wagtail parents are at the nest. The female had just finished feeding the chicks with some insects which she had collected herself when the male arrived with some more. The female took the insects from him and continued to feed any chick which still had its bill open, though by then there were fewer chicks still hungry. The female waited a moment in the nest until one of the chicks excreted, which often happens after they have just been fed. The young of all passerine birds void excreta in a gelatinous sac; this helps the parents keep the nest clean. Below right, the female is leaving the nest with such a sac. Indeed it was always the female of this white wagtail pair which removed these sacs from the nest. Moreover she also seemed to bring food for the chicks more often than the male. Whilst it was raining he was nowhere to be seen, but as soon as it cleared up he re-appeared, all dry and spruce, with food for the young. He had clearly found shelter whilst it was raining! Below is a white wagtail chick foraging for food on the bank of a stream on 20 July. A young white wagtail's plumage is much duller than an adult's and there is no black on the crown.

10. TOWN AND FARM BIRDS

The **REDPOLL** (*Acanthis flammea*) is the second smallest Icelandic bird, only 13 cm long. It is a little bigger than a wren (12–13 cm long), but smaller than a meadow pipit (15 cm long). In its summer plumage it has brownish-grey upper-parts streaked with dark brown. The tips of the wing and tail-feathers are light-coloured. The crown is bright red and the chin black. On its chest and rump the male is pale red, but the female grey. The Icelandic redpoll is classified as a resident bird and belongs to a special sub-species, *Acanthis flammea islandica*.

The redpoll is a woodland and brushwood bird which feeds chiefly on various kinds of seed, including birch and rowan berry seeds, as well as insects during the summer. It makes its nest in birch and spruce trees, often in cultivated woods or in gardens in towns and villages. The nest can be at various heights, depending on the circumstances. The female builds the nest out of withered grass and lines it with wool. To get the right shape inside the nest she presses herself into the centre and then turns around a few times. The main breeding season starts in April and continues throughout May into June. The redpoll usually lays 5–6 pale bluish-green eggs; the incubation period is 11 days, and both parents share the sitting. They feed the chicks on insects, and after 2 weeks the chicks leave the nest and begin to rove about with their parents. By the time they are 4 weeks old they are self-supporting. The redpoll is a gentle, lively, and sociable bird which often flies around in small flocks.

The 2 white wagtail chicks (left) are almost fully fledged. Right: a redpoll is sitting in its nest in a spruce tree near human habitation.

10. TOWN AND FARM BIRDS

10. TOWN AND FARM BIRDS

The above picture of a starling was taken early in spring (16 March). It looks black in appearance with a bluish or bronze-green metallic sheen closely speckled with white. The bill is pale-coloured in this picture, but becomes a bright lemon-yellow during the summer. The starling is a sociable bird and is often seen in large flocks, especially at twilight before settling down for the night (picture on the left). The picture top right is also of a starling early in spring. The bill is dark during the winter, but is now beginning to turn paler and more yellow. Bottom right are a redwing and a starling feeding on titbits left out for them by a householder. The starling's bill is now summer-yellow (23 May).

10. TOWN AND FARM BIRDS

The **STARLING** (*Sturnus vulgaris*) is a recent settler in Iceland, the first nest being found in 1912. The first nest in Reykjavík was found in 1935, but there was no breeding. A nest was next found in Höfn in Hornafjörður in 1941, and the starling has bred there ever since. Breeding starlings were found at Fagurhólmsmýri in Öræfi in 1950 and 1951, and in Akureyri in 1954. The starling began to breed in Reykjavík in 1960 and its population has increased rapidly since then, there now being an estimated 3,000–4,000 resident starlings in the city and its suburbs. The starling is certainly a beautiful and industrious bird, but it has become undeservedly unpopular with residents of blocks of flats because of the inconvenience it can sometimes cause. As the starling likes to breed in or on buildings, especially in open ventilation shafts, the fleas (*Ceratophyllus gallinae*) which live in its nest can, unfortunately, get into people's homes. The fleas suck the starling's blood, and their larvae survive all winter in the nest, becoming fully grown the following spring. There is really no need, however, for this beautiful bird to cause any more trouble than any other bird. It is well known that all kinds of insects, including fleas, live on most birds, the only difference being that the starling likes to live near humans. Wire netting across open ventilation shafts could easily solve the problem and still allow people to enjoy the proximity of these tame and tuneful birds and to live in harmony with them. The starling sometimes plays the mimic, and can successfully imitate the calls and songs of other birds. – The starling is a little bit smaller than the redwing and is, in fact, distantly related to it. Some people believe that it drives away the redwing as it is a tougher and bossier bird. The fact is, however, that these 2 species appear to be able to live in close proximity to each other without any serious friction between them.

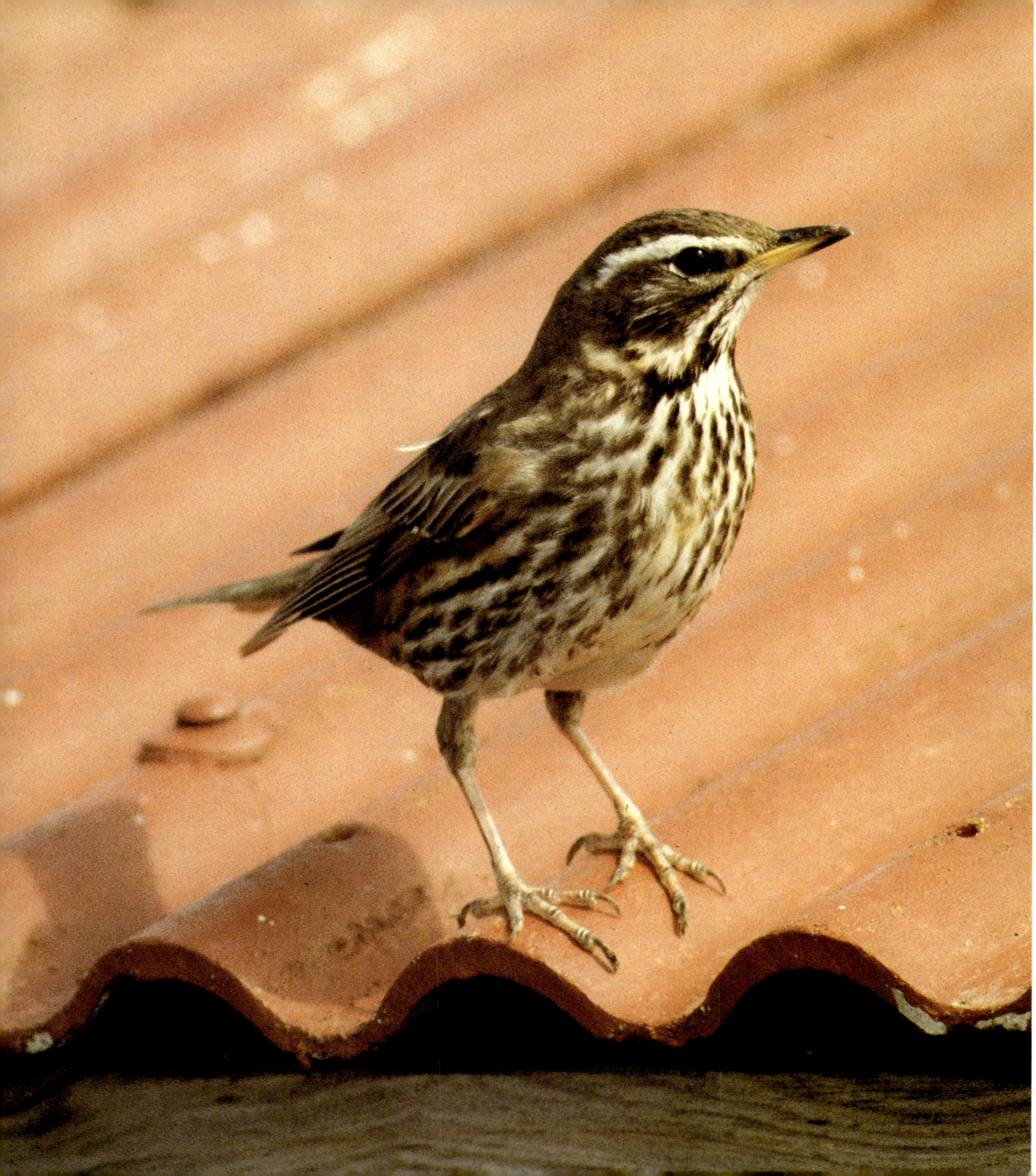
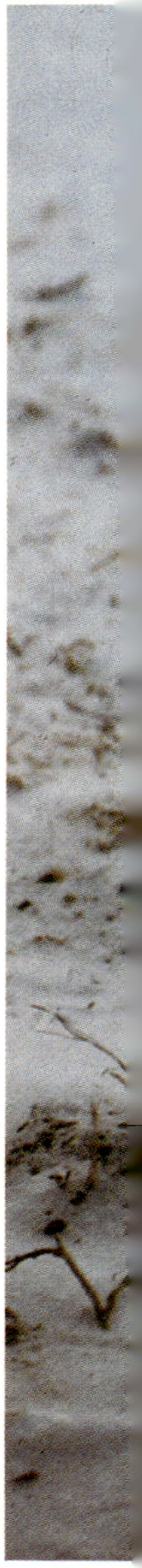

10. TOWN AND FARM BIRDS

On the left is a redwing toddling about on the roof of a farmhouse on a bright summer's day. It had made its nest in a nearby woodpile and seemed to enjoy having the farm folk as neighbours.

The picture above was also taken at a farm, but in rough snowy weather during the winter. A flock of snow buntings had arrived and the farmer's wife had put out bread crumbs for them.

The close proximity and companionship of birds gives many people a great deal of pleasure, both in summer and winter.

11 The highlands

11. THE HIGHLANDS

The **PINK-FOOTED GOOSE** *(Anser brachyrhynchus)* has pale blue-grey upper-parts, a very dark head and neck, a short bill, and pink legs. It weighs around 2.5–3 kg and is thus a bit smaller than the greylag goose (3–4 kg). The pink-footed goose breeds almost exclusively in the highlands, the greylag goose in the lowlands. The Þjórsárver is the main breeding ground of the pink-footed goose in Iceland and has one of the largest goose colonies in the world. There are an estimated 10,000 pairs of pink-footed geese breeding there, with a further approximately 2,000 breeding pairs in smaller nesting sites elsewhere in the central highlands. In addition there are around 4,000 non-breeding pink-footed geese dwelling in the highlands of Iceland in the later part of the summer, again chiefly in the Þjórsárver. Pink-footed geese also breed in eastern Greenland, and these birds sojourn in Iceland as passage migrants in the spring and autumn. The total pink-footed goose population of Greenland and Iceland in the autumn has been estimated at 90,000 birds, all of which winter in England and Scotland.

The **Þjórsárver** *is the name of a region of fertile wetlands on the south-eastern borders of the Hofsjökull glacier in the central highlands of Iceland. Most of these wetlands lie between the glacier and the River Þjórsá and are intersected by glacial tongues (see picture on the left). The Þjórsárver are partly tundra, i.e. boglands which are always frozen to a certain extent. The main breeding grounds of the pink-footed goose in Iceland are in this region. On the right is a pink-footed gander in the Þjórsárver.*

11. THE HIGHLANDS

A total of 32 species of birds have been sighted in the Þjórsárver, 22 of which breed there. For a very long time now, however, the most characteristic bird of this region has been the pink-footed goose. Right up until the late 17th century both moulting adult geese (and thus flightless) and their well-grown young were rounded up in pens and slaughtered; the remains of some of these goose-pens can still be seen today. The hunting of pink-footed geese was stopped around 1700, and indeed the goose population must have been very small by then. Above is a nest of a pink-footed goose with 3 eggs and a gosling. Above left is a pink-footed gosling foraging for food, and on the left are 2 goslings in a pool. Pictured on the right is a pair of pink-footed geese; the goose is incubating the eggs, and the gander stands by the nest. All these pictures were taken in the Þjórsárver which was declared a nature reserve in 1981 because of its beautiful tundra landscape and the magnificent pink-footed goose breeding grounds. The pink-footed goose arrives in Iceland in April or May, generally laying its eggs around 20 May. There are usually 4–5 eggs and they hatch around 20 June, the fledging period being a further 3 weeks. The number of goslings which become fully fledged is estimated to be only about 1.6 per adult pair which began breeding. This low reproductive rate is caused by internal breeding problems, such as infertility, and the activities of predators, especially arctic skuas, great black-backed gulls, and foxes. A shortage of nutritious food (e.g. horsetails and dicotyledonous plants) may also account for the death of many pink-footed goslings.

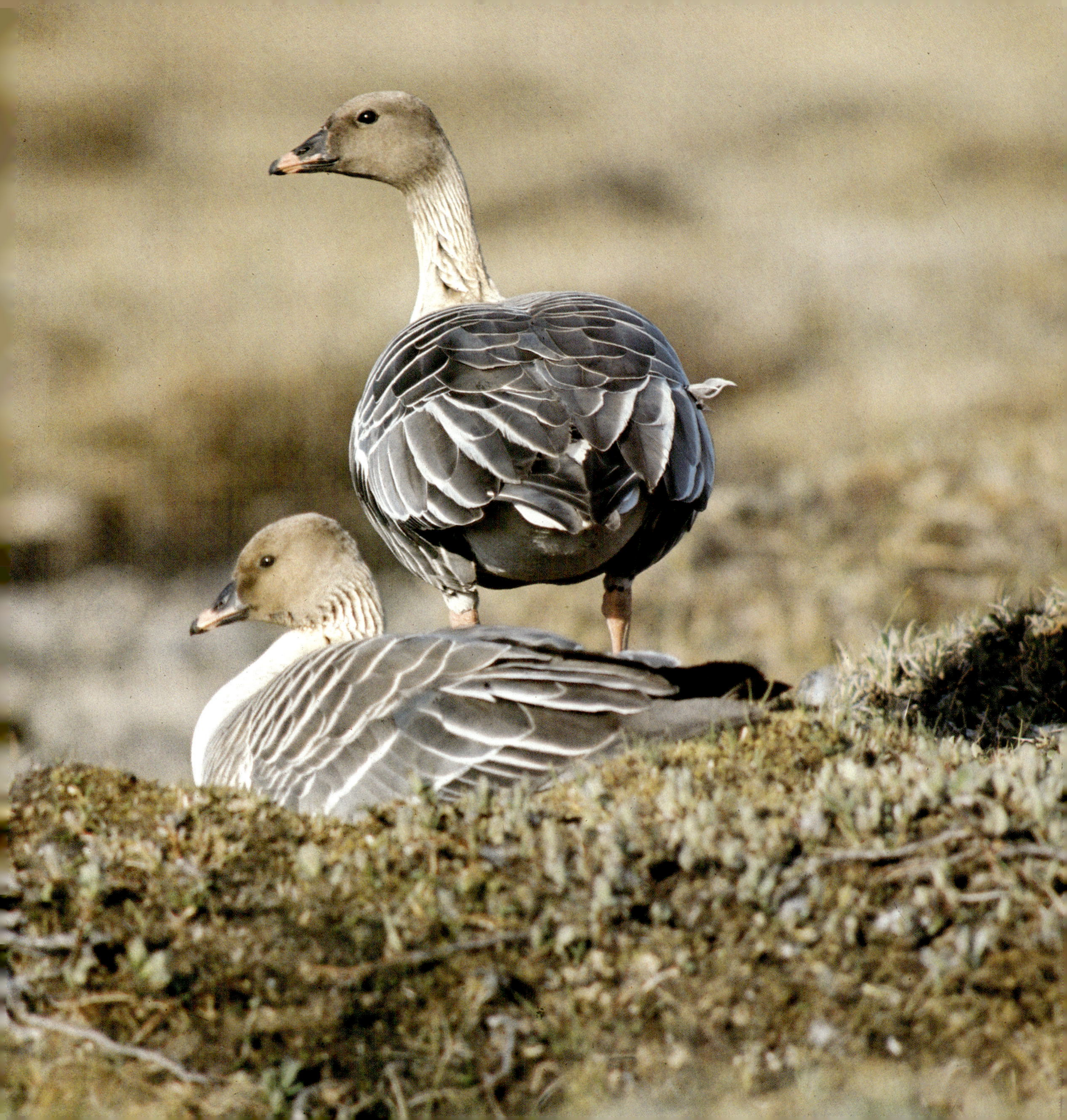

11. THE HIGHLANDS

11. THE HIGHLANDS

The **PURPLE SANDPIPER** (*Calidris maritima*) is a small stocky bird, 21 cm long, a little larger than a dunlin. In the winter it has a slate-grey head, breast, and upper-parts, and is greyish-white on its belly and speckled on its flanks. Its upper-parts are lighter in colour in the summer. The purple sandpiper is a common breeding bird in the highlands of Iceland, where it remains until its young are fully fledged. Its nest is very simple, just a shallow depression in vegetation lined with moss and straw. Little or no attempt is made to hide the nest, but it is generally sited in such surroundings that it is very difficult to see it. The breeding season is in late May or early June and there are usually 4 eggs. The incubation period is around 25 days. The young leave the nest soon after they have hatched out, and the male bird takes care of them. They become fully fledged at 3 weeks of age. At the end of July or the beginning of August, the male and the young leave the nesting area for the coast, where the female birds have already gathered some time before. During the winter the purple sandpiper is a beach and shore-bird, haunting shingle-beaches, mud-flats, and sands where it can feed on various small animals such as sand hoppers, snails, mussels, and acorn barnacles. In the mountains the purple sandpiper lives on various insects, flies, midges and their larvae. For the most part the purple sandpiper seems to be a resident in Iceland.

The picture on the left, of a purple sandpiper in its nest in the Þjórsárver near Hofsjökull glacier in the central highlands of Iceland, was taken from a hide on 24 June. There had just been a hail-storm and white spots of hail can be seen on the bird's back. Top right is the same nest after the hail-storm had passed. There are 4 eggs, as is usual with purple sandpipers. On the right are a group of purple sandpipers on the seashore, 5 May.

255

11. THE HIGHLANDS

The **SNOWY OWL** (Nyctea scandiaca) is a very large white owl, 53–66 cm long. The male is more or less completely white except for a few dark brown spots. The female is barred with dark brown.

The snowy owl is an arctic bird which breeds in the most northerly countries of the world including Greenland. It keeps to the rocky and tundra regions of the north, where it can mostly feed on lemmings. In earlier times, any snowy owl seen in Iceland was presumed to be a rare visitor from Greenland, but in 1932 the first snowy owl nest was found in the rough and difficult terrain of the Ódáðahraun in the central highlands. It was a large nest with 4 almost completely round white eggs, similar in size to a gyrfalcon's. Two large white birds were seen on the wing above the lava-field. A further snowy owl nest was found in the Ódáðahraun on 22 June 1939 and contained 3 newly hatched owlets. In the spring of 1940 another 3 snowy owl nests were found; in one of them there was just a single egg, but there were 3 and 4 respectively in the other two. A further search for snowy owl nests in 1945 ended with 3 being found. One of the nests was a large but shallow bowl in the earth, 32 cm in diameter and 5 cm deep, and contained 3 eggs. It was lined with a lot of moss and quite a few feathers, both large and small, from the owl itself. There were 5 hatched eggs in each of the other nests discovered in 1945. These nests were 44 cm in diameter and about 8.5 cm deep.

The snowy owl seems to like having a good vantage point and chooses its nesting sites accordingly; all the snowy owl nests found in the Ódáðahraun were on rocks or other parts of the lava high above the surrounding area. There was usually considerable vegetation around these points, the owls' own droppings being a contributory factor.

Although no nest was found before 1932, it is very likely that the snowy owl had already been breeding in the Ódáðahraun for quite a few years

The picture above left is of 2 stuffed owls in the Icelandic Museum of Natural History. The almost totally white bird on the left is the male; the female, barred with dark brown, is on the right. On the left is a snowy owl flying over the black and rugged lava of the Ódáðahraun on 26 June 1985. The snowy owl is especially wary of humans, and indeed very few people ever venture into its regions of the Ódáðahraun.

11. THE HIGHLANDS

before then. This would seem quite natural bearing in mind that during the spring, the owl's main breeding season, the lava terrain is difficult and rarely frequented by man. By mid-summer, however, when the lava-fields are more passable, the young have become fully fledged and all the owls have left their breeding grounds. The incubation period for snowy owls is reckoned to be 32–33 days. The female incubates whilst the male hunts for food and guards the nest. The snowy owl is a very wary bird. Its main diet in Iceland is probably various other birds, especially ptarmigans. It is also reputed to seize fish from rivers and lakes with its claws.

Breeding snowy owls were also discovered in the Ódáðahraun in 1957 and around 1974, but no nesting site has been found since then. Snowy owls have been seen in flight every year, but these birds could be vagrants from Greenland. In June 1985 an expedition was made into the Ódáðahraun to ascertain if the snowy owl was breeding there once more. A search was made of the area the bird is known to frequent, and old snowy owl nests were examined, some of which had snowy owl feathers around them. No breeding birds were found, however, although one snowy owl was sighted in the area.

Above right is a snowy owl, probably a male, perching on a crest of lava in the Ódáðahraun, 26 June 1985. It always perched on a good vantage point as it seemed very curious about the expedition and kept a close watch on all its movements. If approached, however, it immediately flew to a high point further away. Below right is a probably old snowy owl nest high up on a mound of lava in the Ódáðahraun. There were some snowy owl feathers by the nest, which was 35 cm in diameter and 7 cm deep. There are still a few such nests in the Ódáðahraun, but no breeding birds were found in the area during the 1985 expedition.

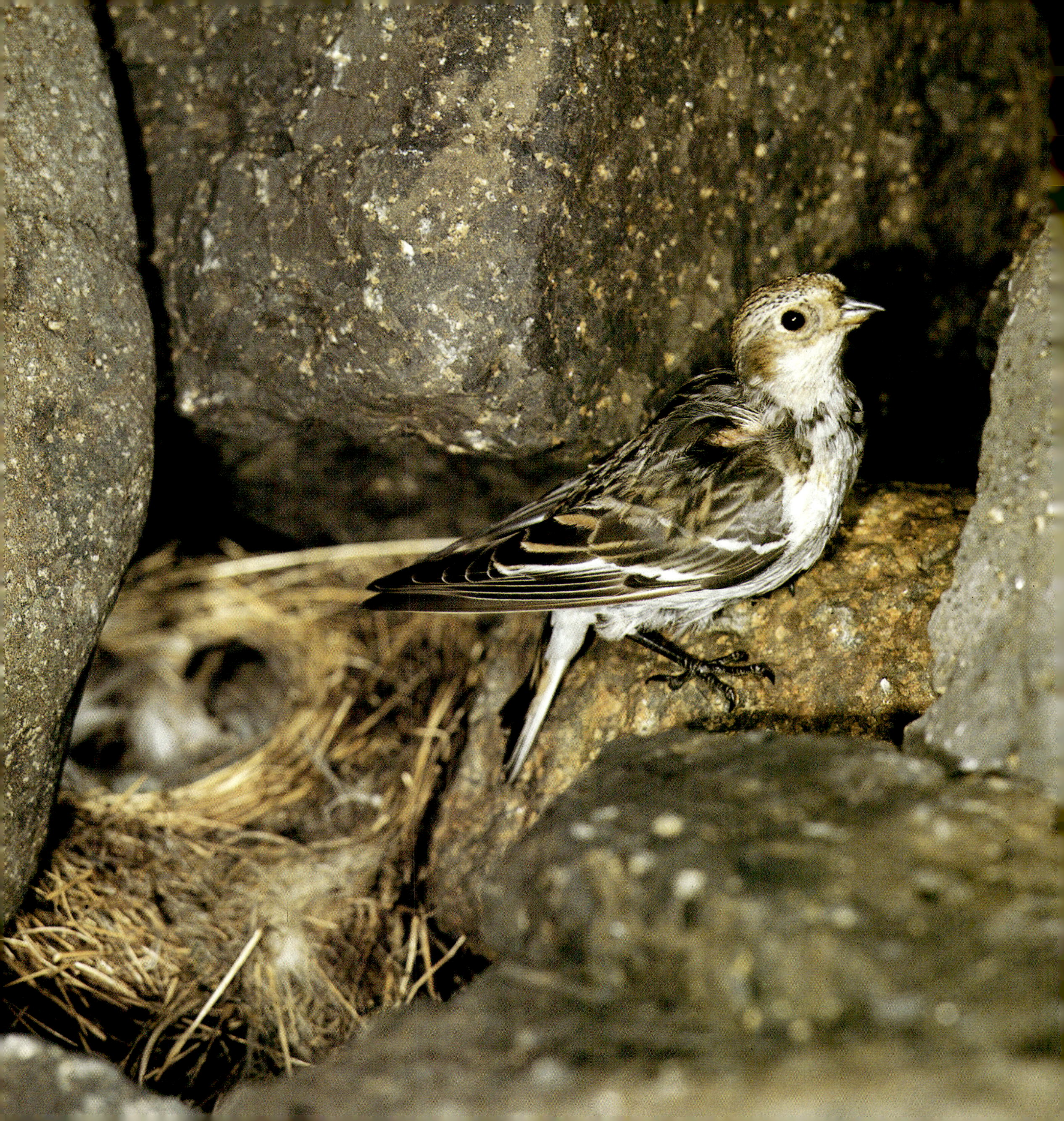

II. THE HIGHLANDS

The **SNOW BUNTING** (Plectrophenax nivalis) is slightly larger than a wheatear, being about 17 cm long. During the summer the male has a black back, primaries, and central tail-feathers, but is otherwise snow-white; indeed it appears to be completely white when seen on the wing from below. The female, on the other hand, is greyish-brown with dark streaks on its head and back. In its winter plumage the male snow bunting is pale brown on its crown, breast, and cheeks, and has whitish-yellow front and under-parts and a brown back. The female's winter plumage is similar except for rusty-yellow under-parts.

The snow bunting is an arctic bird and breeds in all the northernmost countries of the world. It lives a great deal on insects during the summer, but otherwise feeds on seeds. Icelandic snow buntings are generally considered residents, but some of them probably migrate to more southerly countries. On the other hand, there are snow buntings from more northerly countries which winter in Iceland or stop-over here in the spring and autumn. Snow buntings mostly breed on stony ground in the mountains or by the sea. The nest is woven out of straw and lined with thin plant stems, wool, and feathers. There are usually 5–6 eggs and the female does the sitting, the incubation period being just under 2 weeks. Once the chicks have hatched they remain in the nest for just under a fortnight. The parents feed them chiefly on insects.

Late in the summer the snow buntings begin to gather in flocks and to move to the lowlands and the coast in search of food. The snow bunting is a lively bird, constantly trotting and hopping about in between short bursts of flight. It is a hardy bird which can tolerate frosty weather much better than most other birds, provided it has sufficient food.

On the left is a snow bunting (female) leaving its nest. Above is a female sitting in the nest. Below is a snow bunting with its bill full of insects on the way into its nest to feed its young. Snow buntings feed their nestlings on insects for the first 10–12 days.

Snow buntings.
Above left is a male arriving with insects for the chicks. The nest is completely hidden in the rocks and the entrance is under the flat stone on which the male is standing. Below left, the female has come out to take the insects which the male has brought. She will then re-enter the nest to feed the young whilst the male sets off in search of more insects.

The above picture of a female snow bunting was taken on 5 June. Below left is a male (22 June), and below right is a female feeding on the shore, 5 May. All these birds are in their spring and summer plumage.

261

12 Lava-fields and woodlands

The **PTARMIGAN** (Lagopus mutus) is the only gallinaceous species (Galliformes) which lives in the wild in Iceland. Many other species of gallinaceous birds are, of course, domestic, e.g. the hen.

The ptarmigan is a common resident in the northern parts of the world and belongs to the grouse family, *Tetraonidae*. The Icelandic ptarmigan has all the main features of a gallinaceous bird. It is fairly large, stocky, and ungainly, and weighs, on average, about 500 g. It has a very muscular body, a short neck, and a small head. Its wings are short and stubby, and its legs, though short and feathered, are powerful.

During the winter both sexes are almost entirely white, as can be seen in the picture on the right of a ptarmigan pair in their winter plumage on 2 May. In the summer, however, the ptarmigan is brown, its change in plumage being an effective camouflage against predators, especially as it coincides with the change of season. In the winter, when there is snow on the ground, the ptarmigan is white, and in the summer, when the earth is bare, the ptarmigan is brown. It thus has a protective coat all year round. It must be borne in mind, however, that the cock remains white until late in spring, for although the summer plumage of both sexes begins to grow at the end of April, only the female attains its new plumage by the end of May, when it starts to incubate the eggs. The cock does not attain its full summer plumage until late in June. This period, late April until mid-June, is a time of maximum danger for the cocks, for this is when they are busy courting females and claiming and defending nesting sites. To do so they must openly flaunt and disport themselves, and with their snow-white plumage they become very conspicuous against the bare dark background and are easy prey for predators. Indeed to a very great extent the Icelandic gyrfalcon lives on ptarmigan at this time of year, and it has been estimated that up to one third of all ptarmigan cocks which have claimed a nesting site become their victims. This high mortality rate among cocks is not believed to have any serious effect on the overall ptarmigan population, however, as it is the female which incubates the eggs and rears the young and other young cocks soon move into the nesting areas of fallen predecessors. The ptarmigan is one of the few land-birds which does not leave Iceland in the autumn, but remains to defy the winter weather conditions, even though it is almost exclusively plant-eating all the year round.

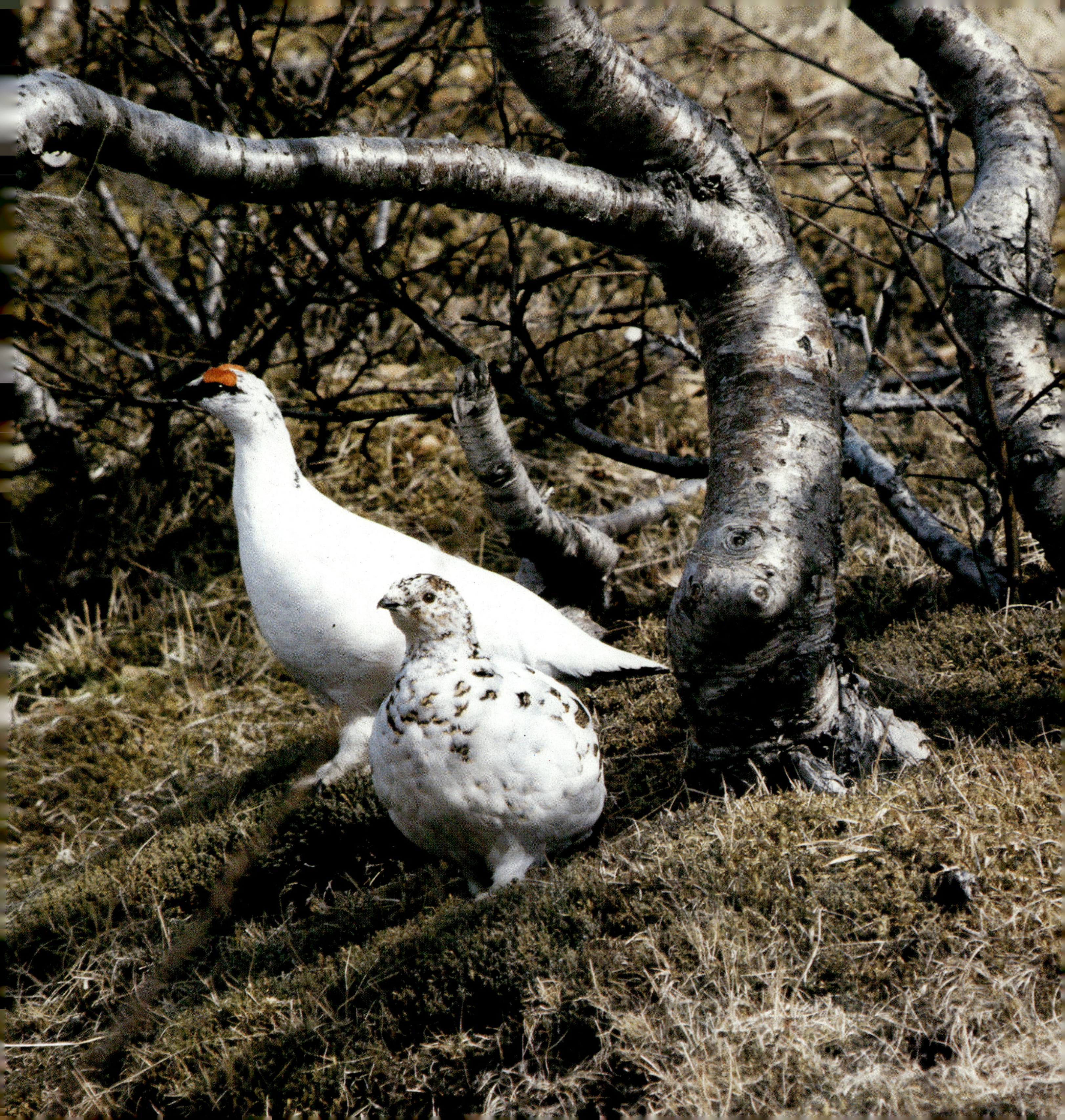

12. LAVA-FIELDS AND WOODLANDS

The **ptarmigan** above left is incubating its eggs in a birchwood copse, 27 June. The bird is well hidden in such surroundings, and remains motionless even when an intruder reaches the nest. The ptarmigan chick pictured below left is also well hidden and can hardly be seen as it crouches perfectly still. On the right is a ptarmigan cock in its summer plumage on Skaftafellsheiði Moor, 16 June, and on p. 266 (overleaf) is a female in its summer plumage in the Vestfirðir. The ptarmigan is a harmless and peaceful bird, but it is greatly sought after by carnivores – including man. Ptarmigan hunting was formerly a professional occupation and in the late 1920s about 250,000 birds were exported annually. According to present legislation, however, the hunting of ptarmigan is only permitted between 15 October and 22 December and is now more of an amateur sport than a means of making a living. The Icelandic ptarmigan's breeding grounds are almost exclusively in copses, woodland scrub, and heather. In the mountains it rarely occurs higher than the vegetation line. The ptarmigan is the only Icelandic bird which lives all year round almost entirely on plant food. Young ptarmigan chicks feed to a certain extent on insects, but the adult birds feed almost exclusively on foliage, flowers, and berries during the summer, and on buds and stalks in the winter. The ptarmigan usually lays its eggs between the end of May and the first week of June. There are usually 10–11 eggs and the incubation period takes around 3 weeks. The chicks thus hatch late in June and become fully fledged after 10 days, although they are not fully grown until they are about 10 weeks old. To grow so quickly they need energy-rich food, especially insects and knotgrass. The chicks begin to try and fend for themselves as soon as possible, and the female assiduously defends them from the weather and predators. When they are about 4 weeks old the young are independent of their mother and, together with adult female birds, they gather in flocks in areas where there is plenty to eat. As the summer wanes the adult birds leave for higher ground. The young birds follow later, and by the beginning of October the majority of ptarmigans have arrived at their winter feeding grounds. In the mountains the ptarmigans often find shelter against the weather by burying themselves in the snow. Shortage of grazing and hunger can temporarily drive the ptarmigan down to the heaths and copses of the lowlands.

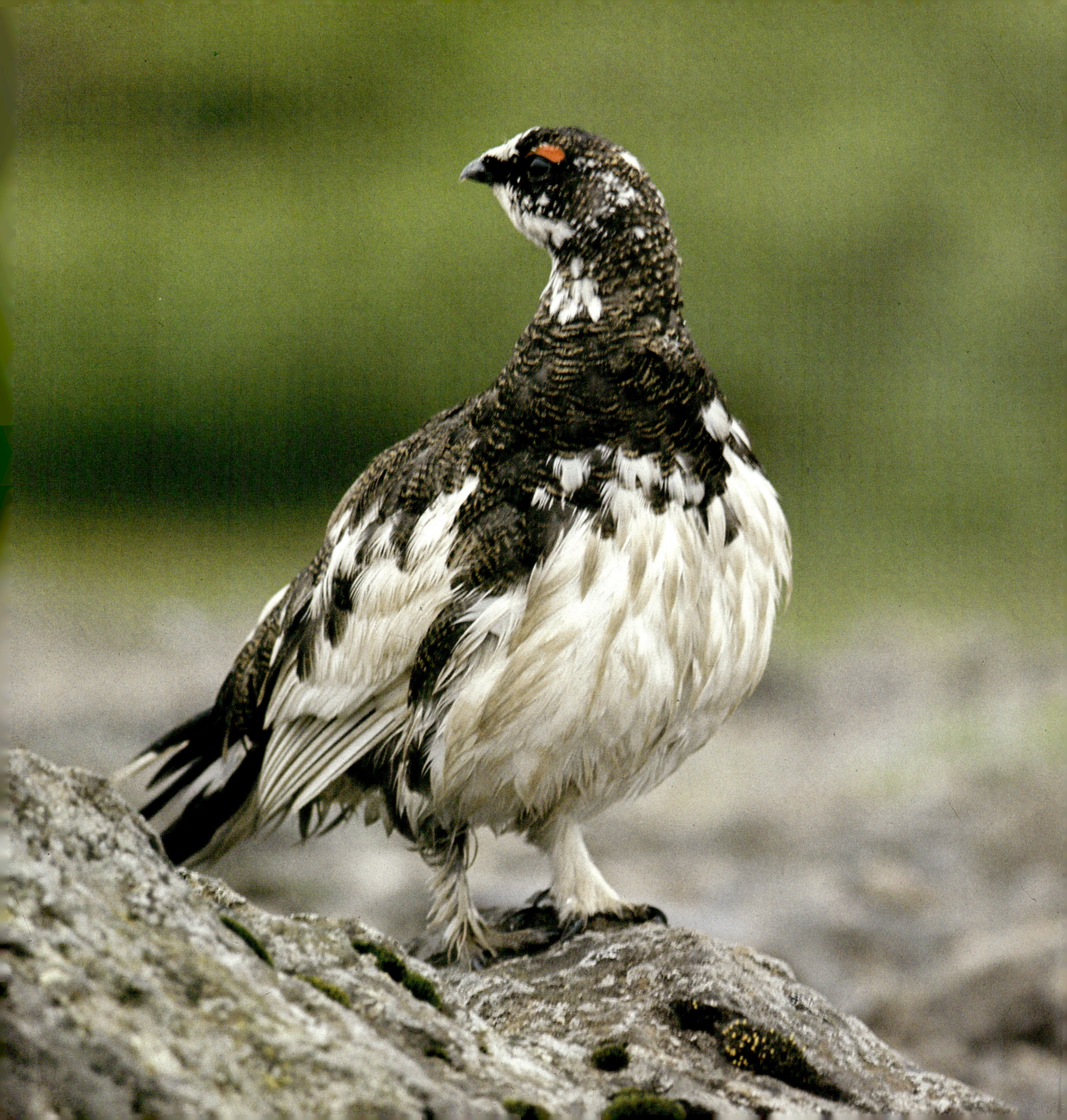

12. LAVA-FIELDS AND WOODLANDS

The **SNIPE** (*Gallinago gallinago*) is very common in the lowlands all year round, but rarely occurs in the mountains. Its choice habitats are bogs and fens, but in Iceland it is also frequently found on dry land and in copses and woodland. It is a migratory bird, arriving in Iceland early in the spring (April) and remaining in the country until late in the autumn. In the south and south-west it is not unusual to find individual snipes which stay throughout the winter, keeping close to brooks and springs which remain unfrozen. An occasional snipe may also be found on the shore, but Icelandic snipes otherwise migrate to Ireland, where there are extensive boglands and the winters are mild.

The snipe feeds chiefly on various invertebrates, foraging for worms, insects, and snails in mudbanks by pools and ponds, or in drains and ditches. Its bill is very long and straight and its tip is soft and sensitive. The snipe forages for food by stabbing its bill into the mud and then jerking it around, immediately sucking up anything alive with which it comes into contact. The snipe is very active at night, but during the day it tends to hide in thick vegetation in order to rest or sleep. If approached by man, it will crouch down and remain motionless until the intruder is almost upon it, when it will suddenly take to the air, uttering hoarse rasping calls. It then usually flies away, keeping very low and with a fast zig-zag flight path. It soon drops to earth again and immediately disappears into thick vegetation.

This is not the snipe's only flight pattern, however. In the spring and during the breeding season, and even late in the summer, snipes will often indulge in aerobatic display-flights high in the air, producing the characteristic drumming sound for which they are renowned. This phenomenon is discussed in more detail on p. 269.

The snipe is particularly fond of bogs and fens. Above is a snipe bathing in a small pool near Lake Mývatn on 26 May. On the right is a snipe nest with 4 eggs in a birch copse near Lake Mývatn on 23 June. In April, soon after the snipe arrives in Iceland from its winter quarters in Ireland, it begins to prepare for breeding. It is a very noisy bird during this period, but once the eggs begin to be laid it generally quietens down. It breeds widely in woodland scrub and in the shelter of birch trees. The snipe is by nature a very shy bird and its nest is always well hidden, as in the picture on p. 268. There are usually 4 eggs and only the female sits, the incubation period being around 3 weeks. The chicks leave the nest as soon as they are completely dry. They are very good at hiding themselves, and the female always tries to entice any uninvited guests away from them. The parents feed the chicks for the first 1–2 weeks and they become fully fledged when about a month old.

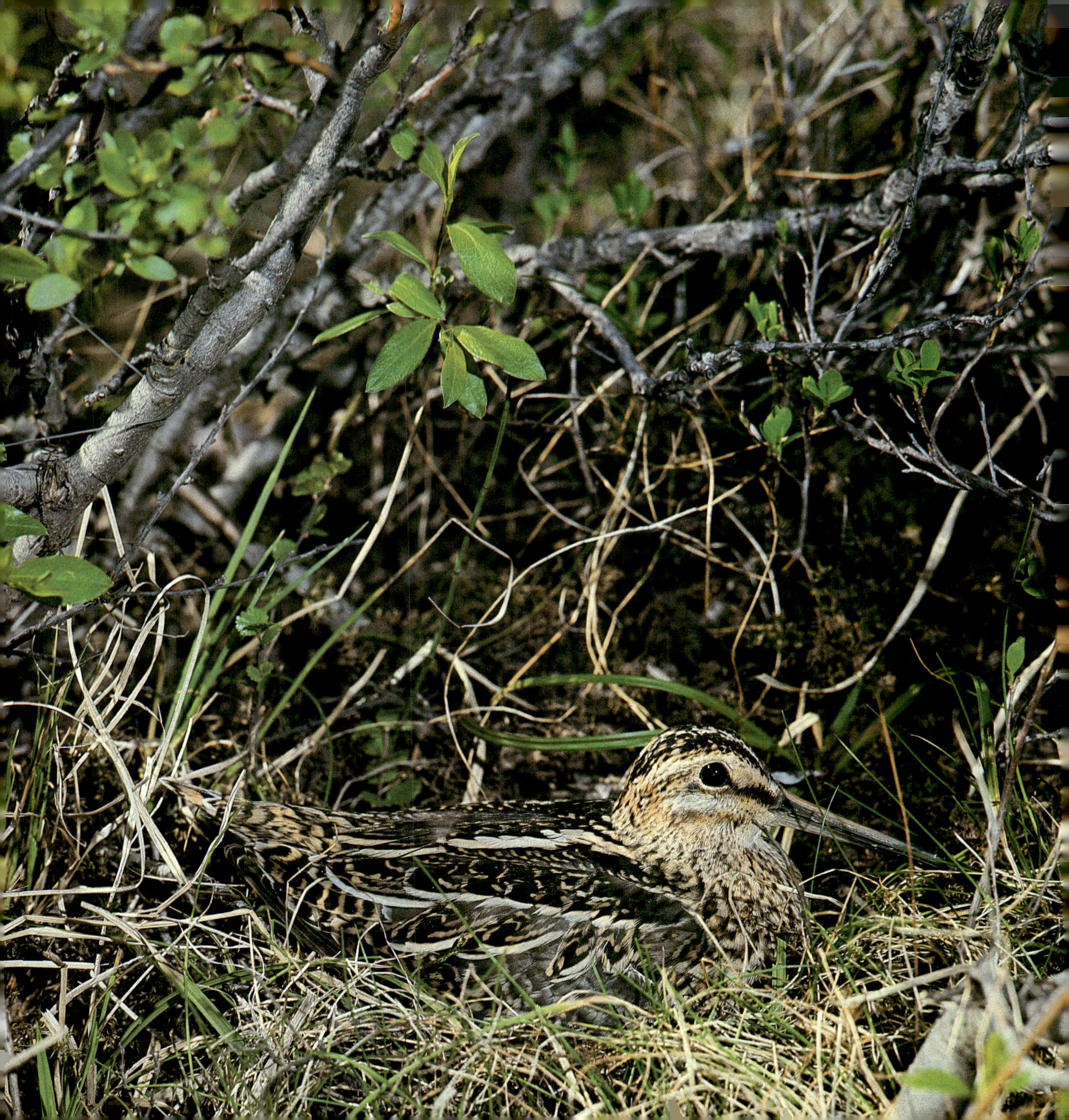

How does the snipe drum?

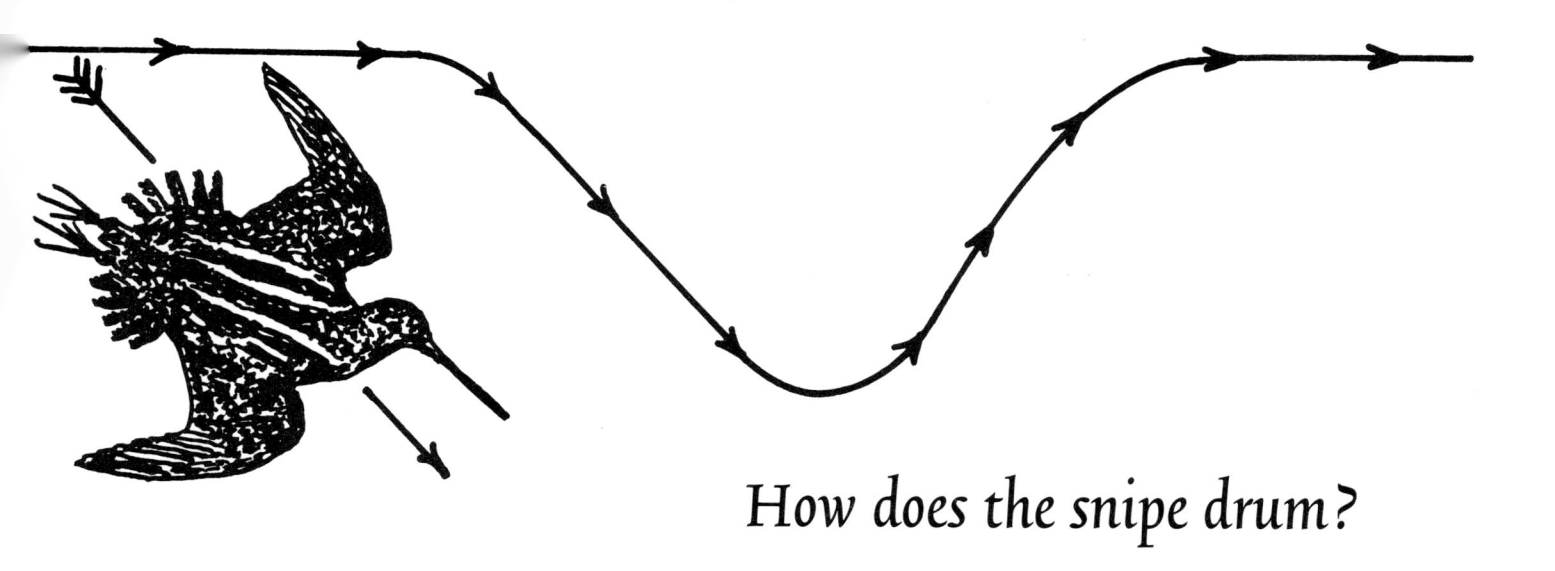

The **drumming of the snipe** has for centuries roused the curiosity of both learned and laymen, and there were many different explanations as to how this sound was produced.

Originally no one actually associated the drumming sound with the snipe, or indeed any species of bird at all. It was believed to be the call of supernatural creatures and many folk tales were written about them and naughty children often threatened with them. Nature lovers soon realised, however, that the sound came from the snipe, although it was first assumed to be the bird's call and to originate in its voice-box. In 1804 a German farmer and ornithologist, Naumann, put forward the theory that the snipe produced this sound with its wings. This was much disputed, but in 1855 the German Altum produced convincing evidence for his own theory that it was the **vibration of the tail-feathers** which caused the drumming sound, and not the bird's flight-feathers. Later experiments, e.g. by the Swede Meves in 1856, proved that this theory was indeed correct.

A description of how the snipe produces this drumming sound is as follows: During the breeding season the snipe can be seen in display-flights, flying, with fast and rhythmic wing-beats, in a circle up to half a kilometre in diameter, and usually at a height of 50–100 m. This horizontal flight is disrupted, with increasing frequency, by an oblique dive at 45°, the bird usually falling 10 to 15 m and for no longer than 2 seconds. It then sharply ascends to its former height with rapid wing-beats. The flight path of the snipe and the position it adopts as soon as it begins to dive are illustrated in the drawing above. The tail is stretched out so that its rear edge almost forms a semi-circle, and its outermost tail-feathers are so extended that they face directly into the back edges of the wings. Instead of its former rhythmic flight, the snipe now uses rapid and abrupt wing-beats. Experiments in a wind-tunnel with a model snipe in the drumming position have revealed that the sound originates in the outermost tail-feathers. If the wings are motionless, a single uninterrupted tone is produced, but if the wings are beaten rapidly, the currents of air flowing onto the outermost tail-feathers are constantly interrupted, thus causing them to vibrate and produce the distinctive and well-known drumming sound. In other words, the outermost tail-feathers are a musical instrument upon which the snipe can play its wings.

This is not a unique phenomenon in the animal world, and there are many equivalents of the snipe's ability to drum. The buzzing sound of various flies and the noises made by grasshoppers and other insects are similar examples. Various other species of birds can also produce special and characteristic sounds with their flight-feathers.

12. LAVA-FIELDS AND WOODLANDS

12. LAVA-FIELDS AND WOODLANDS

The **WREN** (*Troglodytes troglodytes*) is the smallest of all Icelandic birds. It belongs to the *Troglodytidae* family, is resident in Iceland, and classified as a special sub-species (*Troglodytes troglodytes islandicus*) as it is larger, darker, and more streaked than the wrens of neighbouring countries. Icelandic wrens are 12–13 cm long, whereas other wrens are 10.5–11.5 cm long. Its small size, stocky build, and erect tail when perching – which it rarely does for long – all easily distinguish it from other birds. Because of its size, colour, and behaviour, folk tradition has more often associated it with mice than with other birds, and in earlier times it was sometimes referred to in Icelandic as 'the mouse's brother.' Its behaviour does in many ways resemble that of a mammal rather than a fledged bird. It feeds almost exclusively on flies and small insects, which it finds on the ground, in vegetation, or in holes and crevices. It also eats worms and the pupae of insects. It is very quick in all its movements and flies short distances at a time with rapid wing-beats. If alarmed it will quickly disappear into a hole, crack, thick undergrowth, or earth-bank, or else under tree roots or any other convenient hiding place. In Iceland it can usually be found in woodland scrub in lava-fields or in gullies with streams and dense thickets. Its nests are primarily found in such habitats, but they are not easy to locate. A wren's nest is a special structure, being a spherical ball neatly woven out of straw (see picture on p. 272) with a small hole in the side. The nest is often situated in moss-banks in lava-fields, in earth-banks, under thick roots in birch copses, or else in holes and crevices. The male frequently weaves more than one spherical nest, and, once the female has selected the one she likes most, they both take part in lining it with moss and feathers.

Pictured on the left is a wren on the way to its nest with food in its bill. The nest was built under a grassy overhang which jutted out from a 3 m high rock in a gully in Öræfasveit. The chicks had hatched on 7 June, and both the parents brought them food. They always perched on the same branches in the birch scrub on their way to the nest, this branch being the last port of call before they flew up into the nest at the top right of the picture. Above are 2 young wrens just as they are about to leave the nest on 16 June.

12. LAVA-FIELDS AND WOODLANDS

Above is a wren's nest. It is a neatly woven ball of straw which is usually situated in a mossy tussock or hidden under brushwood. This is a nest the male had built but which the female had rejected in favour of another, which they then both lined with moss and feathers. Wren's nests are rarely found as they are well hidden and the birds quickly disappear if disturbed. They usually lay 7–8 eggs in the early part of May.

The **MEADOW PIPIT** (*Anthus pratensis*) is considerably smaller than a white wagtail, being about 15 cm long, although it otherwise resembles it in build, apart from the tail, which is relatively much shorter. The meadow pipit has a basic olive-green colouring with dark stripes and streaks, especially on its upper-parts, but a dirty-white breast and under-parts. Both sexes have the same appearance. The meadow pipit's choice habitats are grasslands, heathery moors, and birch scrubs. Its favourite nesting sites are besides tussocks and in thick vegetation. The meadow pipit is a common breeding bird all over Iceland. It mostly forages for food on the ground and feeds mainly on insects and their larvae.

The meadow pipit is migratory in Iceland, its winter quarters being on the south-western coasts of Europe, as far south as Spain and even Morocco. The meadow pipit's breeding season can sometimes begin in mid-May, but usually starts at the end of May or the beginning of June. The male meadow pipit is one of Iceland's best songbirds, and often cheerfully sings in its nesting territory, ending its song with a beautiful warble. The meadow pipit sometimes lays a second clutch of eggs in July. There are usually 5–6 eggs and the incubation period is 13–14 days. The chicks of the first clutch thus usually hatch before mid-June. The female does most of the sitting, and the male hunts for worms and larvae for the young. The chicks become fully fledged within 2 weeks, but the parents continue to feed them for a little longer. The meadow pipit is a quick and lively bird, always trotting, running, or hopping about in between short bursts of flight. In the late summer, flocks of meadow pipits sometimes descend on a farm where they can forage for food in the newly mown homefields or in piles of dung.

12. LAVA-FIELDS AND WOODLANDS

Above is a meadow pipit on a jagged edge of lava, and below is a meadow pipit chick on 23 June. On the right is a meadow pipit sitting in a typical nest in a hole in a grassy tussock. The nest itself is small and lined with soft blades of grass. Pictured overleaf (p. 274) is a meadow pipit trotting about in grassy land near its nest, 6 June.

12. LAVA-FIELDS AND WOODLANDS

12. LAVA-FIELDS AND WOODLANDS

Meadow pipits (pictured left) can be fairly tame birds if they are not unduly alarmed. Between the end of August and mid-September, most of the meadow pipits leave Iceland for their winter quarters.

The **REDWING** (*Turdus iliacus*) is the smallest of the most common Nordic thrushes, being about 21 cm long. It is partly migratory in Iceland, and a common breeding bird all over the country. There is hardly an Icelander who cannot recognise a redwing, either from its appearance or its song. Its plumage is variable depending on the season, but its basic colouring consists of brownish-green upper-parts, light-coloured under-parts, a dark head and neck, and distinctive chestnut flanks and creamy supercilium. The redwing usually arrives in southern Iceland early in April, or even in the last days of March. It is not usually seen in the north, however, until mid-April. At first the redwing keeps to the coastline or near to human habitation where there is a greater likelihood of food at that time of year. As April passes it begins to disperse all over Iceland, its favourite habitat being woodland or scrub. The male then chooses a breeding territory, which it will allow no other male to enter, and begins to sing with great gusto, both to attract the females and to proclaim to other males his presence in the area. Where many redwings have settled in the same neighbourhood there can be tremendous competition, and their singing can go on both night and day! The redwing is one of the very few Icelandic birds which sometimes breeds twice in the same summer. It has even been known to have 3 or 4 clutches in one year, though the parents do not generally rear the young from the last clutch. The redwing often used to nest on the ground, usually in well hidden places under tree roots or in thick scrub. It now more commonly nests quite high up in trees, both in gardens and in cultivated woodlands. From at least 1930 onwards, redwings have regularly nested on houses or other buildings in towns and farms and seemed to have developed a liking for suburban areas.

In September and October most redwings start to leave the country, often stopping for a while in gardens to tuck into delicious red rowan berries to prepare themselves for their flight over the ocean. The main winter quarters for Icelandic redwings are in Scotland, Ireland, western France, and the Pyrenees. A few thrushes seem unable to tear themselves away from the rowan berries, however, and spend the winter here in Iceland.

12. LAVA-FIELDS AND WOODLANDS

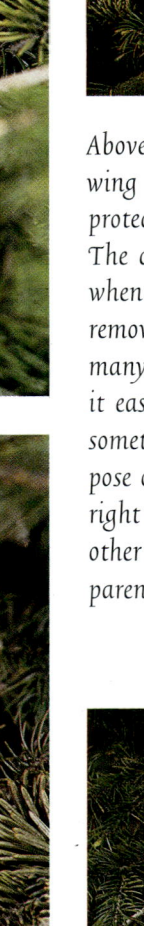

Above left are newly hatched redwing chicks. Below left is a redwing brooding the same clutch of nestlings, both to warm and protect them. Above is a redwing feeding its young in the nest. The chicks which demand the most, receive the most! Only when they are full will they close their bills. Below is a redwing removing the young's excreta from the nest. The excreta of many passerine chicks is voided in gelatinous sacs which makes it easier for the parents to keep the nest clean. The parents sometimes actually eat these sacs, but they more often just dispose of them at some distance from the nest. Pictured on the right is a redwing arriving at its nest with an earthworm and other titbits for its young. In the picture overleaf (p. 278), both parents are present in the nest at the same time.

12. LAVA-FIELDS AND WOODLANDS

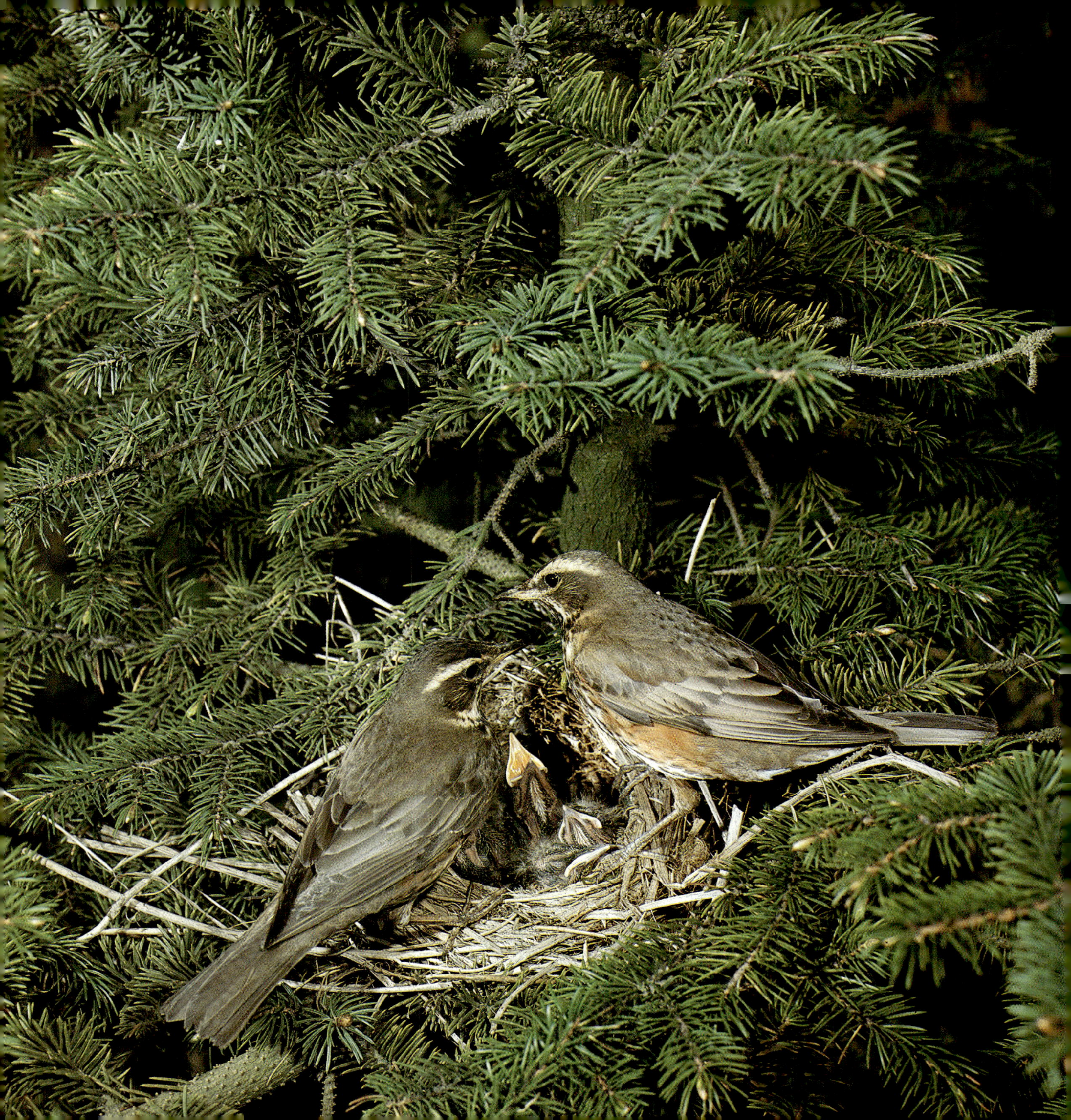

13 Birds of prey

BIRDS OF PREY are classified as belonging to the order *Falconiformes* which has 5 families, the 2 largest being the **falcon family** (*Falconidae*) and the **accipiter family** (*Accipitridae*). In Iceland there are 2 species of falcons, the **merlin** (*Falco columbarius*), and the **gyrfalcon** (*Falco rusticolus*) and one species of accipiter, the **white-tailed eagle** (*Haliaeetus albicilla*).

Most birds of prey, or raptors, live mainly on the animals they kill. Their prey is not always birds or mammals, however, for some species of raptors feed mainly on fish or insects, and yet others live to a great extent on carrion. All birds of prey have the characteristic features of a hooked bill, powerful legs, and sharp talons, and the female is generally larger than the male. Although owls are predatory birds and have similar behaviour to raptors, they are not classified as birds of prey and are totally unrelated to these species.

Man has always been impressed by birds of prey, especially their noble appearance and their flying and hunting skills. Emblems of birds of prey have often been proudly used on many national flags and coats of arms. Indeed the highest honour to be awarded in Iceland is the Order of the Falcon. But there is also another way of viewing the species: raptors kill other creatures for food (as man does) and can therefore be considered as merciless and cruel – and justifiable objects of persecution. The fact is, however, that birds of prey only kill to feed themselves and their offspring; moreover their powerful bills and claws have been perfectly designed by nature to ensure that their prey is killed swiftly and efficiently. Those who regard raptors as cruel often forget that even many small birds hunt insects and worms for food. It must be remembered that all life on earth is bound together in one ecological chain, and that birds of prey are just another link in that chain. All forms of life are dependent on each other for survival, and it is thus very dubious to claim that only man should have the right to kill for food.

13. BIRDS OF PREY

13. BIRDS OF PREY

The **MERLIN** (*Falco columbarius*) is only 27–32 cm long, which is very small for a falcon. Indeed the merlin is the smallest bird of prey in Iceland and is classified as a special sub-species (*Falco columbarius subaesalon*). The male is about 27–30 cm long and weighs around 170 g, whilst the female is 30–32 cm long and weighs about 250 g. The male has slate-blue upper-parts and reddish-brown under-parts with distinctive dark streaks. The tail is barred both light and dark brown. The female has greyish-brown upper-parts and lighter under-parts streaked dark brown. Downy merlin chicks are completely white at first, but gradually become greyer, and the immature bird resembles the female in colour. The merlin's nesting sites are on rocks and stacks in rugged lava-fields, and occasionally on the ground. The nest is not very elaborate, usually just a slight depression in the vegetation of a rocky ledge. The merlin generally lays its 3–5 eggs in late May or early June. The female does most of the sitting and the incubation period lasts 3–4 weeks. The young are fully fledged by the end of July.

The merlin is the commonest Icelandic bird of prey. It nests all over the country, but very dispersively, so its exact population is unknown. It is mainly a migratory bird, the majority of merlins leaving the country in September or October for their winter quarters in south-western Europe. There are a few merlins, however, which spend the winter in Iceland. Although it is not a very large bird, the merlin is a cunning and daring hunter which lives mostly on such small birds as meadow pipits, snow buntings, wheatears, and redwings. To feed its family, it will also kill such larger birds as golden plovers and redshanks. It has a lot of stamina when hunting and is a very agile flyer, chasing and seizing its prey in mid-air. On the ground it will seize the unfledged young of various birds, including ptarmigan, ducks, and whimbrel. The behaviour of many small birds can often indicate the presence of a merlin; they become very uneasy and try to hide themselves by crouching on branches as near to the tree-trunk as possible, and they will not dare to move again until the merlin is long out of sight.

Pictured on the left is a merlin on its way to its young in the nest. The nest is not an elaborate affair, merely a depression in the vegetation on the rocky ledge. Below are 3 merlin chicks in the nest. The downy young are at first completely white, but they gradually become light grey, as in this picture.

13. BIRDS OF PREY

The **GYRFALCON** (*Falco rusticolus*) is the largest of all the species of falcons, and there is a noticeable difference in size between the sexes. The male, or tiercel, is 51–56 cm long and weighs around 1200 g, whereas the female is 56–60 cm long and weighs about 1800 g. The Icelandic gyrfalcon is grey on its back and has a pale yellow breast with long dark brown stripes. The young are white at first, but quickly begin to darken, and immature gyrfalcons are considerably darker than the adult birds. The talons of the immature birds are bluish in colour, but the talons of adult gyrfalcons are bright yellow. The Icelandic gyrfalcon is a resident bird and its population has been estimated at around 200 pairs. It is not very common in any particular part of the country, though it occurs mostly in northern Iceland and in the Vestfirðir. The breeding season begins early in spring, usually in April. The gyrfalcon's nest, or eyrie, is usually sited in places which are difficult if not impossible to reach, as on the rocky cliffs of mountains and river canyons. It hardly builds a nest at all as such, but merely uses a depression in the vegetation of a rocky ledge. It will also often utilise an old raven's nest, which can be quite a large structure made out of branches and brushwood. The gyrfalcon usually lays 3–4 eggs and only the female sits, the incubation period lasting about 4 weeks. The chicks thus often hatch in the latter part of May. The female remains constantly in the nest at first, brooding and defending them. Whilst the female incubates the eggs and broods the young, the tiercel guards the nest and brings food for both her and the chicks, the female tearing up the

13. BIRDS OF PREY

prey before feeding it to the young. When the chicks are older the female also goes hunting, and the young are often left on their own for long periods of time. They are fully fledged by mid-July, after 6–7 weeks in the nest. They remain near the nest for another month or so, however, and the parents continue to bring them food until they have learned to hunt for themselves. Once they have become self-sufficient they begin to rove over a wide area.

The ptarmigan is the Icelandic gyrfalcon's most important prey during the spring and summer, though falcons which nest near the sea also eat quite a lot of sea-birds, including puffins. As mentioned in an earlier chapter, gyrfalcons which nest further inland feed mostly on ptarmigan cocks during the spring as they are such easy targets, being white against a dark background. Once the ptarmigan cocks have attained their darker summer plumage, the gyrfalcon begins to hunt other species, including waders, ducks and geese and their young, and also newly fledged ptarmigan. The gyrfalcon can seize its prey both on the ground and in the air. – The gyrfalcon has been a protected bird in Iceland since 1940, and it is illegal to approach or photograph a gyrfalcon nest without the permission of the Ministry of Education and Culture.

There is a clear division of labour between the gyrfalcon sexes. Whilst the female incubates the eggs and later tends the young, the male, or tiercel, provides food for the family and guards the nest from a nearby vantage point, as in the picture on the left. Top right is a picture of a female perching on the edge of a nest in which there are 3 eggs, a couple of which are just visible. The nest is a half-completed raven's nest which the gyrfalcon had simply appropriated. In the middle picture, the female is incubating the eggs, and in the bottom picture are 4 downy chicks in another gyrfalcon nest.

A male gyrfalcon in flight near its nest. Pictured on the right is a female feeding 3 well-grown chicks on a ptarmigan which it holds in its claws; the entire family has blood-stained bills. The female was busy feeding the young when the male arrived with more prey and called to them. The picture was taken at the precise moment they all looked up in his direction. The male never brought food directly to the nest, but called to the female to come and collect it from his perching place.

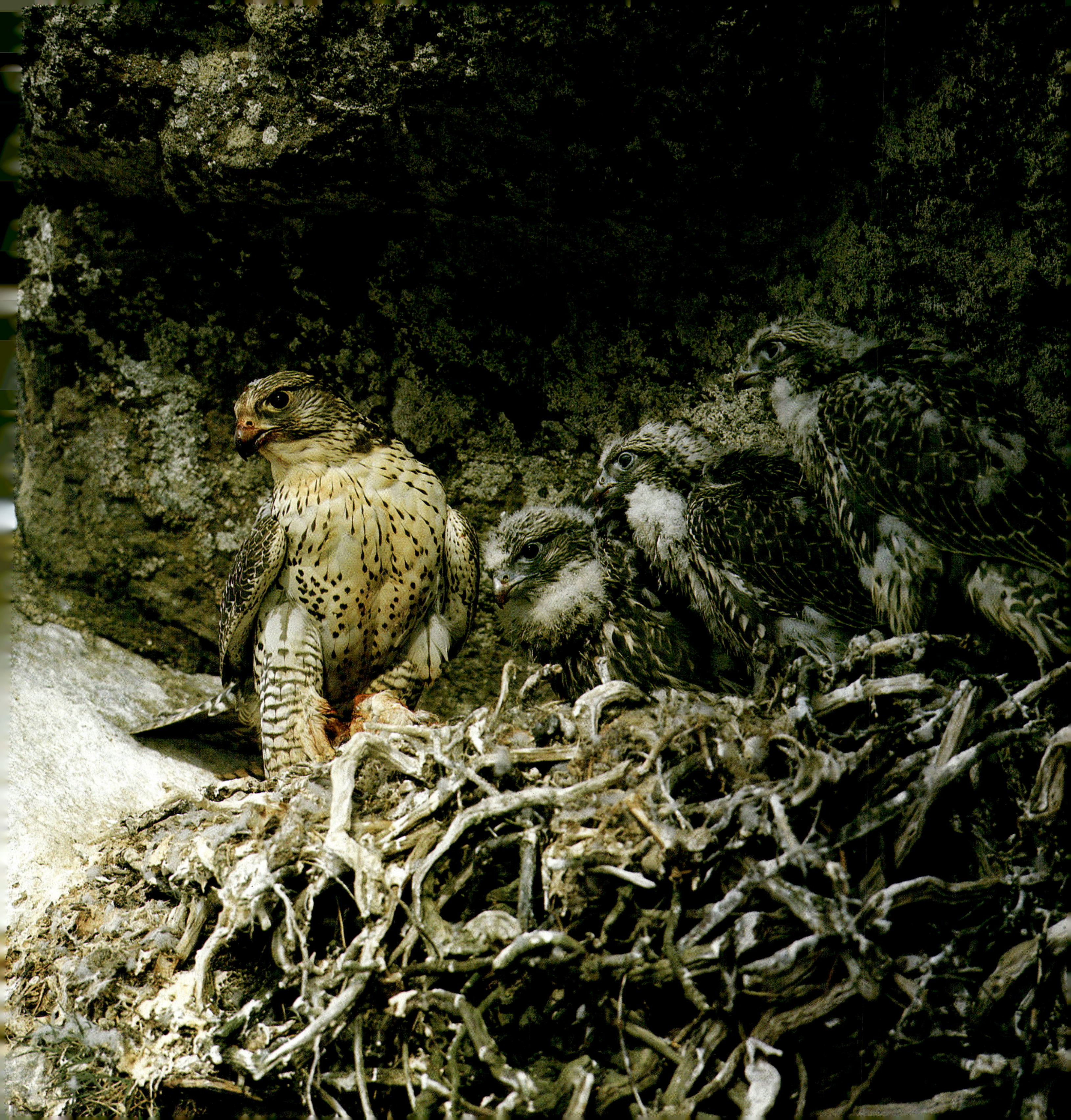

13. BIRDS OF PREY

When the tiercel (the male gyrfalcon) has killed a ptarmigan, it tears off its head and wings and plucks out the feathers on the spot. It then flies with the carcass to a place near the nest and calls to the female to come and collect it and feed it to the young. Above can be seen the feathers of a ptarmigan which a gyrfalcon had killed on Hrísey in Eyjafjörður. Below is a puffin which a falcon had killed in the puffin colony near Skrúðskollur on Skrúður, offshore from Fáskrúðsfjörður. The falcon had been disturbed before it had finished plucking its victim and had flown away. The carcass had disappeared by the following morning. On the left is a female gyrfalcon distributing pieces of ptarmigan to 3 chicks in the nest.

13. BIRDS OF PREY

Below is a young gyrfalcon relieving itself. It raises its tail and rear-end, backs to the edge of the nest and voids the excreta in a long arch. By excreting this way, the young keep the nest clean, but the rocks below become coloured light grey and make the nesting site visible from a distance. Gyrfalcon pairs often change nesting sites from year to year, but always within the same breeding territory which they have established and remain loyal to for years. The fact that no eggs can be found in a known nesting site is no proof, therefore, that the gyrfalcon population is decreasing.

Above is the face of a young gyrfalcon which is just less than a year old, taken on 31 May. Once young falcons have left their parents they begin to rove over a wide area and the first winter is the most difficult period of their lives. They often move to the coast during this time as there is usually more chance of finding food there.

△ Above is a female gyrfalcon feeding a well-grown chick in the nest on 24 June. The gyrfalcon is without doubt one of Iceland's most majestic birds. It was once used as an emblem on the country's coat-of-arms, and the nation's highest honour, awarded by the President, is named after it. The Icelandic gyrfalcon has for centuries had a good reputation as a hunting bird and was earlier exported from the country for falconry. Nowadays Icelanders are determined that the gyrfalcon's status as a protected bird be respected, and the general public is always on the look-out for anyone behaving suspiciously near a gyrfalcon nest.

On the right are a pair of white-tailed eagles near their nest. The ▷ white-tailed eagle is the largest Icelandic raptor, and to see it soaring across the sky on outstretched wings is a magnificent sight. Its wings are very broad and long, the wing-span reaching up to 2.5 m. Its tail is short and wedge-shaped. The female is considerably larger than the male, and adult white-tailed eagles weigh between 4 and 7 kg. They are brown in colour, but paler on the head and neck. The tail of the adult eagle is white.

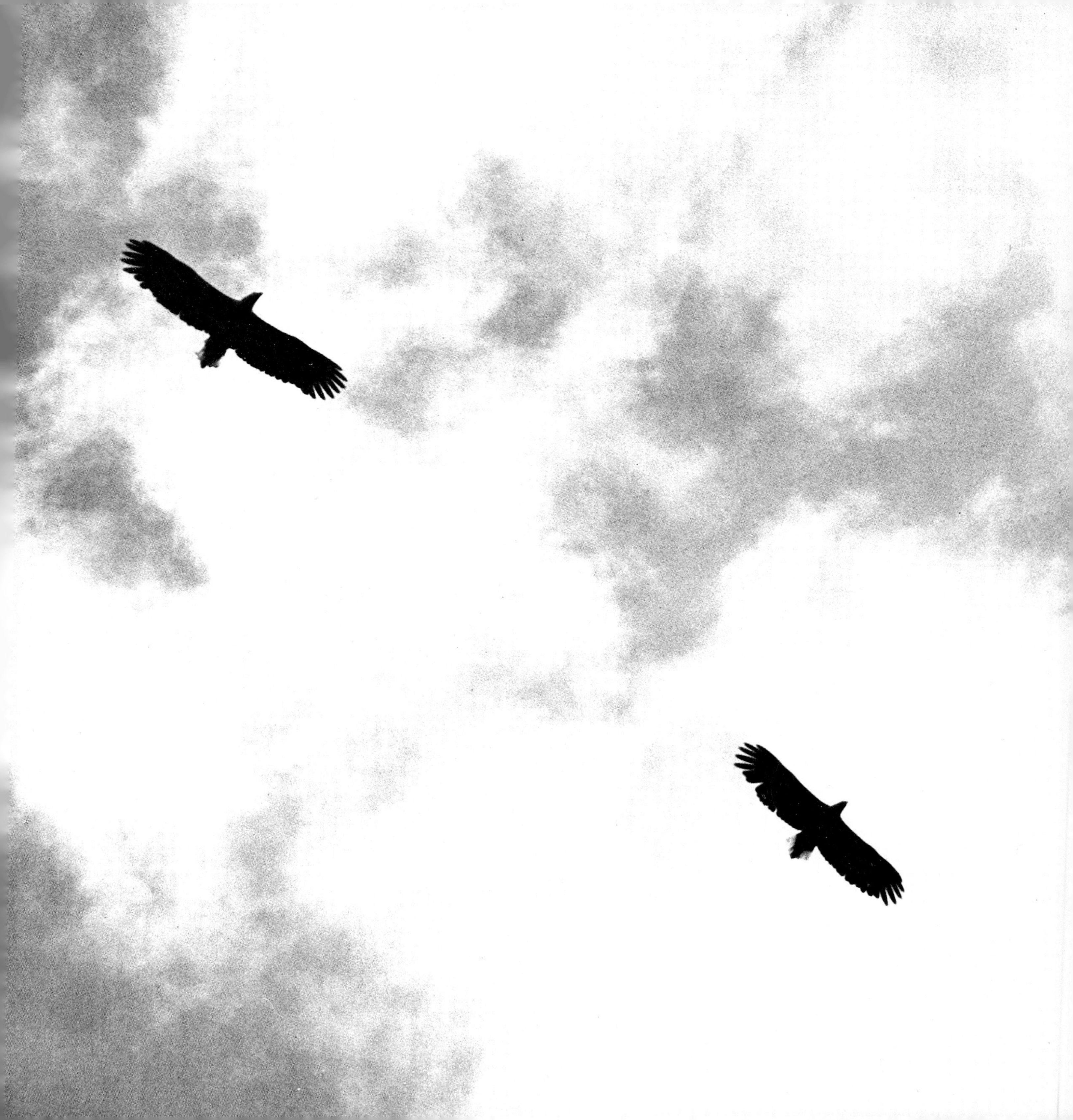

13. BIRDS OF PREY

The **WHITE-TAILED EAGLE** (Haliaeetus albicilla) is the largest Icelandic bird of prey. It has very long and broad wings, its wing-span reaching up to 2.5 m. An adult eagle is 69–91 cm long and weighs between 4 and 7 kg, the female being considerably larger and heavier than the male. The bill is large and thick, its legs are big and powerful, and its talons are grooved to enable it to grasp slippery fish in its claws. Adult white-tailed eagles, often referred to as sea-eagles, are brown in colour, apart from a greyish-brown head and neck and a white tail. The bill is pale yellow and the feet yellow. Newly hatched eaglets are greyish-brown at first, but then attain a dark grey down. A juvenile eagle less than a year old is consequently much darker than an adult, but in its third year its head becomes lighter in colour and the middle tail-feathers become white. By the fourth year the whole tail is almost white, and by the fifth the young bird greatly resembles an adult eagle, though it still does not attain its full adult plumage until it is 6 years old.

There are 8 related species of sea-eagles in the world; they live along coastlines or by rivers and inland lakes, but only one of these species can be found in Europe: the white-tailed eagle, Haliaeetus albicilla. A species very closely related to the white-tailed eagle is the **bald eagle** (Haliaeetus leucocephalus) which breeds in North America and Canada and has become the national emblem of the United States.

Although the white-tailed eagle existed in Iceland long before man ever set foot there, it is believed that there were originally only a few of them. Foxes were then the only land mammals in Iceland, and white-tailed eagles could only have lived on the fish and birds it could catch as well as anything edible washed up on the shore. Once Iceland had been settled, however, the large influx of sometimes neglected or abandoned livestock provided the eagle with a more plentiful and varied means of sustenance. The white-tailed eagle population then probably increased considerably, especially as disease and exposure ravaged sheep and cattle and ensured a regular supply of carrion. The eagle's situation changed dramatically at the end of the 19th century with the increased use of drugs against livestock diseases and improved control of stocks of hay over the winter months. Moreover farmers began to dump poisoned carcasses in the outer fields in an attempt to reduce the number of foxes, and plans were drawn up for a systematic extermination of all birds of prey. This combination of direct persecution and the drastic reduction of its food supply has had such a devastating effect on the white-tailed eagle population in Iceland, that since the beginning of this century it has been in constant danger of extinction.

The ornithologist Dr. Finnur Guðmundsson has done special research into the history and behaviour of the Icelandic white-tailed eagle. He has pointed out that large raptors demand extensive individual territories and thus always breed very dispersively. In his opinion, therefore, there was an absolute maximum of 200–300 pairs of eagles in Iceland at any one time, and that it is possible that there were never more than 100–200 pairs.

The sudden decline in the numbers of white-tailed eagles in Iceland in the late 19th century soon attracted a lot of attention. Some people, especially farmers, were pleased with this development, but others believed that the demise of the white-tailed eagle would be extremely regrettable and thus wished to try and prevent its extermination. By 1913 the situation demanded urgent action if the eagle was not to become extinct, and on 10 November that year a law was passed protecting the bird for 5 years. When this period expired the law was renewed for a further 20 years and has never been repealed to this day. The white-tailed eagle has thus been a protected bird in Iceland since 1913.

One of the main instigators of the protection of the eagle was Peter Nielsen, a store-manager in Eyrarbakki. This worthy cause was later supported and promoted by the Icelandic Natural History Society under the leadership of Dr. Bjarni Sæmundsson. In the summer of 1959 it was estimated that there were at least 38 adult white-tailed eagles still in existence in Iceland, and ever since then the species' population has been under annual surveillance by the Icelandic Society for the Protection of Birds. Judging by the number of nests used annually for breeding, it would appear that the white-tailed eagle population in Iceland remained fairly static for many years after 1913 in spite of the protective laws, but at least the species was saved from extinction. In 1964 it was further protected by a law forbidding the poisoning of carcasses in order to kill foxes as it became known that young eagles also died from eating such poisoned carrion. It is now estimated that there are around 35–40 adult pairs of white-tailed eagles in Iceland as well as additional juvenile birds.

The eagle is not believed to be fully sexually mature until 5 or 6 years of age when it finally attains its adult plumage. It is quite common, however, for eagles to form pairs in which one of the birds is still too young and immature to breed, even if they both build a nest and live in it as if they were breeding. If the female is sexually mature, it might lay eggs, but they will be infertile. Such breeding incompatibility is relatively common in places where eagles are rather scarce, for it can be very difficult for 2 sexually mature eagles to meet and mate. The white-tailed eagle population of Iceland is a good example of this as it appears that only two thirds of known eagle pairs annually breed successfully. It is possible that one of the partners of the remaining pairs is infertile, but then even sexually mature pairs occasionally refrain from breeding and do not lay eggs every single year. Moreover an unusually large number of eggs and young are lost every season, possibly because of human interference or the parents' lack of experience, especially if they are breeding for the very first time.

Those unfamiliar with the white-tailed eagle generally assume that this large wild bird only nests on precipitous cliffs where its nest, or eyrie, is completely inaccessible. This is far from the truth, however. Eagles do nest on high cliffs if they have suitably broad ledges or platforms, but it is far more common for them to nest on steep mountainsides which have occasional rock faces and crags, for there are often rocky bluffs and outcrops in such places and these provide perfect nesting sites. Eagles will also nest on rocky stacks in the lowlands, or on isles and skerries offshore, or on mounds or outcrops of rugged lava. The nests on skerries are often on low crags which are preferably covered with high grass. As with the gyrfalcon, the white-tailed eagle pair often has more than one nesting site within its territory. Some eagle pairs change nest frequently, but others will breed in the same eyrie for a decade or more before suddenly moving to another place and breeding there for an irregular length of time. It has even been known for an eyrie to have been used every year for more than a century, though not by the same birds, of course. Whenever a mate died, it was presumably always replaced by another sexually mature eagle, thus guaranteeing the continuing presence of a breeding pair at the ancient nesting site.

As some eagle pairs do change nests frequently, a deserted eyrie is no real proof that a pair has died or simply not bred that year. The same birds could well have another nest many kilometres away. Some eagle pairs, for example, will nest on an offshore skerry one year, and a nearby mountainside the next. Most white-tailed eagles nest near to the sea however, usually by shallow fjords and bays where there is a large ebb-tide and where it is relatively easy to catch fish and sea-birds.

The nest of the Icelandic white-tailed eagle is generally very unpretentious, often only a hollow in vegetation lined with a bit of moss or seaweed. Other materials are sometimes used, especially if the nest is situated on a bare outcrop of lava or on a rocky ledge. Once a nest has been in use for several years it is often surrounded by quite a bit of vegetation which has been fertilised by discarded food scraps and the birds' own droppings.

Adult eagles are geographically very localised and always remain within the territories they have either established or inherited. These territories are generally very extensive as such large birds of prey need to cover a wide area to find food. Eagles are also loyal to their partners and mate for life. Eagle pairs will often establish a nocturnal roosting place near the nest and this roosting place is also used outside the breeding season, for once their young have become fully fledged, the adult eagles rarely keep to their nest and between October and December will hardly ever be seen in its vicinity. At the beginning of January they begin to return to it once more, and in February and March they indulge in flight-displays, the usual precopulatory behaviour prior to the breeding season. If a nest has to be built, both birds will share the work in finding the requisite moss and twigs. As the time for egg-laying approaches, they will both frequent-

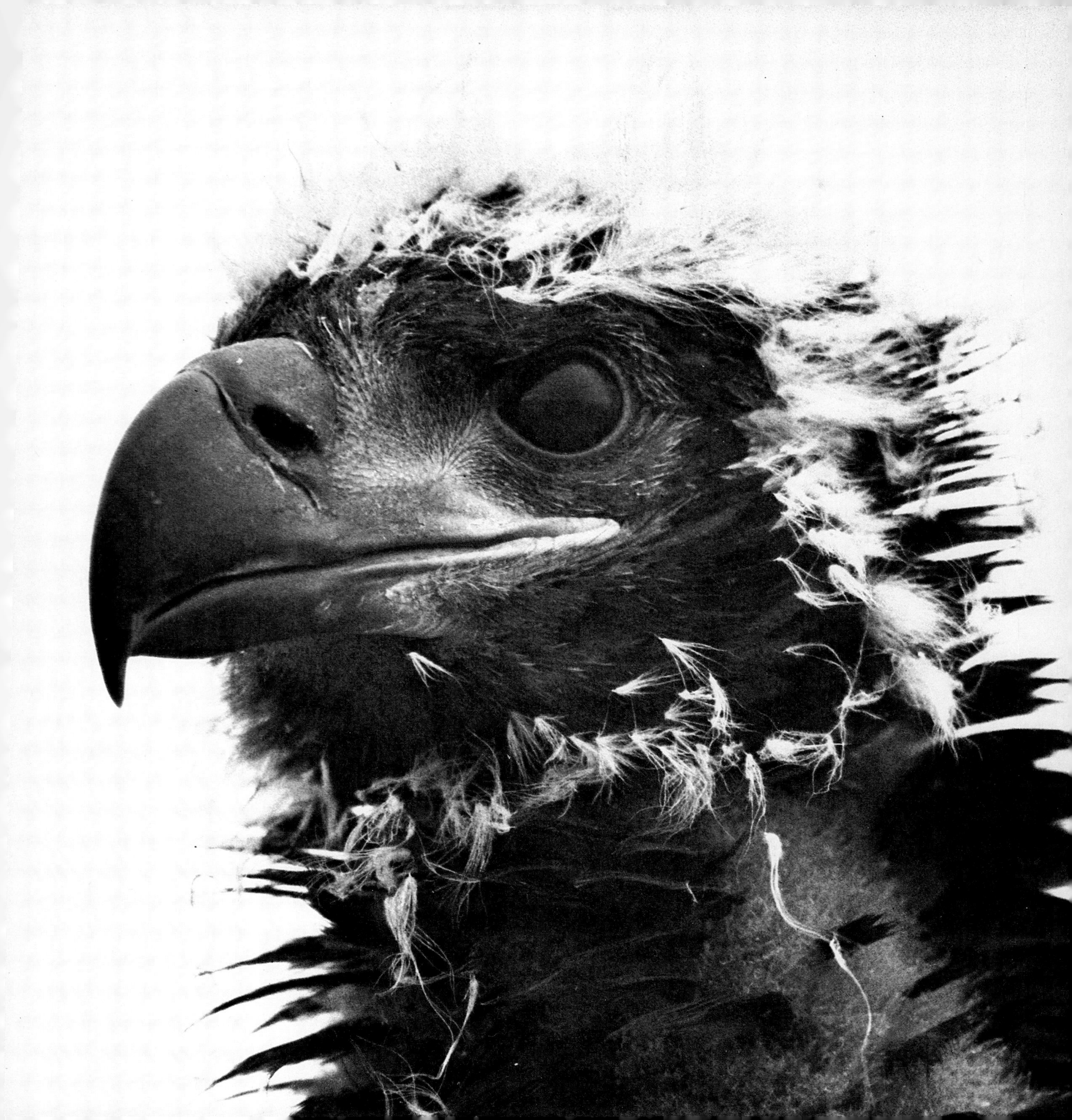

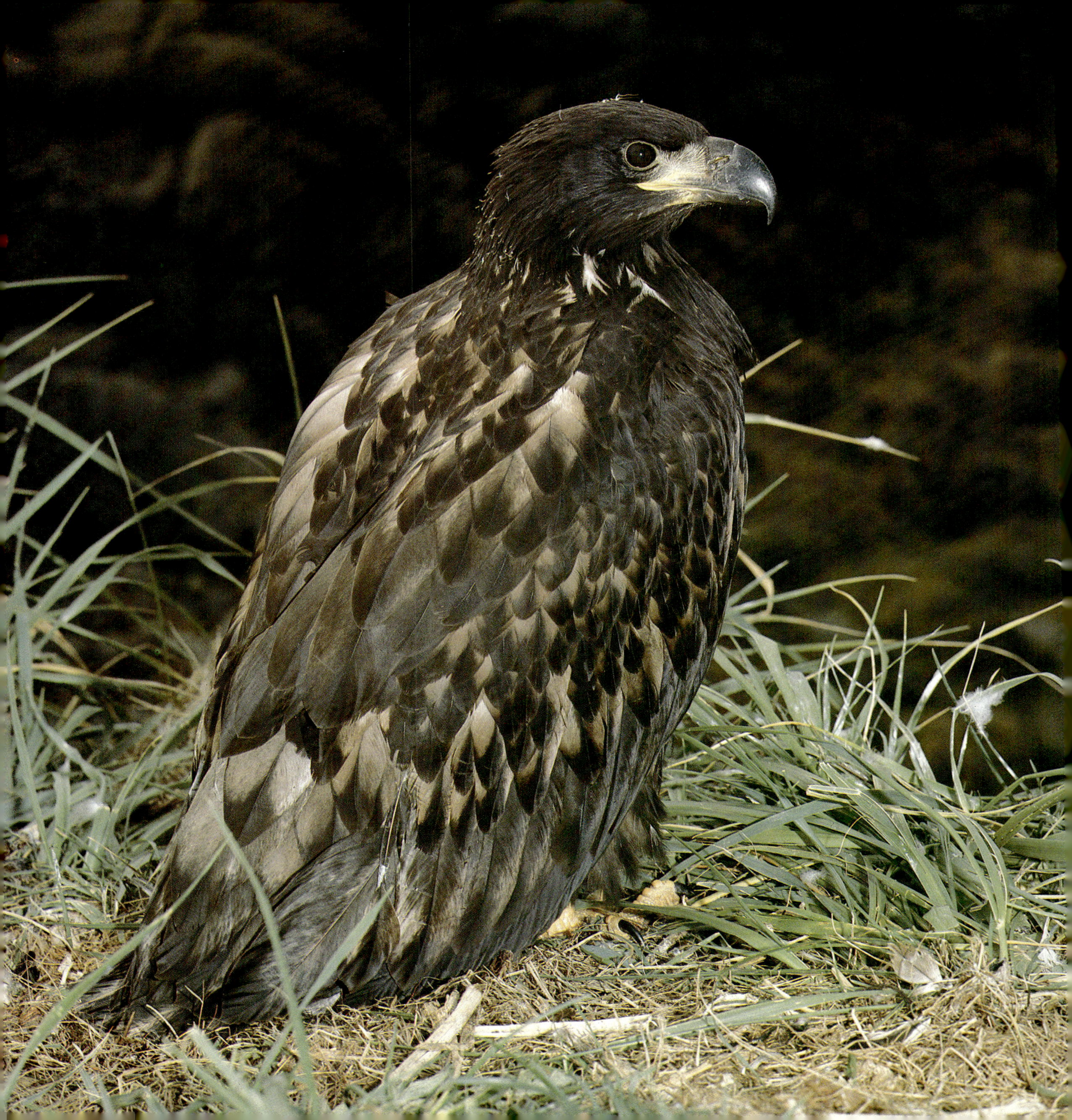

ly sit together in the nest for hours at a time. Eagles have been known to lay their eggs at the end of March, but the Icelandic white-tailed eagle does not generally lay its eggs until mid-April at least. There are usually 2 eggs, rarely 3 or only 1. The eggs are white and rather small in relation to the size of the bird. Eagle's eggs can be compared with other Icelandic birds' eggs in the picture on pp. 36–37.

There is a 2–4 day interval between the laying of the eggs, but incubation begins immediately the first egg is laid. Although the male also assists, the female does most of the sitting, especially towards the time when the eggs will hatch. The incubation period lasts for 38 days, during which both birds hunt for their own food. The male will also occasionally present prey to its mate in the nest. This is believed to be a ritual gesture and not simply just a case of the male providing the female with food.

Once the young have hatched both parents tend them in the nest and hunt to provide them with food, although the female hardly ever leaves the nest for the first 3–4 weeks, and looks after the eaglets very conscientiously, sheltering them from the sun and rain and defending them from any approaching danger. The male is very busy procuring food during this period, always handing over the prey to the female to prepare and feed it to the young. When the eaglets are 4–5 weeks old they are capable of feeding themselves, but the mother continues to feed them herself whenever she is in the nest. As they grow older she gradually becomes less attentive, and the eaglets are often left on their own for hours at a time whilst both parents are away hunting.

On the left is a well-grown white-tailed eaglet in its nest, and on p. 293 there is a close-up of its face.

Many eagle eggs and young are lost in spite of all the parents' care and labour. As there is a 2–4 day interval between the eggs they do not hatch at the same time. This can mean that the bigger and stronger elder eaglet eats food also intended for the younger one, and only one of the young thus survives to adulthood. Moreover it is also common for one of the eggs to fail to hatch at all. If the food supply is good, however, 2 eaglets can be reared successfully in one nest, and in recent years in Iceland it has even been known for 3 white-tailed eaglets to have been raised in the same eyrie.

By the time the eaglets are 8 weeks old they have attained their juvenile plumage and begin to leave the nest, spending some time every day perching in its vicinity. The parents continue to procure food for them during this time, returning with prey which they leave around the nesting site. At 10 weeks of age the eaglets are more or less fledged, but they cannot as yet fly very far, and it is not until they are 11–12 weeks old that they start to accompany their parents on their hunting trips and to eat prey where it is actually killed. They also begin to look for food themselves, though at first they can manage little more than carrion or fish and birds washed up by the sea. About 5–6 weeks after the young have left the nest, the parents leave them to fend entirely for themselves. This is a very difficult phase for young eagles as they have to cover a very wide area in search of food, and often wander into completely unfamiliar places. Their only real hope of survival is to come across carrion fairly regularly, but many young eagles cannot find enough to eat and just slowly waste away and die of starvation.

The white-tailed eagle feeds on both live animals and carrion, so it is both a bird of prey and a scavenger. The animals which it mainly hunts are fish, birds, and any mammal it can cope with. The

Above left is an eaglet in a typical nest on a low crag on an island. On the left is an eyrie on a rocky ledge in which there are 2 cold eggs. Above is a well-grown eaglet in its nest. Dr. Finnur Guðmundsson, the ornithologist, is checking to see if there is a second egg which had failed to hatch. Above right, Dr. Björn Guðbrandsson is searching for eagles through his binoculars during the annual population survey by the Icelandic Society for the Protection of Birds. On the far right is an eaglet in the nest, its flight-feathers just beginning to grow.

limited research done on the white-tailed eagle's feeding habits during the breeding season seems to indicate that lumpsucker fish provide most of its diet, and that the birds it eats are chiefly fulmars, puffins, eider ducks, and gulls. During the winter the white-tailed eagle appears to be much more dependent on carrion; indeed, as mentioned above, young eagles must survive almost exclusively on carrion during their first year.

When hunting for prey the white-tailed eagle can fly quite swiftly, but rather clumsily. It often scours the coastline in case anything edible has been washed ashore. If nothing is immediately on offer, it will perch for hours at a time on one of its many vantage points within its territory, hoping that some kind of prey will eventually come into sight. Perching for protracted lengths of time in one place is a common characteristic of the white-tailed eagle.

The only fish the eagle can readily seize alive, e.g. lumpsuckers, are those found in the shallows or on the surface of the water, though it can also obtain fish by stealing them from other predators, especially the great black-backed gull. The eagle can rarely seize other birds in mid-air as it is too ungainly for nimble aerobatics.

In Iceland, as in many other countries, the white-tailed eagle has been viewed with fear and loathing as a dangerous and destructive bird. This attitude can be found in the very earliest ornithological observations on Icelandic bird life in which the eagle was accused of collecting lambs in its eyrie and even of carrying off children. To this day one can still be aware of the older generation's deep-rooted antipathy to the bird. The various stories of the eagle's cruelty are clear evidence, however, that it is its great size and comparative rarity which have fired people's imaginations and inspired all kinds

13. BIRDS OF PREY

This white-tailed eagle had become covered in liver-oil from a seal's carcass and was in poor condition. It was taken to the Icelandic Museum of Natural History to have its feathers cleaned. When it had recovered its strength, it was released again near to where it had been found.

of folk tales. The actual facts of the eagle's life pattern and behaviour could never have given rise to such wild and exaggerated stories. The truth is that the white-tailed eagle is a ponderous and relatively harmless scavenger which also happens to hunt fish, birds, and small mammals. As far as daring and hunting skills are concerned, the eagle is a far inferior bird to the gyrfalcon. Part of the white-tailed eagle's bad reputation rests on the claim that it steals new-born lambs and thus causes farmers great losses. Remains of lambs have certainly been found in and around eyries, but this is no proof that the eagle actually killed them in the first place. In most cases the eagle probably found a lamb's carcass and simply removed it to its nest. The white-tailed eagle is also accused of disrupting eider nesting sites by killing or frightening away the ducks. Eagles do admittedly hunt eiders, and eiders are therefore very afraid of them, but the white-tailed eagle population is so small that it could never seriously threaten eider-farming as an industry – not even if the numbers of eagles were to increase quite considerably. Complaints of regular depradation by eagles in specific locations must certainly be investigated, but in many such cases, loss or damage could probably be avoided by the provision of carrion for the eagles in places inaccessible to foxes.

The white-tailed eagle has been a protected bird since 1913, but this has not led to the increase in population one might have expected. This is mostly due to the bird's failure to propagate successfully. White-tailed eagles are exceptionally sensitive during the breeding season, and the loss of eggs and young in the nests may well be the result of the adult birds being unduly alarmed or disturbed. Eagle admirers and photographers, both native and foreign, can cause untold harm through ignorant behaviour or by letting curiosity get the better of them. No eagle's nest should ever be approached, therefore, until the young are quite well-grown, for this may help ensure that a greater number of eaglets survive to adulthood.

Dr. Björn Guðbrandsson was the main driving force behind the formation of the Icelandic Society for the Protection of Birds in 1959, and he is still the life and soul of the society, which from its very beginning has energetically promoted the safety and welfare of the white-tailed eagle. Many people who live near eagle breeding grounds have also given their time and energy to protecting the eagle's nests, eggs, and young, even to the extent of providing food for the eaglets. The long-lived and deep-rooted antipathy towards the bird does not seem to be shared by the younger generation, and undoubtedly the majority of people now believe that it would be a tragic loss to Icelandic wildlife if this large and magnificent bird were no longer to be seen soaring on outstretched wings over the country's shores and skerries.

14 Visitors and irregular breeding birds

There are just over 70 species of birds which breed annually in Iceland and, as explained in an earlier chapter, it is these species which are defined as Icelandic, even though some of them are only present in their breeding grounds for 3–5 months of the year. A total of over 300 species have actually been sighted in Iceland, however. Most of these birds are vagrants, winter visitors which arrive in the autumn and depart in the spring, or passage migrants which sojourn in Iceland in the spring and autumn on their way to and from southerly winter quarters and northerly breeding grounds. Some of these visiting birds have bred in Iceland on one or more occasions, and a brief survey of some of these visitors and irregular breeding birds follows in this chapter.

There are 2 species of passage migrants which sojourn in Iceland in the spring and autumn whilst migrating between their winter quarters in the British Isles and their more northerly breeding grounds: the brent goose and the barnacle goose. The **brent goose** mainly skirts the west coast of Iceland in the spring and autumn (the route marked A–B on the map below), stopping at the mud-flats of Faxaflói Bay and Breiðafjörður where there is plenty of eelgrass. The **barnacle goose** mostly crosses Iceland over the central highlands, often following the largest rivers (route C–D) and usually stopping at Húnaflói and Skagafjörður in the western part of the north in the spring. On the way south in the autumn, it often sojourns in the southern parts of the central highlands.

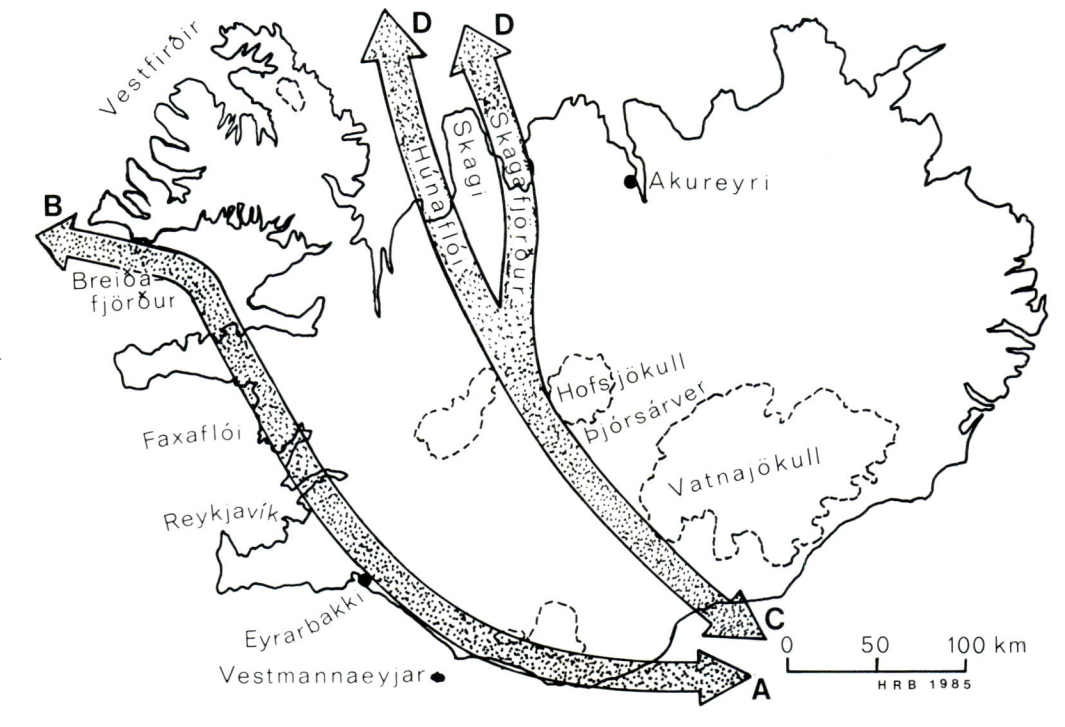

299

The **BRENT GOOSE** (Branta bernicla) is one of the 3 species of geese which winters in the British Isles and breeds to the north and west of Iceland, briefly stopping here when migrating in the spring and autumn. The brent goose is the most marine of the 3 species of geese and thus travels along the western coast of Iceland, as can be seen on the map on p. 299. It usually dwells in shallow firths and creeks where there are large ebb-tides, extensive mud-flats, and plenty of eelgrass or other maritime vegetation on which it chiefly feeds.

Pictured above are brent geese on May 17 near the President's residence at Bessastaðir on Álftanes. Reykjavík can be seen in the background. Above right is a group of brent geese at Bessastaðir, and below right are brent geese on the wing.

As these pictures illustrate, the brent goose has a black neck and breast with a little white spot on its neck. The sub-species which visits Iceland in the spring and autumn (**Branta bernicla hrota**) has pale under-parts. Brent geese often arrive in Iceland early in the spring, even as early as the turn of March and April if the climate is good, and remain in the country until June. The brent goose breeds in North Greenland and on the most northerly islands of Canada, so when it leaves Iceland it heads directly across the Greenland Glacier. In the autumn the brent goose arrives in late August or early September and dwells in Iceland until October.

The brent goose has a very small population, and as it has even been considered in danger of extinction in recent years, it is a protected bird in Iceland.

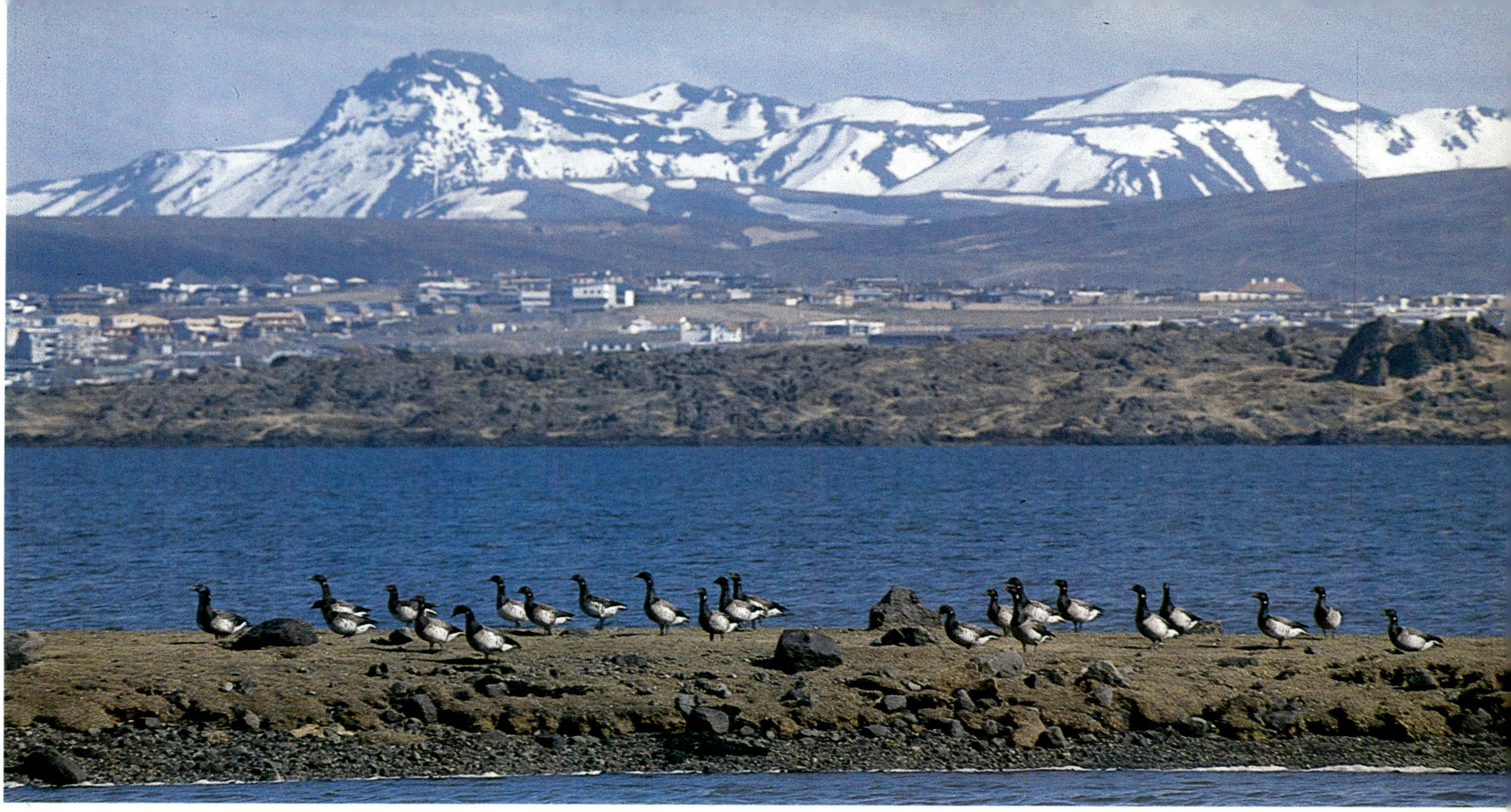

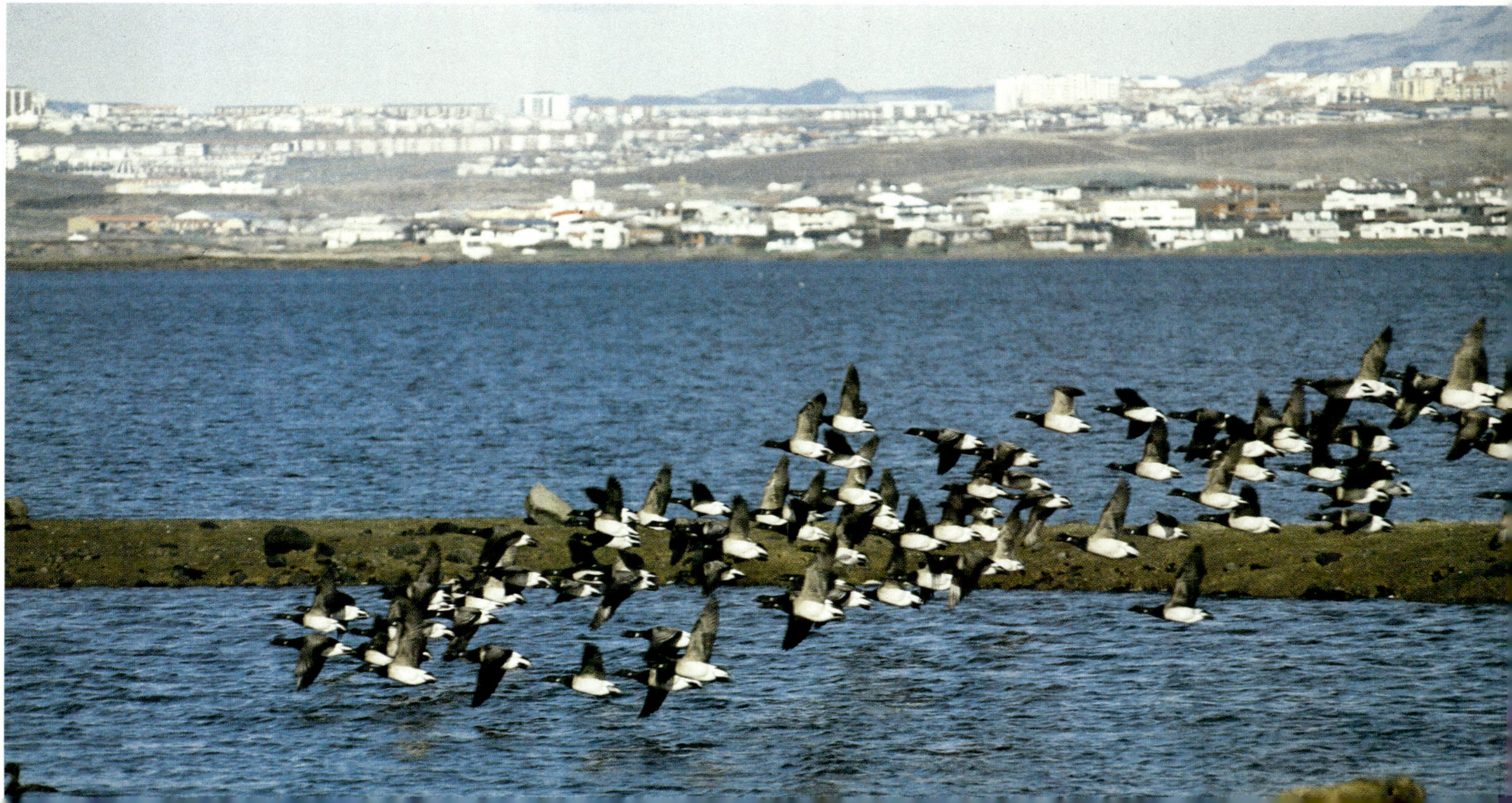

Above are **brent geese** swimming near Hjörsey at Mýrar in Faxaflói Bay on 21 May. The brent goose is about 59–64 cm long and weighs 1500–2000 g. It is just a little smaller than the **barnacle goose** (pictured on the right) and resembles it in appearance; indeed these 2 passage migrants are often confused. The third species of goose which stops in Iceland in the spring and autumn is the West-Greenland race of the **whitefronted goose** (Anser albifrons flavirostris). All of these species have rather small populations, although there are around 35,000 barnacle geese.

Pictured on the right are **barnacle geese** (Branta leucopsis) on Æðey in Ísafjarðardjúp on 6 June. This pair stayed on the island for a few days. According to the map on p. 299, they appear to have strayed from the main migratory route of the barnacle geese, though they probably continued their journey north later.

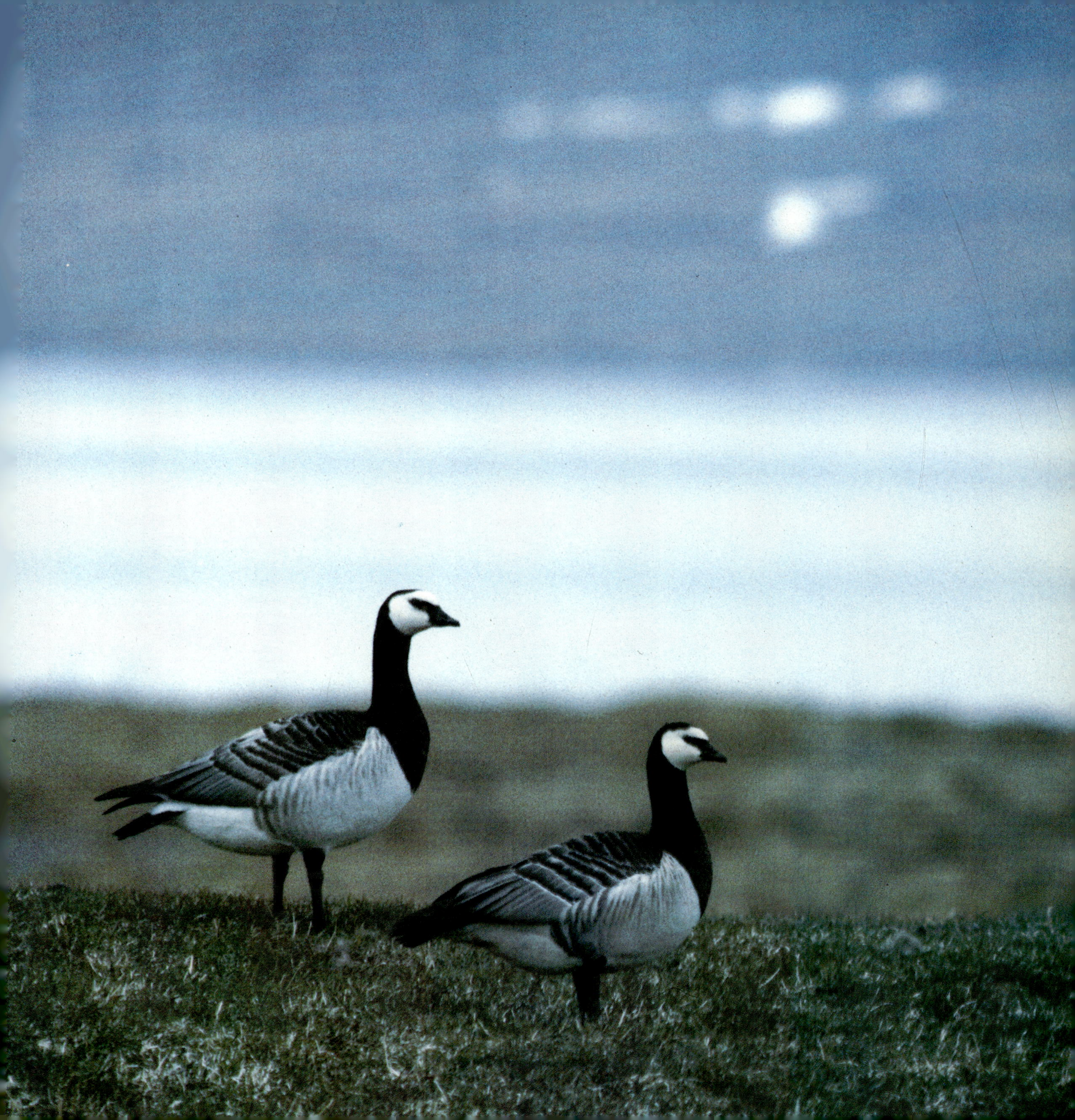

The **BARNACLE GOOSE** (Branta leucopsis) is 58–69 cm long, just a little smaller than the pink-footed goose. It has a contrasting black and white plumage, especially its black head and neck and white chin, cheeks, and forehead. The white face and forehead is the feature which mostly distinguishes it from the brent goose, another passage migrant with which it is often confused. The brent goose also has a distinctive white spot on its black neck.

The barnacle goose is an arctic bird which breeds in crowded colonies on steep cliffs in north-eastern Greenland. Until recently it was believed that any barnacle geese seen in Iceland in mid-summer could only be immature birds which had failed to reach any further on their journey from their winter quarters in the British Isles. It is now known, however, that barnacle geese have sometimes bred on skerries in Breiðafjörður.

Pictured above are 4 barnacle geese in flight near a barnacle goose nesting site in Breiðafjörður on 8 June 1984.

Top right on the next page are some barnacle geese grazing at the northern end of Skagi between Húnaflói and Skagafjörður which is on the migration route over Iceland, C–D on the map on p. 299. A large number of barnacle geese sojourn here in the spring, especially from late April until mid-May. Barnacle geese are grass-eaters like all other species of geese, except for the brent goose, which feeds on eelgrass as mentioned above. Once the barnacle goose has rested and fed sufficiently to have restored its energy, it begins to prepare for its departure, and with the coming of a strong and helpful wind from the south, the whole colony quickly leaves the country.

As stated earlier, a few barnacle geese have occasionally remained and bred in Iceland. In the middle picture on the right are 2 barnacle geese on a skerry in Breiðafjörður. The female is on the nest, on the left of the picture, and the gander is standing on guard on the right. There were a total of 3 barnacle goose nests on this skerry in 1984, and one of them is pictured bottom right; it contained 5 eggs. There were also 5 eggs in one of the other nests, and 4 in the third. There were no breeding barnacle geese on this skerry in 1985, however. In its more northerly breeding grounds the barnacle goose begins to lay its eggs in June. There are usually 4–5 of them, dull white in colour. The down in the nest is grey, as can be seen in the picture on the right. The barnacle goose leaves its nesting sites in north-east Greenland early in September, and has arrived in Iceland by the middle of the same month. It continues its journey southwards in October.

The barnacle goose is considered one of the most beautiful species of geese, perhaps because of its contrasting white face and black head. It also has a black stripe from its bill to its dark brown eyes. There is no noticeable difference in colouring between the sexes, but as with most species of geese, the gander is larger than the female.

305

◁

The **COOT** (*Fulica atra*) is a stocky, slaty-black wetland-bird about 38 cm long and belonging to the *Rallidae* family. Its head is jet-black with a conspicuous white frontal shield and bill, as can be seen in the pictures on the left, which were taken at Höfn in Hornafjörður on 27 April 1985. The coot is a very secretive bird and is rather reluctant to fly, and even then only for short distances. Its behaviour is thus rather similar to a water rail's, and the 2 birds are indeed related. The coot is a common bird in Europe, but it is classified as a vagrant in Iceland, usually being sighted here every year. It has also nested in Iceland, but it is not known if it has ever successfully reared any young here.

The **WHITE STORK** (*Ciconia ciconia*), as most people will ▷ know, is a large white long-legged bird about 100 cm long. Its flight-feathers are black, but its long bill and legs are red.

A white stork was first known to stray to Iceland in 1969, but unfortunately there was no photographic record of the event. The second time a white stork was sighted here was on 27 March 1975, and this time it was recorded on film for posterity. The picture on the right was taken on 3 April that year near Dyrhólaey on the southern coast of Iceland. The stork was extremely shy and sensitive, and so the picture was taken at a great distance through the window of a car. The stork occasionally fed on capelin when down by the shore, but it was frequently harassed there by great black-backed gulls. Further inland it foraged for food in pools, ditches, and boggy streams where it could find various kinds of small animals – though this must have been a meagre diet for such a large bird, and not at all what it was used to in its homelands. It had probably been blown off course to Iceland whilst migrating to Europe from its winter quarters in South Africa. It was last definitely sighted on 4 June. Hopefully it departed from Iceland in a south-easterly direction and eventually reached mainland Europe.

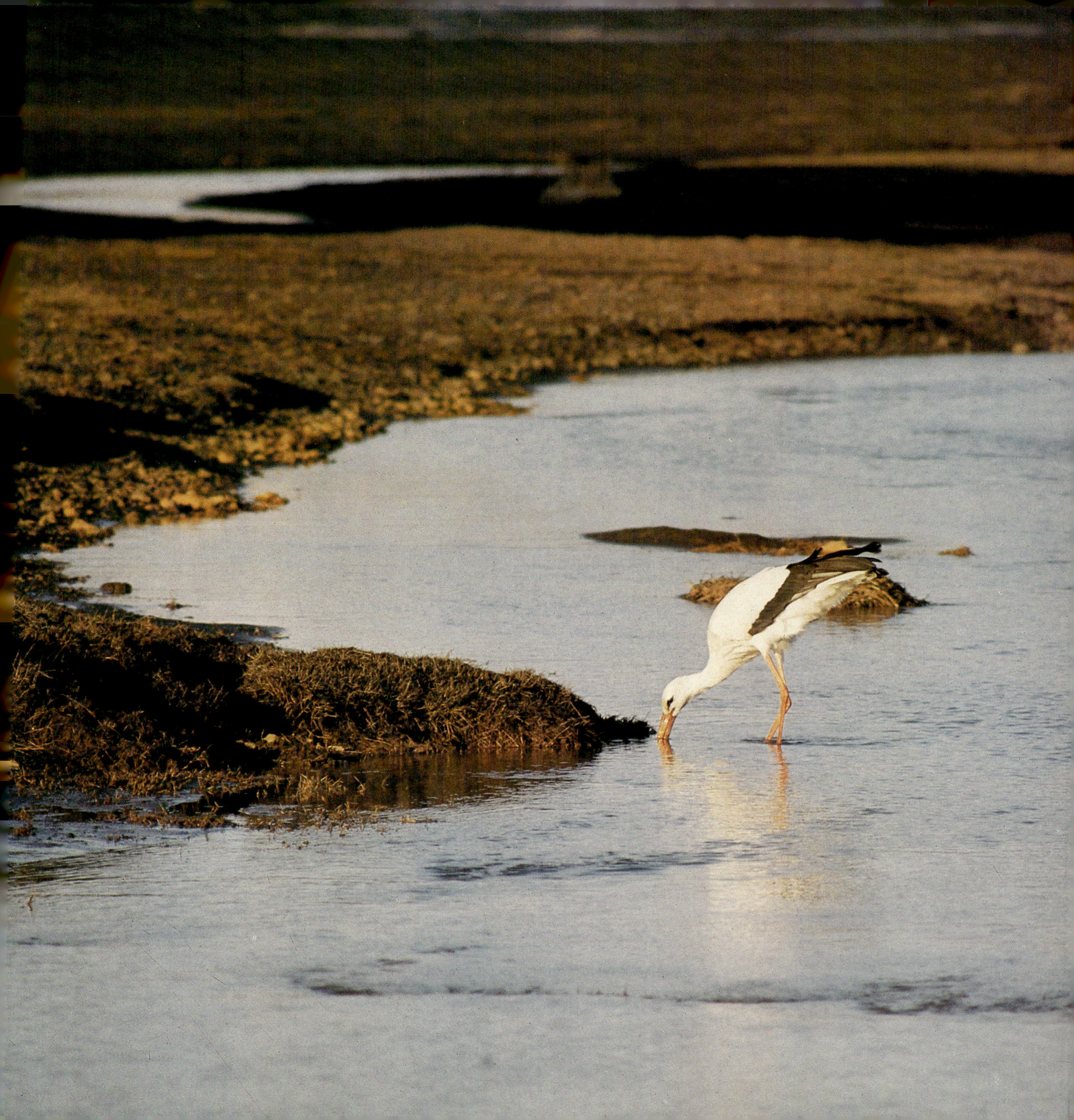

The **TURNSTONE** (*Arenaria interpres*) is one of the 3 species of waders which are passage migrants in Iceland. The other 2 species are the **sanderling** and the **knot** (both described later). All of these species breed in Greenland and the northern islands of Canada and visit Iceland in the spring and autumn when migrating to and from their winter quarters in Western Europe. A few birds of each species will occasionally also winter in Iceland, especially the turnstone. The turnstone also breeds outside of the Arctic Circle, even as far south as the isles, skerries and beaches of Scandinavia and Denmark. It is a stout shore-bird, about 23 cm long, streaked with black, white, and chestnut-red, and with orange legs, as in the pictures on this page. The one above was taken by the River Bugða in Hvalfjörður, and the one on the left on Flatey in Breiðafjörður.

The **SANDERLING** (Calidris alba) is a passage migrant which, like the turnstone, visits Iceland in the spring and autumn on its way to and from its winter quarters in Western Europe. Far fewer sanderlings visit Iceland than turnstones, however. Above is a flock of sanderlings on the sandy shore of Sandgerði on 19 May, and on the right are a sanderling and a turnstone foraging for food on the same beach. The sanderling is a small wader, about 20 cm long, and in the summer has pale rusty-brown upper-parts, speckled with black, and a contrasting white belly. Its main haunts are sandy beaches, where it can be seen trotting about at an amazing speed, one of its main characteristics being to chase frantically after receding waves.

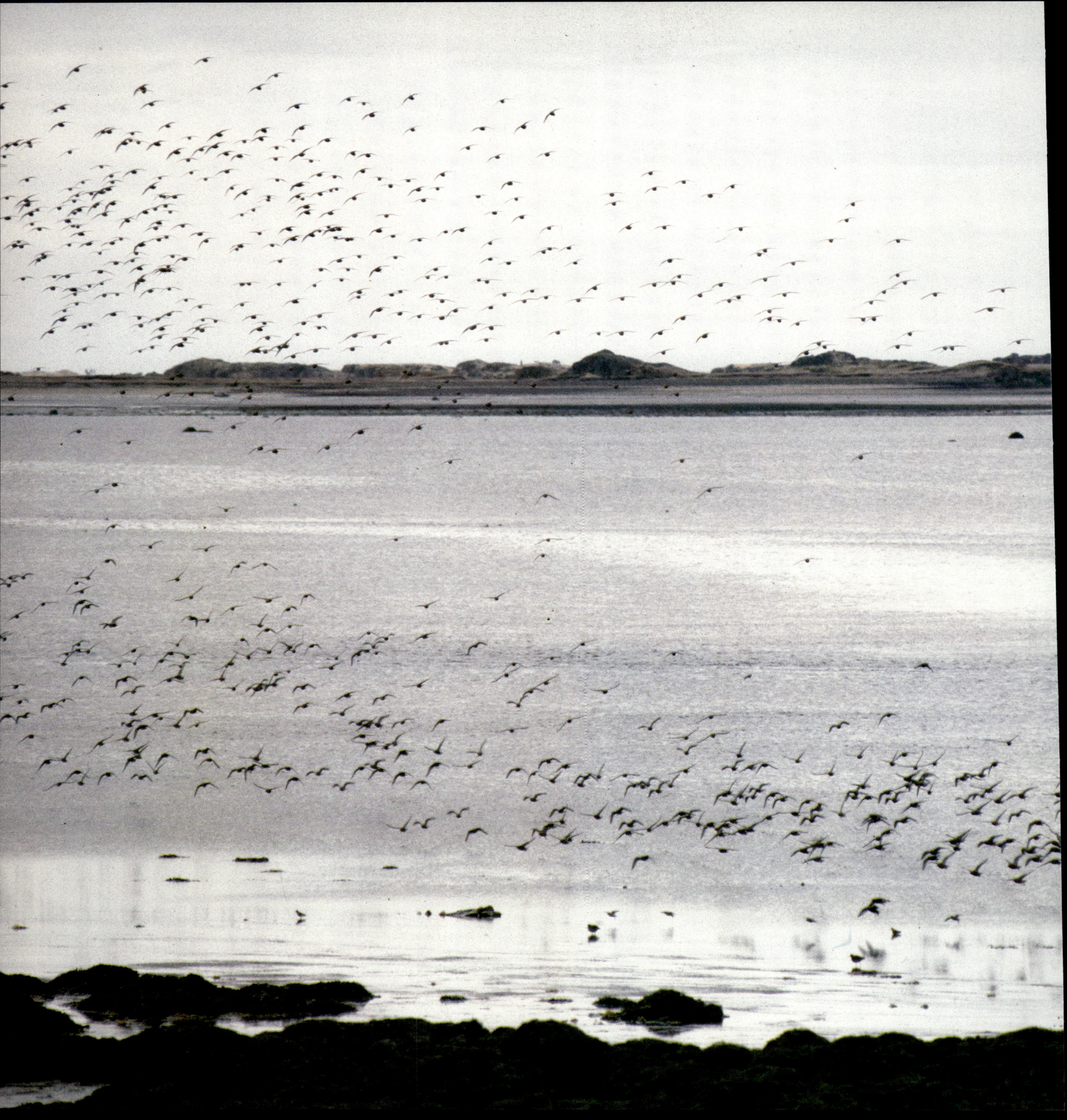

The **KNOT** (*Calidris canutus*) is the third species of wader which is a passage migrant in Iceland, visiting the country in the spring and autumn. It is a stocky bird, about 25 cm long, and in the summer has very mottled chestnut and black upper-parts and a reddish-brown head and under-parts. Around 200,000 knots visit Iceland every year, arriving from the British Isles in very large flocks in April and the first part of May. It remains in Iceland for around 3 weeks, mostly on the country's western and south-western coasts where it feeds on various molluscs, sand hoppers, and flies. Pictured on the left and below are flocks of knots in flight and on mud-flats in Faxaflói Bay.

△
The **BAR-TAILED GODWIT** (*Limosa lapponica*) is about 38 cm long, just slightly smaller than the black-tailed godwit, from which it can be distinguished by its more upturned bill, much shorter legs, and closely barred tail. The bar-tailed godwit is an irregular visitor to Iceland. A few have occasionally been spotted on the shore during the winter, as in the picture above; this was taken near Sandgerði on 24 March 1985 and shows an oystercatcher and 3 bar-tailed godwits foraging for food on the sandy beach.

The **JACKDAW** (*Corvus monedula*) has black upper-parts, dark grey under-parts, a grey nape, and distinctive pale grey eyes. It belongs to the same family as the raven, but is a much smaller bird, being only 33 cm long. Its main breeding grounds are in Europe and Mid-Asia. It is quite a common visitor to Iceland in the spring and autumn, however, and between 1950 and 1979 it was sighted here annually. The jackdaw has also sometimes wintered in Iceland, but then always in urban areas as it probably lives mostly on scraps of food from human habitations. The picture of the jackdaw on the left was taken in the old part of Hafnarfjörður on 14 April 1985.

The **COMMON GOLDENEYE** (*Bucephala clangula*) is mainly a winter visitor to Iceland from Northern Europe, and is mostly found on the rivers Sog and Brúará in the southern part of the country. In the summer it can also be found among Barrow's goldeneyes around Lake Mývatn. These 2 species are closely related and very similar in appearance, though it is relatively easy to distinguish between the drakes. On the left is a common goldeneye drake preening itself on the River Laxá near Lake Mývatn. Above right is a goldeneye drake, and below right is a young goldeneye drake (on the far right) with some Barrow's goldeneye ducks. Common goldeneye drakes seem to show more white on the body, and Barrow's goldeneye drakes more black, but the most distinguishing feature at short range is the white spot in front of the eye: this is round on the common goldeneye drake, but crescent-shaped on Barrow's goldeneye. The ducks of the 2 species are so alike that it can be virtually impossible to distinguish between them in the field.

313

14. VISITORS AND IRREGULAR BREEDING BIRDS

The **HOUSE MARTIN** (Delichon urbica) is about 13 cm long and has white under-parts and blue-back head, wings, and tail. It is often seen in Iceland in the spring and has twice been known to breed and rear young here. The pictures on these pages were taken in 1976, the second time that house martins nested in Iceland. Both the house martin and the **swallow** (Hirundo rustica), also often sighted here in the spring, are skilled hunters of insects, which they catch in flight. The house martin is commonly near human habitation, and builds an enclosed nest out of mud, often under the eaves of houses, as in the pictures here, which were taken in Sandgerði on 24 July 1976.

In the picture above left, the house martin is flying from its nest after having fed its young; 2 of the 3 chicks can be seen at the nest's opening near the top. Below left, one of the chicks has pushed its rear-end through the opening and is relieving itself outside the nest; the excreta is in mid-air. Pictured on the right is an adult house martin by the nest's opening; one of the chicks still has its head out after having had its maw filled with tasty insects. The house martin fills its gullet with flies in flight when hunting to feed its young, and it thus often nests near ponds where there are plenty of flies and midges, the house martin's main diet. Close to the nest in Sandgerði was a shallow lake which the parent birds often frequented to collect flies, flying back at regular intervals to feed their young at the entrance to the nest.

The bluish gloss on an adult house martin's back is clearly discernible in the picture on the right.

The house martin breeds all over Europe and well into the Far East. It is a very common bird in the British Isles, Denmark, Norway, and Sweden.

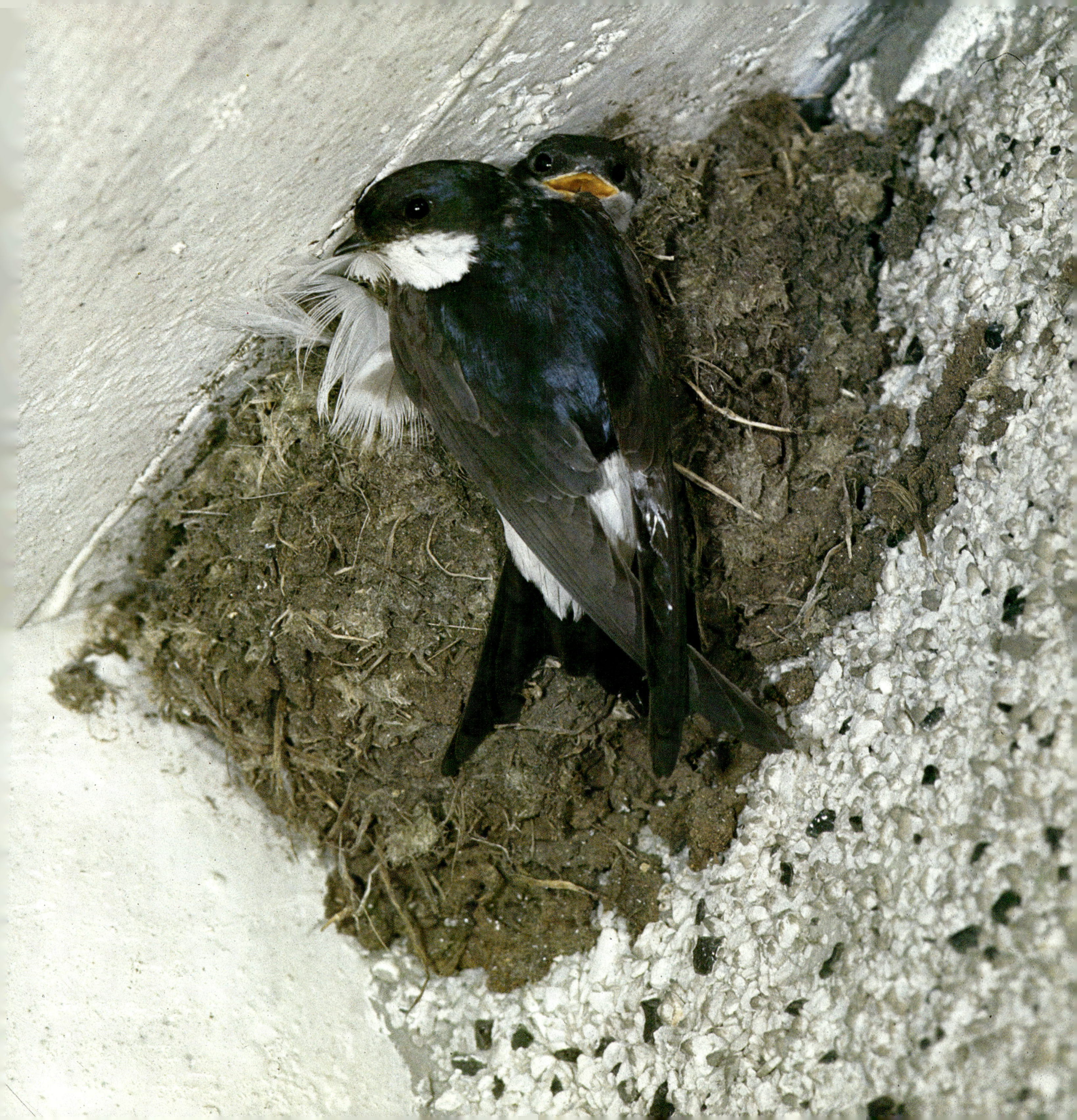

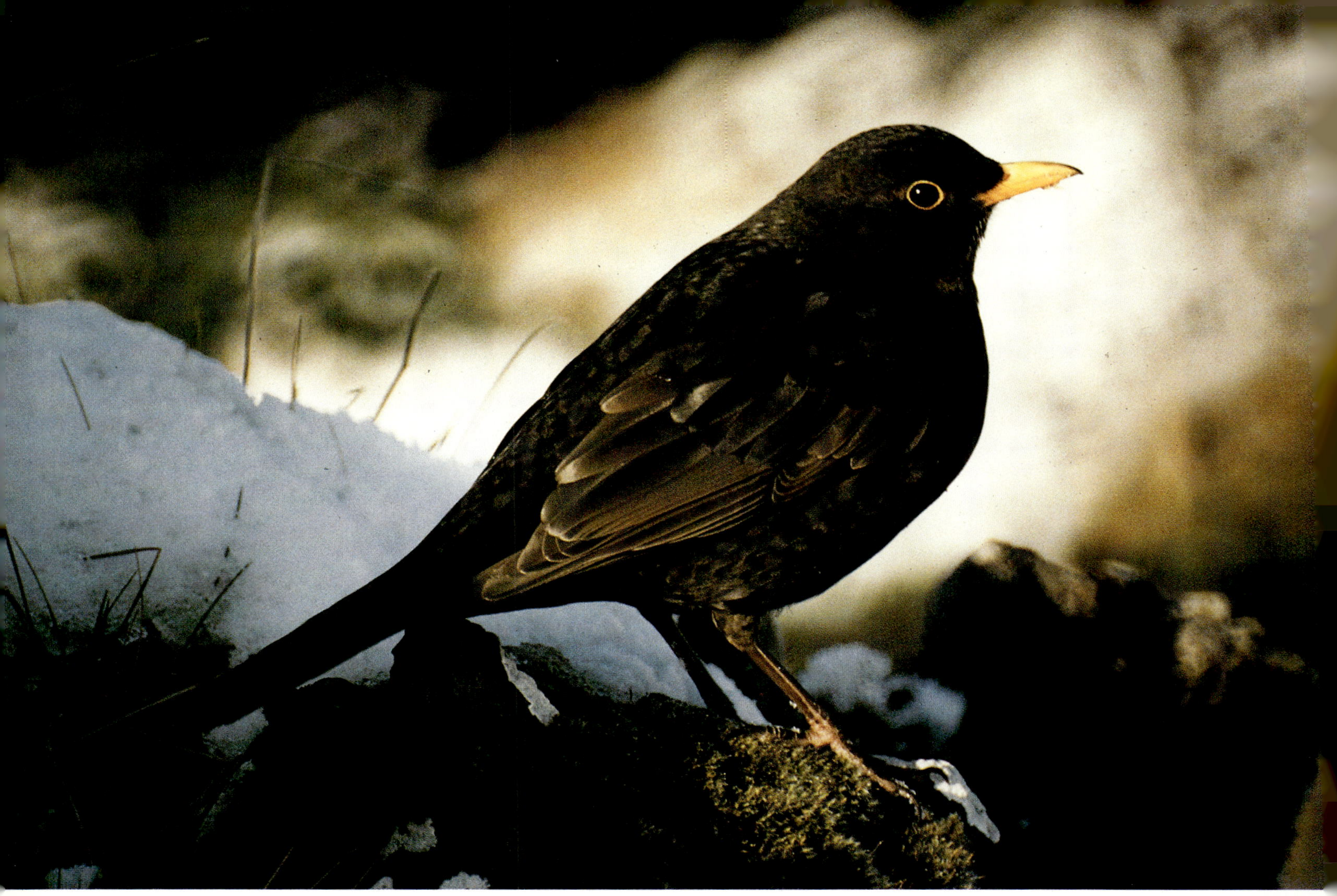
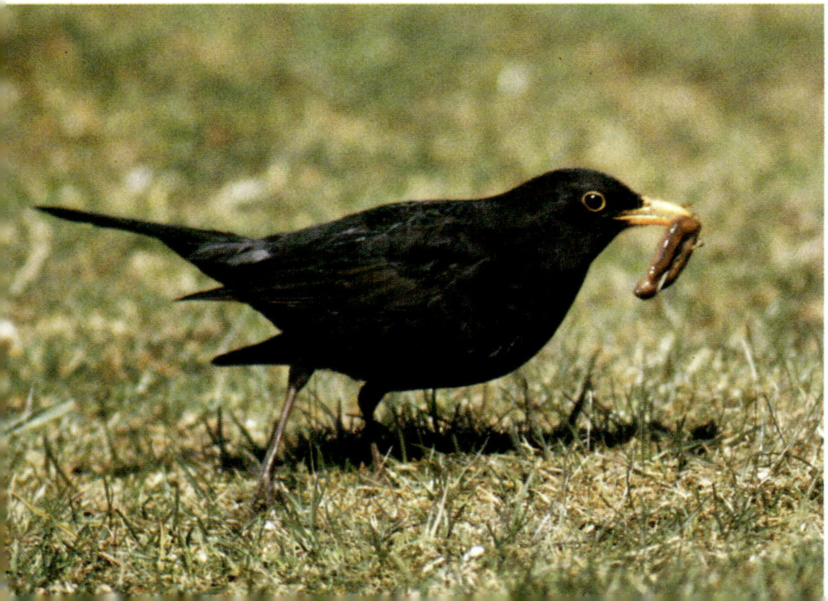
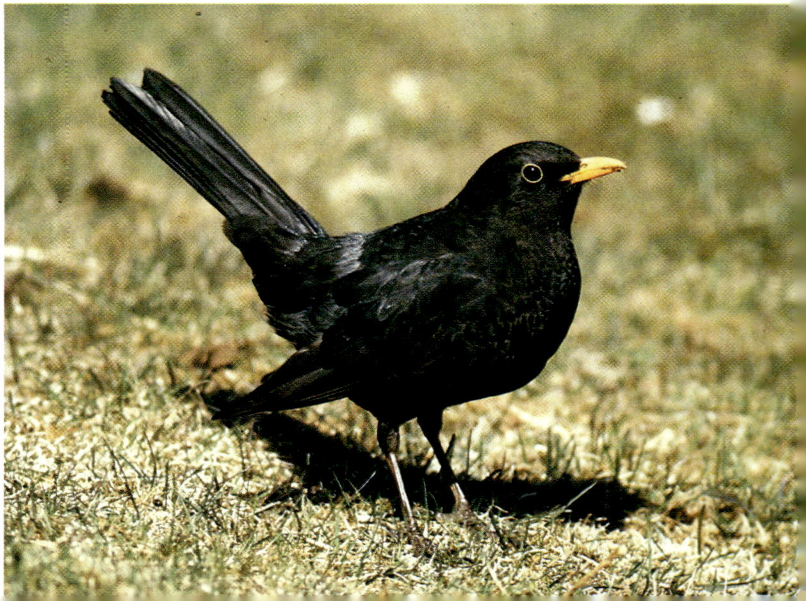

The **LAPWING** (*Vanellus vanellus*) is a large bird belonging to the plover family (**Charadriidae**). At 30 cm long it is considerably bigger than a golden plover. It is greenish-black and white in colour, and is easily recognised by the distinctive wispy crest on its head and its rather erratic flight and slow 'flapping' wing-beats. The lapwing is very common all over Europe, and usually nests on cultivated land or meadows, often near bogs or marshes.

The lapwing is an annual visitor to Iceland, a few birds arriving every autumn and winter, either individually or in small flocks. It has also sometimes spent the summer in Iceland, breeding and rearing young here. Above is a lapwing strolling in grass in Eyjafjörður, 24 June 1985. On the right is a lapwing in flight over the same area; this bird had 2 chicks hidden between some tussocks. The lapwing has not yet settled in Iceland permanently and become an annual breeding bird.

◁ The **BLACKBIRD** (*Turdus merula*) belongs to the thrush family (**Turdidae**) like the redwing, and is slightly bigger than the latter, or about 25 cm long. The male is completely black with a bright yellow bill and reddish-yellow eye-rings. The female is coloured brown with a whitish chin and brown bill.

Pictured above left (p. 316) is a male blackbird feeding on scraps outside a house in Garðabær on 13 March 1985. Below, far left, is a male blackbird with an earthworm in its bill in Höfn in Hornafjörður on 28 April 1985. When a blackbird perches it sticks up its tail and dangles its wings, as the male bird is doing in the picture near left. The blackbird is a common autumn and winter visitor to Iceland and has even nested here, though it has still not settled in Iceland permanently.

The **BRAMBLING** (*Fringilla montifringilla*) is 15 cm long ▷ and a colourful bird. The male is bright orange on its shoulders and breast and has a black head and white rump. The female has light brown upper-parts, paler under-parts, and a white rump. The brambling is quite a frequent visitor to Iceland and has occasionally nested here, though it does not breed here annually.

The pictures on the following pages (pp. 318–320) are of bramblings which nested in Iceland in 1978 and 1983, in both instances in spruce trees in cultivated woodlands. In 1983 the male perched on tree-tops near its nest and sang whilst the female was incubating. The male occasionally brought her food in the nest. Once the eggs had hatched, however, both birds were so busy hunting for food, feeding the chicks, and removing sacs of excreta, that the male no longer had any time for singing.

The **BRAMBLING** has occasionally bred in Iceland. The male (1) is slim and colourful as it perches in the tree-top and sings whilst the female (2) incubates the eggs in their nest in a spruce tree, 3.5 m above the ground. Whilst the chicks were very small the female remained in the nest to tend and brood them (3). She later began to hunt for food for them (4), as did the male (5). The male also removed the sacs of excreta from the nest (6) if any of the chicks relieved themselves, which they often did immediately after being fed. Both parents would sometimes arrive at the nest with food at the same time (7), as the gaping red mouths constantly demanded more to eat. In picture (8) are 2 well-grown young bramblings in a nest on

1 August 1978. On p. 320 is a young fully fledged brambling which has recently left the nest.

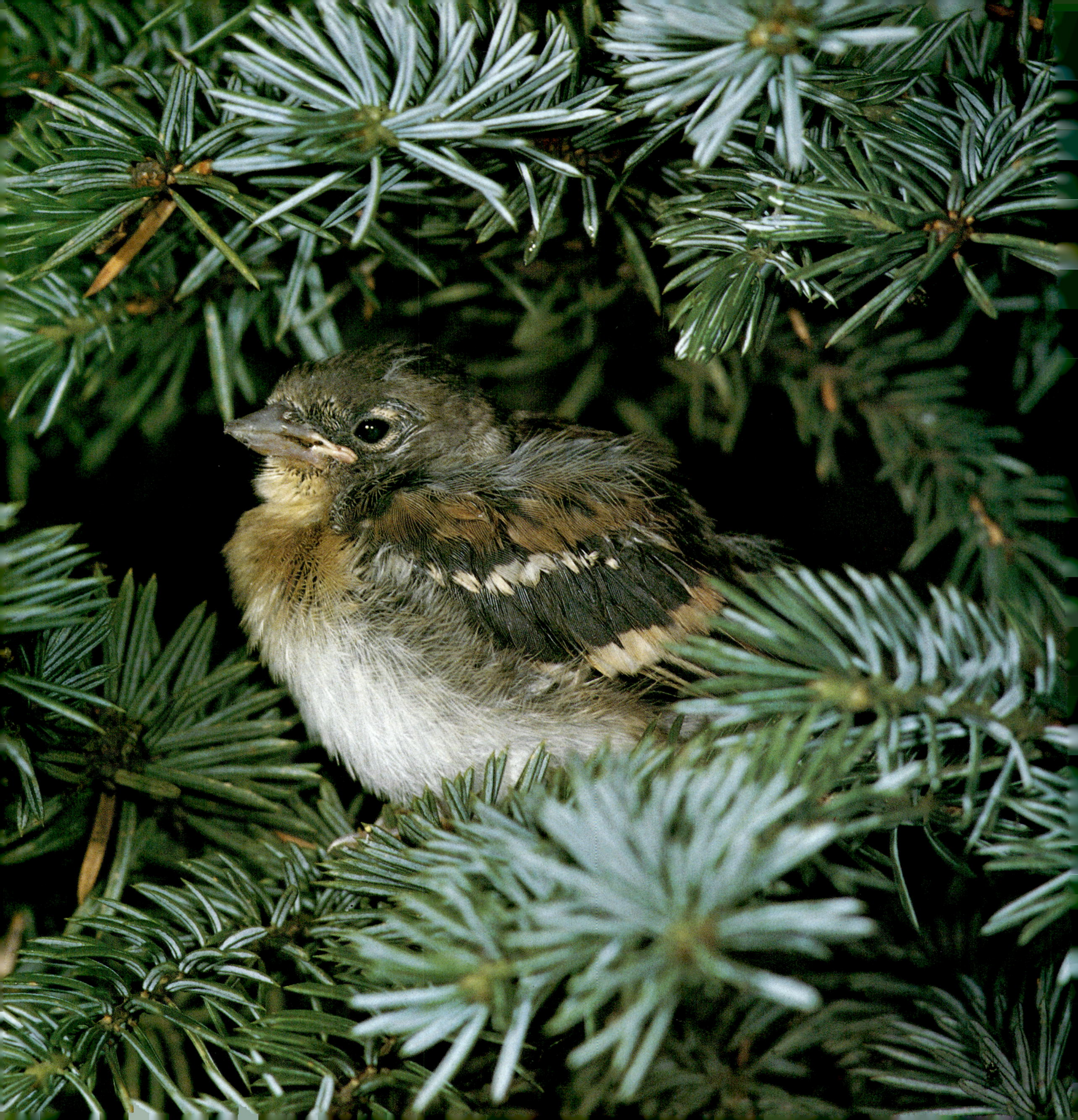

15. Postscript

It is now more than 20 years since I began to concentrate increasingly on the photography of birds. In my earlier books on Iceland, in which I tried to present a comprehensive portrait of the land and its people, the main emphasis was on pictures of landscapes, nature, and people's ways of life, though from the very first book onwards (*Iceland*, Reykjavík 1953), I have always included photographs of birds.

This present book, however, deals specifically with Icelandic birds and their habitats and behaviour. The idea for such a book was born about 15 years ago when my relative, the ornithologist Dr. Finnur Guðmundsson, commented on the need for an illustrated high-quality book on the bird life of Iceland. Accordingly, he actively encouraged my interest in photographing birds and we went on many expeditions together during which I benefitted enormously from his knowledge and guidance concerning birds and their behaviour. I also studied books on ornithology and bird photography and acquired the special photographic equipment necessary, including hides. I also designed a special pylon-hide, a tower with a platform for a hide on top, which could be unpacked and assembled in the field to various heights, depending on the circumstances. In the original plan for the book it was intended that I should provide the photographs and Finnur the main text. It took many more years than expected, however, to take photographs of all the Icelandic breeding birds of a high enough standard to do the book the justice I believed it deserved. Moreover it became increasingly obvious that Finnur's health was sadly failing and that it would be unlikely that he would be able to write the text or see the book in print. Finnur insisted that I continue with our book nonetheless, but that I should also write the text as well as take the photographs. To this end he placed all his work at my disposal. I gratefully accepted this generous offer, and in return obtained his consent to dedicate the book to him.

Now that the book is finally completed, my main thoughts are of the immense gratitude I bear Finnur for all he taught me about Icelandic birds, and for the many treasured memories I have of our expeditions all over the country. Without his encouragement, and without his faith in me to bolster my confidence, it is unlikely that this book would ever have seen the light of day.

Those interested in genealogy may be interested to know exactly how Finnur Guðmundsson and I were related. Finnur's paternal grandfather, Guðmundur Bárðarson, farmer at Kollafjarðarnes in Steingrímsfjörður, and my paternal grandmother, Guðrún Bárðardóttir, were brother and sister. Moreover our fathers, the naturalist Guðmundur G. Bárðarson and the marine engineer Bárður Guðmundur Tómasson, were brought up together at Kollafjarðarnes.

Finnur's writings provided the basic groundwork for much of what is written in this book, but I also found it necessary to do further reading and research, and all the main sources used are listed in the bibliography at the back, along with the titles of many other books and articles, in various languages, which I believe will be of interest to bird-watchers.

Though informative books and articles are useful, there is still no better way of learning about the life and habits of birds than by observing and photographing them in the field. Sitting in a hide for days on end near a nest or avian gathering place provides the best opportunity of all for getting to know and understand birds. Many descriptions and comments in this book are thus based on personal observation, even though they almost invariably confirm previously known facts about birds and their behaviour. I have also learned a great deal from participating in expeditions and discussions with other knowledgeable bird-watchers, and I would like to take this opportunity to express my gratitude to the many ornithologists and bird-enthusiasts who have accompanied me on my various expeditions. On the eagle-counting surveys of the Icelandic Society for the Protection of Birds, I have, along with Finnur Guðmundsson, chiefly travelled with the doctor Björn Guðbrandsson, the society's chairman Professor Magnús Magnússon, and the biologist Baldur Sigurðsson. I have investigated the bird life of Öræfasveit, Ingólfshöfði, Höfn in Hornafjörður, and Skrúður Island in the company of Hálfdán Björnsson from Kvísker. Ragnar Sigfinnsson from Grímsstaðir has often accompanied me in the Lake Mývatn area. I have stayed on Hellisey with the teacher and film-cameraman Páll Steingrímsson and his colleagues, and from there visited Geldungur, Álsey, and other outer isles of Vestmannaeyjar. Hlöðver Johnsen went with me onto Ystiklettur to photograph Manx shearwaters. There were 18 people on the expedition to Eldey on 20 August 1982, the nucleus being a group of 8 experienced climbers from the Vestmannaeyjar. The Icelandic Nature Conservation Council had given its permission for this visit to the bird sanctuary and, being a member of the Council, I was its official representative on the trip. I have visited many of the islands of Breiðafjörður, especially on bird-ringing expeditions, with the ornithologist Ævar Petersen, with whom I have stayed on Flatey; I have also visited many a Breiðafjörður isle with Trausti Tryggvason from Stykkishólmur, and with Jóhann Jónasson, Gunnlaugur Kristjánsson, Gissur Tryggvason, and others. I have visited the razorbill colony on Stóraurð under Látrabjarg with Þórður Jónsson from Hvallátur, and I have observed the bird life of Ísafjarðardjúp and beyond with Jónas Helgason from Æðey. I went round Skagafjörður, the Skagi peninsula, and to Drangey Island with Ingólfur Sveinsson from Sauðárkrókur. I have also roamed the Skagafjörður area with Ingólfur Nikódemusson. On Grímsey I had Alfreð Jónsson from Básar as my guide, and in Akureyri I had the assistance of many people, including Gunnar Egilsson and Arnar Ragnarsson. The teacher Steingrímur Þorsteinsson was very helpful to me in Dalvík. I have photographed ducks and other birds for many years, especially in the Mývatn region, with Grétar Eiríksson. The boat-trip to Skrúður from Fáskrúðsfjörður was organised by Albert Kemp, and I sailed with him to the island along with Úlfar Jónsson, farmer at Vattarnes. The couple Elínborg Pálsdóttir and Benedikt Þorsteinsson greatly assisted me when I was photographing birds in Höfn in Hornafjörður.

I have also been accompanied or assisted on various bird-watching or photographic expeditions by Professor Arnþór Garðarsson, Jón Guðmundsson, Kristinn Haukur Skarphéðinsson, Ólafur K. Nielsen, Agnar Ingólfsson, Kjartan G. Magnússon, Ib Petersen, Sverrir Thorstensen, Erlingur Ólafsson, and Skarphéðinn Þórisson. Jón Ólafsson, Guðmundur Guðmundsson, Einar Þorleifsson, Ingólfur Guðnason, and Jóhann Óli Hilmarsson have all notified me of rarely seen birds which I was subsequently able to photograph.

I would like to express my gratitude to the Icelandic Ministry of Education and Culture for its permission to photograph the white-tailed eagle, the gyrfalcon, the little auk, and the snowy owl.

One of the very first pieces of advice which Finnur Guðmundsson gave me about bird-watching was the need to have good contact with the people who lived in or near places where birds were known to occur or nest. The truth of this advice became very apparent once I began to specialise in photographing birds. Good relations with people can be important in taking landscape pictures and very necessary, of course, when taking pictures of personal or group activities. For bird-watching and photography the goodwill and assistance of local landowners and neighbours of bird colonies is also absolutely essential for good results. In pursuing my interest of photographing birds, I have thus come into contact with so many kind people all over the country, and I know I can never sufficiently express my gratitude and appreciation for their friendship, hospitality, and assistance. I have tried to list as many of them as possible here below, but, inevitably with such a list, there are bound to be inadvertent omissions, and so I would also like to add my sincere thanks to all the un-named well-wishers who have been so kind and helpful to me over the years. I have turned to some of the following people year after year, and to others just the once or twice:

Þráinn Löve, Hjörsey, Faxaflói. – Narfi Kristjánsson, Jófríður Sigurðardóttir and Guðmundur Kristjánsson, Hoftún, Snæfellsnes. – Trausti Tryggvason and Kristborg Haraldsdóttir, Stykkishólmur. – Ingimar Sveinbjörnsson, Króksfjarðarnes. – Þórður Jónsson and Ásgeir Erlendsson, Hvallátrar, at Látrabjarg. – Helgi Þórarinsson and Guðrún Lárusdóttir, and in recent years Jónas Helgason and Katrín Alexíusdóttir, Æðey. – Aðalsteinn Jóhannsson, Skjaldfönn. – Ingólfur Sveinsson and Anna Pálsdóttir, Sauðárkrókur. – Kristmundur Bjarnason and Hlíf Árnadóttir, Sjávarborg, Skagafjörður. – Sigurður Jónsson and family, Syðri Húsabakki, Skagafjörður. – Alfreð Jónsson and Ragnhildur Einarsdóttir, Básar, Grímsey. – Steingrímur Þorsteinsson and Steinunn Sveinbjörnsdóttir, Dalvík. – Sverrir Thorstensen and Þórey Ketilsdóttir, Stórutjarnaskóli, Ljósavatnshreppur. – Þórir Ingjaldsson and Agnar Þorsteinsson and families, Öxará, Bárðardalur. – Tryggvi Harðarson and family, Svartárkot, Bárðardalur. – Hallur Þór Hallgrímsson and Guðrún Pétursdóttir, Árhólar, Laxárdalur. – Hólmgrímur Kjartansson and Kristbjörg Steingrímsdóttir, Kjartan Sigtryggsson and Jónasína Þ. Sigurðardóttir, Hraun, Aðaldalur. – Njáll Friðbjarnarson and families, Sandur, Aðaldalur. – Vilhjálmur Jónasson and families, Sílalækur, Aðaldalur. – Ragnar Sigfinnsson and Guðrún Benediktsdóttir and their families, Grímsstaðir, Mývatn. – Einar Ísfeldsson, Hólmfríður Stefánsdóttir, Auður Ísfeldsdóttir and Elín Helga Einarsdóttir, Kálfaströnd, Mývatn. – Árni Halldórsson and Guðbjörg Jónsdóttir, Garður, Mývatn. – Ívar Stefánsson and Birna Björnsdóttir, Haganes, Mývatn. – Valgeir Illugason and Guðrún Jakobsdóttir, Reykjahlíð, Mývatn. – Árni Gíslason and Gísli Árnason, Laxárbakki, Mývatn. – Jónas Sigurgeirsson and Ingólfur Jónasson, Helluvað, Mývatn. – Jón Aðalsteinsson, Vindbelgur, Mývatn. – Benedikt Þorsteinsson and Elínborg Pálsdóttir, Höfn, Hornafjörður. – Hálfdán Björnsson and family, Kvísker, Öræfi. – Þorsteinn Jóhannsson and Sigrún Pálsdóttir, Svínafell, Öræfi. – Guðlaugur Gunnarsson and Ester Einarsdóttir, Viðihlíð, Svínafell, Öræfi. – Magnús Pálsson and Magnea Þórarinsdóttir, Syðri Steinsmýri, Meðalland. – Páll Steingrímsson and family, Vestmannaeyjar. – Jón I. Sigurðsson, Guðjón Jónsson, Þórarinn Sigurðsson and their families, and Ólafur Jónsson and Oddi Pálsson, Vestmannaeyjar.

———

In returning to the book once more, I would like to record my special thanks to the ornithologist Ævar Petersen, Head of the Zoological Department of the Icelandic Natural History Museum, for his invaluable assistance in reading over the text of the book in manuscript and pointing out where there was room for improvement. I also thank my friend and comrade of many an expedition, Óttar Kjartansson, for a final check on the text and for ensuring that there was conformity between the main text and the picture captions.

Finally, I would like to express my sincere thanks just once more to all those who have helped in the making of this book. I have relied on the knowledge and assistance of a great number of people and have tried to maintain the highest standards of truth and accuracy, but, as always in such instances, the final responsibility for any error must rest with me. It is my sincere hope that this book will make an interesting contribution to the knowledge of Icelandic birds, and that its readers will gain as much pleasure from birds as I myself have done.

16. Dr. Finnur Guðmundsson

Finnur Guðmundsson.
This book is dedicated to his memory.

Finnur Guðmundsson was born at Kjörseyri in Hrútafjörður on 22 April 1909, the son of Guðmundur G. Bárðarson, the naturalist, and his wife Helga Finnsdóttir, daughter of a well-known scholar, Finnur Jónsson.

From his early childhood onwards, Finnur Guðmundsson was greatly interested in all the natural sciences, and he divided his time between biology, ornithology, entomology, conchology, and botany. Ornithology gradually became his main interest, however, as is clearly indicated by his bird-watching diaries which he began to keep in 1918 when not yet ten years old. Finnur's father was one of the first instigators of geological research in Iceland and greatly encouraged his son's interest in natural studies. In 1926 Finnur's father became a teacher of natural sciences at the Reykjavík Grammar School, where Finnur himself completed his secondary education in 1929. From 1929 until 1937 (apart from one year at home in Iceland) Finnur studied zoology, botany, and geology at the University of Hamburg in Germany, where he finally presented his doctoral thesis in zoology on the subject of planktonic life in the seas around Iceland. Despite such learning over a wide field of subjects, ornithology continued to be Finnur's most consuming interest. He returned to Iceland and in September 1937 began working in the fisheries section of the Department of Industrial Research at the University of Iceland, and he was involved in research projects there until 1946. In 1941 he was made supervisor of the Natural History Museum, which in 1932 had begun organising the ringing of birds at the instigation of Finnur and his father. In 1942 Finnur himself became the leader of this bird-ringing programme and remained its supervisor for the next 36 years. In 1947 the Natural History Museum became a state institution and Finnur was appointed its director, a position he held until his retirement in 1977. All Finnur's work at the Museum was aimed at establishing it as a scientific institute, and he was particularly active in building up a complete collection of Icelandic birds. Until a full-time botanist was appointed to the Museum he was also in charge of the botany collection. Finnur was a very conscientious scientist and published around 90 scientific papers as well as many articles for magazines and journals. He quickly became a national figure and was always referred to as an ornithologist even though his actual qualifications were in a much broader field of subjects. He was a keen supporter of nature conservation and was a committee member of the Icelandic Nature Conservation Council from 1956, the year it was founded, until 1975. Two of the most influential and successful campaigns he was involved in concerned the establishment and protection of the nature reserves in the Lake Mývatn region and in the Þjórsárver. From the moment Finnur returned to Iceland he was always in good contact with keen bird-watchers all over the country. He was a pioneer in many aspects of nature studies and many present-day Icelandic scientists once belonged to the group of young men Finnur referred to as 'my bird boys'. He was always prepared to talk about and share his knowledge with young people, and he was especially felicitous in increasing and strengthening their interest in nature.

Finnur was the chairman of the Icelandic Committee for the Protection of Birds from its beginning in 1948, and was Iceland's representative on the International Council for the Protection of Birds. He was also an honorary member of the Jourdain Society, the Dansk Ornitologisk Central, the Ornithologischer Verein zu Hamburg, and the World Pheasant Association. He was an elected member of the British Ornithologists' Union, the American Ornithologists' Union, and the Dansk Ornitologisk Forening. Furthermore he was on the editorial committee of the French journal *Alauda*. Finnur was made an honorary member of the World Wildlife Fund, and was awarded the Order of the Knight of the Golden Ark by Prince Bernhard of the Netherlands. The President of Iceland honoured him with the Order of the Falcon. Finnur was thus internationally known and respected and many of the world's famous scientists were among his personal friends.

Finnur married Guðríður Gísladóttir in 1941 and they had 2 daughters, Helga and Guðrún. Guðríður died in August 1978. Finnur suffered from increasingly poor health in the last few years of his life and died on 27 December 1979.

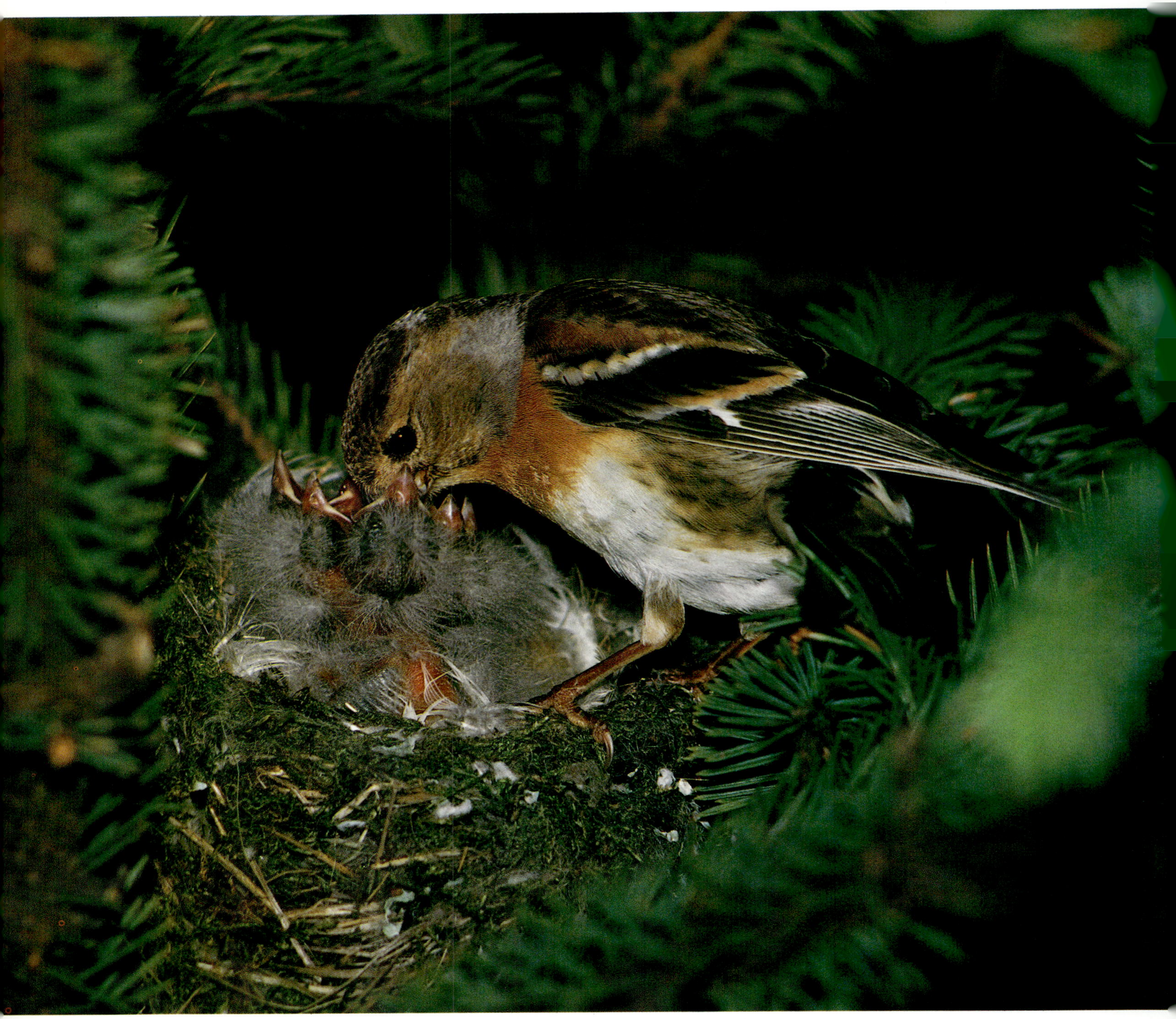

17. Bird photography

'How did you take that picture?' is a question I am often asked, especially about photographs of birds. The answer varies according to the nature and circumstances of each and every picture. Bird photography is a rather special field, even though the photographic equipment used is the same as when taking pictures of landscapes or people. As subjects, most birds seldom keep still, and many of them are so shy and wary that it is very difficult to get near to them at all. The first rule for getting good photographs of birds is to be well acquainted with their habitats and behaviour. There are many fine books available from which one can learn how to recognise birds. These books have detailed information about many different species and are usually illustrated with coloured drawings or photographs in which the birds' distinctive features are cleary marked. The book which most Icelandic bird-enthusiasts use is *Fuglar Íslands og Evrópu*, a translation and adaptation by Finnur Guðmundsson of *A Field Guide to the Birds of Britain and Europe* by Roger Tory Peterson, Guy Mountfort, and P.A.D. Hollom. Finnur Guðmundsson's Icelandic version includes specially expanded sections on Icelandic birds which Finnur wrote himself. Whilst translating the book he also revised all the Icelandic names for birds and created many new ones for hundreds of species, all of which are now in current use in Iceland. Such a book is absolutely essential for any bird-watcher or bird-photographer. It is also advisable to have a pocket note-book in which to record anything of interest in the birds' behaviour. A photograph can also be part of such a record, and it is generally sufficient if the distinctive features of the bird are discernible.

But if photography is to be the specific aim of bird-watching, however, greater demands have to be made as regards the technical quality of the pictures. Special equipment is then usually required, as well as plenty of time and extraordinary patience. Naturally, the first question is usually: 'What kind of camera should I use?' Most of the pictures in this book were taken with a 6×6 cm reflex-camera (Hasselblad) with various lenses, from 50 mm to 500 mm focal length, and in one instance 1000 mm (the white stork, p. 307, with a 500 mm lens and a 2× teleconverter). Several pictures were taken out of doors in sunlight with the help of 2 flashlamp heads. The light from the flashlamps was calculated to brighten up the areas in shadow, though the use of flashlamps is hardly evident in the pictures. The photograph on the opposite page (p. 324) was taken with a Hasselblad from a hide on top of a pylon in thick woodland. The main lighting here was provided by a teleflash (a concentrated narrow beam of light). Although the quality of enlarged pictures is better with a 6×6 cm film, a 35 mm camera (using 24×36 mm film) is much lighter and easier to use when photographing birds on the wing in the open. Long telephoto lenses are also easier to handle on a 35 mm camera, and the pictures produced from a 24×36 mm film are generally of an acceptable quality. A few photographs in this book were taken with a Nikon camera, some with a 1000 mm mirror-telephoto lens, e.g. the pictures of the snowy owl in the Ódáðahraun, pp. 246–7. I mostly use 150–250 mm lenses on a 6×6 cm camera when photographing birds from a hide, and 300–400 mm lenses with a 35 mm camera for pictures out in the open. Although I have mentioned 2 specific makes of camera here, there are many other kinds which are just as good for 6×6 cm and 24×36 mm films. The most important point is that the photographer is very familiar with his camera, for it is this factor which often determines the quality of a photograph rather than the particular make of camera used.

By far the easiest birds to photograph are cliff-birds; fulmars, kittiwakes, puffins, razorbills, common and Brünnich's guillemots are all generally calm and relaxed on cliff-ledges and there is usually no problem in taking pictures and close-ups of them from the cliff-top. Waterfowl can also be very acquiescent in certain places, as for example on Lake Tjörnin in Reykjavík and in many bays and creeks. If small birds are regularly given food in a particular place, it is usually possible to photograph them there without too much trouble. Out in the field there are two main approaches to photographing birds. The first is to carefully reconnoitre an area where birds are known to occur, and then to settle in one spot, wait for the birds to appear, and photograph them from a distance. The other method is to be concealed, e.g. in a hide with an opening for a camera lens. Hides are specially designed for photographing birds and other shy creatures; there is a picture of one in use on p. 154. This hide was raised on a platform on a pylon built of aluminium angles to gain an elevated view of a whooper swan's nest. I have also used such pylon-hides for taking pictures of gyrfalcon nests high up on rock faces. The perforated aluminium angles can be assembled to provide a platform 6–10 m high. The pylon-hide may not be raised too near the nest, however, nor obstruct the bird's approaches to it. The pylon has to be to the side, right against the rock face, and at an appropriate distance. Everything depends, of course, on the various circumstances at each nesting site. The hides which I have designed and used have a base area of 90×110 cm and are 145 cm high as experience has taught me that this is the most suitable size. It is impossible to stand up in such a hide, but it will house a sitting person quite comfortably. I now have 6 such hides so that I can be gradually moving some of them into position whilst photographing in one of the others. The hide is made out of greenish-brown canvas and the struts and roof-frame are made out of aluminium poles which can be dismantled and carried on one's back. There is an entrance at the back which can be zipped up, and in the front section there are holes fitted with canvas sleeves for camera lenses, flashlamps, and tripod legs. Pockets are sewn onto the inside walls for food and other small items, and there are also pockets on the outside, at the base of the hide, which can be filled with sand, gravel, or stones to weigh it down. There are also tent-peg holes around the bottom edges, and there are fixtures at all the top corners of the hide for attaching guy-lines. There are also observation holes on all sides of the hide which are covered with tight netting so that anyone inside cannot be seen from the outside. It is important to have a light and comfortable chair inside the hide as one often has to sit continuously from early in the morning until late at night, day after day, sometimes for up to a fortnight. It may also be necessary to remain in the hide all night so as to avoid disturbing the birds by entering and leaving it. Hides are mostly used for close-ups of birds and their young in the nest, but they can be just as useful in other places, especially lakes, pools, or mud-flats, where birds come to bathe or forage for food. One just has to sit and wait patiently until the birds appear – and the waiting can sometimes be long and very trying to one's patience.

Most birds are often very shy and wary and the slightest unexpected change in the vicinity of their nests can arouse their suspicions. Anyone who thinks he can just go straight up to a nest, raise a hide, and immediately start taking marvellous pictures is simply day-dreaming. Such behaviour would almost certainly frighten the birds into abandoning the nest completely, even though it contained eggs or newly hatched young. All bird-watchers and photographers must let the welfare of the birds and their off-

On the right is a pylon-hide which has been erected for photographing a nest high up on a rock face. The hide is on a platform on top of a tower of perforated aluminium angles which are bolted together. Such equipment is usually necessary for photographing gyrfalcon nests or bird nests high up in trees. The pylon must never be erected too close to the nest or obstruct the birds' approaches to it. Such pylon-hides can be erected up to a height of 10 m, but the tower must then be secured by side-stanchions and guy-ropes.

spring come first – determination to get good pictures must never be allowed to jeopardise birds' lives. It is usually necessary to raise a hide at quite a distance from the nest at first, sometimes up to 100 m away, so as to eventually get a good picture of a bird and its young. The hide is gradually moved closer to the nest in stages, either daily or at intervals of a few days. In the case of very wary and suspicious birds, it can take up to 2 weeks to edge the hide close to the nest. Each time the hide is moved, the nest must be carefully observed from a distance through good binoculars to check that the sitting bird returns to incubate its eggs or brood its young. If the bird in question does not return to the nest within a short period of time, then there is nothing else for it but to dismantle and remove the hide and abandon all plans for photographing that nest that year. It is also important to remember that the hide must never be moved towards the nest whilst it is raining, for if the parent birds are alarmed and keep away from the nest at first, there is a very real danger that the eggs will become cold or the young die of exposure before they return.

As mentioned earlier in the book, individual birds of the same species can vary in their degree of shyness; certain species are also much more wary than others. It can thus be pure chance which determines whether the bird one wishes to photograph is a shy or acquiescent one. Wary or otherwise, there is always one place where every bird can be found for certain during the breeding season: the nest. It is there that the birds fulfil their natural instincts to lay and incubate eggs and then brood and rear their young. Although this is convenient for bird-watchers and photographers, they must never take undue advantage of this fact and disrupt the natural life of the birds. Nests are often carefully hidden in dense vegetation, and it can be difficult to photograph them without 'exposing' them, i.e. pushing aside the grass and foliage until the eggs and young are in clear view. If this has to be done, it must be done very carefully, for if the nest is left 'exposed' once the picture has been taken, it is very likely that the eggs and young will be snatched by a predator before the parent birds return. A nest must **never** be 'exposed', therefore, by actually cutting away vegetation; indeed such a picture would certainly look unnatural and so be useless anyway. Leaves, stalks, and branches can be loosely tied to one side, without being broken or cut, and once the photograph has been taken, be put back into their original position. It is the moral and bounden duty of any bird-watcher or photographer to ensure that the nest is in exactly the same condition after a photograph has been taken, as it was before.

What must be avoided at all costs is the raising of a hide in a place the general public is likely to frequent. A hide can easily attract the attention of a curious passer-by who may frighten the birds into abandoning the nest and thus ruin any chance of a successful photograph. Horses and cows can be just as curious as people and, apart from disturbing the photographer, may even trample on the nest, if it is on the ground, or knock over the hide itself by rubbing themselves up against it.

In the past, hides have been predominantly associated with the photographing of birds and their young in the nest, but, as mentioned above, hides can also be used with very good results in such open places as lakesides and mud-flats, and indeed many of the pictures in this book were obtained this way.

18. Bibliography

18.1 Bibliography of Finnur Guðmundsson on birds.

(Based on a list by Ævar Petersen in the journal Náttúrufr. 49 (2–3), Reykjavík 1979.)

1932 Beobachtungen an isländischen Eiderenten (*Somateria m. mollissima*). Beitr. FortPflBiol. Vögel 8: 85–97, 142–147.
1932 Farfuglar og fuglamerkingar. Náttúrufr. 2: 71–80.
1932 Æðarkóngur (*Somateria spectabilis* (L.). Náttúrufr. 2: 87–88.
1932 Ausländische Beringungszentralen. Island. Vogelzug 3 (3): 139–140.
1936 (with G. Timmermann). Ein Besuch der Mantelmöwenkolonie auf der Insel Sandey im Thingvallavatn (Südwest-Island). Beitr. FortPfl-Biol. Vögel 12: 14–21.
1937 Um fæðu íslensku rjúpunnar. Náttúrufr. 7: 163–168.
1938 Ritfregn (Günter Timmerman: Die Vögel Islands. Erster Teil, 1. Hälfte. 109 síður, 9 myndir. Vísindafélag Íslendinga (Societas Scientiarum Islandica) XXI. Reykjavík 1938. Náttúrufr. 8: 47–48. (Book review).
1938 Fuglanýjungar. Náttúrufr. 8: 164–167.
1939 Nýr fugl. Náttúrufr. 9: 44–45.
1939 Ritfregn. (Magnús Björnsson: Fuglabók Ferðafélags Íslendinga. Árbók F. Í. 1939). Náttúrufr. 9: 148–150. (Book review).
1940 Fuglanýjungar I. Náttúrufr. 10: 4–34.
1941 Æðarvarp og dúntekja á Íslandi. Fylgirit með frumvarpi til laga um friðun æðarfugla og frumvarpi til laga um eyðingu svartbaka. 19 pages.
1942 Fuglanýjungar II. Náttúrufr. 12: 161–188.
1943 Sannleikurinn um hnegg hrossagauksins. Náttúrufr. 13: 163–169.
1943 Skýrsla um fuglamerkingar Náttúrugripasafnsins árið 1941. Skýrs. ísl. náttúrufr. fél. 1941 og 1942. Fylgirit 18 pages.
1944 Fuglanýjungar III. Náttúrufr. 14: 107–137.
1944 Fuglar sem óvinir nytjafiska í ám og vötnum. Náttúrufr. 14: 176–179.
1945 Skýrsla um fuglamerkingar Náttúrugripasafnsins 1942 og 1943. Skýrs. íslenska náttúrufræð. fel. 1943. Fylgirit. 26 bls.
1950 Nýjar súluvarpstöðvar. Náttúrufr. 20: 49–57.
1951 The effect of the recent climatic changes on the bird life of Iceland. Proc. Xth. Int. Orn. Congr. Uppsala 1950: 502–514.
1951 Álitsgerð dr. Finns Guðmundssonar um áhrif veiða á íslenska rjúpnastofninn. Menntamálaráðuneytið. 20 bls.
1951 Skýrsla um fuglamerkingar Náttúrugripasafnsins 1944–1946. Skýrs. ísl. náttúrufr. fél. 1944–1946. Fylgirit 32 bls.
1952 Bird Protection in Iceland. Bull. int. Comm. Bird Pre. 6: 153–160.
1952 Íslenzkir fuglar I. Himbrimi. Náttúrufr. 22: 44–45. (Icel. Birds I. The Great Northern Diver).
1952 Íslenzkir fuglar II. Lómur. Náttúrufr. 22: 76–77. (Icel. Birds II. The Red-Throated D.)
1952 Íslenzkir fuglar III. Sefönd. Náttúrufr. 22: 134–136. (III. The Slavonian Grebe).
1952 Íslenzkir fuglar IV. Fýll. Náttúrufr. 22: 177–180. (IV. The Fulmar).
1953 (with P. Scott and J. Fisher). The Severn Wildfowl Trust Expedition to Central Iceland. Rep. Severn Wildf. Tr. 5: 79–115.
1953 Formáli að Lorenz, K.Z. Talað við dýrin. Þýð.: Símon Jóh. Ágústsson. Heimskringla. Reykjavík. 200 bls.
1953 Fuglamerkingar Náttúrugripasafnsins 1947–1949. Náttúrufr. 23: 14–35.
1953 Íslenzkir fuglar V. Lundi. Náttúrufr. 23: 14–35. (Icel. Birds V. The Puffin).
1953 Íslenzkir fuglar VI. Teista. Náttúrufr. 23: 129–132. (VI. The Black Guillemot).
1953 Fuglaathuganadagur. Náttúrufr. 23: 132.
1953 Íslenzkir fuglar VII. Súla. Náttúrufr. 23: 170–177. (Icel. Birds VII: The Gannet).
1954 Íslenzkir fuglar VIII. Kjói. Náttúrufr. 24: 16–21. (VIII. The Arctic Skua).
1954 Íslenzkir fuglar X. Svartbakur. Náttúrufr. 24: 177–183. (X. The Gr. Black-backed Gull).
1955 Íslenzkir fuglar XI. Hvítmáfur. Náttúrufr. 25: 24–35. (XI. The Glaucous Gull).
1955 Íslenzkir fuglar XII. Sílamáfur. Náttúrufr. 25: 215–226. (XII. The Lesser Black-b. Gull).
1956 Íslenzkir fuglar XIII. Rita. Náttúrufr. 26: 131–137. (XIII. The Kittiwake).
1956 Fuglamerkingar Náttúrugripasafnsins 1950–1952. Náttúrufr. 26: 1–9.
1956 Íslenzkir fuglar XIV. Kría. Náttúrufr. 26: 206–217. (XIV. The Arctic Tern).
1956 Íslenzkir fuglar XV. Spói. Náttúrufr. 27: 113–125. (XV. The Whimbrel).
1958 Report on bird preservation in Iceland. Bull. Int. Comm. Bird Pre. 7: 206–210.
1959 Fuglalífið í Reykjavík. Handbók Veltunnar, vorið 1959. 4 bls.
1960 Some reflections on Ptarmigan cycles in Iceland. Proc. XII. Int. Orn. Congr. Helsinki 1958: 259–265.
1960 Þjórsárver við Hofsjökul. Náttúrufr. 30: 99–102.
1960 Fugladauði á Mývatni af völdum netaveiði. Náttúrufr. 30: 102.
1961 Islandsk Hvinand (*Bucephala islandica*). Bls. 220–226 í Blædel, N. (ritstj.): Nordens Fugle i Farver. 5 Bind. Munksgaard, København. 326 bls.
1961 Strømand (*Histrionicus histrionicus*). Bls. 253–260 í Blædel, N. (ritstj.): Nordens Fugle i Farver. 5. Bind. Munksgaard, København. 326 bls.
1961 Fuglar á förnum vegi. Ferðahandbókin, 1961: 7–15. (Also in Samvinnan, Reykjavík). (1961) 57 (7): 6–7, 25).
1962 Islom (*Gavia immer*). Bls. 136–142 í Blædel, N. (ritstj.): Nordens Fugle i Farver. 6. Bind. Munksgaard, København. 336 bls.
1962 Wildfowl research and conservation in Iceland. Rep. Severn Wildf. Tr. 13: 20.
1962 Fuglalífið á Reykjavíkurtjörn. Fjölrit.
1962 Fuglar Íslands og Evrópu. (Translation). (from R.T. Peterson, G. Mountfort & P.A.D. Hollom). Almenna bókafélagið, Reykjavík. 400 pages.
1962 (?) Bird life in Iceland. A booklet for Icelandair in English, Danish, German and French. 9 pages.
1963 Cyclic phenomenon in populations of *Lagopus mutus*. Progress report for National Science Foundation. 46 pages.
1963 Problems of bird conservation in Iceland. Bull. Int. Coun. Bird Pre. 9: 145–149.
1964 Recent development in bird conservation in Iceland. Bull. Int. Coun. Bird Pre. 10: 177–179.
1964 Diver. Bls. 212–213 í Thompson, A.L. (Ed.) A new dictionary of birds. Nelson, London & Edinburgh. 928 pages.
1967 Haförninn. Bls. 95–134 í Birgir Kjaran: Haförninn. Bókfellsútgáfan, Reykjavík. 205 bls.
1967 Bird observations on Surtsey in 1966. Surtsey Res. Progr. Rep. 3: 37–41.
1970 Bird migration studies on Surtsey in spring of 1968. Surtsey Res. Progr. Rep. 5: 1–9.
1970 Verndun Mývatns og Laxár. Samvinnan 64 (2): 38–40.
1971 Straumendur (*Histrionicus histrionicus*) á Íslandi. Náttúrufr. 41: 1–28, 64–98.
1972 The predator-prey relationship of the Gyrfalcon (*Falco rusticolus*) and the Rock Ptarmigan (*Lagopus mutus*) in Iceland. Proc. XVth Int. Orn. Congr. The Hague 1970: 649.
1972 Ornithological work on Surtsey in 1969 and 1970. Surtsey Progr. Rep. 6: 64–65.
1972 Grit as indicator of the overseas origin of certain birds occurring in Iceland. Ibis 114 (4): 582.
1974 (with B. Clausen). Undersøgelser af dødsårsager blandt fritlevende islandske falke (*Falco rusticolus*). Proc. 12th Nordic Vet. Congr.: 199–200.
1975 Animal life on land. P. 16–19 in Chapter I. Country and population. In 'Iceland 874–1974'. Seðlabanki Íslands.
1979 The past status and exploitation of the Mývatn waterfowl populations. Oikos 32 (1–2): 232–249.
1984 (ritað 1945/46): Í heimkynnum snæuglunnar. Bliki 3: 50–53. (Written 1945/46, Published 1984).

In Newspapers. (Not a complete list).
Lífið í kring um okkur. Dagblaðið Tíminn.

1956	Vestrænir gaukar	11.03
—	Fjallafinkan í Bæjarstaðaskógi	18.03
—	Teistan	25.03
—	Tjaldurinn	08.04
—	Vegvillt kráka	15.04
—	Svartbakurinn	22.04
—	Húsöndin	29.04
—	Haförninn	06.05
—	Helsingjar	13.05
—	Æðarkóngurinn	02.09
—	Álftin	09.09
—	Steindepillinn	16.09
—	Hávellan	23.09
—	Snjógæsin	30.09
—	Rósamáfurinn	07.10
—	Toppöndin	14.09
—	Blinda blágæsin	21.10
—	Fagurgalinn	28.10
—	Spóinn	04.11
—	Hrossagaukurinn	11.11
—	Skógarþrösturinn	18.11
—	Hjálmönd	25.11
—	Krían	02.12
—	Máríatlan	09.12
—	Æfintýri hettumáfs nr. 68813	23.12
1957	Jaðrakan	06.01
—	Um æðarvarp	13.01
—	Lundi	20.01
—	Kúhegri	27.01
—	Skeiðnefur	03.02
—	Gráhegri	10.02
—	Toppklumba	17.02
—	Fjöruspói	24.02
—	Rúkragi	03.03
—	Sefhæna	10.03
—	Skógarsnípa	24.03
—	Bjúgnefja	31.03
—	Keldusvin	07.04
—	Heiðagæs	14.04
—	Rauðhöfðaönd	28.04
1965	Um friðun og ófriðun gæsa. Tíminn	26.10
1965	Eyðing svartbaks. Morgunblaðið	11.11
1969	Framtíð Þjórsárvera. Morgunblaðið	31.05

18.2 Bibliography: The Great Auk.

(Ref. Ch. 2: The last great auk. pp. 18–26).

Guðni Sigurðsson: Geirfuglasker (Great Auk Skerry) is described in: Sögurit XXXIX, Landsnefndin 1770–1771, II. pages 144–147. Text published in Reykjavík 1961.

Reinhardt, Prof. J. 1813. Om Gejrfuglens Forekomst ved Island. In Dr. H. Krøyers Naturhistorisk Tidskrift II. B. p. 533–535. Copenhagen, 1813.

Séra Sigurður Brynjólfsson Sívertsen. 1839. Description of Útskálar parish August 30, 1839; contains information on the Geirfuglasker and its landing-places.

Annálar Björns á Skarðsá, 1639. This annal for 1639 relates how four ships sailed from Reykjanes to Geirfuglasker to hunt great auks. Two of the vessels were lost with all hands, the other two finally managed to reach the mainland. (page 230).

Geirfuglasker. In a manuscript (Lbs. 44 Fol.) in the National Library of Iceland there is a description of the landing-places at the Geirfuglasker (Great Auk skerry). The skerry sank beneath the ocean during earthquakes in 1830 (or 1831). The sketch on page 22 is from the original manuscript.

Steenstrup, Prof. Jap. 1855.: Et Bidrag til Gejrfuglens, *Alka impennis* Lin., Naturhistorie, og særlig til Kundskaben om dens tidligere Udbredningskreds. Videnskabelige Meddelelser fra den naturhistoriske Forening i Kjøbenhavn. Nr. 3–7. Udgivne af Selskabets Bestyrelse, 1855. Publ. Copenhagen 1856–57.

Newton, Alfred, prof. 1861: Abstract of Mr. J. Wolley's Researches in Iceland respecting the Gare-fowl or Great Auk (*Alca impennis*, Linn.). The Ibis, A Magazine of General Ornithology. Vol. III, London 1861.

Steenstrup, Prof. Jap. 1868.: Matériaux pour servir a l'Histoire de l'*Alca impennis* (Lin.) et recherches sur les pays qu'il habitait. BULLETIN de la Société Ornithologique Suisse, Genève-Paris 1868. – The drawing of the great auks on page 25 is from this journal. Lithochromie by E. Vauthey.

Grieve, Symmington. 1885.: The Great Auk or Garefowl (*Alca impennis*, Linn.), Its History, Archaeology and Remains. London 1885. The drawing of the great auk on page 18 is from this book, and the distribution map on p. 19 is mainly based on the same book, except that the

327

map of Reykjanes and Eldey area is drawn separately by the author.

Finnur Guðmundsson. 1955. Geirfuglinn (The Great Auk). Manuscript. Handout for the press when the Icelandic Museum of Natural History purchased the great auk egg and skeleton from Harvard University in USA in 1955.

Finnur Guðmundsson. 1955. Manuscript. Presshandout concerning the great auk bones discovered in the Reykjavík area in 1955.

Art at Auction. London 1970-71. Sale of the mounted great auk at Sotheby's & Parke-Bernet, 4.3 1971. Thames and Hudson, London.

Count Raben-Levetzau. Aalholm Castle, Denmark. A letter of 20.4.1971 to Finnur Guðmundsson concerning the expedition of Count Raben, Faber and Mørck in the year 1821 to Geirfuglasker, and concerning the stuffed great auk sold to the Icelandic Museum of Natural History at the auction in London 4.3.1971.

The purchase of the stuffed great auk in London 4.3.1971 was much in the news at that time. In 'New York Times' on March 6th 1971 it was reported as follows: 'Mounted Great Auk Brings $ 21.600 at London Auction.' LONDON, March 6. – The highest price ever paid for a natural history specimen – $ 21.600 – was paid this week for a mounted great auk at Sotheby's auction house. – The specimen of the flight-less bird, which became extinct in 1844 in Iceland, was sold by Sotheby's to Dr. Finnur Guðmundsson, director of the Icelandic Museum of Natural History in Reykjavík. – The specimen will be taken back to Iceland, where the bird was caught in 1821. The specimen came from Aalholm Castle in Denmark, and was sent to Sotheby's by baron Raben-Levetzau. Dr. Gudmundsson said the money for the bird was collected by the Rotary, Kiwanis and Lions clubs of Iceland. The picture on page 21 is of this mounted great auk.

Bengtson, Sven-Axel. 1984.: Breeding Ecology and Extinction of the Great Auk (*Pinguinus impennis*): Anecdotal Evidence and Conjectures. The AUK, January 1984.

18.3 Bibliography. Books and papers of interest for further reading.

Arnason, E. & Grant P.R. 1978.The Significance of Kleptoparasitism during the breeding season in a colony of Arctic skuas, *Stercorarius parasiticus*, in Iceland. Ibis 120.

Austin, Oliver L. jr. 1962. Birds of the World. Illustrations by Arthur Singer. Foreword by Peter Scott. Paul Hamlyn, London.

Avon, Dennis & Tilford, Tony. 1975. Birds of Britain & Europe in Colour. Blandford Press. Poole, Dorset, 1975, reprinted 1978.

Bárðarson, Hjálmar R. 1975. Sambýli kríu og teistu. Náttúrufr. 45: 37–42.

Bauer, K.M und Glutz, N. 1966–1973. Handbuch der Vögel Mitteleuropas. 5 vols. Frankfurt.

Bengtson, S.-A. 1972. Reproduction and fluctuations in the size of duck populations at Lake Mývatn, Iceland. Oikos 23: 35–58.

Bennett, Linda, and Everett, Michael. 1982. Sea and Shore Birds. Guinnes, Middlesex, U.K.

Bergman, Göran. 1953. Fåglarnas liv. (Oversat til dansk) Fuglenes liv. Schultz, København.

Berndt, R. und Meise, W. 1959–1966. Naturgeschichte der Vögel. 3 vols. Stuttgart.

Bijleveld, Maarten. 1974. Birds of Prey in Europe. Forw.: K.H. Voous. Macmillan, London.

Björnsson, Hálfdán. 1976. Fuglalíf í Öræfum. Náttúrufr. 46: 56–104.

Björnsson, Magnús. 1932. Snæuglur í Ódáðahrauni. Náttúrufr. 2: 122–123. Reykjavík.

Björnsson, Magnús. 1935-6. Rjúpan. Náttúrufr. 5: 161–169, 6: 57–61. Reykjavík.

Björnsson, Magnús. 1939. Fuglabók Ferðafélags Íslands. Árbók 1939. Reykjavík.

Blume, Dieter. 1971. So verhalten sich die Vögel. Frankh'sche Verl. Stuttgart, 1971. Træk af fugles adfærd. (oversat til dansk) Gyldendals Kubusbøger, København, 1974.

Blædel, Niels (ed). – 1963. Nordens Fugle i Farver (7 bind). Ejnar Munksgaard, København.

Boyd, H. & Ogilvie, M.A. 1972. Icelandic Greylag Geese wintering in Britain in 1960-1971. Wildfowl 23 : 64–82.

Brandon-Cox, Hugh. 1974. Arctic quest for the Sea Eagle. Summer of a Million Wings. (North Norway). David & Charles, Devon (UK).

Brown, Philip. 1964. Birds of Prey. Andre Deutsch, London.

Bruun, Bertel. 1973. Birds of North America. London (1973).

Bruun, Bertel. 1982. The Country Life Guide to Birds of Britain and Europe. Illustrated by Arthur Singer. Country Life Books, London.

Brunius, Óran. 1963. Nordisk Fuglelexikon. (oversat til dansk). Branner og Korch, Køben.

Bræstrup, F.W. 1953. Fuglenes Verden. Hans Reitzels Forlag, København.

Campbell, Bruce. 1977. Ill. by Raymond Watson. Birds of Coast and Sea. Britain and North Europe. Oxford University Press, Oxford.

Cerely, Stanley. 1955. The Gyr Falcon Adventure. Collins. London.

Cerný, Walter. 1978. A Field Guide in Colour to Birds. Ill. by Karel Drchal. Octopus. London.

Clausen, B. & Finnur Guðmundsson. 1981. Causes of mortality among free ranging Gyrfalcons in Iceland. J. Wildlife Diseases 17.

Clase, H.J., F. Cooke, T.A. Hill and W.J. Roff. 1960. A survey of the Slavonian Grebe at Mývatn, Iceland. Bird Study 7 : 76–81.

Cramp, S. and Simmons, KEL. (ed.) 1977–1984. The Birds of the Western Palearctic. Vol. 1–4. Oxford University Press. Oxford (1977–1984).

Dalton, Stephen. 1977. The Miracle of Flight. McGraw-Hill Book Co., New York.

Dinesen, G.B. 1926. Nordislandske Fugle. København.

Dossenbach, Hans D. 1974. Fuglenes Familieliv. (Oversat til dansk). Lademann, København.

Driver, Peter M. 1974. In Search of the Eider. The Saturn Press. London.

Dybbro, Tommy. 1972. Fuglene i vore søer og moser. Rhodos, København.

Einarsson, Einar H. 1976. Storkur í heimsókn 1975. Týli, 6 (2): 69.

Einarsson, Oddur. ca. 1590. Íslandslýsing. Útg. Reykjavík 1971.

Einarsson, Þorsteinn. 1939. Stóra sjósvalan. Blik 4: 19–22. Vestmannaeyjar.

Einarsson, Þorsteinn. 1939. Litla sævalan í Vestmannaeyjum. Náttúrufr. 9: 138–144.

Einarsson, Þorsteinn. 1954. Talning súlunnar í Eldey. Náttúrufr. 24: 158–160.

Einarsson, Þorsteinn. 1959. Síðasta förin til súlna í Eldey. Blik 20: 86–93. Vestmannaeyjar.

Einarsson, Þorsteinn. 1979. Fjöldi langvíu og stuttnefju í fuglabjörgum við Ísland. Náttúrufr. 49 (2–3): 221–228. Reykjavík.

Everett, Michael. 1978. Birds of Prey. Orbis Publishing. London.

Felix, Jiri. 1975. A colour guide to familiar Marshland and Freshwater Birds. Octopus Books Ltd., London.

Felix, Jiri. 1978. A colour guide to familiar Sea and Coastal Birds. Octopus Books, London.

Felix, Jiri, & Hísek K. 1978, 1979. The Illustrated Book of Birds. Octopus, London.

Ferguson-Lees, James Quentin Hockliffe & Ko Zweeres. 1975. A Guide to Bird-Watching in Europe. The Bodley Head. London.

Fisher, James. 1952. The Fulmar. London.

Fisher, James. 1969. The migration of birds. Drawings by Crispin Fisher. Bodley Head. London.

Fisher, James. 1979. Thorburn's Birds. Ebury Press. London. Reprinted 1979.

Fisher J. & R.M. Lockley. 1954. Sea-birds London.

Fjeldså, J. 1975. Recent changes in the waterfowl situation in lakes Mývatn and Víkingavatn, Iceland. Dansk orn. Foren. Tidskr. 69: 89–102.

Flächtner, G., Arnþór Garðarsson, Gísli Már Gíslason & U. Halbach. 1982. Ökologische Untersuchungen in Thjórsárver, Zentral-Island. Natur und Museum. 112: 49–61.

Garðarsson, Arnþór. 1956. Stormmáfur, nýr varpfugl á Íslandi. Náttúrufr. 26: 87–93.

Garðarsson, Arnþór. 1967. The waterfowl situation in Iceland. Proc. 2nd. European Meeting on Wildfowl Conservation: 78–80. The Hague.

Garðarsson, Arnþór. 1967. Hvinendur á Íslandi og nokkur orð um ákvörðun hvinanda. Náttúrufr. 37: 76–92.

Garðarsson, Arnþór. 1971. Food ecology and spacing behavior of Rock Ptarmigan (*Lagopus mutus*) in Iceland. Ph. D. thesis. Univ. California.

Garðarsson, Arnþór. 1972. Research in Thjórsárver, central Iceland, and a preliminary account of the Pink-footed Goose. Ibis 114: 581.

Garðarsson, Arnþór. 1972. Íslenskir votlendisfuglar. Votlendi. Rit Landverndar 4: 100–134.

Garðarsson, Arnþór. 1978. Íslenski húsandarstofninn. Náttúrufr. 48. (3-4): 162.

Garðarsson, Arnþór. 1979. Waterfowl populations of Lake Mývatn and recent changes in numbers and food habits. Oikos 32: 250–270. Copenhagen.

Garðarsson, Arnþór. 1981. Population trends in diving ducks at Mývatn, Iceland, in relation to food. Verh. orn. Ges. Bayern 23: 191–200.

Garðarsson, Arnþór. 1982. (ritstj.) Fuglar, safnrit. Rit Landverndar 8. Reykjavík.

Garðarsson, Arnþór. 1982. Rjúpa. Fuglar, rit Landverndar 8: 149–164. Reykjavík.

Garðarsson, Arnþór. 1982. Andfuglar og aðrir vatnafuglar. Fuglar. Rit Landverndar 8: 77–116.

Garðarsson, Arnþór. and Kristinn H. Skarphéðinsson. 1984. A census of the Icelandic Whooper Swan population. Waterfowl 35. Wildfowl Trust.

Génsbøl, Benny. 1969. Grønland. Grønlands natur i billeder og tekst. Under medvirken af Finn Salomonsen. Branner og Korch. København.

Génsbøl, Benny. 1982. Fugle ved strand og sø. Lademann, København.

Glutz von Blotzheim, URS. N. und Bauer, Kurt M. 1966–1980. Handbuch der Vögel Mitteleuropas. Akademische Verlagsgesellschaft. Frankfurt.

Gooders, John. 1975. Birds. An illustrated survey of the bird families of the world. Hamlyn. London.

Gooders, John. 1978. Birds of Ocean and Estuary. Orbis publishing. London.

Goodfellow, Peter. ca. 1977. Birds as Builders. David & Charles. London.

Gordon, Seton. 1942. In Search of Northern Birds. The Royal Society for the Protection of Birds, London. (P. 13–39, Birds in Iceland.

Gordon, Seton Paul. 1980. The Golden Eagle, King of Birds. Melven Press, Perth (UK).

Graham, jr., Frank. 1975. Gulls. A social history. Photogr. by C. Ayres. Random House, New York.

Grant, P.J. 1982. Gulls, a guide to identification. T & AD Poyser, Calton (UK).

Greenoak, Francesca. 1981. All the Birds of the Air, The Names, Lore and Literature of British Birds. Penguin Books, Middlesex. (UK).

Haftorn, Svein. 1971. Norges Fugler. (862 s.) Universitetsforlaget, Oslo.

Hale, W.G. 1980. Waders. London.

Halliday, Tim. 1978. Vanishing Birds. Their Natural History and Conservation. Foreword by Bruce Campbell. Sidgwick & Jackson, London.

Hanzák, J. 1971. Stóra fuglabók Fjölva. Friðrik Sigurbjörnsson þýddi og endursagði með staðfærslu að íslenskum háttum. Bókaútgáfan Fjölvi, Reykjavík.

Harris, M.P. 1984. The Puffin. T & A.D. Poyser, Calton, England.

Harrison, Colin. 1975. A Field Guide to the Nests, Eggs and Nestlings of British and European Birds. Collins. London.

Harrison, Peter. 1983. Seabirds, an identification guide. Foreword by Roger Tory Peterson. A. H. & A. W. Reel Ltd., Wellington

Heilmann, Gerhard og Manniche, A.L.V. 1939. Danmarks Fugleliv. (3 bind). Gyldendal. Køben.

Hjálmarsson, Árni Waag. 1982. Vaðfuglar. Fuglar. Rit Landverndar 8: 117–148. Reykjavík.

Hosking, Eric. & Newberry, Cyril. 1961. Bird Photography as a Hobby. Stanley Paul, London.

Hosking, Eric. 1972. An Eye for a Bird. Foreword by HRH The Duke of Edinburgh KG. London.

Hosking, Eric. with Kelvin MacDonnel. 1979. Eric Hosking's Birds. Fifty Years of Photographing Wildlife. Pelham Books. London.

Hosking, Eric. 1983. Eric Hosking's Seabirds. Text by Ronald M. Lockley. Croom Helm. London.

Hosking, Eric. with W.G. Hale. 1983. Waders. Foreword by Sir Peter Scott. Pelham. London.

Howard, Len. 1953. Birds as Individuals. With a foreword by Julian Huxley and photographs by Eric Hosking. Collins. London 1953.

HRH The Prince Philip, Duke of Edinburgh. 1962. Birds from Britannia. Longmans. London.

Hvass, Hans. 1969. Fugle i farver. Politikens Forlag. København.

Illingworth, Frank. 1978. Falcons and Falconry. Blandford Press. Dorset (UK). Reprinted 1978.

Ingólfsson, Agnar. 1961. The White-tailed Eagle. (*Haliaetus albicilla*) in Iceland. B. Sc. thesis. Univ. Aberdeen.

Ingólfsson, Agnar. 1970. Hybridization of Glaucous Gulls *Larus hyperboreus* and Herring Gulls L. *argentatus* in Iceland. (Kynblöndun silfurmáfs og hvítmáfs). Ibis 112: 340–362.

Ingólfsson, Agnar. 1970. The moult of remiges and retrices in Great Black-backed Gulls, *Larus marinus*, and Glaucous Gulls, *L. hyperboreus*, in Iceland. Ibis 112: 83–92.

Ingólfsson, Agnar. 1976. The feeding habits of Great Black-backed Gulls, *Larus marinus* and Glaucous Gulls, *L. hyperboreus*, in Iceland. Náttúrufr. st. Íslands, Reykjavík.

Ingólfsson, Agnar. 1982. Máfar, kjóar og skúmur. Fuglar. Rit Landverndar 8: 61-76. Reykjavík.
Ivor, Roy. 1968. I live with Birds. Follett Publ. Co. Chicago, New York. USA.
Joensen, Anders Holm. 1966. Fuglene på Færøene. Illustreret af Benny Génsbøl. Rhodos. København.
Johnsgard, Paul A. 1968. Waterfowl. Their Biology and Natural History. University of Nebreska Press, Lincoln, USA.
Jónasson, Pétur M. (Ed.) 1979. Lake Mývatn. Icelandic Literature Soc. in Copenhagen.
Jonsson, Sixten. 1959. Färöarna-fåglar och fångster. Text Nils Linnman. LT's Förl. Stockh.
Jørgensen, Harriet I. 1958. Nomina Avium Europaearum. Munksgaard. Copenhagen.
Kear, Janet. 1967. Feeding habits of the Graylag Goose, *Anser anser*, in Iceland with reference to its interaction with agriculture. Proc. VII. Cong. Int. Union Game Biol. 1965: 615-22.
Kerbes, R.H., Ogilvie M.A. and Boyd, H. 1971. Pink-footed Geese in Iceland and Greenland: a population review based on an aerial nesting survey of Þjórsárver in June 1970. Wildfowl 22. Wildfowl Trust, Slimbridge. (UK).
Kjaran, Birgir. 1967. Haförninn. Safnrit. Bókfellsútgáfan, Reykjavík.
Lambert Terence. 1979. Lambert's Birds of Shore and Estuary. (Paintings). Text by Alan Bitchell. Collins. London.
Leifsson, Kári. 1943. Uglufjölskyldan. Náttúrufr. 13: 68-70.
Lewis, E. 1938. In search of the Gyrfalcon. London.
Linduska, Joseph P. (ed.). 1964. Waterfowl Tomorrow. The United States Department of the Interior. Washington.
Linsenmair, Karl-Eduard. 1968. Warum singen Vögel? Franckh'sche Verlagshandl. Stuttgart.
Linsenmair, Karl-Eduard. ca.1968. Hvorfor synger fuglene? (Overs.) Gyldendal, København.
Lockley, R.M. 1953. Puffins. London.
Lockley, R.M. 1961. Shearwaters. A. Doubleday Anchor Book. The Am. Mus. of Nat. Hist. New York.
Lockley, R.M. 1968. The Book of Bird-Watching. Arthur Barker Ltd., London.
Lockley, Ronald M. 1983. Flight of the Storm Petrel. Ill. by Noel W. Cusa. David & Charles London, 1983.
Lorenz, Konrad. 1978. Das Jahr der Graugans. R. Piper & Co. Verlag.
Lorenz, Konrad. 1978. L'Année de l'oie cendrée. Editions Stock, 1978.
Lorenz, Konrad. 1981. The Year of the Greylag Goose. Photographs by Sybille and Klaus Kalas. Eyre Methuen. London 1981.
Lund, Hj. Munthe-Kaas. 1970. Norges fugle liv. Det beste. Oslo.
Machnally, Lea. 1977. The Ways of an Eagle. Collins and Harvill Press. London.
Magnússon, Kjartan G. og Ólafur K. Nielsen. 1982. Ránfuglar og uglur. Fuglar. Rit Landverndar 8: 165-180. Reykjavík.
Matthews, G.V.T. 1968. Bird Navigation. (2. ed). Cambridge University Press, Cambridge.
Mc Cullagh, Sheila. 1981. Where Wild Geese Fly. with drawings by Peter Scott. Hart-Davis. UK.
Mikkola, Heimo. 1983. Owls of Europe. Ill. by: Ian Willis. T. & A.D. Poyser, Calton, UK.
Muus, Bent; Salomonsen, Finn; Vibe, Christian. 1981. Grønlands Fauna, Fisk, Fugle, Pattedyr. Gyldendal, København.
Nelson, Bryan. 1978. The Gannet. T. & A.D. Poyser, Berkhamstead, UK.
Nelson, Bryan. 1980. Seabirds. Their biology and ecology. Hamlyn, London.
Nethersole-Thompson, Desmond. 1971. Highland Birds. Highlands and Islands Development Board, Inverness, UK.
Nielsen, Ólafur Karl. 1979. Dvergkrákur á Íslandi. Náttúrufr. 49: 204-220.
Nielsen, Ólafur Karl. & T.J. Cade. 1982. Population ecology of the Gyrfalcon in Iceland. Progr. rep. no. 1, Cornell Univ. Fjölrit.
Nielsen, P. 1921-1930. Havørnen (*Haliaëtus albicilla*) paa Island. Dansk orn. Foren. Tidskr. 15: 69-83, 17: 130, 20: 149-152, 21: 82-86, 24: 123-124.
Oddsson, Gísli (Biskup í Skálholti): Undur Íslands (De Mirabilibus Islandiae). Þýðing Jónas Rafnar. Fuglar 12. -15. kap. Útg. Þorst. M. Jónsson, Akureyri, 1942.
O'Donald, Peter. 1983. The Arctic Skua. A study of the ecology and evolution of a seabird. Cambridge University Press. Cambridge.
Ogilvie, M.A. 1975. Ducks of Britain and Europe. T. & A.D. Poyser, Berkhamstead, UK.
Ogilvie, M.A. 1976. The Winter Birds, Birds of the Arctic. Praeger Publishers, New York.
Ogilvie, Malcolm. 1982. The Wildfowl of Britain and Europe. Ill. by: N.W. Cusa & Peter Scott. Oxford University Press. Oxford.
Patterson, I.J., 1982. The Shelduck. A study in behavioural ecology. Ill. by Chris Furse. Cambridge University Press. Cambridge.
Petersen, Ævar. 1970. Fuglalíf í Skógum á Óshólmasvæði Héraðsvatna í Skagafirði. Náttúrufr. 40: 26-46. Reykjavík.
Petersen, Ævar. 1976. Age of first breeding in Puffin, *Fratercula arctica* (L.) Astarte 9: 43-50.
Petersen, Ævar. 1976. Size variables in Puffins, *Fratercula arctica*, from Iceland, and bill features as criteria of age. Ornis Scand. 7: 185-192.
Petersen, Ævar. 1977. Íslenskar teistur endurheimtar við Grænland, og erlend teista við Ísland. Náttúrufr. 47: 149-153.
Petersen, Ævar. 1979. Varpfuglar Flateyjar á Breiðafirði og nokkurra nærliggjandi eyja. Náttúrufr. 49: 229-256. Reykjavík.
Petersen, Ævar. 1981. Breeding biology and feeding ecology of Black Guillemots. D. Phil. thesis. Univ. of Oxford.
Petersen, Ævar. 1982. Sjófuglar. Bls. 15-60 í Fuglar. Rit Landverndar 8. Reykjavík.
Peterson, Roger Tory. 1964. The Birds. Life Nature Library. Time-Life Int. Nederland.
Peterson, R.T., G. Mountfort og P.A. Hollom. 1964. Fuglar Íslands og Evrópu. Finnur Guðmundsson íslenzkaði og staðfærði. 400 bls. Almenna Bókafélagið, Reykjavík. 2. útg.
Peterson, Roger, Mountfort, Guy and Hollom, P.A.D. 1983. A Field Guide to the Birds of Britain and Europe. Collins, London. (4th. Ed.)
Pettingill, Olin Sewall. 1959. Puffins and Eiders in Iceland. Maine Field Nat. 15: 58-71.
Pforr, Manfred and Limbrunner, Alfred. 1981. The Breeding Birds of Europe 1. A Photographic Handbook. Divers to Auks. Croom Helm, London.
Portman, Adolf. 1968. Fuglene og deres verden. Cappelin. Oslo.
Reade, Winwood, and Hosking, Eric. 1967. Nesting Birds, Eggs and Fledglings. Blandford Press. London.
Reader's Digest. 1983. Field Guide to the Birds of Britain. Readers Digest. London.
Reinsch. H.H. 1961. Die Insel Eldey-Brutinsel der Basstöpel im Nordatlantik. Ornitologische Mitteilungen 13: 231.
Salomonsen, Finn, og Rudebeck, Gustaf. 1963. Danmarks Fugle. (2 bind). Branner og Korch. Kb.
Salomonsen, Finn. 1967. Fuglene på Grønland. Rhodos. København.
Salomonsen, Finn. 1967. Fuglene ved vore kyster. Illustreret af Benny Génsbøl. Rhodos. København.
Salomonsen, Finn. 1967. Fugletrækket og dets gåder. Munksgaard. København.
Saunders, David. 1980. Seabirds. Hamlyn. London.
Schlenker, Hermann. 1965. Fuglar. Texti: Broddi Jóhannesson og Steindór Steindórsson. Bókaútgáfa Menningarsjóðs. Reykjavík.
Schonger, H. 1927. Auf Islands Vogelbergen. Neudamm.
Scott, Peter. 1937. Morning Flight. A book of wildfowl. Country Life Ltd., London.
Scott, Peter. 1953. A day trip to Þingvellir. Wildfowl Trust, Ann. Rep. 1951-52. 5: 132.
Scott, P., Fisher, J. and Guðmundsson, F. 1953. The Severn Wildfowl Trust Expedition to Central Iceland, 1951. Wildfowl Trust Ann. Rep. 5: 79-115. (1953).
Scott, P. and Fisher, J. 1953. A Thousand Geese. Collins, London 1953. Kafli bókarinnar er birtur í Náttúrufr. 25 (1955): 1-6, í þýðingu Hermanns Einarssonar.
Scott, P. Boyd, H, and Sladen, W.J.L. 1955. The Wildfowl Trust's Second Expedition to Central Iceland, 1953. Wildfowl Trust Ann Rep. 7: 63-98.
Scott, P. & The Wildfowl Trust. 1972. The Swans. London.
Scott, Sir Peter. (Ed.) 1982. The World Atlas of Birds. Artists House. London.
Sigurðsson, Jón Baldur. 1967. Nýr varpfugl á Íslandi. Vepja (*Vanellus vanellus*). Náttúrufr. 37: 170-178.
Sigurðsson, Jón Baldur. 1974. Rannsóknir á varpháttum og afkomu heiðagæsar (*Anser brachyrhynchus*) í júní og júlí 1972. Orkustofnun. Rvk.
Sigurðsson, Steinþór. 1945. Um snægluna. Náttúrufr. 15: 187.
Skarphéðinsson, Kristinn Haukur. 1982. Spörfuglar. Fuglar. Rit Landverndar 8: 181-208.
Simson, Clive. 1966. A Bird Overhead. Ill. by R.B. Talbot-Kelly. H.F. & G. Witherby Ltd. London.
Sparks, John. 1982. Bird Behaviour. Illustr. by David Andrews. Hamlyn. London.
Steingrímsson, Páll. 1969. Skrofa í Vestmannaeyjum. BLIK, Ársrit, 27: 236-238.
Stillson, Blanche. 1953. Wings, Insects, Birds and Men. Sc. Book Club Ed. London.
Sæmundsson, Bjarni. 1936. Íslensk dýr III. Fuglarnir. Bókaverslun Sigf. Eymundss. Reykjavík.
Terres, John K. 1968. Flashing Wings. The Drama of Bird Flight. Souvenir Pr. London.
Thiede, Walther. 1980. Water and Shore Birds. (Transl. from German). Chatto & Windus, London.
Timmermann, Günter. 1934-1949. Die Vögel Islands. Vísindafélag Íslendinga. Reykjavík.
Tryggvason, Kári. 1941. Snæuglur við Laufrönd. Náttúrufr. 11: 135-140.
Tuck, Gerald. 1980. A Guide to Seabirds on the Ocean Routes. Collins, London.
Tunnicliffe, C.F. 1981. Sketches of Bird Life. Edited with an introduction by Robert Gillmore. Nationwide Book Service. Berkshire. UK.
Þórisson, Skarphéðinn. 1981. Landnám, útbreiðsla og stofnstærð stara á Íslandi. Náttúrufr. 51 (4): 145-163. Reykjavík.
Urry, David and Katie. 1970. Flying Birds. Vernon & Yates. London.
Vaucher, Charles. 1960. Sea Birds. Oliver and Boyd. Edinburgh. London.
Vaughan, Richard. 1971. Gulls in Britain. H.F. & G. Witherby Ltd. London.
Vaughan, Richard. 1979. Arctic Summer. Birds in North Norway. Anthony Nelson, Shropshire. UK.
Vaughan, Richard. 1980. Plovers. Terence Dalton. Lavenham, England.
Víglundsson, Þorstein Þ. 1959. Björgunin við Eldey 1939. Blik 20: 94-98. Vestmannaeyjar.
Wilson, J.R. 1981. The migration of high arctic shorebirds through Iceland. Bird-Study 28: 21-32.
Yeates, G.K. 1951. The Land of the Loon, London.

19. Index

19.1. Birds.
(NA means bird name used in North America).

American Wigeon, NA: American Widgeon: 175.
Arctic Skua, NA: Parasitic Jaeger: 34, 122, 124, 125, 221, **230–231**, 252.
Arctic Tern: 13, 15, 16, 30, **126–132**, 167, 231.
Atlantic Murre (NA), (= Guillemot): 29, 30, 33, 36, **90–92**, 93, 99.
Barnacle Goose: 33, 175, **299, 302–305**.
Barn Swallow (NA), (= Swallow): 314.
Barrow's Goldeneye: 29, 34, 175, **193–197**, 312.
Bar-tailed Godwit: 311.
Blackbird: **316–317**.
Black Guillemot: 9, 15, 30, 39, **80–82**, 131, **132**.
Black-headed Gull: 16, 29, 130, **166–168**, 192.
Black-legged Kittiwake (NA): 29, 30, 33, 58, 75, **83–87**, 91, 166, 231.
Black-tailed Godwit: 30, 35, **164–165**, 311.
Brambling: **317–320**, 324.
Brent Goose, NA: Brant: 30, 175, **299–302**, 304.
Brünnich's Guillemot, NA: Thick-billed Murre: 30, 33, 90, 91, **93**, 94, 99.
Common Goldeneye: 175, **312–313**.
Common Gull, NA: Mew Gull: 33, 39, 62, 63, 72, **77**, 166, 167.
Common Loon (NA), (= Great Northern Diver): 29, 30, 35, 37, **133–137**.
Common Scoter: 34, **198–201**, 206.
Coot: 306.
Cormorant, NA: Great Cormorant: 15, 30, 31, 39, **57–61**, 66.
Dovekie (NA), (= Little Auk): 34, 37, 39, **78–79**.
Dunlin: 30, 192, **225–227**.
Eider: 7, 12, 30, 33, 34, **108–112**, 175, 298.
Fulmar: 29, 30, 33, 91, **94–97**, 231.

Gadwall: 34, 175, **178–179**.
Gannet: 2, 8, 9, 30, 34, 35, 37, **38–49**, 75, 125.
Glaucous Gull: 30, 33, 39, 62, 63, 72, 73, **75–77**.
Golden Plover: 29, **214–217**, 221, 281, 317.
Goosander: 34, 175, 206, **210–213**.
Great Auk: **18–26**.
Great Black-backed Gull: 10, 29, 34, 36, 39, **62–69**, 72, 109, 125, 130, 221, 252, 306.
Great Cormorant (NA), (= Cormorant): 30, 39, **57–61**, 66.
Great Northern Diver, NA: Common Loon: 29, 30, 35, 37, **133–137**.
Great Skua, NA: Skua: 34, 37, **122–125**, 231.
Greylag Goose: 34, 35, **156–160**, 251.
Grey Phalarope, NA: Red Phalarope: 31, 36, **119–121**, 161.
Guillemot, NA: Atlantic Murre: 29, 30, 33, 36, 75, **90–92**, 93, 99.
Gyrfalcon: 9, 12, 33, 34, 37, 221, 262, 279, **282–288**.
Harlequin, Harlequin-Duck: 29, 30, 34, 37, 175, **204–205**.
Herring Gull: 8, 30, 34, 39, 62, 63, **71–75**.
Horned Grebe (NA), (= Slavonian Grebe): 34, **141–143**, 192.
House Martin: **314–315**.

Jackdaw: 312.

King Eider: 33, **111**, 175.
Kittiwake, NA: Black-legged Kittiwake: 29, 30, 33, 58, 75, **83–87**, 91, 96, 166, 231.
Knot: 30, 308, **310–311**.

Lapwing: 317.
Leach's Petrel: 35, 39, 43, **50–53**.
Lesser Black-backed Gull: 34, 39, 62, 63, **68–71**, 166.
Little Auk, NA: Dovekie: 34, 37, 39, **78–79**.
Long-tailed Duck, NA: Oldsquaw: 34, 175, 184, **202–203**.
Mallard: 30, 34, 175, **176–177**, 193.
Manx Shearwater: 35, 39, 43, **50–53**.

Meadow Pipit: 29, 244, **272–274**, 281.
Merlin, NA: Pigeon Hawk: 34, 221, 279, **280–281**.
Mew Gull (NA), (= Common Gull): 33, 39, 63, **77**, 166, 167.
Northern Phalarope (NA), (= Red-necked Phalarope): 29, 34, 119, **161–163**, 192.
Oldsquaw (NA), (= Long-tailed Duck): 34, 175, 184, **202–203**.
Oystercatcher: 30, **116–118**, 311.
Parasitic Jaeger (NA), (= Arctic Skua): 34, 122, 124, 125, 221, **230–231**, 252.
Pigeon Hawk (NA), (= Merlin): 34, 221, 279, **280–281**.
Pink-footed Goose: 14, 15, 35, 157, **250–253**, 304.
Pintail: 34, 175, **183–184**.
Pochard: 34, 175.
Ptarmigan: 11, 33–35. 37, **262–266**, 281, 283, 284, 286.
Puffin: 10, 29, 30, 33, 34, 43, 75, 91, **101–107**, 231, 283, 286.
Purple Sandpiper: 30, **254–255**.

Raven: 11, 29, 221, **232–239**, 282, 283, 312.
Razorbill: 30, 33, 36, 90, 91, **99–101**.
Red-breasted Merganser: 34, 175, **206–209**, 210. 212.
Red-necked Phalarope, NA: Northern Phalarope: 29, 34, 119, **161–163**, 192.
Red Phalarope (NA), (= Grey Phalarope): 31, 36, **119–121**, 161.
Redpoll: 33, 35, 36, **244–245**.
Redshank: 29, 33, 192, **222–224**, 281.
Red-throated Diver, NA: Red-throated Loon: 9, 30, **138–140**.
Redwing: 30, 33, 35, **246–249**, 275–278, 281, 317.
Ringed Plover: 30, **113–115**.

Sanderling: 30, 308, **309**.
Scaup: 34, 175, **186–189**, 198, 206.
Shag: 10, 15, 30, 31, 36, 39, 54, **55–59**, 75.
Short-eared Owl: 34, **169–173**, 221.
Shoveler: 34, 37, 175, **185**.
Skua (NA), (= Great Skua): 34, 37, **122–125**, 231.
Slavonian Grebe, NA: Horned Grebe: 34, **141–143**, 192
Snipe: 29, 33, 34, **266–269**.
Snow Bunting: 29, 35, **249, 258–261**, 281.

Snowy Owl: 35, 36, 170, **256–257**.
Starling: 9, 30, **246–247**.
Storm Petrel: 35, 39, 43, **50–53**.
Swallow, NA: Barn Swallow: 314.

Teal: 34, **175**.
Thick-billed Murre (NA), (= Brünnich's Guillemot): 30, 33, 90, 91, **93**, 94, 99.
Tufted Duck: 34, 175, 187, **189–192**.
Turnstone: 30, **308–309**.

Water Rail: 27, 29, 34, 37, **144–149**, 306.
Wheatear: 29, **228–229**, 259, 281.
Whimbrel: 29, 37, 165, **218–221**, 281.
White-fronted Goose: 30, 35, 175, **302**.
White Stork: **306–307**.
White-tailed Eagle, NA: Gray Sea Eagle: 31, 35, 37, 221, 279, **288–298**.
White Wagtail: 30, **240–244**.
Whooper Swan: 9, 16, 30, 33, 35, 36, **150–155**.
Wigeon: 34, 175, **180–182**.
Wren, NA: Winter Wren: 34, 35, 36, 244, **270–272**.

19.2. Miscellaneous.

Accipiter family: 279.
Aðaldalur: 185.
Africa: 50, 71, 128, 130, 161, 165, 229, 242, 306.
Akureyri: 33, 34, 247.
Álftanes: 30, 300.
Álsey (Ve.): 51, 54.
America: 29, 130, 133, 135, 180, 193, 204, 290.
Antarctica: 25, 124, 128.
Asia: 312.
Atlantic: 18, 19, 25, 46, 50, 87, 119, 124, 128, 130, 161.
Auk family: 90.
Austfirðir: 34.

Bald Eagle: 290.
Bessastaðir: 12, 300.
Birds of prey: 33, **279–298**.
Bird-watching: 12, 13, **27–37**, **325–326**.
Bjarnarey (Ve.): 43, 51.
Borgarfjörður: 30.
Brandsson, Jón: 25.
Brandur (Ve.): 42, 46, 54, 105.
Breiðafjörður: 30, 32, 39, 54, 57–61, 65, 66, 75, 84, 105, 299, 304, 305, 308.

Breiðamerkur sands: 34, 122, 125.
British Isles: 45, 165, 180, 183, 188, 215, 222, 299, 300, 311, 314.
Bryant, Owen: 20.
Búðir: 30.
Bugða (river): 30, 308.
Canada: 204, 229, 290, 300, 308.
Cliff-birds: 33, 75, **83–107.**
Copenhagen Zoological Museum: 26.
Denmark: 20, 23, 308, 314.
Diving ducks: 9, 175, 184, 202, 213.
Drangey: 33, 42, 62, 93, 96.
Ducks: 9, 15, 16, 33, 34, 167, **174–213**, 281.
Dýrafjörður: 33, 109, 111.
Dyrhólaey: 34, 42, 46, 306.

Eggs: 36–37, 90.
Einarsson, Oddur, Bishop: 27.
Eldey island: 18, 20, 22, 24–26, 30, 39–42, 45–47.
Eldeyjardrangur (Eldey Stack): 22.
Eldhraun: 34, 148.
Eldvatn (river): 148.
Elliðaey (Ve.): 43, 51.
England: 23, 26, 157, 251.
Europe: 19, 20, 28, 29, 34, 128, 135, 140, 161, 165, 167, 188, 192, 198, 215, 229, 272, 290, 306, 308, 309, 312, 314, 317.
Eyjafjallajökull (glacier): 124.
Eyjafjörður: 33, 286, 317.

Faber, Friedrich: 23, 24.
Falcon family: 279.
Falconry: 12, 288.
Faroes: 11, 20, 22, 24, 71, 124, 193, 229.
Fáskrúðsfjörður: 46, 286.
Faxaflói (bay): 30, 58, 302, 311.
Finland: 290.
Fish-eating ducks: 175, 210.
Flatey (island in Breiðafjörður): 54, 308.
France: 71, 275.
Funk Island: 20.

Garðabær: 317.
Garðskagi: 30.
Geese: 16, **174,** 175.
Geldungur (Ve): 42, 43, 46, 90, 92.
Geirfugladrangur: 22, 24, 42.
Geirfuglasker (Great Auk Skerries): 22, 23–25, 42.
Gilpin, John: 23.
Grassholm: 45.
Great Britain: 71, 117.
Greenland: 20, 29, 30, 33, 78, 111, 130, 135, 193, 204, 225, 229, 251, 256, 300, 304, 305, 308.
Grímsey: 34, 42, 78, 79, 84, 93, 94, 96, 97, 101.
Grímsstaðir (at Mývatn): 131.
Grindavík: 22.
Grundarfjörður: 30.
Guðbrandsson, Björn: 296, 297, 298.
Guðmundsson, Finnur: 291, 296, **323.**
Guðmundsson, Jón, the Learned: 27, 116.
Gulls: 8, 15, 16, 62.

Hafnaberg: 30, 84.
Hafnarfjörður: 26, 312.
Hafnir: 25.
Hákonarson, Vilhjálmur: 25.
Hansen, Christian: 26.
Hansen, Peter: 23.
Heimaey (Ve.): 34, 92.
Hellisey (Ve.): 38, 42, 46, 48, 54, 90, 96, 105.
Hellnar: 30.
Héraðsflói: 34.
Hofsjökull (glacier): 14, 35, 251.
Hornafjörður: 34, 247, 306, 317.
Hornbjarg: 33, 87–89, 93.
House-duck: 193.
Hrísey (island): 33, 286.
Húnaflói: 33, 299, 304.
Hvalfjörður: 30, 308.
Hælavíkurbjarg: 33, 42, 93.
Höfn in Hornafjörður: 30, 247, 306, 317.

Ibis: 26.
Icelandic Museum of Natural History: 20, 23, 24, 32, 66, 256.
Icelandic Natural History Society: 291.
Icelandic Nature Conservation Council: 39.
Icelandic Society for the Protection of Birds: 291, 298.
Ingólfshöfði: 34, 42, 71, 75, 102, 106.
Ireland: 179, 266, 267, 275.
Ísafjarðardjúp: 33, 111, 302.
Ísleifsson, Sigurður: 25.

Jónsson, Hjalti: 39.

Keflavík: 23, 24.
Kelduhverfi: 185.
Ketilsson, Ketill: 25.
Kirkjuvogur: 25, 26.
Krísuvíkurberg: 30.
Kvíárjökull (glacier): 69–71.

Labrador: 19.
Lagarfljót: 34.
Langanes: 34, 42, 46, 78.
Langey (island in Breiðafjörður): 32, 54.
Látrabjarg: 33, 58, 91–93, 98, 99, 101, 102, 106.
Lava-fields and Woodlands: 262–278.
Laxá (river at Mývatn): 192, 193, 197, 204, 312.
Lónsfjörður: 34.

Marshland-birds: 133–173.
Mediterranean: 229.
Meðalfellsvatn (lake): 30.
Melrakkaey (island in Breiðafjörður): 30, 57, 75, 84, 105.
Melrakkaslétta: 34, 42, 46.
Ministry of Education and Culture: 34, 79, 283, 321.
Moorland-birds: 15, 214–231.
Morocco: 225, 272.
Mývatn (lake): 12, 34, 131, 141, 142, 150, 179, 180, 182, 185, 187, 188, 190–193, 196, 198, 202, 206, 207, 210, 212, 226, 267, 312.
Mýrar (farm in Dýrafjörður): 33, 109, 111.
Mörck LL.B.: 23, 24.

Newfoundland: 19, 20.
Newton, Professor Alfred (Cambridge): 26.
Nielsen, Peter: 291.
Nigeria: 71, 131.
North America: 20, 29, 130.
North Atlantic: 18, 46.
Norway: 11, 290, 291, 314.
Novaya Zemlya: 78.

Ódáðahraun (lavafields): 35, 170, 256, 257.
Odin: 233.
Ólafsson, Páll: 216, 217.
Order of the Falcon: 279.
Orkneys: 20, 124.

Pacific Ocean: 128.
Papey (island): 34, 39.
Passage migrants: 35.
Plover family: 317.
Portugal: 71.
Predatory birds: 14, 279–289.

Raben, Count F.C.: 20, 23, 24.
Raben-Levetzau, Count: 24.
Rallidae family: 306.
Rauðinúpur: 34, 42, 46.
Raven-Flóki: 11.
Reykjanes: 22, 26, 39, 47, 84, 204.
Reykjavík: 12, 16, 23, 26, 30, 127, 128, 176, 247, 300.
River Þjórsá: 14.

Sandgerði: 309, 311, 314.
Scandinavia: 11, 165, 308.
Scotland: 157, 275.
Sea-birds: 8, 34, 39, 58.
Selvogur: 23.
Shetlands: 11, 124.
Shore-birds: 108–132.
Siberia: 29, 204.
Siemsen, Carl F.: 26.
Skagafjörður: 33, 62, 96, 141, 154, 299, 304.
Skagi: 33, 304.
Skeiðarár sands: 34.
Skrúður (island): 4–5, 34, 42, 46, 75, 102, 106, 286.
Snæfellsnes: 30, 42, 92.
Spain: 19, 71, 272.
St. Kilda: 20, 45.
Stóraurð (Látrabjarg): 33, 91, 99.
Súlnasker (Ve.): 42, 43, 46.
Surface-feeding ducks: 175, 182, 183.
Surf-duck: 204.
Svalþúfa: 30.
Sweden: 314.
Sæmundsson, Bjarni: 291.

Thrush family: 317.
Tjörnin (lake in Reykjavík): 16, 30, 128, 176.
Town and farm birds: 232–249.

U.S.A.: 20, 290.

Vatnajökull (glacier): 69, 124, 125, 138.
Vestfirðir (Westfjords): 10, 33, 111, 264, 282.
Vestmannaeyjar (Westman Isles): 22, 23, 34, 38, 39, 42, 46, 51, 90, 92, 94, 96, 105.
Vigur (island): 33.
Vík í Mýrdal: 34.
Vilgerðarson, Flóki: 11.
Visitors and irregular breeding birds: 299–320.

Waders: 15, 16, 34, 167, 222.
Wolley, John (Cambridge): 26.

Ystiklettur (Ve.): 51.

Þjórsárver: 14, 15, 34, 163, 250, 251, 252, 255.

Æðey (island in Ísafjarðardjúp): 33, 111, 132, 302.
Önundarfjörður: 33.
Öræfi: 34, 69–71, 247, 271.
Öxarfjörður: 34.

Books on Iceland
by Hjálmar R. Bárðarson

Ísland farsælda frón
with text in 6 languages; Icelandic, Danish, English, French, German and Spanish. First Edition, Reykjavík 1953. Second Edition 1954. **Out of print.**

ÍSLAND • ICELAND • ISLANDE.
with text in 6 languages; Icelandic, Danish, English, French, German and Spanish. First Edition, Reykjavík 1965. Second Edition 1970. **Out of print.**

ís og eldur, andstæður íslenskrar náttúru.
Icelandic text. Reykjavík 1971.

is og ild, kontrasterne i islandsk natur.
Danish text. Reykjavík 1971. **Out of print.**

ice and fire, contrasts of Icelandic nature.
English text. First Edition, Reykjavík 1971. Second Edition 1973. Third Edition 1980.

eis und feuer, kontraste in der isländischen natur.
German text. First Edition, Reykjavík 1973. Second Edition 1980.

ÍSLAND, svipur lands og þjóðar.
Icelandic text. First Edition, Reykjavík 1982. Second Edition 1986.

ICELAND, a portrait of its land and people.
English text. First Edition, Reykjavík 1982. Second Edition 1987.

ISLAND, Porträt des Landes und Volkes.
German text. Reykjavík 1982.

FUGLAR ÍSLANDS.
Icelandic text. First and second Edition, Reykjavík 1986. Third Edition 1987.

ISLANDS FUGLE.
Danish text. First Edition, Reykjavík 1986. Second Edition 1987.

BIRDS of ICELAND.
English text. First Edition, Reykjavík 1986. Second Edition 1987.

OISEAUX d'ISLANDE.
French text. First Edition, Reykjavík 1986. Second Edition 1987.

VÖGEL ISLANDS.
German text. First Edition, Reykjavík 1986. Second Edition 1987.

---

ice and fire
contrasts of Icelandic nature

ice and fire is a portrait in words and pictures of the striking contrasts of Icelandic nature. Ice and fire, glaciers and volcanoes, have played an important part in the history of Iceland, and from the very first days of the settlement these two elements have often proved formidable foes: drifting ice-floes have occasionally covered fishing grounds and blocked harbours, whilst erupting volcanoes have buried land and livestock under ash and lava. Iceland was first named after the drift-ice seen along its northern shores, but such is the country's nature that it might just as easily have been called 'Fireland' had one of its many volcanoes been active when the first viking settlers arrived.

In the beginning of the book are descriptions and illustrations of the nature, formation, and properties of drift-ice, followed by chapters on glaciers, snowfalls, and icing. The book goes on to deal with geysers, hotsprings, mud-pools, calderas, solfataras, and the many kinds of volcanic activity, including an illustrated record of some of the more recent volcanic eruptions.

ice and fire has 172 pages, 205 photographs (83 in colour), and 15 explanatory maps and drawings, and provides a vivid, informative, and comprehensive survey of all the most interesting geological features of Iceland.

ICELAND
a portrait of its land and people

The book begins by relating the first discovery of Iceland, the voyages of Irish monks, and a discussion on the possibility of an Irish settlement of Iceland prior to that of 9th century Nordic vikings, and then goes on to describe how further viking voyages from Iceland ended in the discovery of Greenland and America. The book traces the origins of the Icelandic nation in the intermingling of the Nordic and Celtic races, and describes how this new nation formed its own unique political and social system based on chieftaincies and a national assembly. The country's subsequent history is recorded and illustrated to show how Iceland finally evolved into a modern welfare state.

Ensuing chapters present a survey of the regions of Iceland in the form of a journey around the island with stops at many historic and interesting places to reveal the way the people live and their natural surroundings. There are also many pictures of Icelandic bird life and flora.

Descriptions of Iceland's glaciers and extensive lavafields are also included, along with an illustrated history of some of Iceland's more recent volcanic eruptions (e.g. Hekla, Askja, and Krafla). There is also a detailed record of Surtsey's dramatic emergence from under the sea, and a day-by-day history of the famous Vestmannaeyjar eruption – and how the thriving community of Heimaey arose again from its ashes.

This attractively bound book has 428 pages, 20 chapters, and 650 photographs (220 in colour) as well as drawings and maps, and provides a vivid, detailed, and lively portrait of the land and people of Iceland, both past and present.

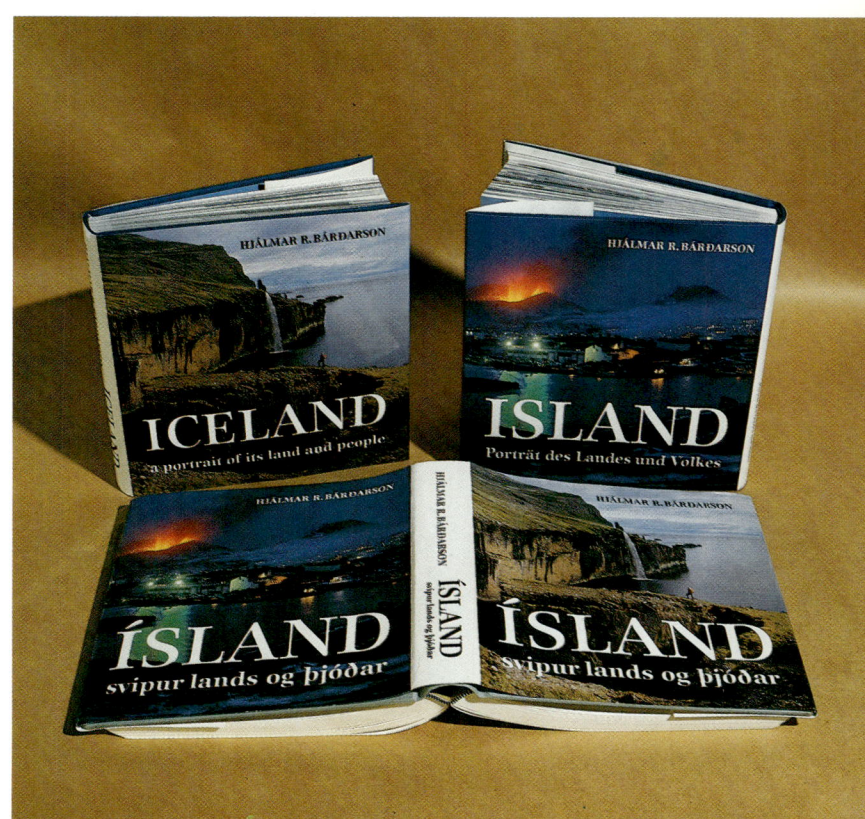

333

20. Glossary of bird names

ENGLISH*)	LATIN	ICELANDIC	DANISH	FRENCH	GERMAN
American Wigeon NA: American Widgeon	Anas americana	Ljóshöfðaönd	Amerikansk pibeand	Canard siffleur d'Amérique	Nordamerikanische Pfeifente
Arctic Skua NA: Parasitic Jaeger	Stercorarius parasiticus	Kjói	Almindelig kjove	Labbe parasite	Schmarotzerraubmöwe
Arctic Tern	Sterna paradisaea	Kría	Havterne	Sterne arctique	Küstenseeschwalbe
Atlantic Murre (NA), (= Guillemot)	Uria aalge	Langvía	Lomvie Langnæbbet Lomvie	Guillemot de Troil	Trottellumme
Barnacle Goose	Branta leucopsis	Helsingi	Bramgås	Bernache nonnette	Weißwangengans
Barn Swallow (NA), (= Swallow)	Hirundo rustica	Landsvala	Landsvale	Hirondelle de cheminée	Rauchschwalbe
Barrow's Goldeneye	Bucephala islandica	Húsönd	Islandsk hvinand	Garrot d'Islande Garrot islandais	Spatelente
Bar-tailed Godwit	Limosa lapponica	Lappajaðrakan	Lille kobbersneppe	Barge rousse	Pfuhlschnepfe
Blackbird	Turdus merula	Svartþröstur	Solsort	Merle noir	Amsel
Black Guillemot	Cepphus grylle	Teista	Tejst	Guillemot à miroir	Gryllteiste
Black-headed Gull	Larus ridibundus	Hettumáfur	Hættemåge	Mouette rieuse	Lachmöwe
Black-legged Kittiwake (NA),	Rissa tridactyla	Rita	Ride	Mouette tridactyle	Dreizehenmöwe
Black-tailed Godwit	Limosa limosa	Jaðrakan	Stor kobbersneppe	Barge à queue noire	Uferschnepfe
Brambling	Fringilla montifringilla	Fjallafinka	Kvækerfinke	Pinson du Nord Pinson d'Ardennes	Bergfink
Brent Goose NA: Brant	Branta bernicla	Margæs	Knortegås	Bernache cravant	Ringelgans
Brünnich's Guillemot NA: Thick-billed Murre	Uria lomvia	Stuttnefja	Kortnæbbet lomvie	Guillemot de Brünnich	Dickschnabellumme
Common Goldeneye	Bucephala clangula	Hvínönd	Hvinand	Garrot à oeil d'or Canard garrot	Schellente
Common Gull NA: Mew Gull	Larus canus	Stormmáfur	Stormmåge	Goéland cendré	Sturmmöwe
Common Loon (NA) (= Great Northern Diver)	Gavia immer	Himbrimi	Islom	Plongeon imbrin	Eistaucher
Common Scoter	Melanitta nigra	Hrafnsönd	Sortand	Macreuse noire	Trauerente
Coot	Fulica atra	Bleshæna	Blishøne	Foulque macroule	Bläßhuhn
Cormorant NA: Great Cormorant	Phalacrocorax carbo	Dílaskarfur	Storskarv Ålekrage	Grand Cormoran	Kormoran
Dovekie (NA), (= Little Auk)	Alle alle	Haftyrðill	Søkonge	Mergule nain	Krabbentaucher
Dunlin	Calidris alpina	Lóuþræll	Almindelig ryle	Bécasseau variable	Alpenstrandläufer
Eider	Somateria mollissima	Æður (Æðarfugl)	Ederfugl	Eider à duvet	Eiderente
Fulmar	Fulmarus glacialis	Fýll	Mallemuk	Petrel fulmar, Fulmar, Petrel glacial	Eissturmvogel
Gadwall	Anas strepera	Gargönd	Knarand	Canard chipeau	Schnatterente
Gannet	Sula bassana	Súla	Sule	Fou de Bassan	Baßtölpel
Glaucous Gull	Larus hyperboreus	Hvítmáfur	Gråmåge	Goéland bourgmestre	Eismöwe
Golden Plover	Pluvialis apricaria	Heiðlóa	Hjejle	Pluvier doré	Goldregenpfeifer
Goosander	Mergus merganser	Gulönd	Stor skallesluger	Harle bièvre	Gänsesäger
Great Auk	Pinguinus impennis	Geirfugl	Gejrfugl	Grand Pingouin	Riesenalk

*) NA: Bird name used in North America.

ENGLISH*)	LATIN	ICELANDIC	DANISH	FRENCH	GERMAN
Great Black-backed Gull	Larus marinus	Svartbakur	Svartbag	Goéland marin	Mantelmöwe
Great Cormorant (NA) (=Cormorant)	Phalacrocorax carbo	Dílaskarfur	Storskarv Ålekrage	Grand Cormoran	Kormoran
Great Northern Diver NA: Common Loon	Gavia immer	Himbrimi	Islom	Plongeon imbrin	Eistaucher
Great Skua NA: Skua	Stercorarius skua	Skúmur	Storkjove	Grande Labbe	Große Raubmöwe
Greylag Goose	Anser anser	Grágæs	Grågås	Oie cendrée	Graugans
Grey Phalarope NA: Red Phalarope	Phalaropus fulicarius	Þórshani	Thorshane	Phalarope à bec large	Thorshühnchen
Guillemot NA: Atlantic Murre	Uria aalge	Langvía	Lomvie Langnæbbet Lomvie	Guillemot de Troïl	Trottellumme
Gyrfalcon	Falco rusticolus	Fálki (Valur)	Jagtfalk	Faucon gerfaut	Gerfalke
Harlequin Harlequin-Duck	Histrionicus histrionicus	Straumönd	Strømand	Garrot arlequin	Kragenente
Herring Gull	Larus argentatus	Silfurmáfur	Sølvmåge	Goéland argenté	Silbermöwe
Horned Grebe (NA), (=Slavonian Grebe)	Podiceps auritus	Flórgoði	Nordisk lappedykker	Grèbe esclavon	Ohrentaucher
House Sparrow	Passer domesticus	Gráspör	Gråspurv	Moineau domestique	Haussperling
House Martin	Delichon urbica	Bæjasvala	Bysvale	Hirondelle de fenêtre	Mehlschwalbe
Jackdaw	Corvus monedula	Dvergkráka	Allike	Choucas des tours	Dohle
King Eider	Somateria spectabilis	Æðarkóngur	Kongeederfugl	Eider à tête grise	Prachteiderente
Kittiwake NA: Black-legged Kittiwake	Rissa tridactyla	Rita	Ride	Mouette tridactyle	Dreizehenmöwe
Knot	Calidris canutus	Rauðbrystingur	Islandsk ryle	Bécasseau maubèche	Knutt
Lapwing	Vanellus vanellus	Vepja	Vibe	Vanneau huppé	Kiebitz
Leach's Petrel	Oceanodroma leucorrhoa	Sjósvala	Stor stormsvale	Pétrel culblanc	Wellenläufer
Lesser Black-backed Gull	Larus fuscus	Sílamáfur	Sildemåge	Goéland brun	Heringsmöwe
Little Auk NA: Dovekie	Alle alle	Haftyrðill	Søkonge	Mergule nain	Krabbentaucher
Long-tailed Duck NA: Oldsquaw	Clangula hyemalis	Hávella	Havlit	Harelde de Miquelon Canard de Miquelon	Eisente
Mallard	Anas platyrhynchos	Stokkönd	Gråand	Canard colvert	Stockente
Manx Shearwater	Puffinus puffinus	Skrofa	Almindelig skråpe	Puffin des Anglais	Schwarzschnabel-Sturmtaucher
Meadow Pipit	Anthus pratensis	Þúfutittlingur	Engpiber	Pipit farlouse Pipit des prés	Wiesenpieper
Merlin NA: Pigeon Hawk	Falco columbarius	Smyrill	Dværgfalk	Faucon émerillon	Merlin
Mew Gull (NA), (=Common Gull)	Larus canus	Stormmáfur	Stormmåge	Goéland cendré	Sturmmöwe
Northern Phalarope (NA) (=Red-necked Phalarope)	Phalaropus lobatus	Óðinshani	Odinshane	Phalarope à bec étroit	Odinshühnchen
Oldsquaw (NA) (=Long-tailed Duck)	Clangula hyemalis	Hávella	Havlit	Harelde de Miquelon Canard de Miquelon	Eisente
Oystercatcher	Haematopus ostralegus	Tjaldur	Strandskade	Huîtrier pie	Austernfischer
Parasitic Jaeger (NA) (=Arctic Skua)	Stercorarius parasiticus	Kjói	Almindelig kjove	Labbe parasite	Schmarotzerraubmöwe
Pigeon Hawk (NA) (=Merlin)	Falco columbarius	Smyrill	Dværgfalk	Faucon émerillon	Merlin
Pink-footed Goose	Anser brachyrhynchus	Heiðagæs	Kortnæbbet gås	Oie à bec court	Kurzschnabelgans
Pintail	Anas acuta	Grafönd	Spidsand	Canard pilet	Spießente

ENGLISH*)	LATIN	ICELANDIC	DANISH	FRENCH	GERMAN
Pochard	Aythya ferina	Skutulönd	Taffeland	Fuligule milouin / Canard milouin	Tafelente
Ptarmigan	Lagopus mutus	Rjúpa (Fjallarjúpa)	Fjeldrype	Lagopède muet	Alpenschneehuhn
Puffin	Fratercula arctica	Lundi	Lunde	Macareux moine	Papageitaucher
Purple Sandpiper	Calidris maritima	Sendlingur	Sortgrå ryle	Bécasseau violet	Meerstrandläufer
Raven	Corvus corax	Hrafn	Ravn	Grand Corbeau	Kolkrabe
Razorbill	Alca torda	Álka	Alk	Petit Pingouin	Tordalk
Red-breasted Merganser	Mergus serrator	Toppönd	Toppet skallesluger	Harle huppé	Mittelsäger
Red-necked Phalarope NA: Northern Phalarope	Phalaropus lobatus	Óðinshani	Odinshane	Phalarope à bec étroit	Odinshühnchen
Red Phalarope (NA) (=Grey Phalarope)	Phalaropus fulicarius	Þórshani	Thorshane	Phalarope à bec large	Thorshühnchen
Redpoll	Acanthis flammea	Auðnutittlingur	Gråsisken	Sizerin flammé	Birkenzeisig
Redshank	Tringa totanus	Stelkur	Rødben	Chevalier gambette	Rotschenkel
Red-throated Diver NA: Red-throated Loon	Gavia stellata	Lómur	Rødstrubet lom	Plongeon catmarin	Sterntaucher
Redwing	Turdus iliacus	Skógarþröstur	Vindrossel	Grive mauvis	Rotdrossel
Ringed Plover	Charadrius hiaticula	Sandlóa	Stor præstekrave	Grand Gravelot	Sandregenpfeifer
Sanderling	Calidris alba	Sanderla	Sandløber	Bécasseau sanderling	Sanderling
Scaup	Aythya marila	Duggönd	Bjergand	Fuligule milouinan / Canard milouinan	Bergente
Shag	Phalacrocorax aristotelis	Toppskarfur	Topskarv	Cormoran huppé	Krähenscharbe
Short-eared Owl	Asio flammeus	Brandugla	Mosehornugle	Hibou des marais / Hibou brachyote	Sumpfohreule
Shoveler	Anas clypeata	Skeiðönd	Skeand	Canard souchet	Löffelente
Skua (NA) (= Great Skua)	Stercorarius skua	Skúmur	Storkjove	Grand labbe	Große Raubmöwe
Slavonian Grebe NA: Horned Grebe	Podiceps auritus	Flórgoði	Nordisk lappedykker	Grèbe esclavon	Ohrentaucher
Snipe	Gallinago gallinago	Hrossagaukur	Dobbeltbekkasin	Bécassine des marais	Bekassine
Snow Bunting	Plectrophenax nivalis	Snjótittlingur	Snespurv	Bruant des neiges	Schneeammer
Snowy Owl	Nyctea scandiaca	Snæugla	Sneugle	Chouette harfang / Harfang des neiges	Schneeeule
Starling	Sturnus vulgaris	Stari	Stær	Étourneau sansonnet	Star
Storm Petrel	Hydrobates pelagicus	Stormsvala	Lille stormsvale	Pétrel tempête	Sturmschwalbe
Swallow NA: Barn Swallow	Hirundo rustica	Landsvala	Landsvale	Hirondelle de cheminée	Rauchschwalbe
Teal	Anas crecca	Urtönd	Krikand	Sarcelle d'hiver	Krickente
Thick-billed Murre (NA) (= Brunnich's Guillemot)	Uria lomvia	Stuttnefja	Kortnæbbet lomvie	Guillemot de Brünnich	Dickschnabellumme
Tufted Duck	Aythya fuligula	Skúfönd	Troldand	Fuligule morillon / Canard morillon	Reiherente
Turnstone	Arenaria interpres	Tildra	Stenvender	Tournepierre à collier	Steinwälzer
Water Rail	Rallus aquaticus	Keldusvín	Vandrikse	Râle d'eau	Wasserralle
Wheatear	Oenanthe oenanthe	Steindepill	Stenpikker	Traquet motteux	Steinschmätzer
Whimbrel	Numenius phaeopus	Spói	Lille regnspove	Courlis corlieu	Regenbrachvogel
White-fronted Goose	Anser albifrons	Blesgæs	Blisgås	Oie rieuse	Bläßgans
White Stork	Ciconia ciconia	Hvítstorkur	Hvid stork	Cigogne blanche	Weißstorch
White-tailed Eagle NA: Gray Sea Eagle	Haliaeetus albicilla	Haförn	Havørn	Pygargue à queue blanche / Aigle de mer	Seeadler
White Wagtail	Motacilla alba	Maríuerla	Hvid vipstjert	Bergeronnette grise / Lavandière grise	Bachstelze
Whooper Swan	Cygnus cygnus	Álft (Svanur)	Sangsvane	Cygne sauvage	Singschwan
Wigeon	Anas penelope	Rauðhöfðaönd	Pibeand	Canard siffleur	Pfeifente
Wren NA: Winter Wren	Troglodytes troglodytes	Músarrindill	Gærdesmutte	Troglodyte / Troglodyte mignon	Zaunkönig

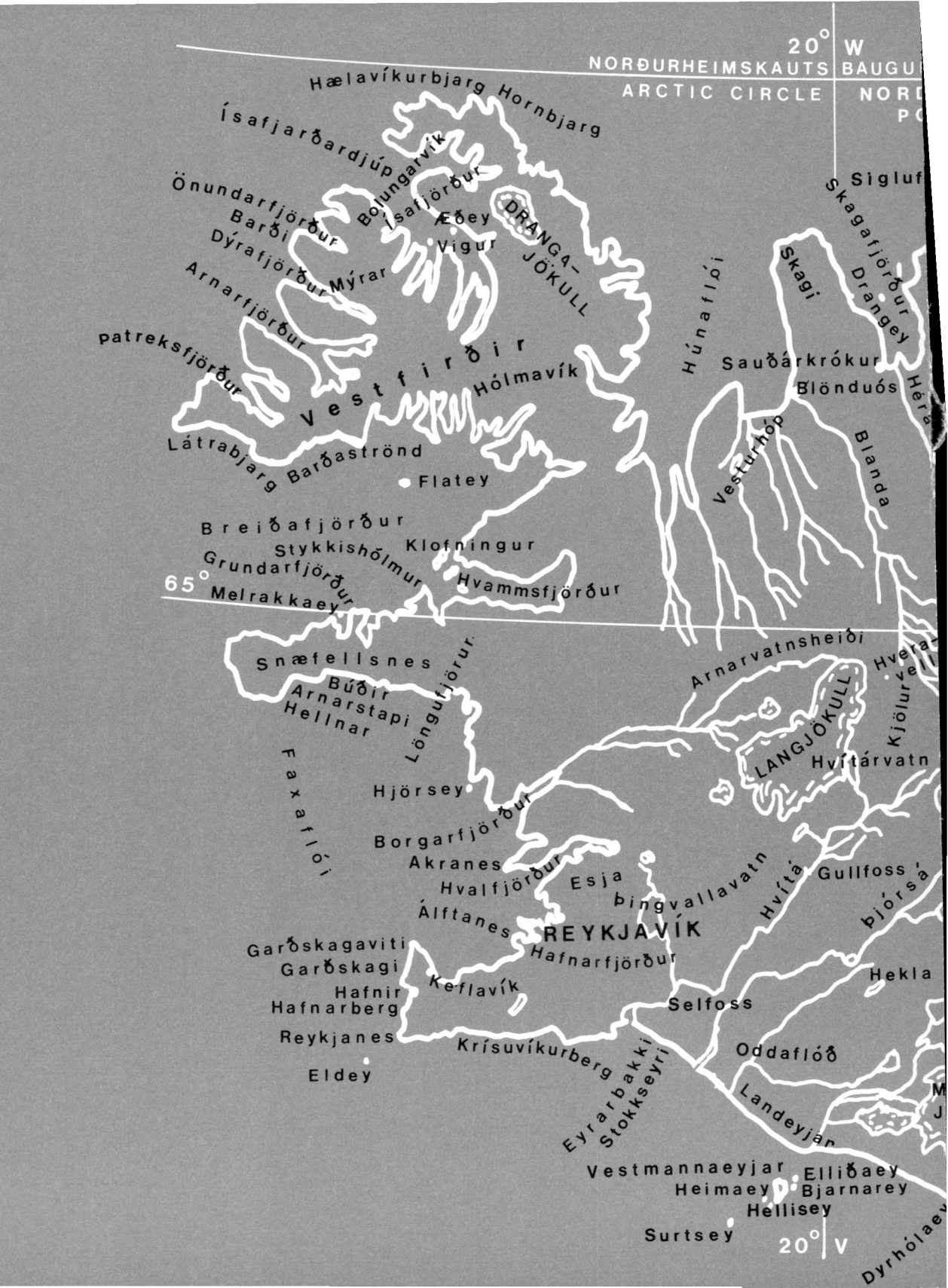